TechnoMage

Disclaimer

The accuracy and completeness of information provided herein and opinions stated herein are not guaranteed, nor are they warranted to produce any particular results. The advice, strategies and techniques contained herein may not be suitable for every individual. The author shall not be liable for any losses, injuries or fatalities incurred as a consequence of the use and application, directly or indirectly, of any information presented in this work. Neither does the author condone or encourage any activity described herein that may be illegal in any particular jurisdiction. Whilst I hope you find the contents of TechnoMage interesting and informative, the contents are for general information only.

TechnoMage

by

Dirk Conrad Bruere

Technological paradigms for the modification of Reality in Consciousness and Magick

A Textbook of Technoshamanism

Science and Technology as a Magickal Belief System

© Dirk Conrad Bruere 2009

All rights reserved. No part of this book may be reproduced, transmitted in any form or by any means, electronic or mechanical, including photocopying, recording or by any information storage or retrieval system without permission in writing from the copyright holder.

Published by Dirk Bruere

22 Milburn Road
Bedford
England
MK41 0NZ

ISBN: 978-0-9567587-0-5

Acknowledgments

Special thanks to the following for their insights, support and aid in this project:

Fiona MacKenzie – Seer
Marc Power – Engineer of Reality
Ian Read – Master of Fire and Ice

The front cover art features Fiona MacKenzie and is used with her permission. The NeoPax logo on the back cover was something I created for my website:

www.neopax.com

email:

dirk.bruere@gmail.com

If for some reason either of those addresses disappear, then search for me on the Net – I have a distinctive name!

I would also like to thank Sara MacKenzie for help with artwork

Dedicated

to

Fiona

Contents

Table of Contents

Contents 5

Introduction 13

1 Semantics and Spells 19
    Energy, Power, Force 19
    Karma 22
    Spirit – Definitions 27
    Spirit as Inner Essence 27
    Spirit as Incorporeal Consciousness 29
    Soul – Definitions 30
    Reincarnation 31
    Etymology – Casting a Spell 34
    Etymology – Spell 35
    Etymology – Casting 37
    Etymology – Enchanting, Incantation and Charm 38
    Etymology – Fascinate 39
    Etymology – Glamor 39

2 Science and Magick 43
    Science 43
    Magick 46
    Science, Proof and Power 46
    Magickal Paradigms 48
    A Magical Theory of Everything (TOE) 49
    Quantum Mechanics 52
    The Many Worlds Interpretation 56
    Quantum Immortality 58
    Time Travel and Doppelgangers 61
    Randomness and Chaos 62

Mathematics and Magick..*63*

Interdimensional Communications...*66*

3 Psi and the Occult..**71**

The Scole Experiment...*71*

The Owen Experiment..*75*

Psychological Factors...*78*

Disembodied Intelligence?...*79*

A Religious Context..*80*

Objects of Power...*81*

Questions..*81*

The PK Party...*83*

Prayer and Healing Studies – a brief review..*85*

Caveat Emptor...*86*

Ultraterrestrial Workings..*87*

Summary..*94*

4 Gods and Daemons...**97**

Agents and The Society of Mind..*97*

Filters and Censors...*99*

Memetics..*101*

Jung and Archetypes..*103*

Entities..*104*

A Game of Ouija..*106*

Safeguards...*112*

Dynamic Archetypes..*113*

Godform Genetics..*117*

Daemon Communications..*117*

Communicating – Evocation and Invocation......................................*118*

Hosts and Conspiracies..*120*

Sacrifice...*121*

Coincidences and Omens...*121*

Health and Healing...*125*

Black and White Magick..*126*

Summary...*128*

Contents

5 Hypnosis **131**
    Early History...*132*
    Theories of Hypnosis...*134*
    The Hidden Observer..*136*
    Susceptibility Testing...*137*
    Induction Techniques..*140*
    Eye Fixation..*141*
    Progressive Relaxation..*142*
    Misdirection Induction...*143*
    Shock Induction..*145*
    Confusion Methods...*146*
    Physical Methods..*149*
    Deepening the Trance...*152*
    Testing Trance Depth..*152*
    Stage Hypnotism...*154*

6 Mind Tools **157**
    Anchoring...*157*
    The Conditioned Response...*159*
    The Post Hypnotic Command..*162*
    Remote Hypnotism...*164*
    Brainwaves and Entrainment..*166*
    Photic Driving..*168*
    Sonics and Binaural Tones..*169*
    Personality Reconstruction..*171*
    False Memory Creation..*175*
    Sensory Deprivation...*177*
    Visualization...*178*
    Lucid Dreaming..*178*
    Cold Reading and Selling...*183*
    The Third Wave..*187*

7 Subliminals **193**
    Neuro-Linguistic Programming (NLP)..............................*195*
    The Meta Model...*197*

The Milton Model 199

Eye Accessing Cues 203

The Boyfriend Destroyer 204

Swish 205

Decision Destroying 205

Values Elicitation 205

Emotional Elicitation 206

Timeline Manipulation 207

Subliminal Images 207

The Subliminal Flash – Technology 208

Subliminal Speech 210

Subliminal Audio 213

Sigils 215

Magnetics 217

The Hypnogogic State 218

Sleep Learning 219

8 Psi and Science 223

Information: 223

Physical Effects: 224

Intelligent Entities: 224

Princeton Engineering Anomalies Research (PEAR) 225

Temporal Paradox and Retro-Causality 229

Changing the Past – Magickal Operations 231

A Note on Random Number Generators 233

Remote Viewing and STAR GATE 234

The Interviewer or Controller 237

Lessons learned, from all sources: 237

Global Consciousness Project 238

The Geopsyche 239

9 The Electromagnetic Domain 243

Transcranial Magnetic Stimulation 243

Natural Electromagnetic Fields 249

Alfar, Fae and Aliens 252

Contents

The Schumann Resonance...*253*
Direct Electrical Brain Stimulation...*256*
Direct Current Brain Stimulation...*257*
Electric Field Coupling...*257*
Ionization of Air...*258*
Skin Resistance Measurement..*259*
High Frequency EM Field Modulation..*260*
Psychotronic Weapons..*262*
HAARP..*264*
Psychic Terrorism...*265*
Experiment and Ritual...*266*

10 Machines...**271**
Ideomotor Divination..*271*
Electronic Voice Phenomena (EVP)...*274*
Random Number Generators...*277*
Computational Demonology – The Quantum Oracle.......................*279*
The Psychomanteum..*283*
Signal Generation..*286*
Field Coils..*288*
The Helmholtz Configuration..*291*
Electrical Brain Stimulation Technology...*293*
Red Light and Healing...*295*
Infra Red Brain Stimulation..*296*
Magnetometers..*297*
Dream Machines..*298*
Symbolic Machines..*299*
The Hieronymus Machine..*299*
The Wish Machine...*301*
Wilhelm Reich and Orgonomy..*303*
The Orgone Accumulator..*305*
The Reich Cloudbuster..*305*
Ultraterrestrials and Orgone weapons..*306*
Conclusions...*307*

11   The Great Work 309

The Magickal and Religious Dimension 311
The Gnostic Connection 319
The Tree of Life 321
The Symbol of Life 324
The Transmutation of Matter 326
The Messiah 327
The Apocalypse 331
The Call of Cthulhu and the PostHuman Condition 334
Resurrecting the Dead and the Transmigration of Souls 335
The Magickal Act of the Great Work 338

12   Fermi, Doom and Simulation 341

The Fermi Paradox 341
The Doomsday Argument 342
The Simulation Argument 344
Levels of Simulations 346
The High Level Simulations 349
The Low Level Simulations 350
Magick in the Sim 353
Features of a Computation 356
Ethics and the Problem of Evil 359
The Boltzmann Brain Scenario 361

Appendix A – Frequencies of Interest 365

Appendix B – Drugs 371

Appendix C – The Laws of Magick 375

Appendix D – Traditional Ritual Techniques 377

Appendix E – The Mindset 379

Appendix F – Levels of Initiation 385

Index 389

Contents

Introduction

"Any sufficiently advanced technology is indistinguishable from magic"
Arthur C Clarke

or

"Any sufficiently advanced magick is indistinguishable from technology"

Generally, I never bother to read introductions to books. So in the belief that you are like me, I will keep this brief and to the point. Having said that, who is this book aimed at? Well... people like me. That rather rare breed who mix science, engineering and magick into what I have termed TechnoShamanism. A more common spelling is Techno-shamanism but in keeping with the spirit of the word I have spelled it as if it were a variable name in a computer programming language. Beyond that anything I claim is merely my view of this particular and very modern religious-spiritual genre. For me, one of the early starting points was the above statement by Arthur C Clarke. We are now living in an age of magick the like of which the world has never seen, yet if you venture into a New Age bookshop you will see the shelves stuffed with every variety of garbage, from "Atlantean Crystal Magick" to "101 Spells For Lovesick Teenagers" and whose working assumption is that magick is a lost art with all power and authenticity lying in the (mythical) past. What you will seldom see next to the "Spell Books for the Gullible" are works on Hypnosis and Neuro-Linguistic Programming (NLP) which really do deliver what the garbage only promises. So, if you are that lovesick teenager, skip forward to those chapters in this book but be warned – unlike twirling three times on Halloween and calling out the name of the one you love to the Dark Powers or whatever, learning the real thing takes intellect, effort and practice. Ah... do I sense you are about to put this book down? Anyway, the point I am trying to make is that not only are powerful magickal techniques a thing of the present and future rather than the past, but that it seems the populist New Age genres appear to steer well clear of anything that actually *works*. In other words, they are mostly harmless. This book, on the other hand, contains information that is far from harmless and could quite easily get you killed or maimed if you do not take the utmost care and precautions.

Having said all that, what is "magick"? Personally, I rather like Aleister Crowley's succinct definition which is that magick is: "The altering of Reality in accordance with Will" since it neatly encompasses just about everything. Of course, the major problem here is one that is usually glossed over. It is the precise understanding of what is meant by "Reality" and "Will" – both very non-trivial concepts and ones that may ultimately have *no* final definitions or explanations at all. Both are fundamental ongoing areas of investigation in religion, philosophy and science and are the core areas of study for the would-be magician. The other major point of this introduction is that in all operations we are dealing with the Human mind. Consequently what follows are methods for engineering a variety of states of consciousness and beliefs. These methods vary from the "traditional" such as hypnotic ritual and drugs to the technologically bizarre such as direct magnetic, electrical, optical or acoustic stimulation of the brain and the use of Symbolic Machines. Furthermore, the emphasis is on doing this with groups of people rather than individuals. The reasons for this focus is twofold. First, group workings are more reliable in that they do not depend on psychic superstars. Second, the technology of manipulation of group consciousness is crucial, from that of a closely integrated coven or lodge to that of conventional politics and on to the larger scales of Godforms and dynamic archetypes. A group can compensate for weaknesses in individual members, whether temporary or chronic. We all have off days, character flaws and personal idiosyncrasies that may hamper or bolster the effects we seek during magickal operations. In a group the negative aspects can be smoothed out and the positive accentuated far more easily than in an individual.

It is also crucial to note that the material presented in the following chapters is in a very information dense format. There is little in the way of inessential padding to get the word count up, and each chapter could quite easily be expanded into a book in its own right. Indeed, each chapter can be considered to be a condensation of the core information of several books, or research publications, in the area it covers. As such this work is an introduction to the field – more a textbook than a fun read, unless you are a serious magician. The aim is to provide a brief, albeit partisan, overview of the application of science and technology to modern magick with references provided to enable the magician to research the topic to greater depth. However, because this book began as a series of individual essays each chapter can almost be read as a stand-alone piece with only minor references to other areas. Nevertheless, there is one feature that may appear to be confusing to a novice when reading this work. It is that quite often multiple and sometimes contradictory explanations may be put forth for various effects. This is because the most important aspect of a technological approach to magick is simply to get your Will made manifest and in the best tradition of Chaos Magick one chooses the theory or belief that gets the work done. So, choose the belief that works for you, because that is what every great magician ultimately does and which is why in traditional magick the student never exceeds the master unless he breaks away and creates his own path.

Another feature worth noting concerns my attempts to clarify terminology. Many occult terms have almost exact cognates in modern scientific nomenclature. This is quite important for a number of reasons. The first concerns why scientifically trained people are so dismissive of the occult when they first encounter the terminology used. There is no better way to annoy a scientist than horribly misusing a well-defined scientific vocabulary – unless it's misusing a well-defined scientific vocabulary that has been thoroughly discredited for a century or more.

Introduction

The second reason to update terms concerns the method by which we record and manipulate knowledge. All knowledge is symbols and metaphor, whether written in a book, stored on a computer or held in ones brain. Only Reality is the "real thing", all else is description and analogy. Of course, some metaphors are more useful, or descriptive, than others, but it is a characteristic of metaphors and analogies that eventually when pushed far enough they break down – the map is not the territory. Even so some have more utility than others and can take one further into uncharted territory in a meaningful manner. In the hard sciences such as physics (and here "hard" means "precise" rather than "difficult") words have generally been found to be inferior to mathematics. For while words can encapsulate a quality, they cannot easily and precisely furnish quantities. Yet even in its precision, mathematics can tell us with certainty that there are mathematical truths that mathematics cannot reveal to us. Thus ends that particular metaphor. So why persist with a ghetto vocabulary when modern science has been refining its terms for two centuries or more? The amount of scientific effort put into defining "energy" for example is literally millions of times greater than that put in by occultists and other magicians. By using a more updated terminology we can take the magickal metaphor to a new level of understanding and hence utility, after science has done most of the hard work for us. Such a work is overdue, even though a good start was made with the analysis that resulted in Chaos Magick. The counterargument to this is that many New Age books are filled with references to Quantum Mechanics and Relativity. However, how many books have you encountered that actually derived new magickal techniques from those concepts rather than merely used them to bolster some old ideas?

Finally, magick can be considered as a game[1]. If we run with this metaphor we can look to the board game Monopoly™ as our illustration. When we sit down to play we agree to constrain our actions by a set of fairly arbitrary rules – the rules of Monopoly. We choose to become a shoe, or a top hat or one of the other movable icons. Of course, we are not *really* a shoe or a top hat just that we *pretend* that we are for the sake of the game. We move by throwing dice and using the resulting number to determine how many squares we can move. Again, we can in reality get up and walk out of the room, but we have agreed to play with these restrictions. When we land on someone else's hotel we have to pay them some money, or if they land on ours they have to pay us in turn. There are no hotels and no money – we just make believe there are in order to continue with the game. Sometimes we end up in jail, or are lucky enough to have a get-out-of-jail-free card. Alternatively we get bankrupted and lose, or perhaps we win and own the entire board. We don't really lose, or really win. There are no jails, or cards to get us out of them. It's a game. It is the same with magick. We are playing a game, a much more complex game admittedly, with a certain set of rules. One of the rules might even be that we do not know all the rules, or even that we are not told that we do not know all the rules! Or perhaps the rules are allowed to evolve as the game is played, more

---
[1] Example furnished by Marc Power of Reality Engineering

players enter and others leave. However, we do know some of the constraints we have agreed to play under. The names of these constraints, as the game is played in the book you are reading, are science and logic. Now, the clever bit is that we are allowed to get around some of the rules by using technology, and some of the rules seem to be a bit dubious as to whether something is permitted or not – for example the paranormal. The key rule is that if we can make something work it is not illegal! And if we can get something to work really consistently, and which seems to be against the rules, the rules can be changed in our favor! Let us play…

Introduction

Semantics and Spells

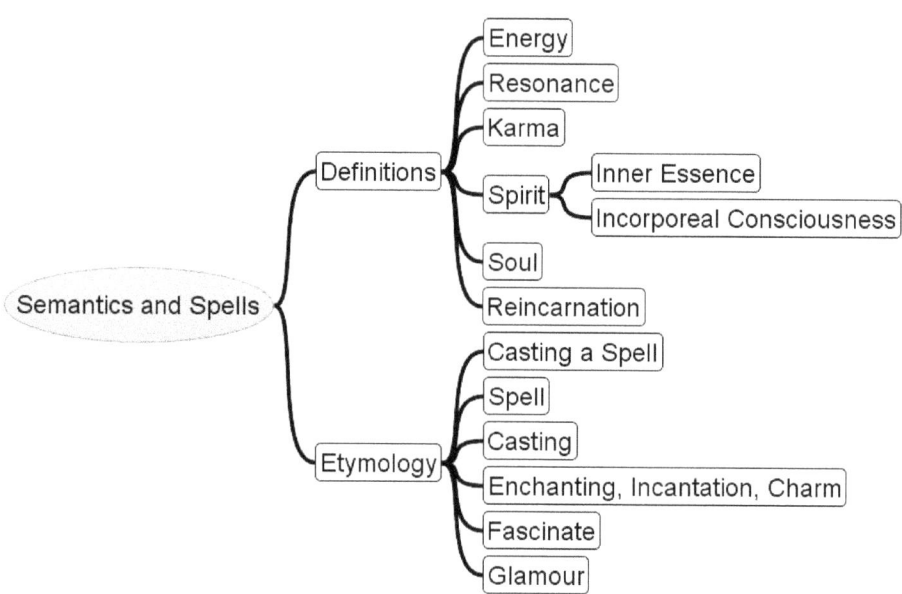

1 Semantics and Spells

"If once we can produce our perfect work - the Materialist Magician, the man, not using, but veritably worshiping, what he vaguely calls Forces while denying the existence of "spirits" – then the end of the war will be in sight."
C S Lewis, The Screwtape Letters

Definitions and origins of words and concepts employed in occult and New Age terminology and their relationship to science are crucial in what is to follow and so the entire chapter is devoted to these topics. Specifically, it sets a up a semantic framework that links the two fields such that people coming from a scientific background can translate what sounds like nonsense into a language they can understand. Conversely, those who are used to using words such as *power, force* and *energy* in an esoteric context can see how differently these are analyzed in modern scientific terms and where confusion arises. However, in common to all systems that defines and analyses language there is often an unspoken subtext, or theory, of how the world operates. What follows is no different and it is worth explaining here and now the spirit of the particular worldview being promoted in this work. Essentially it is one of using an absolute minimum of unprovable or untestable notions, and of sticking as closely as possible to conventional scientific explanations for various phenomena. The only major concession made is to acknowledging the strong possibility of the objective reality of paranormal or Psi effects. Even here there will be an absolute minimum of theorizing as to what is "really" going on and the emphasis will be on outlining possible effective techniques for its utilization under engineered states of consciousness. In short, this is *almost* a manifesto for the Materialist Magician. So, on with the semantic orientation…

Energy, Power, Force…

…Chi, Ki, Prana, Kundalini, Vril, Mana, Lifeforce, Animal Magnetism, Orgone, Bioenergy, Eloptic Energy, Pneuma, Od, Bioplasma, Subtle Energies, Universal Energy…

There are probably as many names again for a concept that has existed for millennia and spanned continents. The concept is that there is a vital "something" that pervades and underlies reality in general and life in particular and which endows it with special transcendent properties. It is often described as "energy" although it has nothing to do with anything science currently recognizes as such, for example in mechanics, electricity, or the nuclei of atoms. It is not scientifically measurable by any known instrument and is believed to be not only the source of life, but of health as well. There are no joules, watt-seconds, electron volts or Newton-meters by which it is measured and it is seemingly outside the bounds of scientific control or study. Only people with special sensitivities can channel or control it and many alternative therapies are concerned with unblocking, harmonizing, unifying, tuning, aligning or balancing it. The problem is that the above is a good description of a metaphysical theory known as *vitalism*, which is the doctrine that living organisms possess a non-physical inner force or energy that gives them the property of life. It is a theory that has been dead in the scientific West for over a century, for very good reasons. Yet it seems to be an article of faith amongst the scientifically ill-educated that the universe is all about such "energy"; which seems to beg the question as to whether these notions of vitalism can somehow be reconciled with modern science.

    A good way to illustrate the issue is by analogy, in this case the modern metaphor for the mind, namely a computer. It is as if a person claims that it is not merely electricity that is responsible for its operation but that there is in addition some mysterious subtle energy that manifests in various ways depending on which keys are pressed. The skeptic will then point out that this is utterly wrong since no such energy can be detected, and that the operation of the computer can be fully accounted for by conventional science. It is only when there is a realization that the "subtle energies" being claimed as the underlying principle of operation of the computer are actually software programs that things become clear and all parties can agree on what is happening. Taking the analogy further the "power" and "force" of a computer comes from the execution of those programs which results in structured and meaningful changes in the data they operate upon. In other words, in the computer world power and force are metaphors for *information processing*. And so it is in the real world. The reason why occult energies are not detectable in a consistent consensus reality manner by scientific instruments is because they are not actually energy but *information*.

    Information is to do with the *arrangement* of and *change* of *patterns* of matter and energy. It is this crucial yet nebulous essence that is really what life is about and what defines it. In particular, it is the essence of what constitutes a mind, a consciousness, a spirit or a soul however one cares to define them in either occult, magickal, religious, New Age or scientific terms. The world is not a duality of matter-energy but a trinity of matter-energy-information by which life and universe become manifest. Mind and magick are manifestations of information of which matter and energy are merely the medium.

    Increasingly modern science is concerned with Information Theory in its many forms as it appears to be deeply connected with fundamental issues. For example, it is directly involved in classical thermodynamics and communication theory as well as Quantum Mechanics. There is also a limit on the amount of information, measured in bits that can be encompassed by a particular area, called the Bekenstein Bound that appears in descriptions of Black Holes. Information is also intimately related to time and its apparent direction (from past to future) which

Semantics and Spells

may in turn be connected with the expansion of the universe. And the reason that this universe can support life at all is because it started in a very low state of entropy (high information content). That is, it emerged in a very ordered state in the Big Bang for reasons unknown. *Entropy*, a measure of disorder, is another very important principle used in modern science, especially the realization that in all *closed* systems entropy can only increase with time. In other words, things wear out, break down, decay, cool, and get more mixed up.

Returning to more mundane matters, how can we account for the descriptions people give of, say, Chi or Prana? Well, ignoring the more obvious answer that we use words like energy and power as metaphors in contexts as varied as politics and personal motivation, it certainly *feels* like energy. Or, to be more precise, it feels like bodily sensations often involving tingling, heat, trembling and a feeling of flow (often along the spine) coupled with changes in consciousness and awareness as well as occasionally auditory and visual hallucinations and time distortions. The simple answer is that we all have a mental model of our body. It's why we can localize physical feelings such as temperature, pain, pressure and so forth to precise parts of our body. The body feeds data to this model, but it is not purely a one way process. Alterations to the mental model of the body, the body image, affect that model and that in turn can affect the body. It's a real Voodoo Doll that each of us has in our head. Heal or harm the doll and we heal or harm the body. The mind and body are not separate things – they interact, influence and depend upon each other to create a unified person.

> Change the body, change the mind.
> Change the mind, change the body.
> Change the mind and feel it in the body.
> Change the body and feel it in the mind.
> Change the mind, change the world.
> There is only information and change.
> Energy is controlled by information.

As for how we can effect these changes, this is what magick is all about.

Resonance and Phase

Or more familiarly, being "in tune" which is a metaphor springing from music and more recently from radio and television technology. The notion of resonance is important for any phenomena that involves waves, vibrations, pulses and so on which, considering that all matter and energy have wave characteristics, means almost everything. The best way of understanding resonance is to use an analogy with which most people are familiar, namely water in a bath. If one starts moving a hand backwards and forwards through the water then most of the time nothing much happens besides some splashing. However, if the timing is just right so that when the wave has been reflected from the end of the bathtub the hand pushes it again it gets bigger and bigger until it rolls over the edge. This is resonance. The number of pushes per second or minute has to be just right for the size of the bath, and the wave has to be pushed on exactly the right part. That is, the frequency has to be correct and the phase just right. If the phase is wrong energy can be subtracted from the wave instead of added and everything gets damped down. Traditionally the size of the resulting wave is called the amplitude, which in music corresponds with loudness.

The reason why resonance is so important in almost all spheres of endeavor is that it is the mechanism by which physical energy is most efficiently transferred between systems. The systems can be as varied as a hand and water, light and vision, violin strings and sounds, and nuclear forces in an atom. Furthermore the same simple equations describe all of theses types of resonance no matter what their character. In general, when two systems are vibrating at the same frequency and in a particular phase energy can be efficiently moved between them even over quite large spatial separations. Indeed, it is often only by using resonance that information and energy can be transferred over large distances. Resonance is the underlying mechanism that makes TV and radio possible. When systems are in resonance surprising things can happen.

Karma…

… Tao, Wyrd, Kismet, Fate, Law of Return…

These are all terms that crop up across various religions from Buddhism to Wicca and although they are not identical concepts they are related in terms of being a perception of how the world is connected. The most famous is the Indian notion of Karma, which is a Sanskrit word meaning "action" or "doing". It is often wrongly associated with some kind of cosmic law of retribution but in its original and simplest form reflects the fact that all actions take place in a universe in which everything is interrelated. It has also come to mean also the law of cause and effect – something that lies at the heart of modern science under the name of Causality. Karma's relation to Fate needs clarifying. It does not mean that everything is predestined, but that one cannot escape the consequences of ones deeds. However, as far as the deeds themselves are concerned we are free to choose. So a person's Karma is simply the circumstances under which they live which results from the choices they have made. Yet the idea that we inherit Karma when we are born is also true. Each of us is born into unique circumstances that are determined by the choices of others, not least our parents. The connection with the notion of reincarnation, and what it is that gets reincarnated, is examined later.

There is no universal morality attached beyond that of the natural world nor do the full consequences of those choices inevitably return unerringly to the doer except in a rather statistical manner. Every evil deed is not punished nor is every good deed rewarded. However, consistently bad or good actions will narrow the odds considerably that similarly morally charged consequences will impact the

Semantics and Spells

person either directly or indirectly no matter what moral system exists. It's no more mysterious than realizing that someone who engages in dangerous sports is likely to be injured at some point, that someone who is a chronic thief will eventually be caught and punished or that an honest person will be trusted. There is, for example, no mechanistic and inevitable "Law of Threefold Return" as espoused by certain Gardnerian style Wiccans, just a tendency.

More interesting from a magickal point of view is the Tao. As the famous first verse of the Tao Te Ching says: "The Tao that can be told is not the eternal Tao" … in which case we will have to make do with an approximation. In some ways the Tao can be likened to the flow of a great river of events from the past to future. In this stream there are natural and easy directions of flow as well as various eddies and currents that can seem like the True Way but are in fact deceptive. These eddies can last for minutes, hours, days or occasionally centuries and often seem like the real direction because most people can only see that which immediately surrounds them. The Tao Te Ching is the text that attempts to codify this Way so that one can recognize where we are in this flow of events and define the best direction to take. In magickal terms this is very important for several reasons. Mainly the value is being in possession of the "big picture" and of clarity – knowledge is power and as the saying goes, "in the kingdom of the blind the one eyed man is king". It can be very useful to recognize such uncharacteristic eddies in order to take advantage of them, especially if they can be recognized before we arrive at them. How this is done using a text that says things like:

> A perfect warrior is not warlike.
> A perfect fighter shows no wrath.
> A perfect winner is not aggressive.
> A perfect leader is humble.
> This is the power of not-contending,
> Using the strength of others.
> It is called Matching Nature.

or

> Tao only moves by returning;
> Only acts by yielding.
> All things come from being;
> Being comes from non-being

and

> Without leaving your door, you can know the whole world.
> Without looking out the window, you can see the way of Nature.
> The more you seek it, the less you know about it.
> The sage knows without seeking,
> sees without looking,
> accomplishes without doing.

requires an entire book. However, texts on the Tao and its related philosophy of Zen can provide deep magickal insights to those sufficiently advanced.

Magickal workings should always take account of the prevailing flow of events as well as any unusual and temporary conditions. In many ways magick is like navigating on that river. Most people are carried along with the flow, but magicians can choose to take advantage of the currents if they can look ahead. Eddies can either be avoided or consciously entered. In extreme cases they can be created by magickal acts, which is magick of a very high order when those eddies persist for more than a short time. Another way of viewing those eddies are as illusions. That is, they are essentially distortions of reality if not outright fabrications that tend to entrap normal consciousness. An example is the Nazi and Communist periods where just such an illusion was created on a vast scale. In common with all such eddies, currents and illusions they eventually dissipate because they actively require energy for their maintenance. The more powerful and deep the illusion the more energy it takes and the shorter it lasts before reality once again asserts its influence and it implodes. Typically the energy either comes from either the victims of the illusion or the magician. In this sense one can define magick as Black or White. The former deals with illusion and the energy of others, the latter with reality and ones own energy. Black creates and leads into illusion while White disperses illusion and leads to reality. In these terms this book deals with technologies that can be applied to either endeavor.

The scientific equivalent of the above is called the *Principle of Least Action* and was first formulated in 1746 by Pierre-Louis Moreau de Maupertuis. It is one of the greatest generalizations in all physical science, although not fully appreciated until the advent of Quantum Mechanics in the 20th Century. Maupertuis arrived at the principle from a feeling that the perfection of the universe demands a certain economy in Nature and is opposed to any needless expenditure of energy. Natural motions must be such as to make some quantity a minimum. He discovered that it was the product of the duration, or time of movement within a system, multiplied by the kinetic energy. What this means is that Nature prefers to use a lot of energy for only a short time, or not much energy at all for a long time and preferably none at all for no time. Having found the quantity that tends to a minimum, Maupertuis regarded the principle as all-inclusive:

> "The laws of movement and of rest deduced from this principle being precisely the same as those observed in Nature, we can admire the application of it to all phenomena. The movement of animals, the vegetative growth of plants ... are only its consequences."

In simple terms, Nature always takes the path of least resistance. Exactly how Nature knows what that path actually is only became clear with the development of Quantum Mechanics. It revealed that on all scales from the subatomic to the transgalactic Nature takes *all* paths, but does so in such a manner that the least efficient ones tend to cancel each other out leaving the preferred route. It's as if

Semantics and Spells

Nature tries out everything in advance and only chooses the best. This also generalizes to the corresponding magickal law that in any successful undertaking Nature will satisfy the requirements with the minimum effort or largest probability (another facet of information theory). For example, if you cast a spell for "some money" the most likely successful outcome will be discovering a small coin lodged down the back of the sofa! Related to this, and often mentioned in modern magickal works is the Butterfly Effect of Chaos Theory. This is used as an example of the extreme sensitivity of some systems to small perturbations in initial conditions. The idea is that a disturbance so small as a butterfly beating its wings can, over the space of a few weeks, be amplified by natural processes into a hurricane. Of course, this is a spectacular and extreme example since in reality most butterflies do not do this! A better illustration is to consider a frictionless pool table and ask how far ahead one could predict the trajectory of balls once they had been set in notion. Assuming a computer controlled cue and perfectly round balls the answer is maybe a few seconds. Anything beyond this requires more and more information being factored into the computations, for example air pressure and temperature, deviations in the gravitational field due to large nearby objects (mountains, skyscrapers), noise… and so on. Even if we could do all this, and had a perfect table and cue down to the subatomic level, we could still not predict where the balls would go for more than a few tens of seconds. To predict for as long as a minute would require us to know the distribution of matter throughout the galaxy down to the subatomic. Or another way of putting it… a single electron moving on the edge of the solar system could ultimately determine where the balls go after a few tens of seconds. Now, all systems are not so sensitive, but some are and it is these that magickal practices can target effectively by providing just the right nudge at the right time. However, this again depends on two factors. The first is that no consciousness is working against the magickal operation, and the other is allowing enough time for the operation to work, although given that some Psi[2] effects appear to have an effect moving from the future into the past this is not necessarily always true. Note that for the above mechanism to work we cannot calculate the outcome of our magickal butterfly but instead have to look ahead in time to directly perceive it and choose accordingly. It is precognition as causation.

Of course, the way that events are closely linked has long been recognized not only in the East with the notion of Karma but more explicitly in Western religions, notably the Greco-Roman and Germanic. In these we have the Fates, or Norns weaving and spinning the web of life in which no one, not even the Gods could escape. In the Germanic religion the three women are Urth or Wyrd (the past), Verthandi (the present), and Skuld (the causal connection to the future). The metaphor is always either one of cloth, with its interwoven structure with threads going from not only from past to future but being linked sideways, one to another, or of a spider's web and its more open and obvious linkages radiating from a central point. This structure is generally known as the Web of Wyrd.

---

[2] Psi – shorthand for "Psychic" or paranormal, also denoted by the Greek letter (psi) Ψ

A perfect illustration of this is the idea of "six degrees of separation" where it is believed that on average any two people anywhere are connected by about six "friends of friends" to each other. In 1967CE American sociologist Stanley Milgram devised a way to test what he called "the small-world problem". He randomly selected people in the American Midwest to send packages to a stranger located in Massachusetts, several thousand miles away. The senders knew the recipient's name, occupation, and general location. They were instructed to send the package to a person they knew on a first-name basis who they thought was most likely, out of all their friends, to know the target personally. That person would do the same, and so on, until the package was personally delivered to its target recipient. Although the participants expected the chain to include at least a hundred intermediaries, on average it took only between five and seven to get each package delivered. Milgram's findings were published in Psychology Today and inspired the phrase "six degrees of separation". In 2001CE, Duncan Watts[3], a professor at Columbia University, continued his own earlier research into the phenomenon and recreated Milgram's experiment on the Internet. He used email messages instead of packages and after analyzing data collected by 60,000 senders and 18 targets in 166 countries, Watts found that the average number of intermediaries was indeed, six. One of the important conclusions was that email has, so far, not fundamentally changed the way social ties are created and hence made the world a closer knit community. Only some six percent of the links in the chain were Net only. However, this may well change as technology progresses and higher data rate communications becomes common. By far the most successful bonds were found to be work-related ones, and messages were also more likely to reach their target if they were forwarded to someone of the same sex. One surprise was that message chains did not rely on a few highly connected individuals but were widely spread.

These are of course the causal links between two people chosen at random. Once we move into a particular field of endeavor the number of links shrinks to two or three. It does not matter what those fields are, whether magick, politics, show business, advertising, "being famous", "being rich"... and so forth. One amusing example is the possible connection between the first President George Bush of the USA (and of course his son, the second President George W Bush), and Aleister Crowley, the great magician. The story starts in 1924CE with a certain Pauline Pierce who was married to the head of the McCall Corporation and her lone sojourn in France, leaving behind her two children. There she met Aleister Crowley and allegedly "assisted" him (along with her friend Nellie O'Hara) in a rather special working concerning his elevation to Ipsissimus[4]. She returned home from Europe pregnant and gave birth to a daughter, Barbara. Barbara Pierce married George H W Bush, who eventually became the 41st President of the United States. So George

---

[3] Science (vol 301, p 827), New Scientist 07 August 2003

[4] The highest possible grade in his style of magick – and outside the scope of this book

Semantics and Spells

W Bush the 43rd President may well be the grandson of the most notorious magician of all time!

Spirit – Definitions

Now, this word and its derivatives get a lot of use in our line of business. There are all kinds of spirits – spirits of trees, rocks, of the Earth itself. Spirits of people both dead and alive; holy spirits and evil spirits; team spirits and the spirit of superstition and gullibility. Then of course we have the adjective "spiritual" – nobody seemingly wants to admit that they are not spiritual, the implied default being some kind of dull "materialism".

However, ask exactly what all this means and the dissembling begins, often with vague arm-waving descriptions of "higher" things, unseen dimensions, vague intuitions, and that catch-all, "God", which lodges the definition with the unprovable. So, taking the noun first, and seeing what the dictionary says concerning the religious aspects we can distill two relevant definitions. These are the "essential nature, vital principle or animating force", and "incorporeal consciousness".

They are usually considered connected aspects of "spiritual reality" as viewed by many people. For example, the simplistic notion of a soul is considered to be the essential essence of a person that survives the death of the body and persists in some incorporeal state. However, such a connection need not be so and for the purposes of this analysis will not be assumed a priori. In order to clarify the issue what follows is initially an analysis of an inanimate object, specifically a sword, rather than the superficially more confusing case of a Human Being.

Spirit as Inner Essence

We begin by first examining the former definition. What, in a rational, scientific, consensus reality sense, is a "spirit" when used as a synonym for "inner essence"?

A spirit actually consists of a number of components. Let us take, for example, the spirit of a sword and examine what it is in terms of information. Obviously, it is a sword – but what is a sword, and how do we recognize such a thing? In our minds we generally have a list of possibilities, each characterized by a cluster of properties, which we compare to what we are looking at. For example, a sword is solid, can be large or small, is long and sharp (but not inevitably so), is usually made of metal, may have one or two sharpened edges, may be pointed etc. These things are, in essence, the "spirit" of the generic sword. That objects have spirits consisting of the characteristics that define them is a notion first expounded upon in detail by Plato, several thousand years ago. He posited a *Platonic Realm* of *Ideal Forms* of which our world was only an imperfect shadow. The notion of Platonic perfection is still present today in branches of modern physics, some highly speculative, and much of mathematics.

We now know the "spirit of sword". It is not much of a leap to extend the idea to encompass type and individuality, that is, to imagine that a particular sword type might have a more highly defined spirit. In the case of a Viking sword, the attributes of "sword" become more specific; namely its steel alloy, its unique shape of blade, guard, pommel and decoration. One can further refine all this to the point where a particular Viking sword is recognized. These are the overt material attributes of the "sword spirit". However, there are three more components or aspects that contribute to its spirit that have nothing to do directly with the sword itself – they lie in the eye of the beholder, or more accurately, the mind.

The first aspect applies to all swords. It is the archetype that "sword" invokes – the images conjured up in the mind by the word and its associations. Clearly these are cultural artifacts, but in general a sword is recognized primarily as a weapon, not a tool. A sword is meant to maim and kill, and is intimately associated with warfare and death. However it has also come to be associated with law and justice, which it often symbolizes.

The second aspect is the history of the sword itself, if known. For example, it may be a new sword, or it may have a detailed history attached to it if it is old. It may be cheap, or incredibly valuable. It may actually have been used in battle, or on ceremonial occasions. The owner(s) may have left their mark on it either literally in terms of decoration, or figuratively in terms of wear. These factors affect the way one sees, and feels it metaphorically.

Finally, there is the interaction in use between the sword and mind/body. This includes the physical effects of weight distribution and grip, which is a very individual thing dependent on ones size and strength. Then there is the psychological effect of holding what may be a dangerous weapon. A "live" blade where even a light touch to flesh will cut deeply has a very different spirit and feel to that of a blunt training sword.

All these aspects interact in a manner unique to an individual to create the spirit of a particular sword. To summarize, the spirit of an object is a composite entity. The first component is essentially "what it is" using a definition that is relatively unchanging – atemporal. The second component is the collection of properties that differentiate it from others of its kind and which may vary in time. Then there is the history and especially the knowledge of its history and its psychological associations. This is most definitely rooted in time. Finally we have the ongoing interaction between a person and the item in question. If we now extend this analysis to a person we find:

- A Human Being – a definition that is almost unchanging over many millennia

- Differentiated from other Humans by ancestry such as DNA, family environment, placental environment etc.

- Made unique by external culture, natural environment, and experience:

Semantics and Spells

- Defined in the moment by interaction with others.

Finally there is one other quality that a Human possesses and which a sword does not

- Self-motivation.

In short, the spirit of a person is a combination of Nature, Nurture, Interaction and Will. Note that it differs from an inanimate object only in terms of self-motivational aspects, that is, internally directed information processing, or Will in magickal terms. Crucially though, the spirit of any object or person is something that is not constant but is changing moment by moment. As the Buddha noted 2500 years ago in the Diamond Sutra:

> "All composite things (samskrita) are like a dream, a phantasm, a bubble, and a shadow; are like a dew-drop and a flash of lightning; They are thus to be regarded."

Spirit as Incorporeal Consciousness

In many ways this is both the easiest and most difficult definition of spirit to cover. One could simply state that no reliable scientific evidence exists of anything resembling consciousness not connected with matter and leave it at that. Most scientists generally believe that consciousness is an *emergent phenomenon* of certain types of computing systems – ones complex enough to model themselves as well as their environment.

However, there is a major problem with this view that has still not been overcome. It is that nobody has successfully defined consciousness at all! The above belief is an assumption, and one that is challenged by a minority of the physics community. The most notable exponent of this minority view is by the famous mathematical physicist Roger Penrose[5] in his books. He believes that consciousness is derived from deep properties of a yet-to-be created theory linking Quantum Mechanics and General Relativity of which the brain takes advantage at the microscopic level.

Another radical view is based around the notion of mathematics as being a foundation for the universe as we see it. The great philosophical problem concerning mathematics that remains unresolved is whether it is discovered or invented. Strong cases can be made for both positions, and both positions also have their weaknesses. Suffice to say that if mathematics is "discovered" it strongly implies that the Platonic Realm mentioned earlier is real, at least for mathematics, and is somehow located beyond the matter-energy-information that we think exclusively defines our reality. It also implies that we have an interaction with that

---

[5] Roger Penrose, 'The Emperors New Mind' Penguin (Non-Classics); Reprint edition (January 1, 1991) ISBN: 0140145346, Roger Penrose, 'Shadows of the Mind' Oxford University Press; Reprint edition (May 1, 1996) ISBN: 0195106466

realm in ways that are not understood, although Penrose and Hameroff[6] have a number of speculations. A related notion is that of the "All Universes Hypothesis"[7] created by Max Tegmark which posits that underlying reality is mathematical, and that all consistent mathematical schemes (an infinite number!) result in entire universes, most of them radically different from ours. That there is nothing but mathematics and our universe only exists because it is a schema complex enough to encompass consciousness. In fact, there is no "physical reality" at all.

Of course, this may or may not be so, but it does illustrate where a not very radical analysis of materialist science is leading, and what questions have to be given serious thought. As the philosopher, scientist and theologian Teilhard de Chardin wrote in "Sketch of a Personalistic Universe":

> "…pure spirituality is as inconceivable as pure materiality. Just as, in a sense, there is no geometrical point, but as many structurally different points as there are methods of deriving them from different figures, so every spirit derives its reality and nature from a particular type of universal synthesis."

Soul – Definitions

So where does this leave the idea of a soul, as distinct from a spirit, at least in this work? If the spirit of a person is a definition of what they are at a particular moment in time then the only thing a soul can be is the summation of the spirit over an entire lifetime. It is in fact a full record of a person for every moment of their life.

The problem is that we do not have such a record of a person. However, it appears that Nature does, and it is called "the past". One of the two great scientific revolutions of the last century was Einstein's Theory of Relativity in the Special and General forms. Both demolished the previously held view of space and time as being a mere backdrop upon which events played out and replaced them with the concept of space-time which was a player in its own right. Previously people could agree on whether two events happened simultaneously and how much time passed, or on how long a particular ruler might be and how much it weighed by close observation. In the new scheme observed lengths and masses change according to how fast one is moving relative to them, and the duration of an event also changes in the same way. All that remains from the old way of understanding the world is the order of events, that is all that people can agree upon is that a cause preceded an effect – in other words, Causality. This has a peculiar side effect with regards to time. Before Einstein the past was gone and finished and the future did not yet exist. After Einstein both past and future had to co-exist in a specific manner, that

---

[6] Orchestrated Reduction Of Quantum Coherence In Brain Microtubules: A Model For Consciousness? Stuart Hameroff & Roger Penrose, In: Toward a Science of Consciousness – The First Tucson Discussions and Debates, Eds. Hameroff, S.R., Kaszniak, A.W. and Scott, A.C., Cambridge, MA: MIT Press, pp. 507-540 (1996)

[7] Max Tegmark, Annals of Physics 270, 1-51 gr-qc/9704009 New Scientist magazine 6 June 1998 for the popular account

is, the past was *not* gone and finished. The past (and future) is as real as anything else in our universe. What this amounts to is that there is a new model of the world with four dimensions, three of space and one of time, tied together in such a way that past present and future can be depicted as a static entity. Objects as they move through space and travel through time from the past to the future trace out what is called a *worldline* that seems, in the bigger 4D picture, to be like unmoving statue. A slice through that statue at any point in time tells us what it was like at that particular instant of "now" – in other words, their spirit. If that statue is a person, the bottom of it is the point in time when they were born, and the top is the point at which they died. That eternal statue as a whole is the soul, and from a time-bound point of view within the lifetime of the person it is something that *grows*.

Naturally, the reality is not as neat as presented above largely because of that second great revolution of the last century, Quantum Mechanics (QM). As we shall see in the next chapter, the implications of QM can be extremely bizarre and literally open a universe of possibilities. This is one reason why it features so much in New Age books and in theories of magick and Psi. For example, reinterpreting the 4D concept of soul by throwing into the mix a particular interpretation of QM we get not merely a worldline but an infinite number of them across yet another dimension. They branch out from the moment of birth like a vast tree, and not all of the branches terminate – in some of them there is no death. There is now no longer a well determined path being traced but the soul-tree taking all possible routes to the future. Interestingly, this is intimately related to the Least Action Principle, but instead of most paths canceling out they extend into other universes.

The problem with all of this speculation arises from something still unresolved by science. It is that Relativity deals with the very large and QM deals with the very small and both have been tested to great precision experimentally and no failures have been found in either. Yet it is known with certainty that either or both are wrong, or at least only parts of a larger theory, because they are fundamentally incompatible with each other. That larger undiscovered theory has come to be known as the Theory of Everything.

On a final note for this section, the frozen knowledge held in space-time bears an uncanny resemblance to that hypothetical occult repository of all knowledge – the Akashic record.

Reincarnation

An explanation of reincarnation in the light of the above rounds out the particular worldview being defined in this work. Unfortunately no magickal insights or technologies flow from it directly. Indirectly it is included in order to foster the creation of a particular mindset suitable for the safe application of some of the technologies later outlined.

For most of history the Indo-European peoples believed in reincarnation because they saw that there was a great deal of evidence in favor of its objective reality. Simply stated, they saw the same people returning, most often in the same family. The latter is a feature of the doctrine of reincarnation that was prevalent in the Germanic religion, which is one of the Western religions that evolved from the Proto-Indo-Europeans. More familiar are the doctrines of its great Eastern derivatives of Hinduism and Buddhism.

The reason people came to believe in reincarnation is straightforward. Consider the circumstances of the great majority of our people throughout history. Most lived in small tribes or communities and seldom ventured far beyond them. They almost always married someone who lived in the locality and continued to reside there. Life changed little over the decades and centuries and the environment in all senses remained virtually constant. The social structure was unvaried, as was the diet, the land, climate and architecture. Occupations were fixed, most people were illiterate and the stories told around the hearth were the ones they had heard from their parents and grandparents.

A child is born into the family – what will he or she be like as an adult? The answer is that a mixture of genetics and environment determines a person. The genetics determines the physical attributes such as height, body type hair and eye color and so forth, as well as emotional tendencies and other features of the personality including intelligence to a significant degree. Yet we have seen that the community is quite inbred, so there are certainly going to be people of very similar appearance and disposition appearing repeatedly down the generations. This is greatly accentuated by the constant environment to which the growing child is exposed, so it is no wonder that people believe in rebirth especially within the family line.

There will obviously be exceptions as random unusual variations arise, but this would be taken as evidence that the incarnating soul comes from farther in the past or perhaps from outside the family line altogether. Such exceptions result in a refinement of the concept, while the bulk of similarities reinforce the central notion of reincarnation. This is obviously a reworking of the definition of "spirit" above, with Nature, Nurture and Interaction being the constant features, which leaves Will.

In many societies, especially those of ancestral Europeans, the naming of a child required the utmost care as it was believed that this had a major impact on the type of person they would become. Indeed, in the Germanic religion there was something of a taboo against naming a child after a living relative, which stemmed from the belief of rebirth through ones descendants. Hence naming a child after a living member of the family tended to interfere with the process in various ways. The idea that a name confers certain characteristics on a child is far from being mere superstition, especially in societies where names have particular associations. For our ancestors names came with stories attached, and indeed the name itself often indicated the particular quality to be conferred. The child was expected to know and to live up to, and to take on the best characteristics of the former owner as remembered by the family, tribe or nation As we will see later, the importance and power of such social spirits, also known as *dynamic archetypes*, is vastly

Semantics and Spells

underestimated. This is still common today but unfortunately much of the power has been lost because it is done through ignorance of its true function. Instead a child is named after a transient figure such as a popular singer or movie star or, if named after a relative it is done as a kind of honor to them without any attached story. More often a name is chosen simply because it sounds pleasant, or is fashionable, without even a cursory investigation as to what it means. In my view naming a child without knowing what that name really means is a form of spiritual abuse.

Anyway, that's the "rational" explanation as to why a reincarnation myth develops. The missing piece of the puzzle is the memory of past lives that some people, mostly children, claim to possess. Additionally we have the phenomenon of past life regression via hypnosis. In both instances there are cases where such information has been checked and found to be accurate not only in outline but in considerable detail. If we accept this at face value there is a serious problem even apart from trying to devise a mechanism. It is the question of what, precisely, gets reincarnated. Despite the way New Age books dealing with such topics tend to gloss over this question it is one that a number of religions have addressed in detail, most notably Buddhism. All have acknowledged that a Human Being is a composite entity although how the non-physical components are defined varies. However, in general two elements are reborn. The first is pure consciousness and the second is Karma in the sense of consequences of past actions being incarnated in new minds. This latter aspect is often fully not appreciated or understood in the West, so we will use that all round exemplar Adolph Hitler to illustrate the point. He is a figure that dominates the 20th Century and the actions and ideas he set in motion have rippled down the decades in the politics of Europe from attitudes towards race, militarism and empire to the way the current borders are drawn. Everyone who has been born into that milieu has absorbed that Karma into their being, which constitutes most Europeans. We are who we are because of who he was and what he did and it is almost impossible to escape from his shadow for either good or evil. The very fact you have just read this illustrates the point since another minor consequence of his existence has been incarnated in your mind through me, the author.

Contrary to many people's beliefs, personality and memory are generally not directly reborn and arise through the causal mechanism of Karma, which includes the transmission of genetic information from parents to child. The nature of mind and consciousness is examined in much greater detail in the following chapters.

Finally, there are two other possibilities at opposite ends of the plausibility spectrum. At one end we have the unconscious mind accumulating detailed information and fabricating a story which appears as false memories. As we shall see later in the book, the unconscious has incredible powers of information acquisition and synthesis that go far beyond what one might reasonably expect. At the other end of the spectrum we have the New Age version of reincarnation as simply being an aspect of Psi, specifically clairvoyance. All that is happening is that some of the memories of someone who once lived are being accessed and interpreted as "self", although it seems likely that such is not a random access but is directed by unconscious elements of the reincarnated person. Or maybe time is an illusion and we are all aspects of one of more psyches spread across time. You choose – but remember that each story you decide to tell yourself has its own ramifications, advantage and drawbacks. Choosing, knowing and using is the essence of the art of the mage.

Etymology – Casting a Spell

We have just used contemporary science to illustrate and interpret ancient concepts but we can go in the opposite direction and examine what our ancestors literally meant when they used certain words. It can be very enlightening because they often had a more precise knowledge of that which they spoke than we do today.

Language itself is often a source of hidden insights. As Wittgenstein noted, language is crucial to thought. It both guides and limits what can be thought and expressed, which is one reason why all sciences and technologies come with reams of carefully defined jargon designed to encapsulate new understandings about the nature of consensus reality. What is seldom realized, however, is that ordinary language also encapsulates some very interesting and useful insights into Mind and Nature. This is not too surprising given that language capability seems to be "hard wired" into the brain via genetics. However, as our language evolves, especially English, the true meaning and origin of words often fades and is replaced by a superficial understanding which bears only a shadow of its former power. Many words literally have occult, that is hidden, meanings that lie dormant in the unconscious of both individuals and societies. In this sense one might surmise that a Golden Age of understanding, or at least precise expression, once existed. For example, one of the oldest and purest of the Indo-European languages (of which English is a member and descendant) is Sanskrit. Its precision, grammar and sheer logical structure is unsurpassed. Perhaps the modern mind has sacrificed depth and clarity of thought for breadth, and magick was once so obvious that it was never considered as a separate category of knowledge at all.

Words are magickal and what they represent in the mind is magickal. They act to bind together facets of mind into something coherent and meaningful in which they can enjoy some sort of autonomy (for a while). And equally important, words can transfer information, knowledge, meaning, emotion, intent and so forth both from mind to mind and as we shall see later from one part of the mind to another. They can even transfer all of that across time and space in the form of writing, which to illiterate peoples appears truly wondrous. To hear the dead speaking in our minds to us across the millennia…

The evolution of words is also the evolution of the psyche and society that uses them. They are tied together inextricably. So although one might decry the loss of purity of the language, with words now taking on multiple meanings, we have

Semantics and Spells

also gained the ability to encode a great deal of context sensitive information into a single word. In terms of this capability English is probably foremost as it has undergone the most radical changes over the recent centuries. One result is that although we might believe we are saying one thing, we are also often unconsciously adding subtexts that may well be meaningful to unconscious aspects of our mind as well as the minds of other people. Indeed, this is superficially recognized in classical psychiatry whether of Jung or Freud, to name but two of the most famous schools. As English speakers we also have the greatest vocabulary to choose from with more than a million words. Most educated people have a working knowledge of less than five percent of this.

So when looking into etymology, especially with regard to words that have deep roots and significance in the collective psyche, one is looking directly into the occult, that is, the hidden. One can consider it as "fossil knowledge" that has been buried deep in our language, or alternatively, perhaps it can be considered as knowledge refined over the centuries and encoded by our collective unconscious in the way we speak and write. I tend to assume that when various meanings coalesce into a modern usage it is not purely coincidence. In fact, one word may expand in use simply because it sounds like another even though they may originally be unrelated. The word has undergone an evolution or mutation that makes it more fitting for a changed environment. That environment can be cultural, technological, geographical or spiritual – and the environment of the English language has undergone vast changes in the past four centuries as it spread with Empire and was augmented by the Industrial Revolution. Furthermore, what is true in one context remains true even when that context evolves and the use of the word changes. Rather, the word accumulates layers of truths like sediment in the ocean of mind. This is especially true of words that have deep religious or spiritual connotations. When we analyze the language used in such contexts we often find that what is really being said is significantly different from what we naively expect.

In order to illustrate the above we can analyze the words used in, and surrounding, the phrase *casting a spell* – something rather appropriate given the theme of this work, and one which leads to some interesting insights and possibilities to be explored in depth later in the book.

A major tool in magick is the *spell* – but what is it? Basically, one *casts a spell* by various means in order to effect a specified magickal change in or to something. What is the mechanism and outcome of *casting a spell*? It may *enchant* by means of an *incantation*, which is both *fascinating* and *glamorous* as well as *charming*. Let's examine each word in detail.

Etymology – Spell

There are several diverse meanings and roots which have come together to create the modern definitions, some actually very recent. Perhaps the most interesting feature of the magickal definition, "a set of words with magical powers, incantation, charm", is the fact that it was first recorded 1579CE. So it seems to be a relatively recent term that appeared after the Middle Ages when the language was undergoing a quite rapid evolution.

The earliest root of *spell* is the Proto-Indo-European word *spel*, meaning "to say aloud or recite". The later meaning, that of writing or saying the letters of a word, can be traced back to around 1400CE. Of course, this is not too surprising when one considers the prevalence of the spoken over the written word in societies where most people were illiterate. Whether it was a coincidence that the printing press appeared in the West around the time the word expanded its role one can only speculate. One of the most recent expansions of utility is traced to as recently as 1940CE in American English, namely using *spell out* to mean, "explain step by step". That too may have had to wait until the complexities of life in the machine age called it forth as a metaphor. Why is speech so important? There are several reasons.

First, speaking has a unique effect on ones own mind. Some facets seem to have poor communications skills and quite often speaking aloud gets their attention more readily than thoughts. It's as if some facets can best hear via the ears, and are poor at intercepting the internal mental dialog. That's why (auto) hypnotism courses are almost always audio recordings and not books or videos. Any visual components of hypnotic induction tend to be ones to lull that particular sense while keeping the audio channel open. The use of vision for communication, apart from gestures and body language, is only some 6000 years old in the form of writing. It is still not natural for Humans to use this method, and neither static nor moving pictures have the immediacy and flexibility of spoken language. Furthermore our technology is not capable of translating thought to image as a means of real-time interactive communication, although it may do so one day. Second, telling others of the spell magnifies its effect. It uses other minds as carriers, whether willing or not.

Returning this time to Old English we have the word *spelian*, of uncertain origin, meaning to "represent, substitute for, take the place of". It may perhaps be related to *spilian*, "to play". Now this may not seem at first sight to have much relevance to the magickal spell, but it does encourage some very interesting speculations.

For example, consider the experiment in "ghost creation"[8] undertaken by the Toronto branch of the Society for Psychical Research in the early 1970s and which is described in greater detail in the chapters on Psi research. They discovered that the optimum atmosphere conducive to the manifestation of physical phenomena by their creation "Philip" was one of playfulness with jokes, singing, music, poetry recital and casual conversation. In addition they had objects related to Philip, including a portrait and items associated with him. Bear this in mind as we progress…

It may also be relevant that in Chaos Magick part of the technique is to

---

[8] Conjuring up Philip by Iris M Owen with Margaret Sparrow, ISBN 0-7701-0005-8

intentionally hide the spell by forgetting about it in order for the unconscious mind to do the real work. It could well be that the playfulness is one component of the mix that serves a similar purpose by fooling the conscious mind into not noticing the importance of what is happening, and hence not impeding it. Then there is the practice of *sympathetic magick* where an item substitutes for the real target and becomes the focus of the working. The most familiar example is the Voodoo doll[9], but it could equally be a photograph or belonging – anything, in fact, with a connection. The operation can be either harmful or beneficial depending upon the intention of the operator.

Etymology – Casting

Superficially one might assume that *casting* simply means "to throw" or "to send forth", which is of course an aspect of what one does with a spell. However, there are several subsidiary definitions that may well play a significant role in the process and help explain why *casting* is a more appropriate word than, say, *hurling* or *sending*. The first is the use of the word to mean *forming*, as in (say) "a sculpture is cast in bronze". This latter meaning comes from the act of throwing the *casting* out of the mold and underlies several subsidiary definitions that follow. Related to this are also "arrange" and "devise" as qualifiers to forming. For example, one can "cast a book into several parts" or "cast a plan". Then there is also *cast* meaning to calculate, as in "cast a horoscope". Clearly a spell is something which is formed and is carefully crafted and deliberately arranged for a calculated purpose or effect. It is not just an arbitrary impromptu process. It is, in fact, something that should be "spelled out" in some detail.

If we carry on delving into the dictionary we come upon other unusual meanings that have gone out of fashion. Cast can also mean to "warp or twist", as in "floorboards cast by age". This is where we move into the realm of speculation. What, exactly, is being warped or twisted in the process of casting a spell? I would suggest that it is the words themselves, as a spell is almost always a verbal, or occasionally written, construct. So, it might pay to look into the possibility that the words are warped or twisted in some manner to heighten their effect. We will look at these possibilities in greater detail later in the book.

Then there is "search", as in "to cast about". However, although this is a variation of "throw", what one is doing when *casting about* is throwing out our senses in order to find something. What that something may be we will return to when we get to examine *fascinate*.

Finally we have cast is in "cast of actors". Now this may not be of direct relevance to a spell unless there is a *cast of deities* involved to which one is appealing

---

[9] Actually a European innovation, not African. Also named a "Poppet" circa 1300CE, related to "Puppet".

for aid in the delivery of effect. Was that one obvious…?

Etymology – Enchanting, Incantation and Charm

Charming, of course, comes from the Latin *carmen* meaning a song or verse and took on its magickal connotations around 1300CE. One current usage, that of a charm being "a small trinket fastened to a chain" was first recorded 1865CE. However, that particular definition will play no further part in our analysis. *Enchant* and *incantation* both derive from the Latin *cantare*, meaning to sing, with the prefix "in" meaning "upon" or "into".

Again, we have moved forward a little. A spell could involve something put into, or upon a song. The difference between the two is indicative of the purpose to which the song is put. The words of the spell could be put *into* the song, or laid *upon* the song. The latter would be the case, for example, when music is used to evoke a particular mental state or feeling in order to facilitate the spell itself, without being an integral part of it.

A chant is a special form of singing, notably "a short, simple series of syllables or words that are sung on or intoned to the same note or a limited range of notes". Crucially singing, chanting and music in general have consciousness altering properties. The various rhythms can alter brainwaves by a process called entrainment whereby the brainwaves start to follow the (low) frequencies of the music. For groups, there is a convergence of mental states based around the music. Probably the most effective ancient method is the use of percussion, particularly drumming.

The most well known forms of magickal chanting specifically designed to alter consciousness are Mantras, that is, single words or short phrases chanted repeatedly. A variation on this is probably the Galdr of Germanic Heathenism whereby the letters of the old Germanic alphabet known as Runes, or Rune combinations, are intoned. Here the meaning is already encoded into the Rune as a series of associations since each Rune has a specific meaning as well as simply being a letter. Ironically those meanings themselves were recorded in ancient times in poems, with each verse telling of an individual Rune, presumably as an aid in memorizing and transmitting the lore.

Which brings us to certain types of poetry. Here we have another method of evoking particular emotional states by using a combination of evocative words coupled with a rhythmic delivery. This in turn is related to the kind of soft toned sinuous prose designed to induce hypnotic states. So we see what *cast* might mean when it implies something warped or twisted.

Semantics and Spells

Etymology – Fascinate

Meanwhile *fascinate* is derived from the Latin *fascinum* meaning "to bewitch" which has roots in the words *fascis* – to bind. Another possibly is that it was connected with the word *fas* that indicates "divine law or command, destiny, fate", which would make sense as the *fasces* was the ax with a bundle of rods bound to the haft which was the symbol of law and power in Rome. On the other hand, perhaps it is one of those occasions where two similar sounding words of different origin form a symbiosis in the minds of those using them.

    Bear in mind that any successful outcome of a magickal working will always have a conventional explanation and mechanism (and here we include Psi phenomena as being part of the natural world). This being so, and all other factors being equal, the course of events which has the highest natural probability will likely be the more successful. A bit like the joke concerning the man who kept praying to God for a lottery win. Eventually God tells him: "Meet me half way – buy a ticket!".

    Determining the flow of events connected with the desired outcome of the spell vastly improves its efficacy if the spell is cast in accordance with that "divine law, destiny, fate". Of course, what is being referred to goes under several names depending upon the religious tradition as we have already seen: Karma, Tao, Wyrd, Fate… It is this "thing" that one *casts about* for with the senses both internal and external. By seeing a Way we create a Way.

Etymology – Glamor

Glamor itself is another word that has been (seemingly) distorted by its late 19th Century, usage. It entered modern English language by way of the Scottish *gramarye* which means enchantment. However, even this is relatively recent, being traced to the 18th Century. Before that we can go back to French, Latin and Greek where it refers to scholarship, especially of the occult kind, as well as study of the rules of language, which is where the modern word "grammar" arises. So, we are back once again to words…

    Words can cast a glamor because they are capable of overriding the information provided by all our other senses. The particular words to prefix the most common spell used to accomplish this magickal act are: "Let me explain…" All that is required to illustrate the power words have to twist reality is to watch the television news with the sound off.

    So next time you hear of something being *glamorous* think carefully what is really being said. Sometime, almost certainly during the 20th Century, the meanings of some key words have been twisted through one hundred and eighty degrees. Where our ancestors once considered the glamorous to be illusory, dangerous and consequently undesirable we are now encouraged to seek it out. In the process we are to consider it a bonus to be *enchanted* and *fascinated*. To be *disillusioned* and *disenchanted* is not viewed as being a positive state to be in, and *unglamorous* is used as a synonym for boring and tedious. On the contrary, we are supposed to value pleasing unreality over hard truth. Where this reversal happened is rather hard to pinpoint, but a good guess might be Hollywood (Holy Wood) and show business which is, after all, in the business of selling *dreams*. This word too has been distorted from its straightforward use as description of the hallucinations that occurs sleep to replacing the previously used *aspirations*. The use of *dream* in this context dates from 1931CE. So once again a word denoting the unreal has been used to replace something fairly concrete, although on closer inspection it might be worse than this. If we look at the word *aspiration* we see that it derives from the Latin *aspirare* meaning "to breathe upon" and "to seek to reach". In turn this latter word derives from *spirare* meaning "to breath", which connects it directly with the root of the word *spirit* which also derives from breathing.

As to why this has happened, or been allowed to happen by the psyche of the English speaking peoples, the reason is uncertain. However, it does seem extremely likely that this is but one manifestation of a spiritual sickness.

Moving in the opposite direction, we have words such as *holy*. The latter word is derived from the Indo-European root *hailo* or *kailo* meaning "free from injury, whole", whence comes also English *hale* as in "hale and hearty". Related to this notion of wholeness is *integrity*. If our mind is not integrated, we lack *integrity* that in modern use means that we are viewed as being untrustworthy or dishonest. As we shall see later, the divided mind is weakness incarnate. It can be pushed and pulled in many different and conflicting directions with ease, and because this is so, it cannot be predicted or trusted. It is one of the major sources of unease that people experience around some types of the mentally ill and around those people who are fickle, "shallow" or "self" centered. And worth bearing in mind is the religious notion of being *blessed*. This too is normally seen as being a positive thing, especially in connection with a deity or its representatives. Its origins however, lie in completely the opposite direction. It actually means "wounded" and we will see exactly what this means in the chapter on Godforms.

For anyone who wishes to further investigate the linguistics of magick and evolution of spiritual world-views the Net[10] often provides decent resources but a good dictionary, particularly an etymological dictionary[11], is the best.

---

[10] http://www.etymonline.com

[11] The Oxford Dictionary of English Etymology, Oxford University Press

Semantics and Spells

The final word I shall leave to Terry Pratchett, a quotation from his book "Lords and Ladies":

> "Elves are wonderful. They provoke wonder.
> Elves are marvelous. They cause marvels.
> Elves are fantastic. They create fantasies.
> Elves are glamorous. They project glamor.
> Elves are enchanting. They weave enchantment.
> Elves are terrific. They beget terror.

The thing about words is that meanings can twist just like a snake, and if you want to find snakes look for them behind words that have changed their meaning. No one ever said elves are nice. Elves are bad."

Science and Magick

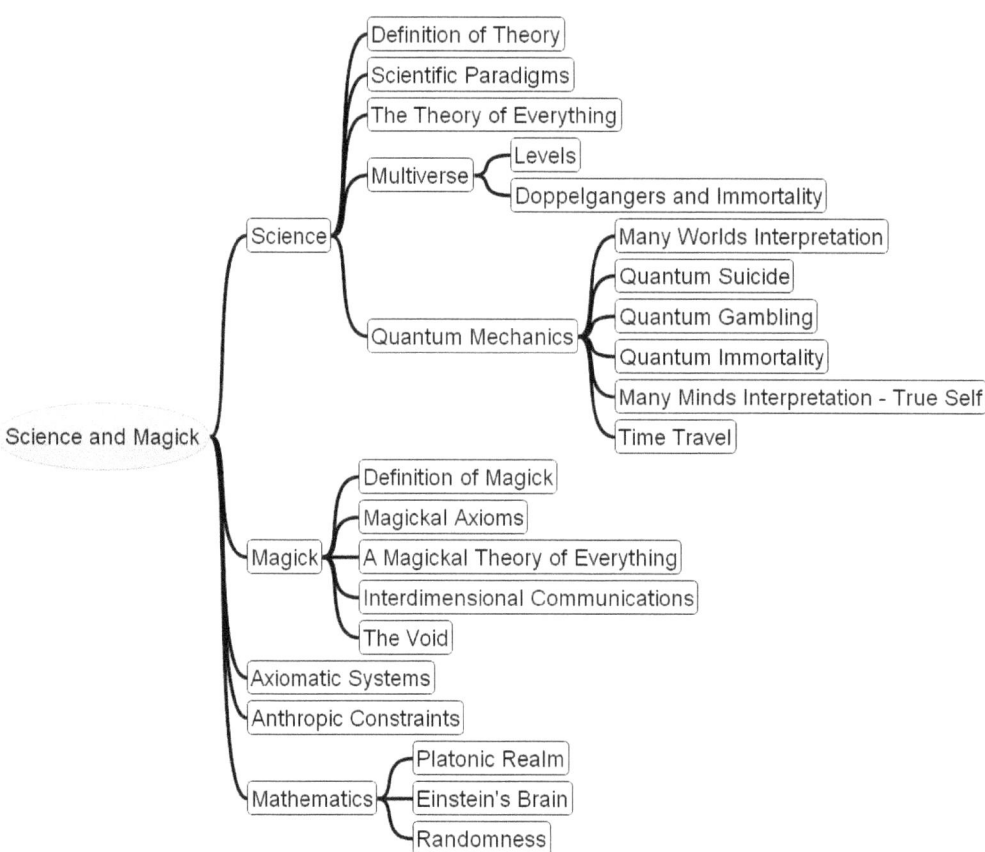

2 Science and Magick

Science

Before we take a look at the nature of science and particularly the notion of what constitutes a theory, we need to understand what a *paradigm* actually is, especially in the context of magick. This is important since we will be seeing a lot of this word as much of the book is devoted to presenting new magickal paradigms in the context of science and technology. Anyway, if we look in a dictionary we get the definition as:

> "A set of assumptions, concepts, values, and practices that constitutes a way of viewing reality for the community that shares them, especially in an intellectual discipline."

It is crucial to note that the same set of known facts can generate quite radically different paradigms. Take, for example, the game of Ouija that we will be looking at in much greater depth later. The facts are that people gather around a lettered board all touching a planchette on its surface, then ask a question. The planchette moves to spell out an answer. The usual paradigm the participants embrace is one where unseen intelligent entities of the spirit world use the energy of the people involved to spell out the messages, which are typically attributed to someone who has died, or "passed over" as the paradigm's specialist vocabulary puts it. Yet a completely different paradigm can be assigned to that set of facts and practices that involves no spirits, or afterlife or anything supernatural at all and which involves group psychology and unconscious manipulation of the planchette. So one set of facts can give rise to, or support, diametrically opposed world-views.

What we are going to do is take aspects of science and technology and reinterpret them in a magickal context in a manner that lends itself to practical workings, often of unique scope and power.

Needless to say, the greatest overall magickal paradigm, or belief system, that we currently have is science, yet few people know what it is. The most common understanding is a vague notion of "Doing experiments and discovering things about Nature". That, though, is only part of the story. Science attempts to find or define *facts*. That is, seemingly irreducible items of data that (nearly) everyone can agree upon and verify for themselves (in principle at least). These are then linked into a *theory* in such a way that it makes *predictions*. These predictions, or pointers to new facts, are then tested by experiments to see whether those supposed facts actually exist. If they do, the theory continues onwards. If not, the theory is shown to be false. A theory is deemed *scientific* if it makes testable predictions that distinguishes it from existing theories and which could in principle falsify the theory. Overall, it is a fairly good way of going about things and has indeed led to the modern age. However, it does rely on a number of generally unspoken assumptions. These are:

- That there is an external reality that we can all agree upon.
- That it is logically consistent.
- That this reality is independent of our belief in it, a corollary of which is that consciousness has no physical effects and that the experiment and experimenter can ultimately be separated.
- That at base this reality is essentially unchanging.
- That the regularities discovered, called the Laws of Physics, are a consequences of more fundamental Laws. In other words, it is all linked into one undivided whole. It is this latter belief that spurs the search for a Theory of Everything or TOE for short.
- That mathematics can describe deep aspects of this reality and that the logic underlying mathematical processes is the same as that which governs reality.
- That we can ultimately understand the nature of reality

There are some other lesser working assumptions that are of interest. These are:

- *Occam's Razor*, which states that given two possible explanations for a particular phenomenon the simplest is more likely to be correct.
- A prejudice that says that the most aesthetically pleasing theory is the one to be preferred, all things being equal. Which is remarkable in its own way for being an acknowledgment that reality shares our sense of beauty, or more likely that we get our sense of beauty from the deepest features of the world around us.
- And finally the concept of *Causality*. This is the belief, which is looking increasing shaky, that causes must precede effects and information can only travel forwards in time.

To understand these further we need to take a different view of the nature of theory. This is best done by using an analogy, specifically the children's picture book game of "join the dots and make a picture". Typically there are dozens of dots on a page, seemingly random, and each dot is numbered. As the dots are joined together by moving a pencil from one to another in numerical sequence a recognizable picture appears.

In science the dots are facts, or data elements and the picture one draws is the theory. The complications arise from a number of sources. First, the dots are not numbered so we do not know in what order they need to be joined. Second, we do not know how many dots there are, or whether we have missed any in our current part of the drawing although we do know with certainty that we do not have all the dots. Additionally, we do not know exactly where to look for our missing dots except by joining up the ones we have as best we can and seeing if the resulting picture suggests an area worth a looking at in greater depth. It's a bit like saying: "I think this might be the nose of a dog – let's have a look for some dots where its nose should be!" So, we have a look and find some more dots there and people say: "The picture must be a dog". That's the dog paradigm.

However, there is a lively debate between those who think it's a dog, and those who think it's a cat. Then a heretic comes along and claims the picture is actually a Tyrannosaurus Rex! After a while, when it is obvious that the animal has very short front legs, very big back legs and a very long tail there is a paradigm shift, and now the picture is that of a dinosaur. Then a crank comes along who says that it's not *really* anything anyone has seen before and that the best way of joining the dots is not to make a picture at all but to make the shortest possible line that can link them all together. Amid much ridicule the crank persists and shows beyond doubt that his method leads to the discovery of a far greater number of dots than the "looks like an animal" method. Now it is claimed that picture is not of an animal but of an abstract painting of beautiful and subtle symmetries. So we come to the modern view of a scientific theory, that it is just the most efficient way of joining the dots that leads to more dots.

This is in fact strongly related to another facet of the nature of a theory, which is that it is the shortest explanation for linking diverse numbers of facts by looking at what they have in common. For example, we have the diverse facts that if you drop a brick it falls. If you drop an apple it falls. If you drop an elephant it falls. What could possibly link bricks, apples and elephants? The answer is the Law of Gravity – that if you drop (almost) anything it will fall. So we have joined the *brick*, *apple*, *elephant* and *falling* dots and come up with a famous picture, and in doing so have reduced millions of such facts down to one simple idea, or in terms of information theory, we have created an *algorithmic compression* of the data. The Laws of Physics (or any science) are then simply the large scale patterns or symmetries that we see in our abstract picture. The problem with this efficient new method is threefold.

- Except for very simple systems there is no way, even in principle, that one can determine whether one has the best picture. Indeed, there may well be better ones or any number of others that fit the facts just as well. It means that if we come up with a TOE that fits all known facts it is very likely we can never prove it is the best, or only, such theory.

- We mistake the picture we draw for being reality. The map is not the territory.

- The picture gets drawn solely from using data points everyone can agree upon. That is, it's a map of consensus reality and by definition cannot handle subjective information. The problem here being that all we have to work on is a theory our brains builds from sense impressions. Indeed the very idea of brains and sense impression is itself a theory concocted by our mind in order to explain itself. A manifestation of this latter problem occurs in at least one area of science, that dedicated to understanding the nature of consciousness, and many scientists suspect that it may well spill over into other areas from Quantum Mechanics to Artificial Intelligence to cosmology.

So, we are going to take a rather partisan look at modern scientific theories to see what magick we can mine from them. There are the usual New Age suspects like Quantum Mechanics, but also a few others of a more speculative nature. However, we look to them not because they are "true", but because they embody the Zeitgeist of the contemporary world of thought. So do not take any of this too literally, and certainly not to the extent my Victorian predecessors did who tried to put the occult on a scientific basis by invoking cutting edge 19th Century physics with notions of "vibrations" and "ether"! It's all just pictures – let their utility speak for itself.

Magick

This leads to interesting views of magick. One such is it that it is an engineering of states of consciousness within the above "gray areas" of the scientific paradigm. The other is that mind underlies everything and that science is merely one manifestation of magick. Peripherally related to this is the kind of science mythology whereby facts lead to theories which lead to more facts plus technologies based upon the successful theory. The true situation is that it is often the other way around, and that theory follows on from engineering and technology, or to put it another way, invention precedes theory rather than follows it. In a magickal paradigm where *belief is all* the only thing that makes any sense are the results. And in the game we are playing the most intractable of the rules are known as *The Laws of Physics*. However, like all the rules we can revise or change them by joining the dots differently (and maybe only temporarily) to draw a more suitable picture. All we have to do is create one. It does not even have to be true – just useful!

Science, Proof and Power

An incredibly powerful magickal technique is to base ones spells (in the widest sense of the word) upon non-disprovable propositions that are then logically expounded and developed in all their consequences. It means that they have a foundation that is immune to scientific attack and can only be overturned by a greater Act of Will bolstered by an axiomatic system of equal or greater power. Traditionally such systems have been extensions of conventional theologies which have been stripped of their pseudo-scientific baggage of explanations for physical phenomena. In the West we have examples such as the Cabala, and in the East Buddhism with its axioms being *The Four Noble Truths*. The key requirement is a set of propositions, or axioms, that not only are not amenable to testing but offer a base of sufficient complexity that a self extending structure of logical consistency can be built upon them. Finally we need a method of tying that derived logic to the desired spiritual or material aims of the practitioner. In summary, these points are:

- Untestable proposition that cannot be derived from simpler ones

- Propositions that are sufficient to support a logically derived structure of sufficient complexity

- A method of tying that structure to "reality"

Usually, that method is one of the initial axioms which posits that $X = Y$ where X is some element of the new system and Y corresponds to an element of the world or of the magician.

In the modern world one specific variant of the above is that of mathematical axioms which lead to the whole of mathematics. And when, (say) X is mapped to a physical property such as time or space we end up with the immensely powerful magickal construct of mathematical physics. However, in more conventional magickal operations X is usually mapped to an internal mental or spiritual state of the practitioner. Even more conventionally, we end up with belief systems that are in effect religions, political ideologies or ethical frameworks.

By now it should be obvious that the set of rules known as the "Ten Commandments of the Old Testament" are a crude attempt at creating an ecological system of belief and control capable of affecting, predicting and manipulating the behavior of individuals and societies. It does this by the mapping X (which is "God") to the internal elements of self interest and assorted desires for control and stability inherent in all higher lifeforms. The problem is, however, that each of the Ten Commandments can be broken down into simpler propositions simply by questioning them, once one of them is denied. Namely, if an axiom of a competing system states "There is no God" all the others fall once it becomes legitimate to ask "why?". The reply "Because God commands it" is no longer sufficient and falling back to a second tier of explanation for each of the commandments further dismantles the overall original construct. For example, each of the commandments then becomes conditional. "Thou shall not steal" becomes a question and answer session about needs, Rights, political power and the very definition of theft. However, before that dismantling happened two subtle conditions needed to exist. The first was a recognition, or assumption (an axiom of a new system) that "God" used logic and logic was permissible in analyzing religion and religious belief. Initially this led to complex theologies that bolstered the existing system, but it also led onto what by now had become legitimate questioning of the motives for God's decisions. The Commandments were no longer beyond analysis and they fell, slowly but surely, from their pedestals. Nevertheless, the construct could adapt to that as we see today, even though it bears little resemblance to its original forms. The second element followed from the first, which was the notion of testing for truth by experiment, and led to the development of modern science. While it did not disprove a key axiom of the old system, it sidelined it.. "God" is no longer viewed as being a necessary element for explaining the entirety of the physical world, despite what a minority of "Creationists" might claim. Once this happened it was natural to ask why one needed the concept of a God at all.

The lesson for the magician is plain – choose your axioms wisely, and do not have too many of them. Whether one can have too few is an interesting point given that a rather powerful one is "There is no reality". So, a summary of the requirements for choosing the propositions to underlie a new magickal systems are:

- The axioms must be untestable
- The axioms must be consistent with each other
- They must be incapable of decomposition into simpler statements
- Do not choose too many, or the complexity will explode to unmanageable levels
- Choose at least one of the axioms to be a mapping to True Will

Like all good magickal advice, by negating any or all of the above one can create a rather interesting variant that does have its uses, but I will not elaborate on that!

The key axiom, and one which is often hidden as an underlying assumption, is the question of how the system is mapped to any kind of reality. Usually this is swept under the carpet by assuming a set of "Magickal Laws", in which case all the magician is doing is tacking on some trivial extension to an already existing paradigm. No doubt this explains the mediocrity of most such New Age alternatives, and doubly so if the underlying assumptions are not spelled out or even consciously known by whoever is creating the extension. The entire notion of Magickal Laws are themselves a parody of the "Laws of Nature" discovered by scientists, and called Laws because there is (as yet) no understanding of any underlying mechanism. Indeed, the whole of science is dedicated to reducing their number and creating an ever simpler framework. Contrast that with magick, which seems at times to seek to expand complexity.

This work that you are reading adopts two approaches, or paradigms. The first is the use an adaptation of techniques from science to operate on either the mind of the practitioner or on the material world. The second is that ultimately there exists no reality at all, and a specific case is analyzed in the last chapter.

Magickal Paradigms

In a similar manner to science, magick also embodies a set of assumptions. Or rather, sets of assumptions depending upon which particular magickal paradigm one is working under. However, the most general are as follows – and apologies if I have added or omitted some that the reader might consider important, since I have chosen the ones underlying TechnoShamanism. These are:

- Reality lies in Mind and Consciousness
- Belief is everything
- Perceived Reality is fluid and conditional
- The Subjective and Objective are equally real
- Space and Time are illusions

Other axioms which are commonly included, for example, "As above, so below" and the so-called "Law of Contagion" I have omitted because they are either irrelevant or can be derived from the above by suitable analysis. For completeness I have included a full list of Magickal Laws from various traditions in an appendix.

In some ways magick and science share the notion of experiment and the testing of theories. However, magickal theories need not be scientific in the sense of needing to be amenable to falsification. Indeed, quite elaborate structures can be build upon untestable foundations and still be very useful and productive. An example of this might be the cosmology of the Cabala with the Tree of Life.

A Magical Theory of Everything (TOE)

Just as science searches for its Holy Grail, let me present a magickal version that, while it is not (at present) scientifically testable and may well never be so, is nevertheless very useful as a belief framework for the TechnoMage. It arises from turning on its head the old question in physics of: "Why something rather than nothing?" The latter question actually carries a lot of hidden assumptions, most notable being that "nothing" is somehow more fundamental than "something". Yet true nothingness cannot have *any* properties whatsoever. In particular, it can have no laws or limitations. In fact, *nothing* can be *anything* that both exists and does not exist simultaneously, that contains infinite chaos and infinite order. Time, space, law and life are but an infinitesimally tiny subset of this realm. It is the Zen Koan made manifest. So, let us use it's magickal name – *The* Void. Actually, that is not it's only name but the other one, *The Abyss*, sounds even more sinister. There's a kind of Zen Koan that sums up the Void:

> To be or not to be, that is the Question
> To be and not to be, that is the Answer

In both ancient and modern philosophy the nearest thing would be the *Platonic Realm of Ideal Forms* which supposedly holds some kind of perfect template of idealized objects and concepts that appear in the material world as mere shadows of their true self. A somewhat restricted version of Neo-Platonism is quite popular amongst physicists and mathematicians. Many view the laws of physics or the mathematical theorems that they discover as being somehow "outside" the material world. It is even embedded into their language. When did you hear of a mathematician who claims to have "invented" a new theorem? They are always "discovered".

The most extreme example in contemporary science probably occurs with Max Tegmark's All Universes Hypothesis. He posits that mathematics is the true basis of reality and that in fact there is nothing but mathematics. That is, our universe is not only made out of mathematics but that every possible mathematical structure (an infinite number of them) corresponds to a particular reality. At the small end there are realities that are simple geometrical constructs, for example a "triangle universe". Obviously not much happening there. However, as the mathematical structures become more complex there arise at some point universes whose complexity is such that elements within it can process information and recursively model themselves. In which case we have a universe with life, like ours, which is once again merely one amongst an infinite number. However, Tegmark's universes are themselves a subset of the Void which is itself unconstrained even by logic. So it would appear that the Void and the Platonic Realm are not necessarily the same thing.

There are worlds "out there" where every conceivable Being exists, where every possible form of life from the humblest virus to Trans-Universal Gods hold dominion along with every possible variation of them in infinite combination. And, of course, an infinite number of realms utterly beyond our comprehension even in principle. So where are they? How do we locate them and can we communicate with or use them in some way? To answer these questions we need to know what makes our reality seemingly so stable.

The answer lies in the word "seemingly". From the magickal point of view our reality is *not* stable, and the things that maintain the illusion are:

- Memory, which anchors the past
- Consciousness, which expresses the present
- Will, which creates the future

There is no "out there" because space and time are fabrications peculiar to our world. The Void lies under the surface of appearances and is eternal and omnipresent.

In fact our universe is dying in infinite variety from attosecond to attosecond and we can only perceive the ones where we are not extinguished as conscious beings. It is a view of a reality analogous to the Many Worlds Interpretation of Quantum Mechanics (see later), but is more robust in that it would endure even if the MWI is shown to be false.

The degree to which incursions of the Void are tolerated is constrained by requirements of our reality manifested at numerous levels. Since there are no constraints on the manifestation of the Void itself the only ones imposed are imposed by us. Manifestations can be arbitrarily large providing they conform to the configuration of our current consciousness. This is determined by the following:

- Continuity of consciousness – creating conditions that extinguishes consciousness causes that consciousness to cease having an effect in that universe
- Self imposed restraints on consciousness such as personal beliefs and expectations
- Restraints imposed by other conscious entities – other entities have their own agendas and have to be brought into line for maximum power.

The first item falls under the heading of the *Anthropic Principle* first elucidated by Brandon Carter in 1974CE, and expanded and popularized by John D. Barrow and Frank J. Tipler in 1986CE with their book *The* Anthropic Cosmological Principle[12]. In it they introduced the principle in order to deal with the seemingly incredible coincidences that in the structure of the universe that allows our existence. This includes, but is not limited to, particular energy states of the electron, the exact level of the weak nuclear force and extends all the way to the number of spatial dimensions. In one sense it is a tautology that simply claims: "We are here because we are here", in that the universe must be the way it is otherwise we would not be around to observe it. However, Barrow and Tipler elucidated three levels of Anthropic Principle:

- **The Weak Anthropic Principle**:
  The observed values of all physical and cosmological quantities are not equally probable but they take on values restricted by the requirement that there exist sites where carbon-based life can evolve and by the requirements that the Universe be old enough for it to have already done so.

- **The Strong Anthropic Principle**:
  The Universe must have those properties which allow life to develop within it at some stage in its history.

- **The Final Anthropic Principle**:
  Intelligent information-processing must come into existence in the Universe, and, once it comes into existence, it will never die out.

One obvious counterargument is that the universe was designed with the intention of supporting life. However, recent attempts at creating a scientific TOE seem to come up with not a single universe like ours, but incredibly vast numbers of possible alternatives. For example, some String Theories have as many as 10^{500} solutions to choose from and the Anthropic Principle has been suggested as a method to prune

---

[12] ISBN-13: 978-0192821478 Oxford Press

that number drastically. The implication being that all these universes exist somewhere and we find ourselves looking at this one because this is one of the universes where the Laws of Physics allow us to exist. Even so, there must also be myriad universes almost identical to ours. As a result, scientists have not only started speaking of the multiverse as the sum totality of reality, but of different types of multiverse. Max Tegmark has categorized them as follows:

- **The Level 1 Multiverse**
  This is essentially the view that the universe is spatially infinite and filled with different versions of the Big Bang that created ours. In other words, beyond the horizon of our universe there are an infinite number of others. Tegmark has even calculated exactly how far away another version of "you", reading this book, actually is. The answer is 10 to the power of 10^{118} meters. A number so huge that there are not enough atoms in the universe to write out the number of zeros after the "1".

- **The Level 2 Multiverse**
  Consists of an infinite number of Level 1 multiverses as a result of the theory known as *Chaotic Eternal Inflation* where the universes thrown up can be utterly different from our own. The differences could be anything from different particle masses to different spatial dimensionality.

- **The Level 3 Multiverse**
  This is the Many Worlds Interpretation of Quantum Mechanics

- **The Level 4 Multiverse**
  Is essentially a description of the All Universes Hypothesis.

These last two need to be examined in much greater detail. However, before we move on it is interesting to note that as I finished the first draft of this book there was a scientific paper[13] published by Stanford physicists Andrei Linde and Vitaly Vanchurin that claims that the limit to the number of possible universes is 10 to the power of 10^{16}. This is determined not by counting universes derived from quantum fluctuations shortly after the Big Bang (Level 1) but by claiming that our ability to distinguish between them is determined by the total number of brain states available to us.

Quantum Mechanics

No work on technology and magick would be complete without a description of the inherent weirdness of Quantum Mechanics (QM). In fact there have been countless books and articles on supposed connections between the two, usually in connection with Psi phenomena and the possible role of QM in explaining consciousness.

However, the weirdness of QM stems from two quite simple experimental

---

[13] arXiv:0910.1589v1

Science and Magick

facts. The first was discovered around the turn of the 20th Century, namely that light has a particle form and these particles, called photons, come with discrete energies. What this means is that if for example we take a beam of green light from a laser and slowly reduce its intensity then at some point our laser detector starts to sound like a Geiger counter as single photons start to arrive. Furthermore, if we look at the energy in a green photon it is always the same value, E[14] – never half E or a quarter E or twice E etc. and that this energy is related to the wavelength of the light involved though a universal constant named *Planck's Constant*. Now that in itself is not too big a surprise, but what followed was and is. To illustrate we need to look at a classical piece of Victorian science equipment called an interferometer. The diagram of the setup is Figure 1.

In an updated form it consists of a laser, four mirrors, and two detectors. The laser is split in two by a half silvered mirror S1 and each beam sent around a different arm of the machine. One beam bounces off mirror M1 and the other M2. Finally, the beams come together on the second half silvered mirror S2. It is at S2 that what is known as interference occurs. That is, if light is viewed as a series of waves then the peaks and troughs of the two sets of waves can either add together or cancel out. So depending on the relative lengths of the arms varying amounts of light comes from the silvered mirror S2 and go to detectors D1 and D2. In the most extreme case, when the lengths of the arms are equal, all the light comes out and hits D1 – just as if it had not been split in two at all. Furthermore, if you put your hand in one of the two beams then it cannot interfere on S2 and so equal quantities of light get through to D1 and D2. Which is pretty standard Victorian science and was well understood. The weirdness comes when we reduce the intensity of the laser to that it is only pumping out (say) one photon per second.

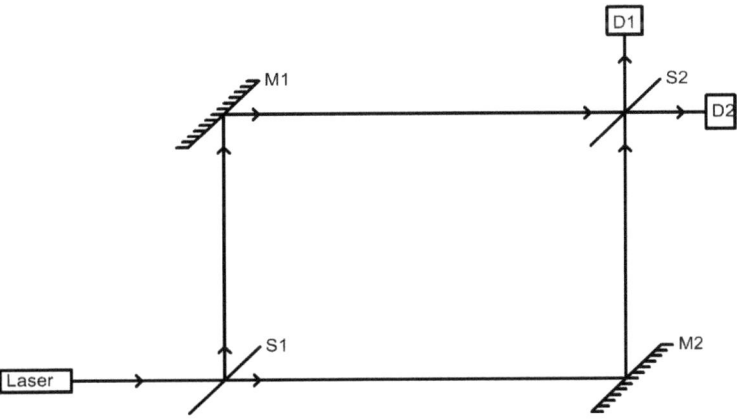

Figure 1

At first, nothing seems amiss. The detector D1 still records one photon per second, and if you put your hand in one of the arms detectors D1 and D2 each register fifty

---
[14] 2.33 eV (electron volts)

percent of the remaining half beam. The weirdness starts to appear when you decide to a hold a detector in your hand and then put it into one of the arms only every other second or so. The usual happens, but this time something odd occurs. On half the occasions your hand blocks the beam the detector you are holding clicks, indicating it has intercepted a photon traveling through that bit of the apparatus, and of course nothing comes out to be registered by D1 or D2 because the photon has been stopped. However half the time the photon is not stopped by your hand but obviously takes the other route. In which case it pops up at D1 or D2 fifty percent of the time. In other words, the interference no longer occurs! (exclamation mark!). Well, you might think, why is that so surprising? And here is the heart of the paradox – if the photon does not travel in the bit of the apparatus your hand is blocking, how does it know *not* to create an interference pattern? How does it know your hand is blocking that path if it does not travel that route? The Victorian answer would have been simple – that single photon would be split in half by the first mirror S1 and half would go one way and half the other. Except, "half a photon" is never seen – only whole photons, arriving either on your hand or at D1 and/or D2. So what is really happening? It is at this point where a number of explanations, or more correctly "interpretations" arise. These generally fall into a number of categories:

- "Shut up and calculate!" This is the traditional response, which is another way of saying that the question of what is "really" happening is meaningless. That is, our notions of reality do not apply, and the mathematics alone is sufficient.

- The photon travels both paths simultaneously and only when it encounters an object (the hand or the final detector D1 or D2) does it decide where it will be. In other words, it is sort of smeared out over the entire system and only a measurement will force it to actually into what we consider to be a real state. This leads to the view that reality only exists because we interact with it – whatever "it" is. And whatever "interact" means. It is the *Copenhagen Interpretation*.

- The photon travels both paths simultaneously and a measurement, caused by the hand, D1 or D2 creates a signal that then travels backward in time back along the arm to the mirror S1 causing the interference pattern to collapse before it is even started. This is the *Cramer Transactional Interpretation*.

- When the photon from the laser first hits S1 the universe splits into two. One where the photon travels the left arm, and another universe where it travels the right. The final mirror S2 blends the universes together again, unless a measurement (caused by the hand) creates a permanent break between the two. In which case a photon will hit D1 in one universe, and D2 in the other. Since both universes have a copy of the experimenter what we see depends on which universe we inhabit. This is the *Many Worlds Interpretation*.

- The entire state of the apparatus remains in a superposition until a conscious observer looks at the results and finally collapses the superposition at random to a definite final state. This is the *Participatory Anthropic Principle*.

In general, when the photon is traveling around the machine the latter is said to be in a *superposition* of states, one where the photon goes left and one where it goes right, and, the final state we see, either interference or no interference, is the result of collapsing the superposition by making a *measurement*.

From this simple setup we can derive a whole set of magickal paradigms. However, before we do this we need to examine two other facets of Quantum Mechanics that have deep magickal ramifications. These are the notions of measurement, and the nature of randomness.

The term "measurement" is somewhat misleading because it implies actually measuring something. In QM it refers to the act that destroys a superposition and puts the apparatus into one definite state. Exactly how, when and if it occurs is a matter of debate. Naturally, we are going to focus on the aspects of that debate which have magickal ramifications. The interesting thing is that from a mathematical point of view QM has nothing to say about where and when a measurement happens and the superposition collapses to the single state we call reality. What it does give is a probability for any given outcome – not a certainty. This leads to things such as the *Schroedinger Cat Paradox*, which is always the example quoted to illustrate the point. Briefly, it is a description from a mathematical QM view of what happens to a hypothetical cat in a box with an enclosed apparatus that contains an flask of poison gas, a radioactive atom with a fifty percent chance of decay within one hour, and a Geiger Counter. If the Geiger counter detects a decay from the atom it triggers the smashing of the flask and the poisoning of the cat. The paradox is that QM predicts that after one hour there is a superposition of an equal mixture of dead and alive cat. Yet, when the experimenter looks in the box they discover not some strange mixture, but a cat that is either totally dead or totally alive. The question is at what point does the superposition of states collapse to a definite value? Claims have been made that it happens at various stages of the process, the earliest being when the Geiger Counter first registers a decay, and the latest being when the experimenter looks in the box.

Eugene Wigner[15] extended this paradox by having a nested series of experimenters and boxes. For example, the entire <cat box + experimenter + laboratory> can be treated as a single system. So, for somebody outside of all of this doing the QM calculations they will get a final result of a laboratory that is in an equal state of <dead cat+unhappy experimenter> and <live cat+happy experimenter> that only resolves itself when the outside party goes in to find out

---

[15] "Wigner's Friend" Paradox

what happened. The implication is that opening the box somehow "infected" (or technically *entangled*) the experimenter and put them into a superposition as well. The way out suggested was that the process is finally resolved by the first conscious being to observe the result. In other words, consciousness itself collapses the superposition to a definite state, at random.

This does not explain which animals, living creatures, or objects have consciousness and which do not. It is also not clear whether measuring devices might also be considered conscious, though generally measuring devices are considered simply to be part of a chain of observations. Some posit that some Beings have a "higher consciousness" and are therefore more capable of collapsing the superposition, whereas others believe all conscious entities have an equal capability. Note, though, that the conscious observer does not get to choose which state is the final one. Of course, most physicists believe that the collapse is triggered by the the Quantum system interacting with its environment in a random manner, usually somewhere when the scale starts to move from the microscopic where QM reigns supreme, to the everyday world of the macroscopic. But nobody knows for sure.

So, QM embodies features involving multiple (almost) identical realities, time travel, questions of consciousness and through the entanglement process an interconnectedness that goes far beyond the old classical physics view of the world. The latter process is quite interesting from a magickal point of view because two things that have been in contact seem to be connected in a very deep way after the event no matter how they are separated in time and space. Experiments show that when the properties of one entangled particle are measured the other *instantaneously* adopts a complementary value. It has even been suggested as the basis of a faster than light (FTL), or backward in time, communications medium. Unfortunately, Nature seems to dislike this idea and so encodes the communication with that pesky randomness once again. The result being that if you want to decode the message you have to bring the two measurements together, which neatly cancels out FTL or time travel effects.

The Many Worlds Interpretation[16]

This is the parallel worlds paradigm par excellence. Simply stated, it says that anything that can happen does happen in some parallel dimension. Normally in magickal discussions it is stated that every decision we make between two courses of action, A and B results in two universes, one where we do A and another where we do B. So every decision point in our lives leads to multiple realities where our subsequent lives follow different paths in an ever branching tree. As to why we choose A or B we have two scientific arguments. The first is a deterministic choice

---

[16] David Deutsch, The Fabric of Reality: The Science of Parallel Universes And Its Implications, Penguin Books (1998), ISBN 0-14-027541-X

whereby we are already following some internal program that makes one or the other choice inevitable. The other is that some quantum effect in our brain triggers a cascade of effects which results in the choice being made. This latter option is the one most magicians associate with Psi effects and notions of True Will. The truth of the matter is more complex in that every quantum transition results in at least one new universe, so we should really think of well over 10^{100} per second being generated.

Returning to Figure 1 above we see two situations arising. The first happens when you put your hand in the beam and either D1 or D2 clicks. At this point you have split the universe into two versions, one where D1 clicks and the other where D2 does so. But if you decide to do nothing only D2 will ever click. As soon as a photon hits M1 the apparatus is in a superposition where the two universes are still mixed up. Putting your hand into the beam *decoheres* them and separates them permanently, whilst doing nothing causes them to merge together again. The really clever thing is that it can detect your hand some 50% of the time without a photon having to touch it. Even cleverer is when you stack several of these together such that you can create an image of what is in the beam without interacting with it at all. It is called *quantum non-demolition measurement* if you want to follow it up on the Net. It is an example of touching without being touched, something that scientists would once have dismissed out of hand as being completely illogical. Unless, of course, you are doing the touching in other universes, ones which do not survive to tell the tale (to put it melodramatically). So what else can one do in these other temporary universes? Maybe a bit of computing perhaps... which brings us to the Quantum Computer (QC). Without getting too technical, what a QC does is split itself into a superposition across lots of universes, like our interferometer did with just two. In each of those universes it does a bit of computation to answer a question. At the end of the process the universes are merged together in such a manner that only the one that came up with the right answer survives to present the result. The defining features of a QC are:

- The process is massively parallel which is why they are expected to be very powerful for certain types of operation. Right now you probably use a PC that has a 64 bit CPU. The QC equivalent would be a CPU of 64 qubits which means it would compute across 2^{64} universes, which is approximately 16,000,000,000,000,000,000 faster than your machine.

- It is only good for certain classes of problem.

- A QC can simulate any quantum system, so if for example the brain does use some form of quantum computing it would still be no problem creating artificial intelligence.

- Under certain conditions, a QC does not even have to be turned on in order to deliver a result of a computation. It just has to be capable of being turned on in those other universes.

The next obvious question about the parallel worlds is: "Can we communicate across them?", perhaps to alternate versions of ourselves. Science at present says not, since once they separate they lose contact permanently. Of course, science might be wrong, so from a magickal point of view we might consider the possibility that we can. In fact, there is one rather extreme way that we can ourselves subjectively move between the worlds.

Quantum Immortality

It stems from a peculiar consequence if the MWI is correct. There may be no such thing as death from a subjective point of view, which leads to what has been called *Quantum Immortality*. This situation arises because as the worlds branch, and all possible outcomes proliferate, there are always branches in which you survive, and the only branches that you can perceive are ones you survive in, not the ones you die in. This is *not* good news. It means that you will live for billions, possibly trillions, of years whether you want to or not and that the world will rapidly become increasingly bizarre in order to support your continued life.

On a related theme we have *Quantum Suicide*. What this means is that if you pointed a loaded shotgun at your head and pulled the trigger the only outcome would be that you saw a misfire. And no matter how many times you tried to commit suicide you would always survive, from your point of view. However, there would be vast swathes of alternate worlds where you would leave a dead body. Only in a tiny percentage or worlds would you survive, those being the ones where the gun did not function properly. This is in fact the only way at present that the MWI can be tested. For example, if no matter how many ways you try to kill yourself if you find you survive by one miracle after another then you can conclude that the MWI is true. To the equally tiny minority who surrounds you as you do this it would seem as if you had a charmed life. However, in the bulk of the worlds they would be looking at a corpse and conclude that you had died. On the other hand, if the MWI is incorrect you will simply die and not even know the degree to which you were wrong. This leads to another game called *Quantum Gambling*.

The scenario this time starts with the purchase of a lottery ticket. The numbers are then fed into a computer that is programmed to scan the lottery results overnight. Also connected to the computer is an explosive charge placed under the pillow on the bed that is sufficient to blow off the head of the sleeper. If the lottery numbers are not the winning combination this charge is to be triggered. So, after setting up the apparatus all you have to do is go to bed, probably with a sleeping pill to calm your naturally nervous disposition! The only world that you will awake to is one where you have won the lottery.

Anyway, that's the theory. In practice a number of things can go wrong. Probably the most common occurrence, if the MWI is correct, is that you will still live but be horribly injured. Alternatively, that the computer will glitch and fail if it is less reliable than the odds of winning the lottery.

We can take this yet another step by replacing the lottery ticket with any arbitrary desirable scenario. Furthermore, suppose that the event that you wish to influence has already occurred. On the face of it, it would seem impossible to use this method to change the past, which (one assumes at this point in the book) to be fixed. However, what is "the past"? It turns out that the past is simply the name we give to a series of records that we use to deduce "what happened". Those records can be anything from geological structures, to fossils to written records to ones own memory. And every record, and especially its interpretation, can be wrong. Admittedly, usually the odds against a record of some major event being incorrect can be astronomical. This is especially true if the event is documented from multiple sources with multiple records, including artifacts – but the probability of *all* of them being incorrect is not zero. So potentially you could change any past where the probability of the records being wrong exceeds the probability of the Quantum Suicide mechanism failing. So given the reliability of power supplies, computers, detonators etc you might be able to wake into a world where the previous day you had a burger for breakfast instead of a bowl of cereal. But waking into a world where World War Two had not happened would almost certainly not work.

Nevertheless, in principle it does provide a method for subjectively switching between alternate timelines. The crucial element though, is that there has to be a "you" in both timelines who are identical with the single exception of the element to be changed. If it works, you have a set of false memories to contend with, and being honest, what is more probable – that you have a bad memory or history has changed? Again, it could be a very subjective thing. This might be doubly so if you tried to change a major event, simply because your memories may well be the weakest link in the probability chain. I seem to recall that World War Two was once called "Great War Two", but maybe I am mistaken...

Related to this in a peculiar way is a method of calculating probabilities developed by the physicist Richard Feynman called the *Sum Over Histories*. What you do to find the probability of (say) a photon getting from A to B is do a mathematical sum over *every* possible route the photon could take in crossing that distance. It turns out that some routes add together and reinforce, and some subtract from each other. When the maths is done you end up with the correct value. In our example with the interferometer above, the two histories are S1 → M1 → S2, and S1 → M2 → S2. However, we might apply this to what people commonly consider to be real history. There are an infinite number of ways to get from (say) 1066CE to now, just as long as we end up with all our *contemporary* records being consistent. So not only do we have a branching tree-like future, but we can also view the past in a similar way with a convergence of events. The only difference being that our possible pasts are more constrained than our possible futures. This constraint on the possible pasts being determined by our records.

This notion of records is where magick and science part company. When science speaks of such records it refers to every element of the universe at a particular point in time, right down to individual photons from the past event winging their way into the sky. When magicians refer to records they refer primarily to the magicians memories and then to a lesser extent macroscopic artifacts. This is because magicians consider that the mind is of paramount importance in determining reality. There is an old philosophical conundrum which asks: Does a tree falling in a forest, with nobody to hear it fall, make a sound? A scientist might well answer "Yes", because the sound would disturb the environment around the tree in such a manner that a later examination could in principle (if not in practice) reveal evidence that a sound was indeed made. A magician would counter by pointing out that no sound was made until the scientist gathered the evidence and created it in their own mind. Now it exists! This provides a lot more scope for altering timeline perceptions.

Still, all of the above does have the rather severe drawback of requiring you to blow your head off in most realities. Is there a better way from a magickal point of view? The answer would appear to center around the notion of "you", which as we will see later is quite a tricky concept. Consider this as an experimental magickal axiom:

> There is only one stream of consciousness across all the realities, between all the myriad bodies. It is this single consciousness that needs to be switched, and it is usually held in place by knowledge and memory.

This is very similar to another, far less popular, interpretation of QM called the *Many Minds Interpretation* (MMI). The concept was first introduced in 1970CE by H. Dieter Zeh and in 1981CE was explicitly called the multi-consciousness interpretation. The final name for it appeared in the work of David Albert and B. Loewer[17] in 1988CE.

The core of this argument is that there is only one universe, but there is associated with each observer a continuous infinity of minds. So instead of each measurement creating a parallel world, what happens is that the infinite stream of minds associated with each of us splits in a kind of schizophrenic way leading to a multiplication of distinct mental states. This obviously has far more appeal for the magician since one immediately sees another definition of the Higher, or True, Self in the infinity of mind. In addition, communication is reduced from one of crossing physically separated worlds to communing with aspects of ones True Self. In all other respects though, it is the same as the MWI.

Anyway, a final note on playing the lottery but this time without the mass suicides. I used to think it a foolish waste of money since statistically you always get back less than you invest – a tax on hope and some people refer to it. However, in a multiverse with infinitely many copies of oneself it can be considered a method of concentrating funds from your other selves to one lucky individual self. Compare this with the case of only one universe, where your money almost certainly goes to some other individual. So, if you believe in MWI or some other version of multiple

---

[17] Albert, D. and Loewer, B. 1988. Interpreting the many worlds interpretation. <u>Synthese</u> 77: 195-213.

Science and Magick

universes then it may well be worth playing. "You" can afford to lose $1, but somewhere $1,000,000 will make a very big difference to "you". The percentage taken by the lottery company can be considered as a cross-universe export tax!

Time Travel and Doppelgangers

Which brings us to one final peculiar property of the MWI (or MMI) concerning the nature of time. Given that every possible thing happens in some branch or other, there must be branches where absolutely nothing happens, where time is effectively frozen. Furthermore, every instant has its own frozen branch. This leads directly to the possibility that traveling backwards in time is equivalent to traveling between parallel worlds. This has the added advantage of removing paradoxes and is now part of "respectable" physics. Note that traveling to such a frozen branch does not mean one also becomes frozen since to the traveler the overwhelming probability is that time will continue to flow normally. We can even extend this to the Level 1 multiverse since in the spatially infinite expanse there are an infinity of states, each of which corresponds to some point in time in our past, and to a lesser extent, our future. Or from a more personal point of view there are an infinity of copies of ourselves "out there", which throws up a peculiar philosophical problem. Simply stated it is this: If two objects are identical in every respect, are they really two objects or only one?

QM really came to the fore in solid state physics by correctly explaining certain properties of metals. Classical physics simply gave the wrong answer when it came to calculating their specific heat. The key to the solving the problem was simple – electrons are identical. Which seems simple enough but had quite significant ramifications when it came to counting the possible states of a system. Consider the simplest, with two particles A and B. In classical physics there are two states if you line up the particles, AB and BA when the order is reversed. However, QM said that because $A = B$ there is only *one* state as AB and BA cannot be distinguished. Plug that fact in and the maths of Quantum Statistics comes out with the correct result.

Naturally though, in this universe we can at least see that we have two electrons, but what about when we compare electrons in two universes? Well, unfortunately we cannot yet do that but we can surmise that there is an additional level of "identicality". Now let's replace the electrons with two identical versions of the same person in two universes, or more precisely, two identical consciousnesses (or even an infinity of them). If one of them ceases to exist in one world, the consciousness continues in the other. Has that person died, or not? And if the particular multiverse is large enough, is that consciousness effectively immortal, as all possibilities unfold? Well, it seems every one of us might find out, whether we want to or not.

Meanwhile, we need to look at another feature that is characteristic of Quantum Mechanics.

Randomness and Chaos

Randomness is an important, interesting and slippery concept. It is often said that there is no such thing as true randomness in the world but strangely, this can neither be proved nor disproved. To illustrate why this is so it is better to examine what "random" means in the context of a string of numbers. The numbers themselves can be the result of measurements, or they can be ones and zeros where a one indicates the presence of something and a zero indicates an absence. Or they can be numbers derived from a mathematical operation or calculation. A very good definition of randomness comes from *Algorithmic Complexity Theory* which states that a string of numbers is random if the amount of information required to describe the string is equal or greater than the amount of information in the string itself. That is, there is no way of compressing the information in the string. An equivalent way of stating this is to say that no matter how many numbers are known there is no way to predict what comes next. Given a string of numbers one can apply tests for the characteristics of randomness. For example, if the string is truly random and very long there should be equal numbers of ones and zeros in a binary string, or if it is decimal then the numbers zero to nine should appear with equal frequency. The problem is that there are numbers that crop up in Nature that satisfy this older criterion for randomness and yet are not at all random. The numbers 31415926535897932382 may look fairly random, and the rest of the numbers in that sequence pass the randomness tests, but it is actually part of the number Pi, the ratio of the diameter of a circle to its circumference. So, if we know that fact it immediately becomes obvious that the string is not at all random. The problem is that no string of numbers can be proved to be random. All we can do is say that we do not know an algorithm that can prove it is not random nor whether one such even exists. In that sense randomness is a measure of our ignorance and we have no way of knowing exactly how ignorant we are.

In physics random numbers seem to show up when we are digging beneath the foundations of reality, where there is no reality. Randomness indicates that we are no longer extracting information because information is not there to be had. This is generally accepted to be the case in Quantum Mechanics where (apparently) truly random numbers are thrown up by measurement. A string of apparently random numbers means that it contains no *usable* information. It may, however, contain information that can be extracted under special conditions.

There is also another peculiar feature of infinite strings of apparently random numbers such as Pi. It is that any arbitrary finite string of numbers can be found an infinite number of times. This means, for example, that the string 0123456789 will be found over and over again. It also means that if one decoded the numbers into letters of the alphabet by assigning 1=A, 2=B... and so on it would not be long before one found simple words being spelled out, and if one went far enough meaningful sentences would appear. Of course, one might have to search billions of digits before the first examples were found, but a few billion are

Science and Magick

nothing compared to the infinite extent of Pi. Eventually one would come across the complete works of Shakespeare, as well as an infinite number of almost complete works of Shakespeare. It's a variant of the old idea of the work turned out by an infinite number of monkeys hammering an infinite number of typewriters at random for an infinite time. In fact, every piece of knowledge is encoded into Pi at some point. One can take this another step by having a powerful computer try to execute Pi as instructions. Obviously if this were done in real life it would crash almost immediately but there must exist sequences of numbers that correspond to meaningful programs. In fact, there must exist an infinite number of sequences representing an infinite number of executable programs. And among those sequences would be extremely large ones representing programs that simulate this entire universe, right down to me typing this sentence. As the joke goes, infinity is *really* big even if it starts off small at one end. All of this coded into the ratio of the circumference of a circle to its diameter. And for good measure, Pi can also be derived from a sum of the following infinite series of numbers:

$$\pi = 4/1 - 4/3 + 4/5 - 4/7 + 4/9 - 4/11...$$

Which leads one to ask: What is the connection between a sum of numbers and the properties of a circle, that is, a two dimensional geometrical construct? If you want to find out, you need a lot more than this book!

Nice theory perhaps, but what of magickal practice? How do we use randomness in magick? There are three fundamental uses:

- As a method of divination by using the patterns the mind imposes on randomness to extract information from the unconscious

- To act as an indicator of Psi activity, when the Void presents non-random sequences as the results of some working

- As one example of a parallel worlds paradigm

The corresponding machinery and uses are illustrated in another chapter. Anyway, that brings us to the Level 4 Multiverse of mathematics.

Mathematics and Magick

Finally, an example of the interface between consciousness, mathematics and magick. So, ignore for the moment any vague notions of consciousness being some mysterious spiritual entity and ponder the ramifications if we limit ourselves to a simple materialist view. In particular, let us look at a computational setup entitled: *Einstein's Brain*.

We begin with (a metaphorical) Einstein upon whom we are about to perform this interesting philosophical experiment. What we are going to do is gradually replace his brain cells with microcomputers that mimic them perfectly through a series of equations that are solved for input and output of each brain cell.

Slowly, his brain is to be changed from an organic computer to one based on silicon circuitry. The contemporary materialist view is that there would be no noticeable change in his thoughts or behavior. It is just the old software running on new hardware, and the hardware is not important. Each time we make a change we ask: "Are you conscious", to which Einstein answers "Yes".

Now we take it another step into absurdity, although a totally logical though impractical absurdity. We decide to run the software manually by writing down in a big book the equations for every cell and working through it by hand with a pencil. What we have is a program that is basically a very big series of mathematical statements, whose solutions are Einstein's mind and consciousness. If we ask the "book brain" the question: "Are you conscious" all we do is solve the equations and out pops the answer: "Yes". So where is consciousness in all this? Can a mere book be conscious once it is complex enough? Or is it the act of solving the equations that generates mind?

It is this latter position which is the most common one, but what does "solving the equation" actually mean? When is an equation solved? Is it only when we actually record the answer somewhere – if so, does $1+1=\ldots$ have no solutions until it is written down? If one answers that such a solution exists even if we do not know the answer, we are back to Platonic Realms again. The question that then arises is why do these mathematics have to be written anywhere at all in order to be a valid consciousness? If truth, at least to the extent of mathematical truth, lies "out there" somehow external to our universe and yet interacting with it then all possible equations and their solutions somehow exist independent of us, or of time and space. It means all possible consciousness' exist in the Platonic Realm, that this realm is a sea of timeless consciousness eternally waiting to be incarnated into the world of matter and energy. Or, if Tegmark is correct, they are already incarnated somewhere.

Finally, such a book represents a frozen consciousness with all of its potentialities. The only difference between its mind and our mind is that it depends for its life on an external agency reading it, doing the sums and writing the results in the book – something the matter in our brains does for us automatically (so we assume, possibly erroneously as we shall see in the final chapter).

Well, we have a book that we have identified as a Human mind and can apply the criteria previously elucidated in order to determine what kind of spirit it has. Clearly its spirit is different from that of a normal Human for obvious reasons and similarly one might expect its soul also to be unique or at least uniquely available. If while we were doing all those calculations by hand in order for it to answer a question we keep a record of all the intermediate results we have what can reasonably be called its soul. Namely, a full history of all that it was (while in book form) with all of its interactions at every moment in time. And if we rerun the calculations from an intermediate stage, we effectively turn back time for Einstein's Brain and undo the past, not that he would ever know. Indeed, the notion of time itself becomes very flexible depending on the point of view. How fast time passes in

Science and Magick

Einstein's book world depends solely on the sequence of equations solved and their values, including values passed to his "senses". From our point of view the book could have been ignored for years, with only the occasional work done on the arithmetic on (say) every Friday afternoon – it makes no difference to Einstein. Time is purely a function of information processing.

Still, it really does not get us any closer to how the Platonic Realm actually interacts with the material, unless of course Tegmark is correct and there is no material world at all. Or perhaps Penrose is right and there is some aspect of matter of which we are currently ignorant. So, perhaps we should move on to explore mathematics a bit more and see what it can tell us of conditions on "the other side".

Well, the answer to that has itself become increasingly uncertain. Back in the Victorian era mathematicians assumed that mathematics was "pure truth" unsullied by the imprecision of the real world, and that one day they would be able to define some fundamental axioms that would underpin the whole endeavor with the result that math would be neatly wrapped up as a complete system of thought. Unfortunately Gödel came along and ruined the whole scheme, along with Turing and Church. The story is told in the best selling book by Douglas Hofstadter, "Gödel, Escher, Bach: An Eternal Golden Braid[18]". The essence is that it was shown that there is a kind of trade-off in axiomatic systems once they get beyond a certain level of complexity (like mathematics). They cannot be both consistent and complete. That is, mathematics will constantly throw up statements which cannot be shown to be either true or false using the existing axioms. So what you do is you take the statement which is indeterminate and generate two more axioms from it, one where it is true and another where it is false. This results in two kinds of unpleasantness. The first is that mathematics turns out to be infinite, which means it will never be "wrapped up". The second is even worse, because those two new axioms generate areas of mathematics that are disconnected and stand like islands in the Platonic Realm.

So how did Gödel discover (or invent?) this? It was from considering self referential systems such as the *Liar Paradox* which states: "This sentence is false." Clearly that statement is true only if it is false, and vice versa. He showed that it applied to math as well as language. Similar results were discovered by Church and Turing concerning what is known as the *Halting Problem*, namely that it is in general impossible to create a computer program that will examine another given arbitrary program and decide whether it will every stop running. Gregory Chaitin in turn took this work further to show exactly how some numbers could arise that are uncomputable. That is, we do not know their exact value and can never know it. The classic example he gave was what he named *Omega*, also known as *Chaitin's Constant* which is a real number that informally represents the probability that a randomly-chosen program will halt. One of its properties is that it appears to be random in its digits. It turns out that math is riddled with randomness, which may

---

[18] Hofstadter, Douglas R. (1999) [1979], Gödel, Escher, Bach: An Eternal Golden Braid, Basic Books, ISBN 0465026567 .

or may not be related to the Void.

The direct connection with magick comes through questions that have arisen concerning consciousness and the brain. For example, it is not known if all of the above applies to us as it does to computers. Or whether (horrors!) that our universe may ultimately be built around non-computable numbers, which would mean the end of theoretical physics. Nevertheless, there is one way in which all of the above might be circumvented, which is to devise a computer with infinite power, known as *hypercomputing*. One possibility would be to use some kind of temporal loop to keep feeding results backward in time so that any number of calculations could be performed in a finite time. Naturally, nobody knows how to do it or even if it is possible. So we end on a riddle: "What do you call a computer with infinite power?" Answer: "God".

Interdimensional Communications

Currently modern science says this is impossible, but obviously we are not going to leave it at that. There are two notable possibilities. The first being a subjective method involving an "inner dialog" with the True Self mentioned in conjunction with the Many Minds Interpretation. The essential magickal paradigm here is one of "All is Mind", possibly bordering on solipsism.

The second is rather more interesting and is examined in detail in other chapters. It stems from the certainty that if other realities exist in infinite multitude then somewhere amongst them there will be entities far more advanced than we are currently. They may be Human, PostHuman, Machine Intelligences, Aliens or if inhabiting universes with utterly different properties or dimensionality something akin to *The Great Old Ones* or *Elder* Gods depicted in the fiction of H P Lovecraft. Somewhere amongst these entities will be ones seeking to make contact with us, either as explorers or something else. So, we rely on their advanced technology or capabilities to do what we cannot, which is to initiate and maintain the contact. The only question then remains as to how to recognize such attempts and how to respond. One might guess that the communication medium would involve randomness and the most complex, versatile and intelligent machine on the planet – the Human brain. Such communications, if they come from an alien source might seem nonsensical and if they come from a space with different laws of nature they may request the building of machines that seemingly have no rational function. They may even lie about their origins and purposes…

Finally another dip into the Cthulhu Mythos, not because I believe it is true but because it is an amusing way to illustrate some points about cross dimensional communications. In this case, it is said that the Great Cthulhu will return when "…the stars are right", which is usually assumed to refer to either a great length of time as measured by the movement of stars, or some kind of pseudo astrological prediction. However, it could be literally true in certain cases. Consider the notion of parallel worlds spatially coexisting as in the MWI previously discussed. If I had an inter-dimensional portal located in my basement that could cross these worlds all I have to do is step through it to a world that diverged from this one a few hours ago and I would appear in an almost identical basement. But what if our worlds had diverged years ago? Well, I step through and find myself either in the basement in this other world or at least the geographical where the basement would have been. Except, maybe not – perhaps I step into a vacuum in deep space. The reason being that while the worlds may start off identical, including in the same relative spacial position to each other, various random effects may cause a small amount of drift in their orbits. Not much at all probably, but over a long period of time enough such that they no longer line up and stepping through the portal would have you breathing vacuum. However, after a very long time "when the stars are right" the worlds would line up again and the portal work as expected. Taking this speculation to its logical conclusion might explain why most ghosts seem relatively modern, at most only a few centuries old and why we seldom see phantom mastodons although maybe the "stars are right" when it comes to the Cretaceous and the Loch Ness Monster! The rest just drift away, most likely manifesting skywards or below ground.

Also related to this question is how an alien entity from one of an infinite number of parallel worlds could actually find, lock onto, and repeatedly return to communicate. Presumably it could be looking for compact information processing devices that operate at least partially at the quantum level, are relatively efficient and respond in a meaningful manner to very low levels of stimulation. In other words, highly evolved brains.

The final problem is how to attract the attention of some other dimensional creature to us, when we are effectively lost in an infinity of Earth's, and possibly an infinity of universes. This is a kind of reversed SETI (Search for Extraterrestrial Intelligence), where instead of us looking we put out some kind of beacon. In both cases it relies on finding a configuration that is highly non-random., and usually comes down to mathematics since only intelligent entities (or their machines) are assumed to perform such operations. Perhaps something as simple as writing down, transmitting or memorizing the binary expression of Pi or some unique structure? In which case an entity might lock onto the carrier of the information, which could be a location, an object or a mind. Alternatively, something that covers a large spatial area could be chosen that contains highly non-random information and also imprints its signature on spacetime. Since we do not have easy access to the weak or nuclear forces, that leaves gravity and the electromagnetic domain. If we choose gravity we need to arrange large masses in a specific non-natural configuration – maybe something resembling a megalithic structure of gigantic aligned stones? However, given the difficulty of the magician creating such an object it might be worth looking at magnetic fields, which are themselves vastly more powerful[19] than the gravitational effects even of stones weighing hundreds of tonnes. That suggests

---

[19] Magnetic fields are typically 10^{36} times more powerful than gravity – which is why a small magnet can lift a piece of iron against the gravitational pull of the whole planet

that small Neodymium magnets spaced at coded intervals might be worth a try.

Science and Magick

Psi and the Occult

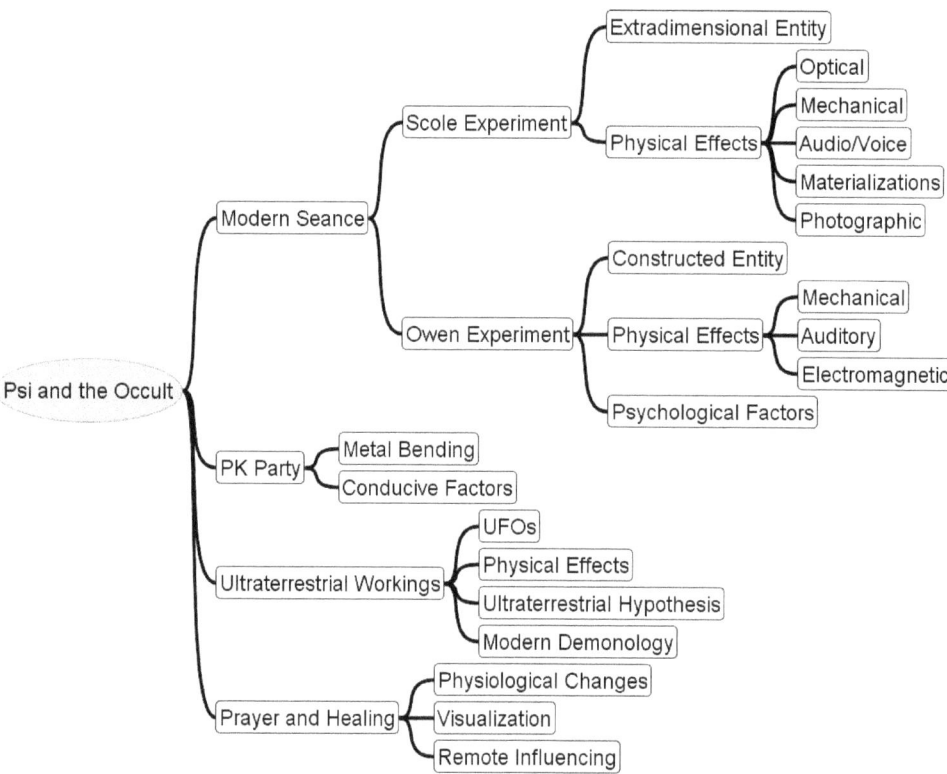

3 Psi and the Occult

The Scole Experiment

This was a series of extended contacts with an entity named Manu and his team of spirit scientists and technicians comprised of personalities who had had an interest in science and technology while alive on Earth. The means of communication was the traditional mediumistic setting. The experiment itself was named after the village of Scole in Norfolk, England, and took place between the years 1993-1998CE. Involved as mediums (channelers) were Alan and Diana Bennett and the work was undertaken in the basement of a house rented by Robin and Sandra Foy. Manu, speaking through Diana, told them that he was the gatekeeper between Earth and the other side, and that he represented thousands of minds from the many other realms of existence. Their plan was to pioneer methods of communication between the two dimensions using combination of spiritual, human and earth-bound energy forces. Manu further explained that it was important that two of the group were able to work as mediums. As we will see, what makes this different from any other number of séances are two factors. The first was the major emphasis on physical manifestations, and the second its thorough investigation by the Society for Psychical Research (SPR)[20] and others over a period of more than two years.

The first physical manifestation occurred when Manu announced that he had brought a gift from his team to their group. There was a loud thud on the table and after the lights were switched on a mint condition coin, a Churchill Crown, was lying on the table. Within six months of receiving the coin, the group recorded that they had witnessed dancing lights, the ringing of bells hung on the roof of the cellar, levitation of objects placed on the table, noisy cracklings and loud thumps. This process culminated one night when the Foys and Bennetts were joined by three other friends they received another message from Manu that he was going to bring a collection of gifts for them. At the end of the session when the lights had been turned on there were seven objects lying on the table. These were: A silver thimble, Two small silver lockets, A silver chain bracelet, A St Christopher medallion, An ornate miniature spoon, A decorated bowl with an inscription in French on the reverse, A small gold medallion adorned with hieroglyphics.

After this the sessions produced even more esoteric phenomena. Dancing lights would appear in the cellar and touch the group members. Among the varied activities of the lights were:

---

[20] The Scole Report: Proceedings SPR Vol. 58, Society for Psychical Research, 49 Marloes Road, London, W8 6LA

- Extremely rapid movements.
- Shape changes.
- Responses to requests to visit and touch the hands of participants.
- Hitting suspended strings of bells, glass jars or the table top with a loud noise.
- Entering and apparently moving around inside people.
- Extremely precise high speed geometrical gyrations.

Often accompanying them were words spoken from mid-air, a technique that came to be known as extended voice, and which seemed to come from all quarters, even from within the walls.

The next series of manifestations began when the Scole group bought a new camera loaded with conventional color film. This was placed on a wooden chair beside Sandra Foy who was instructed by the spirit team to take photographs in the total darkness whenever she was asked to do so. This was to be done without the use of a flash attachment even though there was no source of light in the room. As the ghostly lights moved around the cellar the spirits explained that they would try to project images directly onto the film. Altogether eleven frames were exposed in the darkness and upon development there were recognizable pictures where there should have been none at all. The pictures varied greatly and appeared unconnected with each other. The first and second were images of St Paul's Cathedral during the Blitz of WW2. Two others showed a wrecked bus after a night of bombing in Coventry or London. The fifth showed the front cover of a newspaper from 1936CE and a sixth showed a group of soldiers from WW1 consisting of two officers and seven men. The remaining pictures were not as clearly defined but seemed to be groups of people. Having proved they could use the camera the spirit scientists needed one further test before the group could go public with their findings. They intended to project images directly onto film left on the table without using a camera. The group used a 35mm film still factory sealed and also put out two instant Polaroid films. The latter, when processed by feeding back through a camera, revealed a variety of pictures, star clusters and on one occasion a very clear portrait of Sir Arthur Conan Doyle. As the experiment progressed the images grew more sophisticated and started to include ancient scripts and hieroglyphics as well as excerpts from poems and pieces of literature. At this point Manu suggested that the Scole group invited the scrutiny of more orthodox scientists, and they contacted the SRP via a friend of their who was a member, Montague Keen. The subsequent investigations involved individuals from organizations such as NASA, the Scientific And Medical Network, and various European universities and privately funded research bodies. Investigators from Germany, Ireland, the Netherlands, Spain, Switzerland and the U.S. assessed and reviewed the Scole group's techniques and physical evidence, especially the photographs.

Psi and the Occult

To preclude fraud a special wooden box was built that was just large enough to house the unopened still sealed film. This was then padlocked and held by one of the visiting investigators. However, before the box was used in any of the experiments, it was sent away for examination to ensure that it was not possible to open it without breaking its seals. An "outsider", a highly respected German engineer named Walter Schinneger, was invited to attend a session. He was handed the wooden box and placed his own roll of film inside it before locking it. He then carried both the keys and box to his car where he left the box keys. The car keys he handed to another investigator (Dr Hans Schaer) for safe keeping. In the meantime all the participants agreed to wear luminous wristbands so that their position at any time could be determined. Schinneger then explained what happened:

> "From the moment of locking the box until the time the film was processed immediately after the sitting, the box was solely in my hands. It was never allowed to stand alone and was not even touched by anyone else. In the cellar I held the box on my lap with my right hand, in such a way that my forefinger was on the lid and the lower part of the finger touching the locking mechanism. During the several minutes that followed, with my hand in this position, the table vibrated several times, sometimes so strongly that crystals we had placed on the top started to rattle. On one occasion the pullover and shirt on my right arm were pulled up and a finger circled my wrist; then the clothes were pulled down again. It felt as though at least five hands were touching my right arm at the same time, some of them quite powerful, as if they were seeking to pull my fingers away from the container (which I did not allow) or to apply force to the container, so that some effort was needed to keep the container in place. I held on to the box until after the sitting had finished. Then I retrieved my car keys from Hans, took the box to the car to pick up the padlock keys and returned to make a close inspection of the processing machine to ensure that it was empty. I then inserted the film into the processing machine and started the clearly audible processing mechanism, which took about two minutes. I removed the film myself and we all inspected it. It showed text, symbols and lines over the whole length of the film, together with some German words and handwriting and some strange mirror text."

Although the investigators present were convinced there was no fraud there was still an element of doubt which visiting investigators insisted on removing. Dr Richard Wiseman was brought in to ensure no tricks were being played. He was a former member of the parapsychology unit at Edinburgh University and a specialist in the psychology, methods and practice of deception. He provided another fraud-proof security bag made of opaque triple-layered polythene. Investigators always insisted on bringing their own film.

Approximately four years after the Scole experiment began Manu asked to switch some of their experiments to video. A video camera was mounted on a tripod and angled according to the spirits instructions. The captured images ranged from dramatic surges of color to Human faces emerging from bubble-like spheres. A year later the group saw a rather animated non-Human creature on film they named "Blue".

In the last experiment in 1998 Dr Hans Schaer personally loaded a new tape into the video camera that was focused on a mirror reflecting a brown ceiling[21], making sure that no one else touched it. Alan and Diana Bennett went into a trance and Manu spoke to them, explaining that the work that they had all produced in the past would not continue, as the energy was needed elsewhere. At the end of the session Dr Schaer removed the videotape from the camera, checked his dated signature and carried the tape upstairs where he inserted it in the video player. At the start of the tape was the profile of a man aged between 50 and 60, slightly balding in front, with dark hair and possibly a black mustache, wearing metal-rimmed glasses. After a few seconds the image moved slightly and another face appeared behind the first one of a man wore something like a Russian fur hat. After a further three seconds or so both images vanished. Dr Schaer later concluded in his report that there was no explanation for what had happened.

Perhaps the most astonishing phenomena were those involving dematerialisations. Montague Keen writes:

> "… the event that finally overwhelmed any lingering doubts harbored by Professor Arthur Ellison (former SPR president) about the authenticity of what he was experiencing. It occurred when a small point of light settled on and irradiated one of the four crystals located at the cardinal points on the periphery of the circular table round which the investigators and the Group sat. The three visitors saw, and described for the benefit of the tape recorder (all sittings were recorded and later transcribed) how the glowing crystal then rose before our eyes, and descended into the base of a translucent perspex kitchen bowl from which Arthur was invited to abstract it and replace it. He did so, bending low over the bowl to ensure than no human hand or instrument was at work. He was then asked to repeat the process, only to find that the image of the crystal was simply that: a non-material but clearly visible essence. This experiment was at our request repeated for the benefit of the two other investigators. All experienced the phenomenon of de-materialization and re-materialization of the crystal."

Another notable feature was that the group were given instructions to build a communications device based around a chip of Germanium placed under physical pressure by a screw, and the output fed to a high impedance audio amplifier. Initial tests revealed the output to consist largely of White Noise (see later) which one would expect from such a setup. The claims as to there being faint voices or music present could be put down to either the unit acting as a radio receiver and picking up transmissions on the AM radio band, or to Electronic Voice Phenomena (EVP).

---

[21] Compare this set-up with the Psychomanteum described elsewhere in the book

Psi and the Occult

The group were then asked to bring some film to one of the sessions and it was subject to the usual security. Upon development it showed a modified circuit diagram, where the Germanium was located between two iron cored coils wired in parallel with it. This is reproduced in the Machines chapter.

What are we to make of all this? There are only three possible explanations. The first is that what was reported actually happened as reported, and that Psi phenomena manifested on a massive scale. The second is that all, or most involved, were party to a deliberate fraud. The third option is that a plot of unprecedented sophistication fooled the investigators. For example, the lights might have been caused by numerous computer controlled concealed lasers and the dematerialisations were actually holographically produced. The voices in the air were created by acoustic tricks using multiple hidden speakers. The film in the boxes were exposed to highly focused X-ray beams from hidden equipment, and the video camera was tampered with by including a small television receiver or alternatively using a high power TV transmitter to "infect" its electronics with a TV-like signal. Additionally, much of this equipment must have been portable since these effects were demonstrated in several countries. If so, it suggests a plot requiring large sums of money and several engineers and technicians, all of whom had to keep the secret over the years. They must also have been superbly skilled since not a single instance of fraud was uncovered in two years of investigations. Take your pick! However, for our purposes we will take the phenomena at face value, although maintaining a certain skepticism about the reality of Manu, his spirit scientists, and their story.

One element that keeps surfacing in all such experiments, whether in the lab or field is that of the negative effects of skepticism and the sensitivity of the results to such personalities. This was especially true here with the group requesting "serious and positive" investigators. Also of relevance, and with an interpretation that varies depending upon whether one is a skeptic or believer, the SPR wanted at least one video camera using infrared light to monitor events, but were told that this would seriously inhibit the work. It would seem that although the Psi effects were large, so was their sensitivity to disruption, and like all mediumistic phenomena depended upon one or two "star performers". However, the major problem from our point is view is that this leads nowhere. Consider what has just been presented – a series of bizarre effects not under the conscious control of anybody present, immune from technological analytical scrutiny, and no obvious way of following up the experiment or extending it into any kind of utility. The importance, for us, of this experiment is less to do with the technique than the scope of results that can be obtained. The next section describes a classic experiment that preceded Scole by some twenty years, but has wider implications for group oriented magickal practices.

The Owen Experiment

What follows is an account of a major experiment that was conducted several decades ago by the Toronto branch of the Society for Psychical Research[22]. It is included because it is remarkable not only in what it achieved, but in how positive and unequivocal results were obtained in a group dynamic – something which is of direct relevance to the rest of this work. Whether you believe in psychic phenomena or not, this experiment is illustrative of how "real magick" of the Hollywood witchcraft movie variety might work, either as hard fact or unconscious mass illusion. As we will see elsewhere, it opens up a vast array of possibilities and will enable us to reinterpret existing world-views in a manner sufficient to create a major paradigm shift amongst students of the occult.

The experiment, instigated by Iris Owen, is detailed in a book published in 1976 called "Conjuring up Philip"[23] and details the experiment carried out over several years in the early 1970s. The original aim of the experiment was to create a ghost and have it appear before the group as a consensual hallucination or other similar manifestation. In order to so they deliberately created a fictitious character; one that every member of the group knew could not exist, nor ever could have existed. Additionally it was decided to form a group of ordinary people none of whom claimed any psychic ability whatsoever. The experiment was to be scientifically controlled and as such it was conducted in light sufficient for visual recording.

Initially some fourteen people were willing to involve themselves in the experiment with a schedule of weekly meetings lasting up to one year. As group rapport was felt to be important it was also agreed that if any member felt incompatible with the group or another person then they should withdraw. Eventually the group was whittled down to eight members, four men and four women.

The task of creating a suitable biography for the ghost fell to (Margaret) Sue Sparrow, one of the co-authors of the book. The character was named "Philip", an aristocrat who lived in England during the time of Cromwell, with an interesting story to tell complete with impossible details. His character and history were determined during early meetings of the group and they made themselves very familiar with the agreed upon details of his life. A portrait was even produced by one of the members so that a visual representation existed for them to focus upon.

Simple relaxation and meditation techniques were used with the participants either seated in a circle or around a table bearing items associated with Philip. These meditation sessions were interspersed with conversation and analysis. Philip rapidly became a "real" person in the minds of those present.

Several safeguards were included. The first was that Philip was to be a wholly benign character. Second, that Philip would not be active outside of the group meetings and those meeting were to be confined (initially) to a particular

---

[22] Generation of Paranormal Physical Phenomena in connection with an Imaginary "Communicator", authored by Iris M. Owen & Margaret H. Sparrow, Toronto Society for Psychical Research, 17.10.1973.

[23] Conjuring up Philip by Iris M Owen with Margaret Sparrow, ISBN 0-7701-0005-8

room where his artifacts were kept. All the members agreed not to attempt any kind of individual contact outside of the experimental context.

After one year no progress had been made. It was at this point that the insights, methods and theories of Brooke-Smith and Hunt[24], and Batcheldor[25] came to the attention of the group and a new direction was taken. The meditations were dropped and replaced with some séance techniques used by the Victorians. Specifically, a kind of light-hearted party atmosphere with jokes, singing, music, poetry recital and casual conversation etc. Instead of darkness they decided to use colored lights, but always at the level whereby everything was visible, although the color could be changed throughout the sitting. Crucially, they had to believe it would work.

The first results appeared on the third or fourth session with a vibration being felt in the table, which evolved into a rapping sound. The table then began to slide about the floor in an apparently random fashion even though nobody was consciously pushing. And to make sure such actions were not taking place unconsciously (ideomotor response) paper doilies were placed under the hands of the sitters to make an almost frictionless contact with the table. The phenomena continued.

In true Victorian fashion the group established a code – one rap for "Yes", two raps for "No". The contact with Philip had been made, albeit in a manner not expected by the group.

Subsequently when the group met they each greeted Philip and received a rap by way of reply, without any preamble or warm-up. Seemingly this rap came from under the hand of the person speaking. The table itself was a light plastic topped card table with folding legs. As the sessions progressed Philip was treated as "one of the group" and responded with various noises, including scratching sounds, and quite vigorous table movements including "jumping movements" in reply to questions or conversation. The strength of the noises was often an indicator as to the strength of feeling Philip expressed.

Philip's psychokinetic powers, however, were amazing and completely unexplained. If the group asked Philip to dim the lights, they would dim instantly. When asked to restore the lights, he would oblige. The table around which the group sat was almost always the focal point of peculiar phenomena. After feeling a cool breeze blow across the table, they asked Philip if he could cause it to start and stop at will. He could and he did. The group noticed that the table itself felt different to the touch whenever Philip was present, having a subtle electric or "alive" quality. On a few occasions, a fine mist formed over the center of the table. Most astonishing, the group reported that the table would sometimes be so animated that it would rush over to meet latecomers to the session, or even trap

---

[24] Brooke-Smith, C and Hunt D W (1970) "Some Experiments in Psychokinesis" Journal, SPR Volume 45, No. 744

[25] Batcheldor, K J (1966) "Report on a Case of Table Levitation and Associated Phenomena" Journal, SPR Volume 43 No. 729

members in the corner of the room.

The climax of the experiment was a séance conducted before a live audience of 50 people and under the bright lights of a television studio where Philip's interaction was broadcast on the CBC television show Man Alive as well as other talk shows of the day. One session was also filmed as part of a television documentary. Besides table rapping, creating other noises around the room and making lights blink off and on, the group actually attained a full levitation of the table. It rose only a centimeter or so above the floor, but was witnessed by the group and the film crew. Unfortunately, the dim lighting prevented the levitation from being captured on the film. Even spoon bending popularized at that time by Uri Geller was tried, with some success. The phenomenon was also seemingly capable of extending itself not only into the walls of the room, but both other rooms and on several occasions to the locations of absent members.

Another feature of Philip's conversation was the way his answers occasionally appeared to be elicited "by committee". That is, they would change according to what members of the team were present and what opinions or beliefs those members held. An extreme form of this was the sensitivity the Philip phenomena showed to disapproval or disbelief. It was very easy for one member of the group to banish him, as was discovered by accident when one person voiced the possibility of sending him away. It took the remainder of the session to coax him back.

Also interesting to note is the fact that not all the members had to be present. Philip was quite capable of manifesting, albeit more weakly, when only four were available. And two members did not even have to have their hands on the table in order to get a response. Their presence in the room was sufficient. As to the strength of the psychokinetic (PK) phenomena, two examples will suffice. On one occasion a much heavier table replaced the light one, but that practice had to be discontinued due to damage to the walls caused by collisions. On another occasion a physicist at a university demonstration who was actually sitting on the table was thrown off quite violently.

Psychological Factors

Probably the most important factor was the rapport of the group. In the previous year they had developed bonds of friendship and the ability to relax completely in one another's company. Coupled with this they had a common goal and motivation, plus a detailed object of focus – Philip.

Another requisite was an open-minded approach that could accept paranormal phenomena without, either inwardly or outwardly, expressing disbelief or astonishment. There must be an attitude of "heightened expectancy".

One unique factor involved that separated the experiment from a conventional séance was that there was no one person who was the focus. Instead of the Medium, or "Channeler", being the focus it was Philip via the table. Often the table itself was addressed directly. Hence there was no pressure on any individual to "perform". The atmosphere was one of relaxation – not concentration.

In their interactions both with each other and Philip there was an element of playfulness described as "childlike creativity" by one of the observers. The members of the group were not exhausted by the proceedings despite significant energy being utilized (energy here is used with its scientific meaning). There was also no psychological exhaustion either – just the opposite.   Other similar studies were instituted at this time. The other experiment briefly reported in the book, using the techniques developed above, took only five weeks to come to fruition. However, crucial to this rapid success was the apparently the "hot swapping" of members, to use a term from computing. That is, members of the second team were invited into the Owen group one at a time substituting for original members. In a sense, the technique was literally passed on by personal contact.

Probably the most amazing fact to emerge is that a method has been developed to demonstrate psychic phenomena to order. Overall, the key finding is simple – *belief is everything*.

Disembodied Intelligence?

The obvious question arises as to whether Philip was actually a manifestation of group consciousness, or some disembodied intelligence masquerading as Philip and deliberately (or otherwise) deceiving them. Since there is absolutely no way to determine the truth of the matter it seems reasonable to apply Occam's Razor. Namely, that the simplest explanation is likely to be the truth and that Philip was purely a thoughtform[26].

Another question naturally follows from this – are all spiritual phenomena that seem to exhibit intelligence actually projections from Human Beings? It would certainly simplify matters if this were so. However, the only possible way for an entity to prove it was independent of the Human mind would be for it to impart knowledge that was unknown to anyone, anywhere and additionally had never been known. That is, knowledge that could not be derived by telepathy or clairvoyance (assuming such abilities exist). It would also have to be of a complex non-trivial nature in order to rule out the "lucky guess". As far as I know, this has never been the case.

Thoughtforms also provide neat explanations for such things as poltergeists and other hauntings, as well as explaining the effectiveness of exorcism and other rites of banishment.

---

[26] A major contributor to the literature on thoughtforms, or "Tulpas" in the Tibetan Buddhist tradition, was Alexandra David-Néel who traveled widely in Tibet.

A Religious Context

Years ago it was standard practice, when Christians were discussing history, to disparage our "primitive" Heathen ancestors and illustrate the point by telling of how they foolishly worshiped idols – dead things of wood and stone, or believed in "magickal" objects. Naturally the heroes were the Christian missionaries who rescued them from their ignorance and superstition through the power of Jesus etc. The Philip experiment recasts the whole issue in a new light.

Substitute "idol" or "altar" for "table", "Philip" for the God of ones choice and we have the core of a very convincing religion complete with physical phenomena that backs up and validates whatever worldview the adherents subscribe to. For all practical purposes, and amongst a small group of people, idols and magickal items can be imbued with real power and apparently meaningful communications for good or ill. Conversely the sensitivity of the phenomena to disbelief, or the undermining of belief, gives us insight into the way Christian priests can display the "Power of Christ" over the "Heathen Idols". As always, it is easier to destroy than create.

Which brings us to the "dark side" of this experiment that was not discussed at all. Any force that can throw someone off a table could in principal cause immediately fatal brain damage if directed as a weapon. It becomes a lot more than a "rap on the head".

The experiment also strongly reinforces the theory of deities being gestalt Godforms. That is, living entities that represent the group unconscious of entire cultures across millennia. Naturally, these Gods are potentially orders of magnitude more powerful than anything that a small group of people is capable of creating, but it might be interesting to scale the Owen approach accordingly or at least take steps in that direction. Additionally, given that the phenomena are governed by belief one can deduce quite a lot concerning the success, or otherwise of magickal practice and ritual. For this was a magickal working of a power most would-be magicians can only dream of.

A major lesson concerns ritual. It becomes obvious that the purpose of ritual is to put the participants into the correct mindset whereby the group-mind can create the expected effects. The downside is that ritual then becomes a constraining factor. For example, why draw circles and create protections unless you intend to create something that is inherently inimical to its creator, at least unconsciously? While such elements engender belief, they also shape that belief into creating something to be guarded against, as well as limiting the spontaneity and usefulness outside of the immediate magickal working. Of course, that's not a problem if you want to conjure up a "Demon from Hell", but given that these are "only" projections of the practitioners why do something so potentially self-destructive?

Finally, to end this section and illustrate the degree of malleability of the thoughtforms various members of the experimental groups at a Christmas party in 1974CE conjured up Santa – and no, unlike in the joke they were not dyslexic! It does illustrate though how easy such evocations can become once the initial experience exists.

Objects of Power

Returning to the notion of "power objects", or objects evoking strong psychic events, there is an additional explanation we can derive from the section of the chapter on Remote Viewing. If we accept the results concerning remote viewing we can deduce what might happen when someone, usually a talented individual, either voluntarily or involuntarily performs a remote viewing on the object itself. If it is unfocused as to time they will be drawn to the most emotionally charged event that intersected with the object's timeline. This could be a "natural" traumatic event, for example something involving injury or death, or it could be something engineered from the psyche of a magician. In either event the object will have an impact on the mind apprehending it, and in the latter case that impact could be a contact with the mind of the magician, or at least the intention and emotion of the magician. This may in rare circumstances incorporate aspects of the Owen experiment in transpersonal gestalt creation. The result would then be an "updating" of the created entity and its re-empowerment, albeit on a lesser scale than originally.

Questions…

There are many questions that currently remain unanswered, at least in the public domain. Some that spring to mind are listed below, with comments and some putative answers. These form the core of very broad research program, especially in combination with techniques explored later in this work.

- It certainly appears that either very little progress has been made in the past thirty years, given the lack of headline news in the world, or perhaps progress has been made and kept secret. It is also telling that despite all the publicity about US psychic warfare programs there has never been so much as a hint that anything like the Owen experiment has been tried. Which, considering its amazing success at creating Psi phenomena, is somewhat surprising.

- If it can produce raps, what about more modulated sounds such as voice? Actually, the Scole Experiment may provide an affirmative answer to this.

- What limits the power of the entities? Presumably the same thing that limits poltergeist activity since while the latter might move objects and rearrange the furniture there have been no reports of flying houses.

- Where does the energy come from to create physical effects? It almost certainly does not come from the bodies of members of the group. If some poltergeist effects were taken at face value then the energy expended would probably severely injure a person if it were somehow extracted from their body. For reference, the normal Human body runs at about 100W but can peak for a few seconds at over 1000W, for example on an exercise bicycle. The most likely explanation is that the mind is somehow controlling an energy conversion process. The source of this energy is unknown, but some have speculated that it might be driven by temperature differentials between, say, the inside and outside of a house. This, of course, would neatly account for the well-known phenomena of cold spots associated with "hauntings" as well as the cool breezes felt by the Owen group. To provide some idea of the energy available, a moderate size room could ideally supply some 50kJ of energy just from the air inside if it dropped in temperature by one degree Celsius. Other possible sources of higher-grade energy might be electrical and magnetic fields associated with mains supplies. So, the notions of witches dancing around the high energy bonfire casting spells may more than just a romantic fancy.

- Electrical phenomena are especially interesting given that electricity is a very low entropy energy form. That is, it is very high grade and can be efficiently converted to just about anything else, unlike small heat differentials. The effects on the electric lights are almost as impressive as any table levitation in the Owen experiment. As for the mechanism, that is totally unknown. It could be anything from an alteration of the resistance of the circuit to the suppression of photon emission in the filament of the light bulb. Irrespective of how it occurs it does suggest a method of interfacing a poltergeist to a computer...

- What is the optimum number of people in a group? What are the maximum and minimum numbers of people in a functioning group? The minimum in the Owen group seemed to be four, and the maximum was presumably limited by space constraints especially around a small table in a small room. On the other hand, one might guess a maximum of around a dozen given that this number appears to be the maximum that a person can psychologically bond with. This number is reflected between groups as diverse as covens and military squads.

- What effects do various intoxicants have, ranging from alcohol to (say) LSD? Presumably any drug that facilitated bonding while not totally scrambling the brains of the participants could be expected to enhance the desired bonding state. This could range from small quantities of alcohol to MDMA. Something like LSD may have a powerful positive effect but its drawback could well be the lack of focus on the task in hand. Obviously though, this depends on dose.

- Can separate groups combine their power effectively? Unknown, but ending on a lighter note that underlines some of the observations above we have…

The PK Party

This is a summary of a particular aspect of the work of Jack Houk, a Psi researcher who is famous for instigating social events in order to facilitate massive PK effects, most notably metal bending. The typical PK Party would last between two and three hours and consists of people who wish to experience large-scale PK effects. The size of the party varies but he recommends than no less than 15 people for several reasons. These are:

- That a larger group tends to create larger effects.
- A fun, party-like atmosphere is very conducive to such effects manifesting.
- That a larger group can create a suitable number of mental distractions that seem necessary for the effects to appear.
- The party generally starts with a talk lasting 30-45 minutes so that by the end people are getting to the point where they want the talking to stop and the action to start. The "party protocol" is as follows:
- The first action is to throw the cutlery on the floor to emphasize its worthlessness – an important psychological factor. People then dowse the cutlery with either a pendulum or rods in a yes/no manner looking for a piece that is ready and willing to bend. The overwhelming majority of people will be able to do this successfully. This builds confidence as well as determining if/when the unconscious will allow each particular piece of tableware to be bent.
- The people then move their chairs (if sitting) into a big circle where the presenter then gives the instructions. During this period nobody should be attempting to bend the metal. Then…
- The tableware is then held between thumb and forefinger and rubbed gently while a mental connection is made with the item.
- A point of intense concentration in the head is then visualized, moving it down through the neck, shoulder, arm, hand, fingers, and into the tableware. This process allows the mind to achieve a link to the material.
- Command what is wanted, verbally. In the case of metal bending commands (or shouts) of "Bend! Bend! Bend!"
- Stop the efforts, relax and let it happen. It is at this point where the conscious mind takes a back seat and the unconscious takes over. This is

where the necessity for distraction arises. [Some magicians reading this will recognize techniques utilized by Chaos Magick and other systems.] In the meantime the fingers feel for the small time window when the metal is ready to bend, while occasionally pushing on the object with the other hand to see if the object gives. During this time the organizer can move around and deliberately break people's concentration.

Initially people are given fairly low quality cutlery that can easily be bent by moderate pressure. When they are successful at bending this, as most are, they then go on to much stiffer higher quality utensils that generally cannot be bent without exerting extreme pressure. The successful graduates, some 50%, then attempt metal bars up to 12mm in diameter. A modification of the procedure is to give everyone a fork in each hand that they hold between thumb and forefinger, at the base of the fork. Exerting no pressure the group then repeats the procedure above. Usually within a few minutes the tines on a number of forks begin to bend.

Most parties have the majority of the individuals bending within 30 minutes and people are asked to let the whole group know when it starts to occur. Once someone is successful then the belief system of the rest seems to change, and they too accomplish the feat shortly thereafter. Finally approximately 50% of the people subsequently discover they can perform metal bending outside of the group setting. That is, it is a skill that can be learned.

The metal most susceptible to PK effects appear to be the ones with most stress and dislocations. That is, contrary to what a skeptic may imagine, forged or hardened metal is easier to bend than is softer annealed material. It appears that there is a localized heating along the grain boundaries that results in a partial melting making it easily deformable. The heat is then transferred out through the metal that can then be sensed by the individual either as stickiness or warmth. The easily malleable state generally lasts between 5 and 30 seconds, and it is finding this time window which is critical. This can occur anywhere from a few seconds to several hours after the initial bending attempt. Houk claims, plausibly, that the secret to creating the time at which this window occurs to be as close to the immediate time as possible is the amount of excitement and intent that is generated on the initial attempt. Again it would appear that the mind is tapping energy already stored in the stress of the metal although perhaps a more general hypothesis might be that it is tapping into the most easily available power source. The magickal Principle of Least Action once again.

The PEAR experiments (later chapter) suggest that Psi is not a force or energy. Rather it is the effect of consciousness interacting with the world at the Quantum level and directly skewing the statistical basis upon which everyday reality is built. In other words, Psi is a distortion of reality. If this is so, then the Owen and Scole experiments described above must take this process to a level of statistical improbability that is almost unbelievable. Alternatively, and more plausibly, Nature is taking the shortest route to a result and this distortion is opening new avenues of approach to areas of physics with which we are not yet familiar.

Psi and the Occult

Prayer and Healing Studies – a brief review

It is beyond dispute that "hands on" healing certainly does aid patient recovery, and/or the amelioration of their symptoms. However, much of this can be put down to the amazing efficacy of the Placebo Effect discussed in the chapter on Mind. What concerns us here are the multiple, and admittedly conflicting, studies carried out where this effect was eliminated. This is usually done by allowing no overt contact between the healer or healing group and the patient, nor on occasion allowing the latter to know that anything is being done for their benefit. These studies are what might be termed "remote healing" or in religious contexts "the power of prayer" and generally fall into one of two distinct experimental protocols.

The first type is exemplified by the work of William Braud and Marilyn Schlitz at the *Mind Science Foundation*. They pioneered models for healing that are testable in the lab. The protocol used most often was to monitor the Autonomic Nervous System (ANS) activity of a subject, typically the Galvanic Skin Response (GSR) or skin resistance, while a healer would randomly attempt to create a response. Over a series of 14 experiments Schlitz and Braud found significant differences in the subject's ANS under these conditions.

The magnitude of the effects were quite significant. In one of the studies, participants were also taught to control their own GSR through normal biofeedback. During the self-control sessions, the average GSR shift was about 19%, and in sessions with a distant healer the average GSR shift was around 10%. What is surprising is that the influence of another person, from a distance, is similar in magnitude to the influence we have on our own physiological system. In one particular study subjects were asked to visualize a wall acting as a protection surrounding their body and preventing any external influences from reaching them. In these studies the GSR remained at baseline, indicating that whatever influence was being exerted by the psychic operator was successfully blocked.

These studies are especially interesting from the point of view of the focus of this book in that three major factors in magickal practices are coming together. These are:

- Remote influence of a person's physiology, either to their benefit (healing) or detriment (cursing, "evil eye" etc.)

- The power of visualization, which we return to throughout this work as a major tool of empowerment.

- A basic technique of psychic self defense.

Whether this is the result of PK or some kind of telepathic Placebo Effect is unknown.

The reason why such studies remain disputed is the usual one concerning Psi replication by skeptics. Once again there seems to be an "experimenter effect" where belief, or lack of it, has a major role in the experimental outcome.

Which brings us to the other major branch of investigation, namely that of "the power of prayer" and particularly group focused efforts. While there have been numerous studies done on patient recovery aided by group prayer none have been rigorous enough for the skeptics. Or, if they were rigorous enough then they have not been sufficiently repeatable. This is understandable to a degree given the complexity of Human Beings and their remarkably flexible response to all kinds of external factors.

One such prayer study was conducted by Cha[27] et al. The report's authors, two of whom were faculty members at Columbia University's College of Physicians and Surgeons, claimed to have demonstrated that distant intercessory prayer can double the success rate of in vitro fertilization (IVF). The recipients were in Seoul, South Korea, undergoing IVF in the usual fashion. Approximately half the patients were the unknowing beneficiaries of intercessory prayers by various Christian groups in the United States, Canada, and Australia. The pregnancy rate in the prayed-for group (50%) was essentially twice as high as the pregnancy rate in the non-prayed-for group (26%).

Again, these examples are provided as illustrations not definitive proofs. The literature on such alternative healing practices being examined on a scientific basis is large and growing, with mixed results. Any scientific studies of malicious application of such techniques by, for example, the military of various nations remains classified.

Caveat Emptor

One lesson as old as history that it seems has to be learned over and over again by people contacting alien intelligence is that the overwhelming majority are inherently untrustworthy. This lesson applies to phenomena as varied as séance spirits, conjured demons, UFO aliens, the Faery Folk, Astral Travel or aspects of the unconscious including group gestalts. What typically happens is that some impressive feat is demonstrated and then an explanation is attached by the entity. It could be as modern as a UFO landing and the occupants explaining what they want, or it could be disembodied spirits accurately prophesying major events and showing off their PK powers. Then come explanations or requests that at the time seem reasonable but on later reflection are anything but. There are numerous cases where a whole series of accurate prophecies have led groups to believe that they are in touch with a cosmic intelligence or benign power such as the Hidden Masters or Secret Chiefs of Theosophy. Finally, when belief is total there will be a prophecy concerning some global disaster which results in the True Believers standing on some mountaintop awaiting salvation from the impending End Of The World. The next day things are clearer, although quite often the True Believers assume that it is they themselves at fault rather than their information source. It is why the Trickster

---

[27] Cha KY, Wirth DP, Lobo RA. Does prayer influence the success of in vitro fertilization-embryo transfer? Journal of Reproductive Medicine 46:781-787, 2001.

archetype is common to all shamanic views of the world and many religions. A relatively modern case study was recorded in a book by John Keel entitled "The Mothman Prophecies"[28].

Briefly, for a thirteen month period from November 1966CE until December 1967CE, the town of Point Pleasant, West Virginia, USA was seemingly overrun by UFOs, poltergeists, Men in Black and the usual cattle mutilations that were to become famous in later decades. The appearance of these phenomena appeared to revolve around regular sightings of a winged humanoid that became known as the "Mothman". The Mothman was most often seen around disused North Power Plant, which was part of the dormant West Virginia Ordnance Works complex. The area was used as a shooting range and "lovers lane", and kind of unofficial common. There were hundreds of witnesses to these phenomena including some members of the population who claimed contact with various extraterrestrials. It appeared that anyone even peripherally involved was affected, and Keel, who had arrived from New York to investigate the reports, was no exception. Before long, he experienced the kinds of synchronicities that plague such phenomena. For example, many of his contactee friends from his previous UFO investigations often knew of his future actions before he had himself decided on them. His phone line became almost unusable with untraceable interference, tapping, line cutting, crossed lines, hoax phone calls and people allegedly following him round Manhattan. Keel received constant precise predictions throughout the 13 months that came to be known as the Mothman Prophecies. Unfortunately they had a nasty habit of being almost right but not close enough to do anything about them. Things finally came to a head during rush hour on Point Pleasant's Silver Bridge across the Ohio River. Keel was warned of a nation-wide power outage for December 15th. Instead the bridge failed taking 31 vehicles and 67 people with it into the river killing 46 of them. This incident effectively marked the end of the Mothman story.

It is crucial that the magician does not take the claims of "spirits" at face value – they are only as good as the phenomena they produce. Another thing worth bearing in mind is that this is intended to be a technology, not a propaganda outlet or a club for wild goose chases initiated on behalf of a dubious spirit world.

Ultraterrestrial Workings

There is one area of modern magick that is both rare and dangerous, and that is working within a UFO paradigm with entities that are not so much "aliens" as Ultraterrestrials. Traditionally, UFO sightings are attributed to a number of possible causes:

- Mis-identification of known phenomena

---

[28] The Mothman Prophecies, John A. Keel, Tor Books, ISBN: 0765341972

- Hoaxes of one sort or another
- Unknown aircraft, including secret military technology
- Extraterrestrial spacecraft

Excluding the first three categories, and assuming that the phenomena is guided by non-Human intelligence, the extraterrestrial hypothesis as it has come to be known appears to be untenable. In other words, whatever the "real" UFOs are, they are not spacecraft piloted by "aliens" from another planet. Now, this does not mean the usual debunking as offered by the usual suspects, that is, by the traditional scientific and political establishments. Nor will I elaborate on the obvious, that much of this debunking has been done to discredit quite accurate reports by witnesses of secret military technology being tested in our skies. Indeed, I will be taking some reports, especially the ones claiming contact with alien visitors, as accurate. Or at least as accurate as the perceptions of the contactees. Nevertheless, there is so much "alien spaceship" mythology attached to the UFO phenomena that it obscures what is really happening.

So, why are UFOs not alien spaceships? The simplest answer lies in the chapter on the Great Work. The aliens are too primitive – they are barely more advanced than we are. They are using tools and methodologies that are primitive compared to things that are being tested in our own laboratories right now. Consider Earth in, say, 200 years time. There will likely be no Humans left on Earth, having been replaced by PostHuman societies and individuals whose intellects will exceed ours to the same extent that ours exceeds that of an ant. The tools such PostHumans use will likely not be the crude equivalent of "space spanners" as wielded by our UFO aliens but subtle extensions of their own bodies that can access and analyze structures down to the nuclear level or beyond. Their vehicles will not be spaceships in which they sit tweaking the control console but, again, extensions of their own bodies and minds. And if they do visit another star system and wish to do covert surveillance and take covert samples it will not be by kidnapping the locals and applying the anal probes! Even as I write this there is a report on the use of insects with electronic implants being developed specifically for covert surveillance by the US military. If a real alien did exist and wanted a blood sample from you, it would not need to land the spaceship, drag you aboard and stick a hypodermic into you. A remote controlled mosquito would do the job far better.

Then we have the other parts of the mythology which we can examine in turn, starting with the reverse engineering of crashed UFOs. It's fair to say that if any technology has been discovered in such a wreck it has not leaked into the civilian sector. From before Roswell to today, some 60 years later, there is not a single piece of technological innovation that does not have a fully Human pedigree backed by decades of research publications. Of course, periodically there are such claims, the most notable being that the transistor was not invented by William Shockley, John Bardeen and Walter Brattain in 1947CE but was just such an example of reverse engineering derived from the Roswell crash. The proponents of such claims conveniently ignore a number of patents for the transistor as far back as 1925CE [29]. Ironically, the patent was for what might be considered a more advanced device than the one that eventually made the headlines in 1947CE. Again, it can be claimed that all such technological advances, including antigravity drives and "free energy" generators have been kept secret as part of a parallel military technology. That spending trillions of dollars on conventional aircraft and rockets is just a smokescreen designed to hide the real state of affairs which is controlled by a secret elite. And then we have to throw the aliens back into the mix. The result of this logic is that there is a conspiracy of galactic proportions of which the vast majority of Humanity is ignorant, and indeed a victim.

So, if UFOs are not spaceships, what are they? Well, ironically there may be more to the old "mass hysteria" debunking explanation than was originally intended by the skeptics. In other words, Jung's view as to the nature of UFOs may be far closer to the truth of the matter. He came to the conclusion that UFOs were examples of the phenomena of synchronicity where external events mirror internal psychic states. In his book on UFOs[30] he wrote:

> "As we know from ancient Egyptian history, they are manifestations of psychic changes which always appear at the end of one Platonic month and at the beginning of another. Apparently they are changes in the constellation of psychic dominants, of the archetypes, or "gods" as they used to be called, which bring about, or accompany, long-lasting transformations of the collective psyche. The transformation started in the historical era and left its traces first in the passing of the eon of Taurus into that of Aries, and then of Aries into Pisces, whose beginning coincides with the rise of Christianity. We are now nearing that great change which may be expected when the spring point enters Aquarius."

This is quite close to the view of researcher Dr. Jacques Vallée who in the 1960s began exploring the commonalities between UFOs, cults, religious movements, angels, ghosts, cryptid[31] sightings, and psychic phenomena. Much of this he documented in his book[32]. He came to the conclusion that the phenomenon has been occurring throughout history masquerading in various forms to different cultures, and partially involving non-Human intelligences capable of manipulating space and time. Their possible origin he widens to include other dimensions coexistent with ours and hence they fall into the category of what has been termed "Ultra-Terrestrials". The aim of such UFO phenomena he believes to be social

---

[29] Julius Edgar Lilienfeld on October 22, 1925

[30] Jung – Flying Saucers ISBN-13: 978-0415278379

[31] A cryptid is an animal whose existence has not been verified scientifically – see Cryptozoology

[32] Passport to Magonia ISBN-13: 978-0426157397

manipulation by using deception on the Humans with whom they interact. Vallée also proposed a secondary aspect of the UFO phenomenon involving Human manipulation by Humans in that witnesses of UFO phenomena and contactees undergo a staged spectacle designed to alter their belief system, leading eventually to Human society believing in intervention from outer space with unknown social consequences. The ultimate motivation for this deception is probably a projected major change of human society, the breaking down of old belief systems and the implementation of new ones. Vallée cannot say who or what is behind this scheme, only that the evidence, if carefully analyzed, suggests an underlying plan for the deception of mankind by means of psychotronic technology. It is highly unlikely that governments actually conceal alien evidence, as the popular myth suggests. Rather, it is much more likely that that is exactly what the manipulators want us to believe. These and other reasons can be summarized thus:

- The technology is too primitive. In fact, through the ages and into modern times the phenomena reflects the current public expectations of advanced technology. As we shall see later, Human technology will soon far surpass anything demonstrated by UFOs and their occupants.
- The number of visitations is ridiculously high if one were to assume that these are star ships.
- The occupants are almost entirely Humanoid, which is improbable in itself.
- The occupants mirror mythological creatures, which is understandable if our mythologies are partially based on such visitations. However, they also mirror contemporary mythologies in the making, such as science fiction movies and novels even down to individual plot lines and spoken words.
- Their behavior is seemingly irrational or full of pointless and overblown warnings or trite philosophy.
- They have an unhealthy interest in Human sexuality.

The alien entities are in fact angels, demons, the Faery folk and so forth. Additionally many of their characteristics have far more in common with the paranormal than with conventional science and technology. In fact, the UFO part of their appearance can be viewed as a high energy poltergeist effect, and it may well be a serious mistake to assume that UFOs have "occupants" instead of the UFOs and occupants being essentially the same thing. Vallée has also come to the somewhat disturbing belief that Human groups of some undefined kind may also be associated with the UFO phenomenon, and not merely as perpetrators of hoaxes but for more directed reasons. Still, through the ages this too was a feature, there being people who were "in league with the Devil" or the Faery folk, or whatever. From our perspective it should not come as a surprise, since if the mage wishes to work with the Ultraterrestrial paradigm this is bound to happen. We are certainly not the first and the whole "Men in Black" myth associated with UFOs and latterly

Psi and the Occult

Hollywood, has its origins with the "Man in Black" who made his appearance in medieval sorcery and who was presumed to be the Devil (or in other cultures, a vampire). However, one should not assume an either/or view of such Beings, that they are either supernatural or aliens or Humans. Consider the nature of dynamic archetypes examined elsewhere and how people can play a role without realizing they are manifesting such forces.

The spectrum of encounters, which is what really interests us as magicians, bears more than a little resemblance to classical demonic conjuration with all its attendant dangers. This is especially true given their possible high energy nature. For example, calculations just of optical emissions of some famous sightings have indicated power dissipations in the tens to hundreds of megawatts. There is no doubt that there is to be expected a very serious physical presence and possible threat. This is born out by many reported instances of injuries and occasionally deaths associated with the Ultraterrestrials. Nevertheless there are also reports of miraculous cures and benevolent entities, again mirroring the duality we find in past contacts that were interpreted in religious terms. Other associated characteristics reported are:

- Time distortions, especially lost time and amnesia
- Changes in medical conditions, sometimes beneficial sometimes not
- Physical damage, from crushed trees and grass to sunburn and radiation sickness in witnesses
- Massive electrical disturbance, the classic ones being a failure of car engines, radios, flashlights etc.
- Seeming teleportations or transport over long distances in unreasonably short timescales
- Telepathic communication
- Hauntings and apparitions, for example aliens walking through walls.
- The appearance of marks or patterns upon the skin of contactees (the classic "witch mark"), recently updated with claims of bionic implants as the entities strive to keep up with modern paranoia.
- Sexual overtones to the contact, ranging from intimate "medical examinations" to explicit sexual intercourse.
- Hallucinations

It is this latter aspect that causes a great deal of the problem. People in the vicinity of a UFO seem to enter a different world more akin to a lucid dream than mundane reality. What they claim to see may bear no resemblance to what is actually happening to them. This has obviously been one of the major factors when it comes to their stories being dismissed, and it could certainly account for the nonsensical or sexual nature of much of what is happening if material is being dredged from the unconscious and made manifest. It has even been suggested that this state is caused by the aforementioned electromagnetic disturbances, which seems plausible, but then that only pushes the mystery back a bit further.

So, let's take a rather famous case that occurred in Brazil in 1966CE. This was superficially a UFO murder mystery with a strong pointer to the culprits being extraterrestrials. The story[33] as I originally heard it years ago went as follows.

It starts on a hill named Morro do Vintem in Niteroi, a suburb of Rio de Janeiro, where the bodies of two men were discovered. They were lying side by side on their backs dressed in neat suits and new raincoats with no signs of blood or violence. Next to them were metal masks made of lead and some notes which included basic electrical formulas as well as instructions saying: "Meet at the designated spot at 16:30. At 18:30 ingest the capsules. After the effect is produced protect half of the face with lead masks. Wait for the pre-arranged signal". Their identities were revealed as electronics technicians Miguel Jose Viana aged 34 and Manuel Pereira da Cruz aged 32 who specialized in installing TV transmitters and repeaters. A postmortem revealed no poison and the official verdict was cardiac arrest. At the time these men were on the hill many witnesses reported UFO sightings in the same place, specifically an oval shaped craft that glowed orange and sent out blue rays. This was essentially what was reported in the UFO magazines and books at the time as evidence of some kind of extraterrestrial contact gone wrong. What was omitted was even more interesting.

It turns out that both the men were members of what has variously been described as an occult group or spiritualist organization who were interested in contacting other worlds. At Viana's house police discovered a book on what they termed "scientific spiritualism" with underlined passages on spirits, intense luminosity and masks. The wife of the other man confirmed that she was told by him that they were on a "secret mission". Further intensive investigations over a two years period, including an exhumation and testing of the bodies using neutron activation analysis revealed nothing definitive, and what actually happened remains a mystery. Naturally the police did not pursue the occult connection in any depth.

So, how does one go about evoking Ultraterrestrials? There are a number of clear pointers from various traditions as well as modern (pseudo) science. The essential thing to recognize is that you are performing a demonic (or angelic) summoning, and that the entities involved have themselves evolved to match the expectations of the planetary psyche. They no longer manifest as (say) witches on broomsticks but as aliens in spacecraft. Whereas a few hundred years ago one would cast a circle and go through various incantations and exhortations nowadays the technique must be updated to match the science of the times. Fortunately we do not need radio telescopes and all the paraphernalia of real science because we are essentially performing a series of symbolic actions. So, here are the brief guidelines

---

[33] Confrontations, Jacques Vallée, Ballantine Books, ISBN-13: 978-0345365019

Psi and the Occult

based around classical demonology, specifically from the European medieval tradition:

- The Ultraterrestrials are constrained by both your beliefs and their own (if they have any)

- They believe in machinery. Not necessarily "real" machinery but the kind of Symbolic Machines we will later examine in detail.

- You still need to call them by name or by type. Naming them goes some way to determining what will appear. As in a game of Ouija or a séance, starting with: "Is anybody there?" is asking for trouble.

- The Grays and Reptilians are the modern equivalent of demons. The Nordics the equivalent of angels. Read some UFO literature on who is who.

- You need to set limits on their manifestation in both time (duration) and space (where) by specifying it as part of the summoning.

- The summoning has to be planned, and the plan adhered to.

- There is little point in casting a circle of protection in the conventional sense. A modern update would be some kind of "force field". One suggested method is the use of Orgone (see the chapter on Machinery).

- Be very careful as to whether you are inside it, or the summoned entity is inside it. Bear in mind that if it is a UFO its manifestation is something you want well away from you. A few megawatts of energy being dissipated in your close vicinity will look indistinguishable from Spontaneous Human Combustion. If someone breaks the circle they are on their own. If things go badly wrong consult the medical services, police and/or your local exorcist assuming you are still alive.

- Do not rely on electrical equipment as it may well fail. This includes electrical lighting, so do not forget the candles! However, malfunctioning of equipment can be used as a method to determine whether something is happening, as can the detection of fluctuating magnetic and electrical fields. Beware though, because it is not definitive.

- The summoning itself should be via something akin to the Hieronymus or Wish machine (see chapter on Machines) capable of broadcasting your intent. Even a conventional (real) radio transmitter may do.

- Have a psychic weapon handy – for example, a handheld Cloudbuster. It's the updated wizard's wand.

- It may help to "beam" the summoning at the constellation associated with the alien in UFO mythology

- Know what you want from the entity and spell it out in detail. Be very careful of the wording.
- Be polite – very polite, but forceful.
- Do not be sidetracked, do not break the circle or forcefield.
- At the end, thank the entity and dismiss it. Perform a banishing ritual with psionic weaponry to ensure the area is cleared.
- Do not do this at home, you will not want to live with what might decide to hang around
- NEVER just abandon a working if it appears nothing is happening.

In my opinion, working consciously and with intent within the Ultraterrestrial paradigm is the single most dangerous thing a magician can do. If you intend to follow this path read up on classical demonology and Faerie[34] lore first, because it is about the only source of protective knowledge. And even that may not be enough if you are successful. It is not something to be undertaken lightly, or without preparation, or without a specific goal.

Summary

So, what can we conclude from the above concerning the augmenting of magickal operations? The lessons are numerous and rather than providing radical new insights tend to explain numerous traditional practices.

- Groups are more effective than individuals.
- Mixed groups are better than single sex groups.
- The members of the group should be emotionally bonded together and be able to trust each other.
- Anthropomorphization – the object that is the focus of the group should be something to which the group can bond emotionally, as with another person. In the case of the Owen experiment this was taken to its logical conclusion in which the focus was a personality.
- A light-hearted approach is more effective.
- Belief and expectation are crucial, at least in the early stages.
- Peak events should be emotionally charged.

---

[34] Or as the comedy fantasy author Terry Pratchett put it in "Lords and Ladies": "...bringing all those things traditionally associated with the magical, glittering realm of Faerie: cruelty, kidnapping, malice and evil."

Psi and the Occult

- The importance of speech – not at all obvious but relevant considering the Society of Mind mental model examined next.

- The first manifestations are the most important. Once these occur the rest is easy – it's a positive feedback loop that builds upon its own success.

- The first Psi attempt is likely to be far more successful than second and third. This may account for the fact that most magickal workings involve one-off effects. Correct training can minimize this effect which is generally psychological.

- Psi skills can be taught and learned.

- The most rapid way of passing on Psi skills in certain group workings is to hot swap in new members while taking original ones out while still maintaining the integrity of the phenomena.

- Psi seems to be only loosely timebound and effects may sometimes precede or post-date the intentional effort by a considerable period. The immediacy of the result appears to be connected with the freedom the unconscious mind has been given.

- Temporal effects are apparently maximized by closed loops between past and future.

- The presence of a high-grade, low entropy, energy source may facilitate manifestations. That is, energy sources such as electricity, electromagnetic fields, high temperature differentials etc.

- The information provided by entities should not be trusted.

- If these effects are to be taken into the wider community the group gestalt needs to be hardened against skepticism. There is little or no published research that has been done in this area, although the analysis of cultist conditioning elsewhere in the book may be of use..

Gods and Daemons

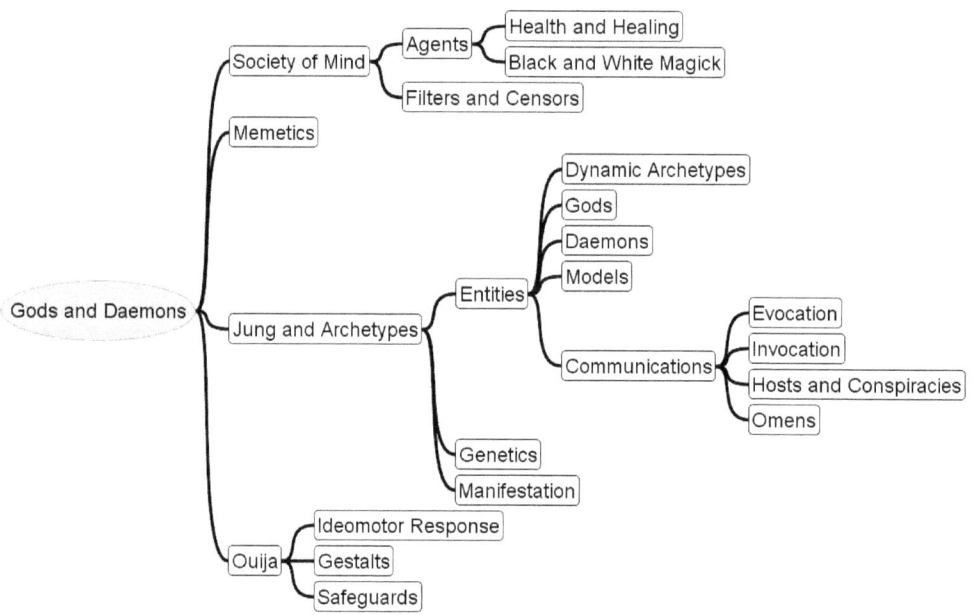

4 Gods and Daemons

Agents and The Society of Mind[35]

Society of Mind (SoM) is a concept developed by the prominent MIT scientist Marvin Minsky, with the aid of Seymour Papert, over several years of work in the field of Artificial Intelligence (AI). It was developed as an analysis of the Human mind in terms that might make it amenable to modeling on computer systems. As such it owes less to modern psychology than it does to engineering, since attempting to build something so complex often provides deep and non-trivial insights into the ways that it must be done and certainly into ways it cannot. Many aspects of SoM anticipated modern advances in cognitive psychology, and in this work it provides a basic theoretical underpinning for later concepts such as dynamic archetypes. Only a brief overview will be presented, with most of the technical descriptions omitted. However, we will retain the notion of *Agents* for later use.

The mind is a community of semi-autonomous Agents, each with limited power and communication abilities. What we think of as Mind emerges from their interactions since Agents by themselves have no significant intelligence. By way of illustration Minsky provides the example of talking with oneself, and how the participants of these imaginary conversations really exist in the forms of Agents or higher level collections of such which in general are referred to as Agencies. There are, in fact, many sub-personalities interacting with one another. Solving even simple problems may involve many Agents, perhaps vast numbers of them. Some may contain knowledge, strategies, warnings and encouragement, while others are concerned with discipline, prohibitions and censoring forbidden thoughts. These are organized into local, quasi-political hierarchies. Each agent can be based on a different type of process with its own distinct kinds of purposes, languages for describing things, ways of representing knowledge, and methods for producing inferences. Overall coherency of personality ultimately emerges not from any clear and simple principle, but from the interactions, under elaborate genetic control, of communities of doers, critics, filters and censors, culminating in agencies for self-discipline that compare one's behavior with fragments of self-images acquired at earlier stages of development.

The notion that Mind is a single unitary thing is clearly false. Having recognized this, the notion of "mental states" then becomes not the state of a Mind, but a description of which Agents, Agencies and hierarchies are active at any particular time. Minsky explicitly uses an analogy that will be expanded upon in far

---

[35] Minsky, M.: The Society of Mind. Simon and Schuster, New York, 1986.

more detail later, namely that of Mind being very similar to a Human administrative organization. On the largest scale are divisions that specialize in such areas as sensory processing, language, long-range planning, and so forth. Within each division are multitudes of sub-specialists, Agents, which embody smaller elements of an individual's knowledge, skills, and methods. No single one of these little Agents knows very much by itself, but each recognizes certain configurations of a few associates and responds by altering its state. This idea is perhaps best summarized by the following quote from Minsky's book:

> "What magical trick makes us intelligent? The trick is that there is no trick. The power of intelligence stems from our vast diversity, not from any single, perfect principle. Our species has evolved many effective although imperfect methods, and each of us individually develops more on our own. Eventually, very few of our actions and decisions come to depend on any single mechanism. Instead, they emerge from conflicts and negotiations among societies of processes that constantly challenge one another."

That is, the Human mind is a gestalt, another crucial concept that will be expanded upon in a magickal context later. A *gestalt* is defined as

> "...a physical, biological, psychological, or symbolic configuration or pattern of elements so unified as a whole that its properties cannot be derived from a simple summation of its parts."

The "Self" is then merely another Agent, one that monitors some of the other Agencies, most notably those involved with sensory inputs and outputs. Even so, the vast majority escape its view and these omissions are collectively known as the unconscious. Even simple introspection reveals that what we habitually think of as our conscious self is at best a composite of competing Agents. For example, close your eyes and think of nothing at all. Unless you have trained long and hard in this particular discipline you will find that an internal dialog develops whereby you hear yourself saying things like: "…I've just done ten seconds without thinking!" or alternatively totally unrelated thoughts will bubble up and spoil the effort. So who is doing the talking and who wants to stop the talking? Clearly someone inside is not obeying orders, yet, the "chatterer" is superficially the one who keeps insisting it stop!

However, there is no proposed model for Consciousness, unlike Self, which can be modeled as a kind of monitoring Agent. The SoM and other theories do not explain Consciousness but instead assume that it somehow emerges from all this complexity. This is, in general, the view of the majority of scientists although there is a notable dissenting minority who hold interesting ideas concerning a possible connection between Consciousness and Quantum Mechanics.

The notion of Agents and Agencies are of critical importance in much of what follows. Part of this is due to the fact that the lines of communication between them do not follow straight lines to or from some hypothetical control center one might consider to be Self. Nor do they line up directly with sensory input and motor outputs, but in fact many chains of Agents can be activated by single inputs, and many Agents can compete for outputs. Additionally, most Agents do not or cannot communicate with each other except indirectly.

This is a piece of crucial information that explains why, for example, spells should be spoken aloud. We automatically assume that if we visualize words in our head, that is we speak them internally without actually saying them aloud, that all aspects of our mind perceive them. This is not true at all. The Agencies responsible for imagining those words have only limited communication abilities. It is a fact that some Agents triggered by hearing are not triggered by visualized words, and that the best way to engage more Agents is to actually speak the words aloud. It turns out that the best way of linking some Agents within the mind is to send the communication outside the body. In the case of words the linking occurs from mouth to ears. Similar bypasses exist for all sensory inputs, most notably the visual but also for touch, smell and taste in decreasing order of importance. Imagining a picture, or Sigil, has less of an effect than seeing one. However, auditory information is the most interesting since it is the channel of language and from a magickal point of view links to more useful Agents than the other senses. That is why hearing is the primary channel for hypnotic techniques (although not the only one). Hearing, and language in particular, is specialized for receiving data that is already encoded with meaning, unlike the other senses. There is also another reason for using externalized communications with ones own mind. It is that different modes of perception have different Censor or Filter Agents monitoring that data input. What may be censored via one input channel may bypass those censors or filters by using another.

Once the censors and filters are by passed many Agents are highly suggestible. They believe what they are told and act upon the data uncritically. One should also not forget that there are Agents that have direct effects on bodily health, and this will be elaborated upon later. From a magickal point of view this model illuminates numerous phenomena, from hypnotism to psychic healing and the placebo effect to the fragility of Psi phenomena and onwards to an explanatory underpinning of transpersonal entities described later.

Filters and Censors

Filter Agents exist to defend the integrity of Mind against both internal and external influences that have been determined to be detrimental to the gestalt, and most have probably been in place since early childhood. Some can be removed or suppressed voluntarily but most cannot. When we walk around we do not see most of what exists about us. Instead our conscious mind is fed a summary of what is there. We do not see every blade of grass on the ground, every leaf on every tree, every link in every fence or the minute surface detail of the ground we walk upon. We get the filtered version that says: "There is a whole lot of green grass, plus some trees and the ground is a bit rough." To illustrate this, and without looking, name all the objects behind you, their colors and their relative positions. Most of what we perceive as we go about our daily lives is an illusion. How little we actually consciously perceive was recently illustrated in a psychology experiment that was set up as follows.

People who were walking across a college campus were asked by a stranger for directions. During the resulting chat, two men carrying a wooden door passed between the stranger and the subjects. After the door went by, the subjects were asked if they had noticed anything strange. Half of those tested failed to notice that, as the door passed by, the stranger had been substituted with a man who was of different height, of different build and who sounded different. He was also wearing different clothes. Despite the fact that the subjects had talked to the stranger for 10-15 seconds before the swap, half of them did not detect that, after the passing of the door, they had ended up speaking to a different person. Some did still not notice the change even when the gender, race or color of the person changed. This phenomenon, called change blindness, highlights how we see much less than we think we do, and more importantly how we continue to see what we expect to see.

No method of problem solving or reasoning will always work so Minsky proposes that in addition to knowledge about problem solving methods themselves, we also have much knowledge about how to avoid the most common problems with those methods. He calls this type of knowledge negative expertise and describes this knowledge as embodied in the form of censor and suppressor agents. Censors suppress the mental activity that precedes unproductive or dangerous actions, and suppressors suppress those unproductive or dangerous actions themselves. What this means is that many ideas, notions, solutions to problems and so forth are never allowed to bubble up to the point where they become conscious and can be acted upon. In other words, "we" even censor our own thoughts.

This is one reason why psychedelic drugs such as LSD are said to expand consciousness. They create conditions where many of the Censor and Filter Agents are rendered ineffective, unedited reality floods in and previously unthinkable thoughts see the light of day. When tripping you actually do see every blade of grass and every leaf on every tree, to the extent that the detail overwhelms the mind. This, of course, is the reason the filters exist, because we do not need to apprehend every blade of grass, while we do need to see and concentrate upon important features of our environment. Evolution endowed us with a set of tools that enable us to filter out grass while emphasizing what we have learned to be vital for our well-being, such as recognizing saber-tooth tigers. Yet it is important to realize that some things are filtered out because the filters established in childhood were educated to perform that function, and what the child did not need to see then may be extremely important for the adult now. The result is a blindness so complete that most people do not even see that they are blind in certain areas of reality and may indeed be extremely resistant even to the notion that this might be so. Nobody likes to think they are mentally crippled, which is of course the reaction of a censor agent. When some of the censors are removed or bypassed all kinds of strange, bizarre and fascinated insights are presented to the consciousness. That is the reason why in the early days of the exploration of the effects of LSD and other psychedelics they were considered to be "creativity drugs"[36] (and still are for many).

The world is awash with messages and meanings, some are real and meant for you, some are real and meant for some part of you, some are parts of your mind talking to itself, some are fabrications, some are only potentially meaningful. Reality itself is conditional upon what, where and who, you are. And vice versa. This is the situation that schizophrenics, or the users of psychedelics, can find themselves in. It is a world of vast complexity and meaning with very few rules or signposts.

Memetics

The concept of the meme was introduced by the biologist Richard Dawkins as the cultural equivalent of genes in biology. Whereas genes contain information that enables them to biologically replicate in suitable bodies memes contain information that enables them to replicate in a host population of suitable minds. They are the equivalent of a mental virus. The simplest forms are easily recognizable and vary as radically as catchy tunes that one cannot stop humming, to funny jokes that propagate rapidly, to simple injunctions like "Stepping on the cracks in the pavement is bad luck" and onwards to far more complex structures such as the God meme. A meme is an idea that embeds itself in the mind and which encourages the host to propagate it onwards and hence infect others thereby replicating it. Like genes they undergo evolution and adapt themselves to their host populations while also often adapting their host to the memetic environment. The most successful memes, such as the Chain Letter promising great rewards if it is passed on and dire consequences for "breaking the chain", pyramid selling/gambling schemes, the monotheistic God meme or those associated with political ideologies, generally have several components. These are:

- The core data. This has to provide something that either triggers the pleasure center in the brain or is perceived to enhance the survival or power of the Self. This perception need not be true, just plausible - especially if there are penalties for non-acceptance.

- An element that immunizes the host against related competing memes.

- An element which creates an urge to communicate it. This need not be specifically included in the meme but may be implicit. For example, spreading it may be viewed as an act of altruism.

- A reward for doing so.

- A punishment for failure to do so.

---

[36] Storming Heaven: LSD and the American Dream, Jay Stevens, ISBN-13: 978-0802135872

In the case of Islam and Christianity we can see each factor coming into play. We have a story that promises a way to enhance survival to the ultimate degree by guaranteeing life beyond death. Additionally that life can be one of perfect pleasure, if the story and its injunctions are followed, or it can be one of eternal torment if the conditions are not met. In both YHVH stories (the God in question) there are commands to proselytize, to spread its message. Both stories have ways of immunizing against other similar memes by claiming that the YHVH meme is the true one and acceptance of another will result in Hellfire. The mutations are numerous, as witnessed by early major evolutionary variants as it mutated and found new psychological niches away from Judaism and into Christianity and then into Islam some centuries later. Of course, there are also countless competing subspecies of almost identical forms. Some, especially those urging physical repression and military conquest, have been very successful. This pattern is later copied by the ideologies that have killed tens of millions of people such as Communism. Ironically, in order to create the same psychological appeal without a deity involved they have often had to elevate individuals almost to that status which is why we start with Jesus who is supposed to be God himself, and end up with the Stalin and Hitler style of personality cult.

Of course these are at the top of the food chain as far as memetic ecology goes and their complexity puts them into a very special category, namely that of Godforms which have stories and actual personalities attached, which we will examine in detail further on. Meanwhile we can define a meme in relation to the previously established description of Mind as:

- **Ideas = Agents + Data**
  That is, we have the mind's control mechanisms acting upon raw data, both internal and external, and selecting coherent messages – ideas – for presentation to the conscious self.

- **Memes = Ideas + Communication**
  Here the ideas are optimized for communication between minds.

The most powerful memes are fairly complex intellectual constructs that share the common feature of claiming to explain major aspects of reality. They are almost invariably religious in nature and the more modern major political memes share this characteristic. We can even analyze modern science and it's quest for the Theory of Everything in these terms.

The tipping point for science came when its meme effectively displaced the God meme in the delivery of perceived material benefits. In this it had an advantage that the God meme did not, namely that while the God meme claimed truth the science meme provided proof or more to the point, disproved elements of the God meme story. The latter then fought back by mutating into a form where it claimed that it was a metaphor rather than a literal statement of fact. An interesting question is whether science actually has something equivalent to God at its core, since it certainly has a priesthood comparable to Christianity at its peak and at least a budget that is comparable in real terms as a percentage of social wealth expended. Which brings us to the link between memes and archetypes.

Jung and Archetypes

The word *archetype* comes from the Greek *arche* meaning *first*, and *type* meaning *imprint or pattern*. Psychological archetypes are thus first prints, or patterns that form the basic blueprint for major dynamic counterparts of the human personality. The concept of the archetype is important in what follows, so it is essential that a definition and critique of Jung's work is offered in order to minimize confusion between the original Jungian view and the use of similar concepts later in this work. To help clarify things here is a quote from a lecture on the topic delivered by Jung in 1936CE[37].

> "The collective unconscious is a part of the psyche which can be negatively distinguished from a personal unconscious by the fact that is does not, like the latter, owe its existence to personal experience and consequently is not a personal acquisition... the contents of the collective unconscious have never been in consciousness, and therefore have never been individually acquired but owe their existence exclusively to heredity... the content... is made up essentially of archetypes."
>
> ...
>
> "The concept of the archetype, which is an indispensable correlate to the idea of the collective unconscious, indicates the existence of definite forms in the psyche which seem to be present always and everywhere. Mythological research calls them motifs; in the psychology of primitives they correspond to Levy-Bruhl's concept of "representations collectives", and in the field of comparative religion they have been defined by Hubert and Mauss as "categories of the imagination". Adolf Bastian long ago called them "elementary" or "primordial thoughts". From these references, it should be clear enough that my idea of the archetype -- literally a pre-existent form -- does not stand alone, but is something that is recognized and named in other fields of knowledge."
>
> ...
>
> "This collective unconscious does not develop individually, but is inherited. It consists of pre-existent forms, the archetypes, which can only become conscious secondarily and which give definite form to certain psychic contents."

From this it seems that Jung believed that the archetypes are genetically encoded. Given our greater knowledge of heritable characteristics it seems unlikely that this is the whole truth of the matter. More probably the archetypal imagery is built by

---

[37] Carl Jung, "The Archetypes and the Collective Unconscious", Collected Works, Vol. 9, paragraphs 87-110.

each of us upon the relatively few universal genetic tendencies that define our minds as Human. It is also clear that Jung did not believe his archetypes were a product of social forces. The connection with mythology becomes clear with this extract from Carl Jung's "The Structure of the Psyche"[38], 1927CE:

> "The collective unconscious -- so far as we can say anything about it at all -- appears to consist of mythological motifs or primordial images, for which reason the myths of all nations are its real exponents. In fact, the whole of mythology could be taken as a sort of projection of the collective unconscious."

Carolyn Pearson[39] identifies twelve archetypes that are fairly easy to understand. These are the Innocent, the Orphan, the Warrior, the Caregiver, the Seeker, the Destroyer, the Lover, the Creator, the Ruler, the Magician, the Sage, and the Fool. Obviously these descriptions reflect major social roles or personalities in virtually all societies. Indeed many have been explicitly encoded into Tarot cards across the centuries, long before modern psychology or psychiatry began to explore these areas.

From the above we can create a simplified, and simplifying, formula:

- **Ideas = Agents + Data**
- **Archetypes = Ideas + Genes**
  That is, ideas that whose acceptance or rejection is partially a function of genetically conditioned tendencies.
- **Gods = Archetypes + Nature + Memes**
  Where Nature defines the physical environment of a population.

Archetypes are essentially static across Humanity and throughout history. These in turn are amplified and differentiated by both the natural environment (Nature) and the evolving cultural milieu to create the culturally specific mythologies we recognize today. Hence a Jungian Archetype is essentially the genetically conditioned framework for the core data structure of a meme. That is, it provides the outline of a type of story that is universally appealing. What it actually appeals to within the mind are dominant groups of Agents. The stories themselves are wide-ranging embellishments around these themes.

Entities

The direction we are moving is from the genetic level through the natural world and its effects to the personal and both conscious and unconscious on our way to the transpersonal and superconscious. Naturally a big stopover has to be made at the most complex level, the one that involves the most directed computing power, and

---

[38] Carl Jung, "The Structure of the Psyche", 1927, Collected Works Vol. 8

[39] Carolyn Pearson, "Awakening the Heroes Within"

around which the world revolves – the Human brain. So, we are going to proceed to the next step beyond simple Agents to those embodying personalities, namely *Entities*. Briefly stated in the notation used above:

- **Entities = Ideas + Personalities**
  Where a personality is essentially a story that we can relate to in the first person.

To give an example of an Entity, consider a friend that you know well. You can imagine in considerable detail their likes, dislikes, tone of voice, mannerisms and can quite easily hold an imaginary conversation with them. If your mental model of them is accurate that conversation might be little different from one held in real life. As we will see later, in the section on the Psychomanteum, this is a particularly relevant analogy especially since we are receptive to far more information about people that we meet than might be supposed. Furthermore, such information resides in the unconscious and is accessible to many unconscious aspects of that model. However, Entities can, and are, created when anything with a detailed personality is encountered, or anything to which we can ascribe a personality – even inanimate objects such as idols. Such an Entity can be a construct that is either non-existent or one we are never likely to meet such as a cartoon character, a pop or movie star, politicians and of course religious figures ranging from dead prophets and messiahs to gods and demons. They can also be personifications of things living or non-living such as pets and cars, or even entire societies.

The strength and depth of an Entity is determined by a number of factors, the most essential of which is that of familiarity and repeated contact in numerous contexts. That's why for most people the strongest models[40] are of their parents and why the rhetorical question: "What would your mother say if she could see you now!" is such a psychologically effective device. Because most of us know *exactly* what she would say and how she would say it!

We use such models all the time since they are indispensable when it comes to communicating with other people, especially in a social context. It is obviously a very valuable talent to know beforehand how someone is likely to react to what one says or does. Not only does it save time finding out but it enables speech, body language or actions to be specifically tailored in order to evoke the desired response from another. This is, of course, a very simplistic view of what's happening because these models are not passive things. The brain is not like a computer in this respect, with particular Entities called as sub-routines when needed and then put back into a limbo state when no longer required. In a sense they are always running in the background, both influencing and being influenced by other mental processes. They *evolve* within the mental environment.

When things go wrong with the way Entities are constructed or manifested there are two extremes that are recognized. At one end we have the spectrum of

---

[40] The term "Model" is used in NLP (Neuro-linguistic programming). In this book "Entity" is a more general form of the term.

autistic disorders where the models are either incomplete or missing entirely. With the latter the results are almost always deleterious and the autistic person cannot predict what something as complex as a Human is likely to think or do, and may not even recognize them as being different from other parts of the environment. Incomplete models may result in what's termed *High Functioning Autism* of which *Asperger's Syndrome* is the most widely recognized. In such cases the incompleteness may arise because Agents normally used to feed information into the creation of such Entity models do not function efficiently. For example, Agents that would normally automatically recognize body language may not be doing their job and in order to build effective models this information has to be explicitly sought through other more conscious learning processes. At the other end of the spectrum we have the situations where the internal control mechanism regulating the use of some Entities is lost and they manifest spontaneously and chronically in an unwelcome manner resulting in rare cases of *Multiple Personality Disorder* or more commonly the voices heard in Schizophrenia. Of course, this is the extreme end of a continuum of problems out-of-control Entities can cause, ranging from various psychotic symptoms to the religiously oriented phenomenon of possession by non-Human Entities. Interestingly in many such cases, especially those involving multiple entities, they may not be aware of each other or if they are it is in a kind of pecking order where the dominant one knows about the lesser but the reverse is not true. In possession cases the person concerned, or at least the model that calls itself "The Self", may not be aware of what the possessing Entity says or does. Possession, unlike Multiple Personality Disorder, almost always has voluntary aspects and is usually a temporary phenomenon. This is true of Spiritualist mediums channeling their once-Human spirit guide to Shamans becoming possessed by their animal guides to practitioners of Voodoo being ridden by the Loa. It has been claimed, although I cannot authenticate it, that no atheist has ever been a subject of Demonic Possession at least in the Christian sense, presumably because they simply do not have the necessary detailed demon model that is instilled into many religious people. Which brings us to the next level…

A Game of Ouija

The concept of the Ouija Board was invented in 1853 by French spiritualist, M. Planchette. The Ouija Board was a large piece of paper and the wedge was heart-shaped with two wheels on each end. The third end had a pencil attached. Then one or more people would place their fingers on it and the wedge would move and draw pictures or form words.

    Elija J Bond and Charles Kennard of the Kennard Novelty Company invented the modern board around 1891CE. A patent was awarded on February 10, 1891CE. He called the new creation "Ouija" because he claimed the board told him that Ouija was Egyptian for "Good Luck" – which it isn't!

    William Fuld reinvented the history of the Ouija board once he took over the company. He claimed he had invented the talking board and that the name came from a combination of Oui [French] and Ja [German] – making the name of the board "Yes, Yes". He also claimed to be guided in business by the board. After Fuld's death from a fall, his children ran the company until 1966CE, when they sold the business to Parker Brothers. Parker Brothers moved the manufacturing of Ouija boards to Salem, Massachusetts. In the first year of production in Salem, Ouija boards outsold Monopoly. Over two million boards were shipped and it is alleged that it is the biggest selling board game of all time.

Ostensibly Ouija is a technique for communicating with the "spirit world". In many ways it is rather underrated, being relegated to the status of a party game for teenagers when compared to "real" seances or the infinitely more prestigious work done in laboratories under scientific conditions. However, it is far more interesting from a psychological point of view and is certainly not a game given the potential mental hazards involved for particularly susceptible participants. Nevertheless, most adults appear to have played it at some point in their lives, so given the numbers involved it is not surprising that there have been stories of adverse reactions.

Typically, the arrangement is as follows. A set of cards bearing individual letters of the alphabet is set out in a circle on a smooth table surface, with two additional cards bearing the words "Yes" and "No" placed at opposite sides of the circle. A free moving low friction pointer called a *planchette* resides in the center of the circle and each participant places a finger lightly upon it. Someone then asks the traditional question: "Is anybody there?" and shortly thereafter the planchette moves to "Yes" (or occasionally "No"!) whereupon the participants put questions to the spirit which then spells out the answers by pointing to the alphabet cards in turn. The number of participants is not especially critical. The upper number is limited by space considerations, and the minimum is obviously one. When it is the latter then the Ouija game is far more akin to traditional *mediumship*, or *channeling* to use the New Age term, in which case it becomes a subset of *automatic writing* (and we return almost full circle to M Planchette).

As the question and answer session proceeds the manifesting entity reveals a personality complete with history, likes and dislikes and various idiosyncrasies. Part of the attraction of playing this occult game also lies in the fact that the information relayed from "beyond" is often a surprise to all the participants. At the same time the spirit might reveal personal or intimate details known only to a few, or often only one, of the participants. Another interesting feature of Ouija games is that many different personalities can be contacted, and that they can interact with each other as well as with the players. In fact, the depth and coherence of the group interaction with the entity is so impressive and convincing that if it were a computer program it would immediately be classified as a true revolutionary Artificial Intelligence capable of passing the Turing Test.

Ouija, though, has rather a bad reputation. This originally arose from a number of sources. The most prominent one is the Christian Church which views all such contact with spirits to be demonically inspired. A second source is Hollywood that is only too happy to take this demonic view and hype it into horror movies. The third source is rumor. I am pretty sure we have all heard stories of "friends of friends" to whom strange and disturbing things happened after playing the game. Finally, in Ouija the power of cultural conditioning and expectation cannot be overemphasized – if you think it's about angels or demons, you get angels or demons.

In fact, when problems arise, as they occasionally do with regard to suggestible individuals, it can almost always be traced to people asking inappropriate questions. The very first question – "Is anybody there?" is rather a bad way to start since it gives carte blanche to every repressed Agent of the psyche to have its say. Other obviously bad questions are ones such as "Who around this table will die soon?" and other dramatic and scary requests for information. In fact, problems begin when a casual game starts to be taken seriously by one or more of the group. Having said that, there is one very strong argument against real spirits being present and responsible for the information. It is that there has never been a single instance of information coming from a Ouija game or séance that has not previously been known to some person at some time, or is not accessible to a Human mind (and I include such hypothetical psychic talents as psychometry here). You might be wondering what kind of information that leaves available for a discarnate spirit to prove its bona fides. The answer is scientific information, and I will provide two simple cases where a few words could have changed the course of science substantially. Both are cases where a major discovery was overlooked. The first concerns the amazing superconducting properties of Magnesium Diboride, which went unexplored for almost a century. A simple message such as: "Magnesium Diboride superconducts at thirty seven degrees Kelvin – tell a physicist!" would have been all that was required. Ditto for the Fullerenes, also known as Carbon Buckeyballs. The relevant information would have been "A new form of carbon is created in a carbon arc in helium, it dissolves in benzene to produce a red colored liquid – tell a chemist!" Nothing like that has ever happened. Both are simple, both would have won Nobel prizes and it's quite likely that other gems are out there awaiting discovery. Just do not count on the spirits to come up with the goods. And let's not even mention cases where famous (dead) mathematicians or scientists have been channeled. The most charitable thing one might claim is that the afterlife is not conducive to further quality work or knowledge in their chosen fields. Plenty of second-rate Mozarts, though.

So, in providing an analysis of the dynamics of the Ouija game we are going to make a couple of very reasonable and conservative assumptions. The first is that there is no supernatural entity being contacted, least of all dead people. We are also going to discount anecdotal accounts of flying planchettes (or glasses used for that purpose) and levitating tables. This is not done because such things do not reportedly happen but because it is not directly relevant to the major thrust of the argument in this section. The second assumption is that nobody is consciously cheating by deliberately pushing the planchette to spell out messages.

So, where do these coherent messages originate? The simple and logical answer is that they come from the unconscious minds of the participants acting in concert. This itself is an *incredible* phenomenon that is vastly underrated, especially in its implications. It means that aspects of the psyche of several people are conspiring to blend together and create a transpersonal intelligence, or gestalt.

Previously the notion of a gestalt was introduced with respect to the Human mind itself as it emerges from the interactions of billions of non-intelligent and microscopic neurones, dendrites, axons, synapses and glial cells in the brain supporting information structures of thousands or perhaps even millions of Agents and Entities. The only difference between these and the gestalt created in Ouija lies in the fact that with the latter the individual components (people) are intelligent entities in their own right, which shifts the mass of complexity underlying the phenomenon from the overall group to the individual psyches of the participants. So, instead of a mass of simple elements creating something complex we have a mass of already complex elements (people) being used as building blocks to host a transpersonal gestalt.

Additionally, that gestalt not only has access to the minds of each participant, both conscious and unconscious to a greater or lesser degree, but also is actually controlling the physiology at least to the extent of exerting a subtle influence over the motor control responsible for moving the planchette. The mechanism by which this occurs is well known and is called the *ideomotor response*. If you have ever used a pendulum, holding its chain or string, and made it move in a particular way simply by thinking, then you have experienced the ideomotor response. This is a result of unconsciously driven minor muscle movements. In other words, your unconscious mind makes the things move by exerting control outside of your conscious experience.

In the Ouija game the method by which the gestalt is formed is quite simple and illustrative of a more general process.

The first step in its creation is for people involved to relinquish conscious control of both their hand movements and intellectual deliberation. They need to be willing to play along and leave their conscious mind open to whatever occurs within the boundaries of their expectation. In some ways the initial stages of a Ouija game is like a mild hypnotic induction.

The second step is to establish the type of gestalt via the types of questions asked. In a sense, everyone asks leading questions in that the posing of the question elicits an answer from the group unconscious that did not exist until the question was asked. It is as if an intelligent entity were in the process of being constructed piecemeal. The more questions and answers, the greater its degree of reality in both the conscious and unconscious minds of those present. Beyond this point the process becomes self sustaining and self-fulfilling as a real personality is filled out and in turn starts to affect the participants. In many cases the group loses control of the evoked personality and such is its strength it can override the conscious objections of individuals involved. Some people will be more conducive to the expansion and expression of the group mind than others. These will be preferentially chosen by it, and asked to participate in the game, whilst those of a hostile or skeptical disposition will be encouraged to leave. This can take various forms varying from peer pressure statements such as: "…the game won't work if you're here", discouraging comments about "negative vibes" from the entity, or explicit and generally empty threats. However, a large part of this process is due to pecking orders being established within the group. It also takes on elements of a popularity contest amongst some.

Furthermore the gestalt is often created from each member's unconscious with all the suppressed desires, frustrations, hopes and dreams that seldom get expressed. This is in many cases simply because the creation process is fairly ad hoc, and totally unlike the ghost creation process previously examined. After all, the vast majority of people who play Ouija are simply doing it for casual fun.

In a sense Ouija is a remarkably effective method of creating a group consensus on particular topics. An analogy would be that of a far more formal method whereby individuals raise questions and then each member in turn provides an opinion. The group would then discuss this until a compromise is reached and an answer presented. However, such a process would be far slower than the Ouija method. Nevertheless, it does resemble other group pastimes such as *Chinese Whispers* where a short story mutates as it is passed between a succession of people, or communal storytelling in an oral tradition over longer time periods.

Critically, like meetings in real life, the contribution of each person is not of equal weight. In practical terms it means that some people have more of an influence than others in the creation process whether by asking particularly relevant or unique questions, or by unconsciously applying more force to the planchette to guide it to a reply. Reasons for the latter are manifold. For example, they may have a greater expectation or desire for a particular answer, or perhaps wish to avoid a particular answer. Perhaps the gestalt has a greater ability to use their ideomotor response due to their particular susceptibility or willingness to acquiesce to the game. In this case it may be that the depth of involvement in the process is strongly correlated with hypnotic susceptibility. The overall result is that a model of the gestalt Entity is built in the mind of each person comparable to those that exist of relatives, friends and other close acquaintances.

There are two essential differences between an Entity model of a friend and the gestalt Entity. The first is that the model of a friend contains much more detail since it is a result of long term interactions in the full complexity of the real world. Another crucial difference is that in reality the friend is a largely independent person who is modeled as being so and who is "not us". Indeed, there are inevitably aspects of all real people, including friends, which do not mesh perfectly with our desires and expectations at a deep level. This is not necessarily true of an Entity created in a Ouija game. Compared with a real person such an Entity is only very vaguely sketched out in terms of facts, but gains its depth from the unconscious of each participant. This means that it has deeper roots in us than the model of the friend does. On the other hand the nature of those roots are almost inevitably different for each person in the group. It is like a game of "join the dots and make a picture" – there are fewer dots, that is facts, and each person has their own picture. The fewer the dots the more variations of the possible picture are available for us to choose, and we choose the one that has most resonance with our mind, both conscious and unconscious. This means that what the Ouija Entity lacks in detail it makes up in depth, plus it has one crucial feature that distinguishes it from other mental models, namely that we allow it autonomy and a degree of control over our bodies. This arises because we have agreed to play the game, and is the reality behind the myth of the vampire, another parasitic creature with hypnotic powers. In that mythology the vampire cannot enter our house without being invited. The degree of control over a participant can be quite significant. One indicative case might be where the gestalt reveals information held by a participant against their overt wishes. It would require a serious degree of control over that person's ideomotor response in order to make them betray their overt wishes.

Having said all this, there is one situation where the "friend" Entity model may take on some of the characteristics of a gestalt, and that is when a group of people who know, or knew, the person in question "call them up" in a Ouija game. Usually this is because they have died but it is entirely possible to do so while they are alive, or even in the same room! It is because of this that people often jump to the wrong conclusion and assume that what is being manifested is a deceptive or evil spirit. In fact, this can be a method of simulating someone in a magickal setting in order to extract information from him or her or testing out their reactions to hypothetical situations. As mentioned, we often unconsciously absorb considerable amounts of information when we interact with people and this is a method of accessing it in an interactive manner.

Anyway, returning to the topic of a normal Ouija session there is one other aspect of the way it usually develops that renders it relatively safe and inconsequential. As the questions and answers gradually flesh out the gestalt it develops in an almost random manner, and as it does so it inevitably takes on characteristics that cease to have deep resonance with all the members of the group. In other words, as the Entity gains definition it loses psychic depth so that as it becomes more real to the consciousness it loses reality in the unconscious. This is not always so as the Owen experiment described previously demonstrates, for reasons that will now be explained.

The key to creating a powerful gestalt Entity is to prevent the above trade-off occurring. We need to make the entity more real to all aspects of the Human minds involved, both conscious and unconscious. This requires two essential conditions; one aimed at strengthening the gestalt on the conscious level, and the other at strengthening it in the unconscious of all participants. The former is accomplished by consciously defining the major characteristics of the Entity to be created by group consensus in formal meetings. The latter is somewhat more difficult in that the participants all need to be focused on the aims of the work and additionally all need to align their unconscious minds with each other. In practice this means getting to know each other to the point where they like and trust one another. This is why, at the start of the Owen experiment, those who felt that they would not fit in were asked to withdraw. The remainder found that a relaxed friendly atmosphere where they got to know each other was conducive to the manifestation. Consequently they meshed together fairly well as a team. Of course, under other circumstances the word *coven* or *lodge* might have been more appropriate.

Safeguards

From the above it becomes apparent why some people experience psychological difficulties. In exceptional cases the fragment of the gestalt that they carry within them can manifest outside of the context of the Ouija game. This can happen for several reasons. The first is where the person concerned is actually suffering from a mental illness such as schizophrenia and the various Agents and Entities are slipping from control. The gestalt then appears as one of the symptoms of the condition. Another mechanism is reminiscent of one of the features of deep hypnotic trance, namely that of a hallucination whose character is determined by the suggestion imparted by the hypnotist. This type of phenomena is examined in far greater detail in the chapters dedicated to hypnosis and magick. At a lower level the gestalt may maintain ideomotor control and subsequently affect physical co-ordination leading to the person being accident-prone. Lower still and the gestalt may appear in dreams. However, a great deal of this depends on the belief and fear feeding back into a reinforcement of the gestalt in the mind of the victim. It has often been said that there is nothing to fear but fear itself, and in this case it is especially true. For those who are familiar with *Chaos Magick* this is one reason why banishment by laughter works well. If in the back of your mind you hold the belief that Ouija Boards are evil, it can grow with use of the board until the fear takes over. Again, this is related to the psychology of the user and his/her perception and beliefs relating to the board. The beliefs of the people using it are critical – if they believe in evil spirits their unconscious can easily oblige. In the case of poltergeists, such fear can increase the stress levels to the point of initiating the feared psychokinetic activity. In fact, such fear and even the belief that weird things happen when people use Ouija Boards can also initiate psychokinetic activity (caused by the unconscious) in apparition and haunting cases. Such stress can also result in a hypnotic induction where imagination and consensus reality become confused, as we will examine in later chapters.

When Ouija is played as a casual undertaking and not taken seriously there is generally no problem. In fact not taking anything the spirits say seriously is the only safeguard needed. However, for more serious work where belief in the Entity created is essential then very specific safeguard procedures are needed. These are discussed in detail in subsequent chapters.

Anyway, if we return to our formula where does a transpersonal gestalt fit into the picture? So far we have:

- **Ideas = Agents + Data**
- **Archetypes = Ideas + Genes**
- **Memes = Ideas + Communication**
- **Entities = Ideas + Personalities**

It would seem natural that the gestalt created in a Ouija game should be a combination of Ideas, Personality and Communications, or in short Entities plus Memes. However, I am going to give this particular type of gestalt a name – *Daemon*. The word is obviously the Greek root of the Modern English word *demon*, but originally it did not have the negative associations later added by Christianity. A daemon was lesser god, guiding spirit or tutelary deity. Today daemon can also mean a supernatural being of a nature intermediate between that of gods and Humans or a guiding spirit. Incidentally, the word is also used for the programs in the Linux computer operating system that run without human intervention to accomplish particular tasks. So we have:

- **Daemons = Entities + Memes**

So, let's end this section with a question, one that makes this esoteric interest relevant to any group of people but especially religion, business and politics: What constitutes a Ouija game? What happens when we vastly increase the number of participants and expand the timescales?

Dynamic Archetypes

Previously we defined a formula wherein:

- **Gods = Archetypes + Nature + Memes**

These Gods are, however, fairly static "things", so what happens when we throw in a daemonic element?

- **Dynamic Archetypes (Godforms) = Gods + Daemons**

Godforms can have effects that can be classified as personal, interpersonal or impersonal depending on the degree and type of communication involved. Personal effects are the ones most often associated with spiritual and religious experience and reflect an internal dialog that can be either conscious or unconscious. An amusing example of this type of interaction occurred when I visited the Theosophical Society in Wheaton a few years ago. There is a statue of the Madonna in the grounds that is apparently fairly famous and I was invited to take a picture by my host Kathy. I joked that it looked like a well-worn and battered Goddess and that I was in two minds as to whether to bother with a photo, but that I would be gracious enough to take one. As I casually lifted the camera it flipped out of my hand and landed lens down in some soft mud at my feet, the only mud in the vicinity. Since I did not have a lens wipe I could not take any more pictures that day even though the camera and lens were undamaged. It clearly was not a PK effect but an ideomotor action triggered by the "Goddess" I hold in my unconscious mind. She clearly taught me a mild lesson in respect. I returned a year or two later and got the picture with no problems, having taken note.

Much more common are archetypal experiences in dreams, which is the classic medium for such revelations and also under the influence of psychedelic drugs when they can burst forth in totally unexpected directions, quite often prompted by the general environment. This is true even when a specific mythology is not known to the conscious mind. The record of one such experience is lodged with the Erowid[41] archive by an individual named *Abdul Rahman* who had ingested seeds of *Datura Stramonium*, known as *Jimsonweed* in the USA.

> "I ran for my life. I had begun to witness the spirit world, the darkest reality, ghost like beings were everywhere, it sickened me. I ran and ran... I saw a glow in the middle of the field... There were seven guys and girls dressed in dark clothes, black hair, and pail skin. They were all enticed basically making love with the plant. They danced around the glowing Datura plant. She was, alive. There was one guy/girl to my left that was very tall and thin he/she seemed to be the plant spirit (the leader)... They all quit dancing... I messed up and I knew it... I hopped the wire and ran up the hill tore through vines, brier, just tearing through I leaped down the other side. Something stopped me and pulled my head up towards the ridge. There was the temptress, and she was after my life. She was capable of transformation and teleportation. I was so scared. I tore through the woods, I had to avoid two black jaguars. It was her, she is so so tricky and evil... I kept running from her. She was so tricky she had this power to dissipate, bow into the side of the road and just vanish, leaving only slightly noticeable energy particles, she could move about so quickly like this. I spent the next hour running in terror. I had to prove my strength and that I wasn't going to give in. She would offer me things like power and drugs, girls...."

So, who does this remind you of? We have tall thin androgynous otherworldly people dancing in the night around a glowing plant of power who is also a beautiful woman. They take offense easily and they play a dangerous game of pursuit and wild flight during which she temps and she tests. She controls two large cats, jaguars. She can transform and move with supernatural ease. She is the supreme mistress of magic. She is intimately and explicitly associated with both death and sexuality. If you are versed in Northern European mythology you will see that this is a classic encounter with the Faery Folk by an American teenager of, presumably,

---

[41] www.erowid.org

non-European descent living in the USA. Also known as Alfar in the Nordic mythology, they are the people of the God Frey and his sister Freya, although whether these are their real names nobody knows since they are actually titles meaning Lord and Lady. Frey is the God of fertility and sexuality and is often portrayed, at least through his ancient priesthood, as being somewhat sexually ambivalent.

You will find few stories of encounters with the Alfar and Freya as detailed, documented and modern. It is also a reminder that the Freya of legend also has a very dark side that is glossed over in modern retelling. She is not only the Goddess of love, but also of war, death and also magick. It is she who commands the Valkyries and chooses half the heroic battle slain to reside with her in her hall Sessrúmnir. The other half go to Odin in Valhalla. It is she who taught Odin the secrets of *Seidr*, the shamanic magickal system that was the preserve of women in Viking times. Her chariot is drawn by two cats and she can shapeshift into a falcon to travel between the worlds. Similarly the Alfar, or Elves or Fae, are not always the kindly wise elder folk as portrayed in movies like *Lord of the Rings*, but they too were feared as well as respected by our ancestors, no doubt with very good reason.

Perhaps here we can see how myths and legends come into being, or are strengthened. Even though one might suppose that Abdul knew little or nothing of North European mythology something was channeled through him that expressed itself in a very precise fashion.

The Daemon type of experience involving Dynamic Archetypes comes through direct interactions with people. A good example is of the story told by John Cooper[42] who (maybe) met Odin. The synopsis is as follows:

> "As we walked up the street, we passed homeless people which, at least at the time, were very abundant in that city [Washington]. I'm a sucker for the homeless. I'll drop some change in their paper cups, or give away half a sandwich, and occasionally I stop to chat... The particular homeless man that I targeted that fateful day didn't look like he was looking for a handout, but he did look homeless. He was an old sun-wrinkled man, with long scraggly white hair and a long unkempt white beard... The wrinkles in his face were obviously put there just as much from laughter as by wind and sun. Which was probably what made me curious enough to stop... He took my quarter in a nonchalant way. I remember he had a strong, friendly handshake and a black patch over one eye. The other eye was bright blue. My friends continued silently up the street, as I shook his hand and began our short conversation.
> "Nice day, huh?"
> He nodded. "You missed the parade."
> "Yeah? Here? I didn't know there was a parade today."
> "Yep" he said, "there was music and everyone was joining in, dancing down

---
[42] Rûna Magazine # 21, published by Eormensyl Hall of the Rune-Gild in London

the street, in all sorts of nice costumes. It was a nice day for it."

It was about noon, with no evidence of any parade activity...

"Well, it's great weather for a parade" I said, glancing up the street, where my friends were still in sight, walking slowly with their backs to us. "Looks like the sun's coming out."

"Nope" he countered, shaking his head slightly, "it's about to rain."

Then, just as I began to say "I don't think so..." it began to rain... "Hey, I have to go, my friends are waiting" I said...

"Alright" he said slowly, still looking into the far distant sky as I turned my back. "We'll see you later, Johnny."

I stopped, mouth open in surprise, and slowly turned to see him turning back from the clouds to smile at me once again. We were now separated by about seven feet. I was suddenly very happy and yelled through the rain -- "Hey! How did you know my name?"

His voice was still calm, though his smile was a little more mischievous. "Oh, we know lots of things, Johnny, Lots of Things."

It only took me a few days to convince myself that I had met Odin. There are many ancient stories of The All-Father coming down to earth to be among mortals for a while. Sometimes to test, sometimes just to observe. He usually assumed the form of an old man in a dark blue or gray cloak, with long beard and blue eyes – one eye was often patched over... A lot of the stories of Odin have to do with him dropping in on some nobleman to see how well that person has been treating the common folk. The moral of such stories seems to be that one should treat strangers with hospitality, because they could be really powerful entities that could ruin your whole life. I don't pretend to have any nobility in me, so maybe Odin was waiting for someone else (there are plenty of big shots in DC) and decided to have fun with me while he was waiting."

Of course, if this story could be checked in detail and the homeless man tracked down it would no doubt be just a homeless man. What he was doing though, was acting as a Medium for a Godform in both body and spirit. Whether he knew it or not is another question. Naturally, examples from other religions are more numerous and I include the above simply because they are from mine – Asatru[43]. In fact, there is a whole genre of New Age lore related to people's encounters with Angels that recount very similar stories.

Finally we have the most powerful type of Godform interaction when it is operating on the largest scale of its environment. Once again we look to Jung and the events of pre-war Nazi Germany about which he wrote in this 1936CE essay entitled *Wotan*. What is particularly interesting is that it is not something concocted with hindsight in order to explain events, but essentially a prediction and description

---

[43] Asatru - From the Old Norse **Ásatrú**, from *Ása* (the genitive of *Áss*, referring to one of the groups of gods and goddesses in the Old Norse pantheon, the *Æsir*) + *trú* (belief), thus, "belief in the Æsir".

of the contemporary flow of events that he saw around him in this unique period. In this he recognized aspects of the God Wotan (Odin, Woden), and he wrote:

> "We have seen him come to life in the German Youth Movement, and right at the beginning the blood of several sheep was shed in honor of his resurrection. Armed with rucksack and lute, blond youth, and sometimes girls as well, were to be seen as restless wanderers on every road from the North Cape to Sicily, faithful votaries of the roving god. Later, towards the end of the Weimar Republic, the wandering role was taken over by thousands of unemployed, who were to be met with everywhere on their aimless journeys. By 1933 they wandered no longer, but marched in their hundreds of thousands. The Hitler movement literally brought the whole of Germany to its feet, from five-year-olds to veterans, and produced the spectacle of a nation migrating from one place to another. Wotan the wanderer was on the move... He [Wotan] is the god of storm and frenzy, who unleashes passions and the lust of battle; moreover he is a superlative magician and artist in illusion who is versed in all secrets of an occult nature. I venture the heretical suggestion that the unfathomable depths of Wotan's character explain more of National Socialism than all economic, political and psychological factors put together."

Godform Genetics

Returning full circle to archetypes and genes there is the rather peculiar possibility of Godforms selectively breeding strains of Humanity as preferential hosts. Although it might sound bizarre and implausible it's as simple as the notion of "like is attracted to like". People with the same dominant characteristics tend to marry each other. Presumably there are no "Godform genes", yet if one admits that genetics accounts for a significant portion of the development of personality, or susceptibility to belief, then such a conclusion is inescapable. Look in the lonely-hearts sections of newspapers and magazines and see for yourself those who specify particular religious beliefs.

Daemon Communications

The methods that Daemons communicate with each other, with Humans and with the world in general have one thing in common. They are all messages superimposed upon what are overtly normal messages, in almost the same way that a voice can be carried by a radio wave. We are drenched in communications that have multiple meanings and which are purely dependent on the context in which the listener places them. The most obvious method of communication is simply choice of subject matter. In defining this we are excluding overt messages, although if someone is almost wholly dominated by a particular Dynamic Archetype this is the major mode of communication. Subtlety is not required in, for example, a priest of a religious sect delivering a sermon. The choice of subject matter is related largely to what interests that person, and what motivates them. The balance adopted in reporting news, deciding what is shown on television, writing screenplays and so forth, in short editorial decision making, can affect millions of people. Given the arguments over bias in the media that already exist in relation to such course grained features as political favoritism it comes as no surprise that more subtle biases go largely unnoticed and unreported. Even in everyday conversation, especially small talk, the choice of topic can range far and wide, and a little push from a Godform that wants to get a word in is particularly easy, as are memory lapses and interruptions when unwanted topics surface, or a change of emphasis is required. Another channel that a Godform can often use is body language. It can be used to reinforce, modify or negate other messages and is particularly good at communicating attitude. The fact that most people do not have conscious control over, or awareness of, their body language means that it is a channel that can be easily used by Daemons and Godforms.

There is one more effect that is characteristic of the experience. It is that time and space do not have the same meaning. The delusions of schizophrenics and psychedelic trippers have one more feature in common. The messages emanating from, say, the television to them personally occur in real time, and often make enough sense to enable a conversation to be held. This can happen even as the channels are changed and different people are speaking. Coincidence, which it is always assumed to be by normal people, runs wild. That it might be anything more is discounted because the programs involved are almost always recorded, and not live. There is one outside possibility if, as we shall see later, events in the past can be altered. If it is accepted that events can be structured retrospectively, that is, history is "constantly" changing then these random, seemingly impossible, conversations take on a new meaning. They are in a sense Daemons talking to each other, and battling for dominance, by the restructuring of events months or years in the past, and brought to a focus at one point in the here-and-now, because the "here-and-now" is the only true reality.

Communicating – Evocation and Invocation

Magickal practices dealing with seemingly intelligent non-Human entities traditionally fall into one of two categories. The first is evocation, where an internal aspect of the mind is evoked, or "called out", from the unconscious and made manifest to the consciousness as if it were a separate entity. The second category is that of invocation where an entity external to the magician is called from another realm in order to perform some service. Traditionally they are either compelled to do so by the magician's Will or the nature of the invocation ritual itself, or alternatively they are cajoled by the promise of some reward.

There is only one essential difference in operational technique between evocation and invocation, and that is the degree of communication undertaken as part of the working. The use of a Psychomanteum (see chapter on Machines) is a prime example of an evocation since only the person concerned is involved, along with the various Agents of their mind to be made manifest, and no communication occurs with other people. On a slightly larger scale, and blurring the boundary between evocation and invocation is the example of ghost creation described in the Owen experiment. Clearly each participant in the experiment carried a large fraction of the total gestalt, which suggests evocation. However, the group itself *invoked* Philip as if it were an external entity and involved quite intense group sessions where interpersonal communications were paramount. At the extreme end of this spectrum lies the invocation of fully archetypal beings – Gods. In this case the vast bulk of the gestalt lies outside of the magician or group performing the invocation, which means that the fraction of it invoked is correspondingly tiny unless the rest of the God can be engaged. To do this successfully requires two things. The first is to make sure that the object of the invocation is in accord with the overall character of the God and does not go against its larger interests. This is accomplished by thoroughly understanding its mythology at a conscious level and then conversing with the fragment held by either the individual or group to confirm the objectives at the unconscious level. Once this is accomplished and an agreement is struck between the magician and the God this must then be communicated to the wider gestalt residing in the global population at large. It is this God in its full aspect that will then work in accord with the magicians Will. How this communication is accomplished is an art in itself and owes more to public relations and propaganda on one hand, and subliminal technology coupled with rumor on the other, than it does to magick. It is this that forms large sections of this book.

From a magickal point of view much of the above might be interesting theory, but how does one actually communicate with, or utilize, Godforms and lesser such Beings in the world at large?

- State your allegiance aloud

- Let the Being know what is in it for them

- Perform sacrifice

- Let your affiliation be known widely, use the most efficient means such as mass communications and the Net.

- Tell others what is required of the Being

- Talk to those who manifest the Being, whether consciously or unconsciously

- Wear their symbol(s)
  As we shall see, visual symbols have a direct impact on the mind and bypass many filters by circumventing the language centers of the brain.

- Take their names
  In other words, create a confusion between yourself and them from a language point of view.

How do Godforms communicate with individuals?

- Through dreams, visions and introspection.
- Through overt personal communications from Godform representatives such as priests.
- Through meaningful coincidence, that is, signs and portents.
- Through the secondary meanings of ordinary conversations with people who host the Being.

Hosts and Conspiracies

The people most likely to host Godforms and Daemons are naturally those who have a detailed knowledge of them, even if it is unconscious. With practice it is possible to see the mostly nameless daemonic facets of personality shifting through the features of ordinary non integrated people. The way they walk, the way their eyes move, body language, words chosen in conjunction with that body language, the actual physical body type, all these can be recognized not merely in one person, but many. These facets exist in very similar forms in most ordinary people, and by observing them it is possible see their expression in the world. A skilled practitioner can call forth these daemons in others and talk to them in a way that is almost independent of the supposedly dominant ego. With practice, it is possible to evoke any of these, or create them, in oneself. By being able to consciously call forth a Godform, under suitable control, a whole new mode of communications with others opens up. By mimicking a dominant daemon that one sees, or calls forth, in other people it is possible to pass oneself off as being "their type". It is the ultimate psychological disguise and a key to the art of invisibility. Systematized, it lies at the heart of Neuro-linguistic Programming.

   Conversely, when a group of people share similar daemonic facets of personality or even Godforms, they mesh together at an unconscious level to create, literally, a "team spirit". Members recognize each other and act to help each other. Or alternatively, to exclude those whose "face does not fit" in a kind of unspoken conspiracy. If such a group exists in a formal sense then quite often bonding rituals are developed to enhance the gestalt. These are where the flows of political power, business, money, information and entertainment converge, and are the nexus and battleground of a war that has been raging as long as Human Beings have existed in civilized societies. The stronger certain archetypes manifest themselves in the people involved the more successful they will be. However, it should be realized that they are also attempting to modify that environment to the benefit of that person and archetype. Survival and domination are the primary aims. There will also exist a selection process whereby those who strongly manifest an archetype will be given preferential entry to this ground by similar creatures. Such a process can be as simple as the "old school tie" test, or as complex and explicit as Freemasonry in its archetype reinforcement and infection process. It's a jungle out there.

The overt result is a kind of psychic conspiracy, or rather, multiple psychic conspiracies. Such a notion is a paranoids charter and should not be taken too seriously in everyday applications, or plots and conspiracies will abound wherever one looks; but just because you're paranoid does not mean it's not out to get you.

Sacrifice

If we examine the notion of sacrifice in the light of the above analysis we see the reasons for its presence in religious ritual and practice, and gain clues as to the best forms. In general most people regard a sacrifice to their God as some kind of bribe or payment for services rendered, hopefully to be rendered, or simply to placate the deity. The question then becomes one of what it is the deity actually wants or requires. Clearly material offered up in sacrifice, whether it is as simple as money thrown into a watery pool, mead poured upon the ground, an animal killed or food burned is of no direct use to any non-material Being. Usually the two fallback answers as to why these things are done are either that they are symbolic or that there is some ethereal energy or life-force that actually migrating from one realm to another. However, there is a simpler explanation, namely that by giving up something valuable, elements of our own mind are being shown that they are subservient to the aspects modeling the Daemons or Godforms. The act strengthens these parts whilst weakening any internal opposition.

Coincidences and Omens

Another indication that reality is being distorted, either internally or externally, is the abundance of coincidence. Jung wrote about *meaningful* coincidence occurring when powerful aspects of the psyche are active, but for most people the nature of the coincidence is simply recognition that strange and unusual things are happening often without any meaning being apparent. For example, a particular number might appear repeatedly throughout the day for no apparent reason. The conventional explanation is that an aspect of the mind has been primed to notice something that it has previously ignored. In other words, part of us wakes up for a brief period and sees a tiny part of the world that has slipped through our habitual filters. This actually makes a lot of sense especially when it is realized that these coincidences are always part of the process of consciousness expansion, whether through meditation, drugs or occasionally stress. Alternatively it can be a sign of mental disintegration, for example in schizophrenia. In either case the mind's habitual hunt for meaning should be kept in check. It is often very tempting to try and interpret the coincidences as signs or portents arising from something external. In a religious context they are often believed to be messages from spiritual entities such as God or Satan in extreme forms, or as warnings or even instructions. However, almost certainly if there is some communication being attempted it is by one part of the mind to another. Nevertheless, most such coincidences arise simply because the censors and filters that restrict our view are being weakened or removed and no message at all beyond this exists. The flip side of the above concerns the parts of the mind that search for meanings, connections and patterns in and between every item of data being received from the senses. Once again it is an indication that control mechanisms are being relaxed through a variety of possible processes. The only practical difference is that the latter is indicative of an enhanced creative capacity as opposed to an enhanced perception.

Then there are the coincidences that are clearly not artifacts of mundane enhancement of perception or creation. These almost always involve physical manifestations that are far less open to generalized interpretation. It is worth looking at one notorious example to see how these might arise. It is by no means unique, but it is probably the best illustration of the process. It concerns the making of the classic horror movie "The Omen" that was released on 6 June 1976CE (6-6-76) and the train of events that not only accompanied it but both pre and post-dated its production. For those who do not know of it, the movie follows the story of an American ambassador to London, played by Gregory Peck, who gradually learns that his son is actually the Antichrist. He comes to this reluctant conclusion after being persuaded by a combination of bizarre accidents surrounding those who threaten the destiny of the Antichrist. These include a group of Christians who already know the truth and are trying to kill his son (and who come to predictably unpleasant ends) plus a random sprinkling of Satanists and evil animals.

The starting point of what is often called *The* Curse of the Omen was the suicide of Peck's own son some two months before the filming started in London. Then on his flight from Los Angeles to London to begin work his plane was struck by lightning and lost an engine. Some hours later the plane carrying the screenwriter David Seltzer was also hit by lightning. The third accident involving aircraft came when the production crew chartered a plane to do aerial shots. After booking the charter company had had a better offer on that particular day from some Japanese businessmen and asked whether the Omen crew would accept a later date at a cheaper price. Since it was a movie on a tight budget they accepted. The jet crashed on takeoff killing everyone aboard. In the process it hit a car on a road beyond the runway that hit another car. In the latter were the wife and child of the pilot, who also died. Apparently the cause was bird strike due to the airfield's bird scarer being inexplicably turned off that day. Numerous non-fatal accidents happened throughout the filming, including a car crash on the first day and problems with the animals involved. This in particular culminated in the events at Windsor Safari Park where the crew shot some scenes involving lions, which were eventually dropped from the movie. The day after they finished shooting an experienced keeper was killed by two of them after making a mistake with the cages.

There was more to come. The IRA bombed the London Hilton in which the producer Neufeld and his wife were staying. They also bombed a restaurant where the executives and actors, including Peck, were expected for dinner on 12 November. Even upon completion of shooting the problems did not cease. The flight taking the negatives to LA had to perform an emergency landing and the worst was to follow some months later.

One of the most shocking scenes in the movie involved a truck carrying sheets of glass. Its brakes fail and it rolls backwards, shedding a sheet that decapitates one of the main movie characters investigating the Antichrist. The stunt was devised and arranged by John Richardson who went on to work on "A Bridge Too Far" which was being filmed in Holland. While there he was involved in a car crash which resulted in his girlfriend being cut in half. Nearby there was a sign which read: *Ommen – 66km*. Of course, this last "fact" may have been exaggerated. Some reports say 66.6km, which is highly implausible for any signpost, and others put it at a rather more likely 20km.

Similar stories could be told of other movies dealing with archetypal occult/demonic themes, in particular The Exorcist and Poltergeist movies. Those interested can do a Net search, as there is plenty of material online.

These stories raise obvious questions, the foremost being: what was going on? There is no doubt that most people fall into one of two camps. These are the atheist-rationalists where it is all dismissed as coincidence and the Christian-religious where the events are attributed to Satanic influence. The latter claim itself divides into two theological branches. The first is that Satan, who likes to work in secret, was trying to prevent the movie being made and awareness of the Antichrist raised. They cite the spike in Bible sales that followed the release and success of The Omen, plus renewed interest in the final chapter – *Revelations*. The alternate interpretation was somewhat simpler and more plausible. Namely that focusing on Satan and the demonic attracted Satanic and demonic forces which predictably did their best to live up to their reputation. Or, in New Age terms, focusing on negative energy attracts negative energy. However, what does this really mean in terms of our preceding analyses of Godforms?

First, we have to view the creation and production process of the movie in a slightly different light – we have to view it as an act of ceremonial magick. One, which, in particular, has elements of Human sacrifice attached. At the same time as the movie concept was coming to fruition the son of the leading actor killed himself. Now, conventionally this has been seen as the first consequence of the curse, as we shall call it. However, more plausibly it was a major factor in triggering or enhancing the events that followed. Peck was central to the plot and indeed, the script revolved around him both as character and actor. The fact that in the script he had to re-enact the death of his son (killing the Antichrist) created a powerful resonance in his mind, according to fellow cast members. So much so, in fact, that he could not go through with the originally scripted final scene. Then we have the script itself that was essentially a recipe for creating a plausible scenario of the birth of the Antichrist, and his murderous behavior aided by demons and Satanists, in the minds of millions of theatergoers. In order to do this cast and crew steeped themselves in the archetypal imagery of Revelations and this specific interpretation of the personification of the Antichrist in the boy Damien. They did this through individual study of the script, group discussions, rehearsals both individual and on set and formally before the camera. They brought Damien into their own reality in the same way the ghost Philip was created by the Owen group. They dressed up for the parts and acted out the story. They went through each of the steps previously described for communicating with Daemons and they did this repeatedly. Each of them carried Damien as a very real Entity of the type already described – even the name of the Antichrist was chosen for its similarity to demon/daemon. The archetypal and memetic components were already in place and familiar to hundreds of millions of Christians. The blending of these elements within the group to create a Daemon and activating it as a powerful Godform followed a natural progression. Additionally, it was a particularly malign Godform – namely, the son of Satan.

One major reason why it was so powerful was due to the nature and impact of archetypal evil. Such Entities feed on the fear they induce. They can create the conditions for harm through omission and commission via mundane channels such as the ideomotor response and "accident proneness", or extraordinary channels such as Psi. Fear is a very powerful and primitive force that easily cuts through the superficial levels of normal habit and rationality and activates the emotions as well as loosening control over Entities within the mind. It reduces people to a childlike condition and as we will see later, it enhances hypnotic suggestibility. The end result was a runaway effect that had few limitations beyond those naturally extant in some of the cast and crew, or those artificially constructed. Of the latter the most prominent was the adoption of Christian protective mythology and symbols. Quite a few people wore the cross for just that reason as most of them recognized that there was an element of the real supernatural being invoked. Interestingly, probably the only person not touched by all this was the child actor who played Damien.

So, who is Daemon fodder? If we look at the above example, we can see that there are several types of people whose resistance to specific daemonic infection varies greatly. In general we have:

- Those who embrace the Daemon/Godform and act as its agent.

- Those who embrace a powerful alternate that acts both as an immunization and exerts a protective effect.

- Those who have a belief system that immunizes, but does not exert a protective blanket. For example, conscious atheists.

- Those who have no major belief system, but have an "open mind" and are receptive to memetic infection when they see it supported by personal physical evidence. That is, they witness "weird shit" and are receptive to a particular explanatory story such as: "Satan did it!" It is these people who are more likely to fall victim to unpleasant coincidences. This group is also the largest in percentage terms of normal Western populations.

Note that all these categories can, and do, act as carriers albeit some more than others.

It is of little use to say that you do not believe in the Christian notions of God and Satan because the fact that so many people do really does distort the psychic landscape to the extent that these entities exert a real and powerful influence over everything and everyone. In other words, your disbelief is of no use if you are being burned at the stake. It can only protect you from yourself. As Robert Anton Wilson once noted, Hell exists for those who believe in it and it is just as bad as they can imagine. And one might add that those people who manifest these entities can make things just as bad as they can imagine for those they perceive as enemies of their masters. There is very little in the way of neutral ground.

Health and Healing

The influence of the mind on the body is something that Western medicine has only recently recognized. At the top of the list is of course stress, with its effect on the immune system and its connection with heart disease. However, we can go further. People grow to resemble their true selves as they age, and if they are dominated by various characteristics or archetypes these will be given bodily expression. This can be understood on a crude level. If someone is chronically unhappy or depressed and frowns all the time then after some years the skin of the face will have those permanent lines etched into it. The way they hold themselves and their entire body language will reflect this. Although most people express a random mix of fairly weak, and weakening, Daemons, some express relatively pure ones and it is these that look outstanding, either in terms of beauty, power or sheer spiritual ugliness. Age is only a factor in that most manifestations only start to clarify during their mid thirties, although some are visible from childhood. The latter tend to be mythologically familiar, such as elves, werewolves, and so forth. One would guess that there is a large genetic component in their expression.

There are also Agents associated with disease. They do not cause disease directly, but either betray, or cause, a susceptibility to particular forms of illness via the connection of mind and immune system. This is one of the reasons that placebos can be so amazingly effective. In one review of the relevant literature, it was found that placebos gave substantial relief to diabetics, peptic ulcer, rheumatoid arthritis, Parkinson's disease, radiation-sickness, and other serious health problems. The clinical study of the effectiveness of minoxidil, the drug that is used to regrow hair in balding men and women, showed the surprising result that 11% of the patients in the placebo condition regrew new hair!

Much of the method of New Age, or Holistic, medicine is implicitly to remove, modify, or balance these Agents, or in rare cases Daemons. Doing so is an art that is difficult to teach as recognition and restoration comes from experience and the healing ability of individuals varies with insight. The ability itself is often unconscious, and a skill of an Agency, Daemon or Godform. These Agents are often visible in the body long before the illness is manifested.

Every movement of the body draws on some aspect of these and by drawing on it and giving it expression thereby strengthens it. The mind and body are a unity, and act and respond as such. After all, most of the brain is concerned with the body rather than the intellect. This is of great importance in such undertakings as ritual magic or religious observance, or martial arts training and psychic healing to give simple examples. Just as it is possible to understand someone through their body language, so deliberately changing that language will result in a change that person's psyche. Some movements, or postures, can help strengthen and integrate the psyche, the classic example being Tai Chi. Others will weaken the person. Naturally, there are no acknowledged formal exercises to weaken people, but every day millions are taught unconsciously to adopt these malignant expressions of body language through many media. The results are plain to see, for those who can see.

There is even a name given to the negative placebo effect, which is the nocebo effect. One notable case was a man (mis)diagnosed who subsequently sickened and died just as his doctors predicted.

> "Take Sam Shoeman, who was diagnosed with end-stage liver cancer in the 1970s and given just months to live. Shoeman duly died in the allotted time frame – yet the autopsy revealed that his doctors had got it wrong. The tumor was tiny and had not spread. "He didn't die from cancer, but from believing he was dying of cancer," says Meador. "If everyone treats you as if you are dying, you buy into it. Everything in your whole being becomes about dying."[44]

Black and White Magick

The issue as to what might define magick as either Black or White, or whether such a categorization is meaningless, is a topic that has generated many opinions over the centuries, not least in ours with the rise of neo-paganism and Wicca. The most common views are as follows:

- Any magick used to harm another person is Black, and any used to benefit another is White. This is the most simplistic view and is logically untenable. The problem here is that harm is relative, as is most morality as one expands the context. For example, is magick used in self-defense also to be defined as Black? And is magick used for personal gain White? Opinions vary...

---
[44] New Scientist magazine 13 May 2009 by Helen Pilcher

Gods and Daemons

- The next most common opinion is that magick itself is neither intrinsically Black or White, but it is the intention of the user that defines it. In other words, it is of the same ethical nature as a knife, which can be a beneficial tool or a murderous weapon, depending upon the user. This is the most modern interpretation – magick as a technology with no inherent moral or ethical qualities.

- However, there is a definition that withstands scrutiny once we move from the realm of morality and ethics to one which looks at mechanism. It defines Black magick as that which is mediated by demonic forces. That is, magick that relies for its efficacy on the intervention of non-Human entities or spirits. Crudely put, magick is not a Humans ability and Humans have to rely on the true workers of magick to do our bidding. Magick is, therefore, a branch of demonology whether one knows it or not.

As might be apparent by now I do not believe in the reality of demons in the Christian sense, although it might well be applicable if the original word from which it is derived, *daemon* meaning "spirit" in Greek, is substituted. In this case the daemons employed are the semi-autonomous Agents of the Human mind which may or may not act as part of a gestalt. This view leads to gradations of Black and White magick:

- The least Black being non-gestalts, that is Agents that do not extend beyond the individual utilizing them and which are intrinsically part of the magician's own mind.

- Next is magick that utilities small group gestalts, for example that of a coven or lodge where a "group spirit" is employed.

- Finally, the Blackest is that which is mediated by daemons that amount to gestalts which are effectively enmeshed in populations so large as to constitute a major aspect of global consciousness – in other words, Gods. This means that supplications to Gods, including Judeo/Christian/Islamic prayer, are forms of Black magick, which many of their followers would no doubt dispute!

Having said all that it now becomes clear what constitutes White magick – namely, magick that does not utilize the Human unconscious but instead proceeds directly from a fully integrated mind and an expanded consciousness. In many respects this is a superior form of magick but one that is exceedingly difficult to perform, requiring as it does the mysterious quality that Buddhists refer to as "enlightenment". As to where that leaves any contact with genuine non-Human intelligent entities, one might simply say that it is no different than interacting with another person, albeit one with special knowledge or abilities. And the mentality of such an entity, as with a person, can be Black or White, good or evil.

This being so, what you are reading is a book largely concerned with technologically enhanced Black magick because it tends to focus on enhancing group working. Naturally, I could change the name of the type of magick from the emotive "Black" to something more neutral such as "Archetypal", but a lot of what follows is about pushing the right psychological buttons in order to create a specific effect – so Black it is…

Summary

- Ideas = Agents + Data
- Archetypes = Ideas + Genes
- Memes = Ideas + Communication
- Entities = Ideas + Personalities
- Gods = Archetypes + Nature + Memes
- Daemons = Entities + Memes
- Dynamic Archetypes (Godforms) = Gods + Daemons

Finally, a note on what it actually feels like to be possessed by a hostile entity, taken from an account by Robert Bruce[45]:

> "…Soon, I began losing control of my body, one part at a time. The first episode of this was while reading; my arm moved on its own, picked up a book, and tossed it on the floor. This shocked me, but I still felt okay. I did not sense anything evil or threatening in or around me. Incidents of brief loss of control increased over the next two weeks. It was not long before I knew I was in deep trouble… The strength of the mental pressure I felt was unbelievable. I did not hear voices or experience insane thoughts. This was not a compulsion. I was sane and rational. I just had no control of my body, as if suddenly struck with physical paralysis and someone else was now running my body. Thankfully, with a supreme act of will and some much-needed luck, I broke free of the puppet-like state at the last possible moment. But I no longer trusted myself after this event."

Since psychic self defense is considered part of standard magickal practices I will not go into much detail on the subject. If you are in the unfortunate position of needing an exorcist, or at least some decent advice, this book is a good place to start.

---

[45] Practical Psychic Self-Defense: Understanding and Surviving Unseen Influences, Hampton Roads Pub Co (July 1, 2002), ISBN-13: 978-1571742216

Gods and Daemons

Hypnosis

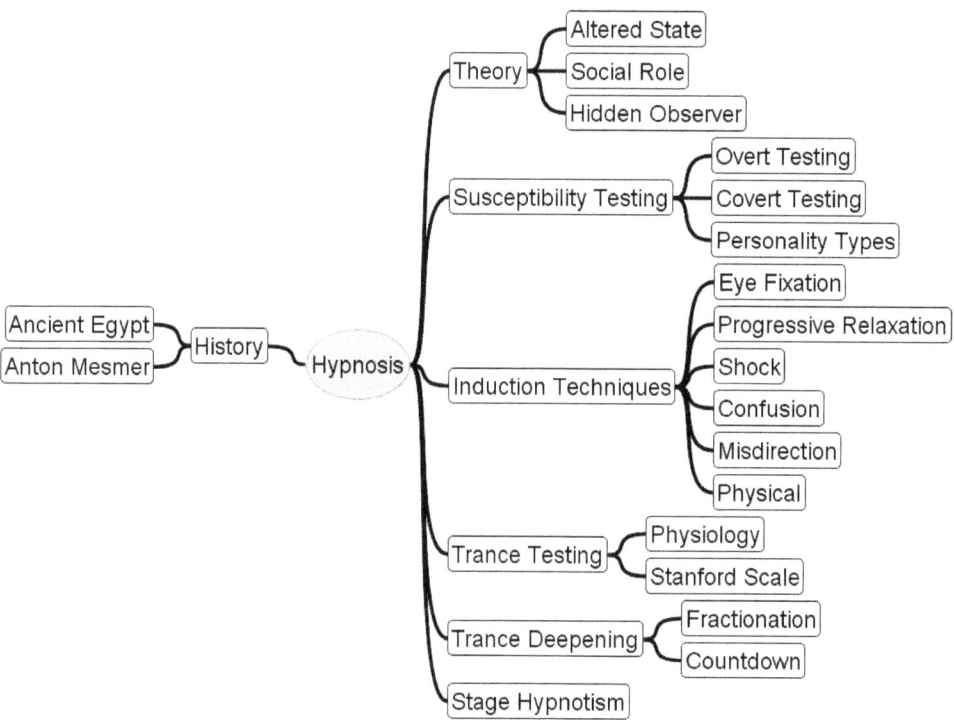

5 Hypnosis

> "Hypnosis is an altered state of consciousness. It happens when a state of mind is achieved in which suggestions alter someone's awareness, memory, or thinking in a way that the hypnotized person responds to the alteration as if it were reality."

In all magickal practices we see hypnotic techniques being used, sometimes effectively but generally not so. Part of the problem is that most people have a poor idea as to what is and is not possible with hypnosis, the nature of the hypnotic state and how it can be induced. This chapter outlines basic theory and techniques and provides enough detail and references for both application and further in-depth study.

We cut to a scene inside Baker Street Underground station in London, at the bank of public telephones. One of them is ringing and after a short while a passer-by, a woman, decides to answer it. She listens for a minute or so and then slumps to the ground unconscious. What could possibly cause such behavior?

The entire sequence of events was being recorded by the production team of a man called Derren Brown[46] for later transmission on his TV show. He is what used to be termed a "mentalist", that is, someone who specializes in psychological magic and hypnosis. The above was a spectacular example of remote hypnosis, in this case across a phone line. Although he does not explain some of his feats, this one he did. At the time of writing it is on his website along with the video. First, and most important, it was no trick. The woman was unknown to anyone involved and was only there because she decided to answer the telephone. This, it turns out, was crucial for more than the obvious reason. It meant she was self-selected as someone who was suggestible. When she answered the phone she found herself on the receiving end of a barrage of complex questions and instructions which were impossible to follow. After listening to this for some time she was given one final instruction which, gratefully, her mind could grasp and act upon – "Go to sleep!" – which she promptly did. The specific technique used is referred to as "Confusion Induction" and will be examined later, along with remote hypnosis.

Hypnotic techniques are of great interest and utility when it comes to accessing different facets of the mind. Common to all is the setting aside of the critical faculty, leaving open other aspects of the mind to directly interact without many of the long established censorship rules and barriers that would normally keep them under control. It has been said that the critical faculty of the mind is the part that passes judgment, and that hypnosis is the establishment of a mode of highly selective thinking that bypasses it. Central to this is either the distraction of the critical faculty, or inducing it to sleep while the rest of the mind remains awake.

---

[46] Derren Brown, Trick of the Mind, Objective Productions Limited for Channel 4 Television

As we will see later, hypnotic technology has a key role in explaining, clarifying and massively enhancing magickal practices.

Early History

Hypnotic techniques have been used throughout history, and it is known that the ancient Egyptians used a form of it in their dream temples, which were extremely popular and subsequently spread through Greece and Asia Minor and eventually to Rome. Among the Romans the famed physician Aesculapius often cast his patients into a deep sleep and alleviated pain by stroking with his hand.

Perhaps the best source of reference to hypnosis in early Egypt comes from the famous Third Century CE Demotic Magical Papyrus[47] which was discovered in the 19th Century in Thebes. The technique describes using a young boy who was in training for the priesthood to gaze steadily into a lamp while a priest recited the following words until a "great light" appeared to the boy.

> "O Osiris, O lamp that giveth vision of the things above, and of the things below the earth. O lamp, O lamp, Amon is moored in thee. O lamp, O lamp, I invoke thee, go thou up to the shore of the great sea of Syria, the sea of Osiris. Go and find Osiris on his papyrus boat, Isis at his head, Nephthys at his feet, and the gods and goddesses about him. Speak O Isis, and let Osiris be told the things I ask, let him cause the god to come here in whose hand is the command of the day, and give me full answer to all I request here today..." and so on. Then the light is invoked saying "Hail O light, come forth, come forth, O light, rise, rise, O light, grow, grow, O light! O that which is outside your vision come in!"

The Priest says this nine times until the light increases and the god appears. The procedure ends when the god answers the operators questions through the boy.

The advent of Christianity forced a decline in the use of hypnosis for all purposes including trance healing as it was considered to be witchcraft. It was only in the aftermath of the Renaissance that it began to surface openly in a variety of forms.

Skipping forward some fifteen hundred years or so we come to Franz Anton Mesmer[48] who was the New Age medical practitioner of the 18th Century par excellence and is credited with being a pioneer of modern hypnotic techniques in healing. A student of Maximilian Hell (and you can't get a better name than that...), his teachings were varied but largely focused around the then mysterious phenomenon of magnetism. He taught of animal magnetism, universal fluids and their proper distribution in healthy bodies, of the magnetization of inanimate (and non-magnetic) objects such as wood and water, the effects of the planets, the

---

[47] London and Leiten, manuscript numbers 10070 and I.383

[48] Franz Anton Mesmer, 1734CE to 1817CE

importance of passing the hands across the patients body and so forth. In particular he believed in the efficacy of various "magnetized" metals in curing specific ailments, a technique called metallo-therapy, and that "animal magnetism" flows accounted for his cures.

However, amid all the baseless theorizing he did achieve seemingly miraculous cures. Such cures occurred as a result of what he called "crises" that his technique of hypnotic induction created. When he had created the proper attitude on the part of the patient he triggered a crisis with its attendant convulsive spasms and trance. After this had passed the patient would go limp and in many cases the illness had dissipated. It was only later that Mesmer chanced upon the passive sleep-like state that we recognize today as a feature of modern hypnotism.

Since his skills were in great demand, of necessity he was also a pioneer of group therapy or at least a pioneer in mass treatments. For example, he constructed a magnetizing tub with up to thirty handles that could direct the magnetic energy to the patients en masse. He added to the gravitas of the proceedings with music and by walking amongst the patients dressed in impressive silk robes, occasionally touching the patients to increase the magnetism and help precipitate the healing crisis.

His downfall came with the report of an investigation committee set up by the French government which included the chemist Lavoisier, Benjamin Franklin, and Dr. Guillotin. They came to the conclusion that although he appeared to cure people his methods were dubious, especially the "magnetism" aspects. They saw that cures occurred even when patients accidentally touched the wrong metals or materials that had not been magnetized when they believed them to be. In short, he suffered the fate of many modern alternative medical practices from "Crystal Healing" to Reiki where the undoubted beneficial effects have nothing to do with the alleged theoretical reasons given for the efficacy of the treatment. It was the belief itself that was curative and the explanation and circus surrounding the event was merely window dressing that created and bolstered that necessary belief.

Because of its demonstrated practical benefits Mesmerism, as it came to be called, continued to be of interest to a physicians through the 19th Century. In 1843CE the English physician James Braid created the term hypnosis from the Greek hypnos, to sleep, although the hypnotic trance is very different from the normal sleeping state.

There were numerous demonstrations of practical applications of hypnosis preceding the discovery of anesthetics during this period with regard to serious pain management. For example James Esdaile, an English surgeon working in India from 1845CE to 1851CE, used hypnosis extensively to control pain and bleeding in both minor and major surgery, including normally traumatic operations such as the removal of large tumors.

The history of hypnosis from this point until the modern era is beyond the scope of this book although obviously some of the debates that have raged over it continue into the present. Nevertheless, the major fruits of those decades are largely condensed into this chapter and it's rather ironic that the technology of mind that flowered in ancient Egypt, one of the most magickal societies ever to exist, is once again being applied to magickal ends in the most technologically advanced society in history – the West.

Theories of Hypnosis

Underlying many theories of hypnosis is the concept of *trance logic* – a state where language processing is altered, words are taken more literally and there is a decrease in critical judgment coupled with an increase in tolerance of incongruity. Here reality and hallucination coexist as equals. If asked to say which object is real, the hypnotized person can usually tell the difference, but the difference does not matter to them. In the trance state they will deal with the real and the unreal in the same way.

From this, a number of theories[49] about trance arose varying from the notion of it being a form of psychological age regression to the *Cortical Inhibition Theory* that focuses on the apparent decrease in the activity of the left hemisphere of the brain. The latter fact has been used as an explanation for the decrease in critical thinking and enhanced suggestibility associated with the hypnotic state but does not appear to be the primary mechanism. However, most modern theories tend to fall into one of two categories, the *Altered State* and the *Social Role* theories.

The Social Role theories, also known as social-psychological and social-cognitive theories, question whether the notions of trance and trance logic, which are rooted in subjective reports, actually exists as any kind of defining characteristic. Furthermore they posit that hyper-suggestibility is simply an extreme of a continuous range of normal thinking and behavior. In this view, subjects in a hypnosis situation enter into a special social role, that of hypnotic subject, and play that role to the best of their ability using various cognitive and behavioral strategies. Good hypnotic subjects try to convince both the hypnotist and themselves that they are good hypnotic subjects, according to their understanding of the subjective and behavioral characteristics of good hypnotic subjects. The hyper-suggestibility is viewed as an end-point to which hypnosis is only one route. Despite this, there seems to be a "trance reflex" in humans and also in primates. Experimentation with Rhesus monkeys[50] has induced a hypnosis-like response in these non-human subjects. Of the 45 monkeys in one study, 6 went quickly into a motionless state when sat in front of a gently oscillating shining ball, 12 others who initially tried to turn away or push away the ball also became motionless after being secured to their chair. Restraint is probably the major factor in other forms of "animal hypnotism", especially at the low end of the intelligence scale such as in chickens. Whether this is

---

[49] Lynn, Stephen, and Judith Rhue (eds.) 1991, "Theories of Hypnosis: Current Models and Perspectives" N.Y. Guilford Press. ISBN: 089862343X

[50] Petrova E.V., Shlyk G.G., Kuznetsova G.D., Shirvinska M.A., Pirozhenko A.V., Hypnosis in Macaca Rhesus is Characterised by Different Phases and Inter-hemispheric EEG Asymmetry

a true hypnotic state rather than a survival reflex, and whether there is actually a difference, is debatable. No doubt such reflexes remain in all animals, including Humans, but the more complex the nervous system the more such reflexes can be overridden voluntarily. Nevertheless, such well-known descriptions as "being paralyzed with fear" suggest that not everyone can overcome such instincts, and almost nobody can do it instantaneously without training. In fact, this is used in one of the induction techniques known as shock induction. In the end, all of the monkey subjects ended up displaying hypnotized behavior in response to the ball and EEG monitoring showed some changes in the hemispheric dominance of the monkeys. Other factors influencing animal hypnosis include emotional stress, the novelty of the hypnotic condition, and physical restraint. Some of these can be generalized to human subjects as well. One model of hypnosis advises operators to take advantage of the first hypnotic experience of the subject as this is when they are likely to go very deep, and animal experiments seem to support this conclusion.

The more traditional view of hypnosis is that it is an altered state of consciousness. The difference between the theories is that this model posits an actual change in the state of the brain while the Social Role theory claims that the subject is acting the way he or she thinks is expected. There are also differences of emphasis on the hypnotic induction process, for example whether any special preparation must be performed to create a hypnotic state, and the condition of hyper suggestibility which apparently results. It seems likely that there are elements of truth in both theories and which one is more applicable depends on the phase and type of induction used, as well as the depth of resulting state and its accompanying phenomena. Some people may start by consciously acting out the role of hypnotic subject and then move to the point where a genuine altered state of consciousness is achieved. Indeed, one type of induction actually encourages the subject to "pretend" that they are hypnotized. However, for the purposes of this book it is convenient to assume that deep hypnosis is actually an altered state of consciousness on a par with those induced by other methods such as hallucinogenic drugs. Overall though, whatever theory turns out to be correct is less important than the utility of hypnotic techniques in magickal operations.

Having said all this there is one specific type of Altered State theory that illuminates a number of magickal paradigms. Hilgard's[51] *Neodissociation Theory* explains hypnosis in terms of dissociation or disconnection between the brain's control system, conscious monitoring, and cognitive subsystems. It is well worth bearing this particular model in mind when we are dealing with group gestalts and archetypes as previously described. Of particular interest with respect to the focus of this book we have Hilgard's discovery of the hidden observer that has exact parallels with the notion of the True Self of magickal theory.

---

[51] Hilgard, Ernest R., 1977, "Divided Consciousness: Multiple Controls in Human Thought and Action" John Wiley & Sons.

The Hidden Observer

While hypnotically induced deafness was being demonstrated a student asked whether there might be some part of the hypnotized subject's mind that could hear. Hilgard tested the idea by suggesting to the subject that there might be some part of him that was aware of what was going on, and if there was, then he (Hilgard) would be able to talk to it when he put his hand on the subject's arm. Subsequently, with Hilgard's hand on the subject's arm, the subject was able hear and with the hand removed he was unable to do so.

Hilgard called the subsystem that has knowledge not available to the hypnotized subject's consciousness, but which can be accessed through special methods such as automatic writing and automatic talking, the *Hidden Observer*. Hilgard hypothesized that the monitoring system is divided, such that one part feeds information to the hypnotized subject's consciousness, whereas another part retains information that is not made available to the consciousness. The dissociated part, the Hidden Observer, of the monitoring system becomes a separate subsystem that can control responses such as writing and talking. In Hilgard's view the Hidden Observer is not an alternate personality, nor is it an enduring part of the person. Rather, it seems to appear in response to certain kinds of suggestions where its function appears to be limited to dealing with the information excluded from consciousness by the suggestion. Of course how deep the suggestion needs to be and whether the conditioning created by everyday life, and especially magickal operations, is sufficient is a moot point.

The subjective experience of the Hidden Observer made by subjects after the termination of various sessions is quite interesting. The following is an extract of quotes by people reporting on various experiments, from the writings of Hilgard:

- The hidden part doesn't deal with pain. It looks at what is, and doesn't judge it. It is not a hypnotized part of the self. It knows all the parts.

- The hidden observer seemed like my real self when I'm out of hypnosis, only more objective. When I'm in hypnosis, I'm imagining, letting myself pretend, but somewhere the hidden observer knows what's really going on. I think this is part of the same process as the tendency in hypnosis to stand back and say: "Look what's happening to you. You're slowly going under hypnosis."

- The hidden observer was an extra, all-knowing part of me. I was not at all aware of it when I blotted out the hearing. It was not there until it was told to be there.

- I can separate my mind and my head from the rest of my body. The hidden part, reporting on the keys, was controlling my body. My mind was not counting key pressing. My mind was reporting what it felt, verbally. I've always been aware of the difference between the mind and the body when I've been hypnotized.

- It's as though two things were happening simultaneously; I have two separate memories, as if the two things could have happened to different people. The memory of the hidden part is more intellectual, but I can't really comprehend or assimilate the two.

A consistent feature of the Hidden Observer is that it is relatively objective and analytical. However there is one puzzle, namely that only about half of the highly hypnotizable subjects have experienced the effect when tested for it.

Having said all this, there have been serious questions raised as to whether the Hidden Observer is actually an artifact of the hypnotic suggestions and not an omnipresent facet of the mind. If this is so then it merely emphasizes that the True Self is something that is actually created in response to a certain set of circumstances. It reinforces the Zen view of Self – that there is no such thing that exists as a permanent feature and all is transitory.

Susceptibility Testing

Contrary to popular belief susceptibility to hypnosis is not a measure of "weak mindedness", gullibility or "lack of willpower". In fact, it is just the opposite. It is an ability to set aside consciousness and its inhibiting effects in order to allow other aspects of the mind to manifest directly and efficiently. Almost everyone has, and desires, this capability whether they know it or not. In the physical realm without it one could not ride a bike or safely drive a car, as every movement would have to be consciously calculated and then consciously executed. Intellectually it would be impossible to read a book for pleasure or enjoy any work of fiction in any medium that requires a "suspension of disbelief". Generally the more imaginative a person is the more susceptible they are to hypnosis. If you have ever been so absorbed reading or daydreaming that you have not heard questions addressed to you, you have been in a light hypnotic state. The same is true of "highway hypnosis" where one can travel for a considerable distance and remember nothing of the trip. Another obvious and notorious example is television. This is particularly true of children and cartoons.

Overall, research has shown (J. Hilgard) that highly susceptible subjects almost always have at least one pathway to trance involving a high degree of imaginative involvement. These are:

- Enjoyment of reading fiction and the ability to identify with the characters emotionally.

- Enjoyment of the dramatic arts in the same way either as an actor or a viewer.

- A serious religious commitment.
- The capability of being moved emotionally by sensory arousal such as by music or appreciation of Nature.
- Being adventurous
- Being involved in some artistic creativity such as painting, poetry, or music.

People of low susceptibility were less likely to have these pathways.

Surprisingly, people with two or more pathways were no more likely to be highly susceptible than were those with only one pathway. Two interests, participation in competitive team sports and majoring in the natural sciences, are negatively correlated to susceptibility. That is, those who exhibited these interests are less likely to be susceptible to hypnosis. So, simply talking to someone about their interests can provide useful insights into the ease with which they may be hypnotized.

It has been estimated that some ten to twenty percent of people are very good hypnotic subjects, and the same percentage again are very poor, with most lying between these extremes. What this means is that some people can be hypnotized very easily and some appear very resistant although ultimately, depending upon hypnotist and the technique employed, virtually everyone can be inducted into the trance state. At one end of the spectrum this may require only a few minutes and at the other hundreds of hours. Milton Erickson notes in "The Collected Papers" Volume One, that on average a total of four to eight hours of hypnotic induction training is required for most subjects.

In order to save time, especially when it comes to selecting subjects from a group of people, it is useful to apply some kind of quick test to discover which members are the most susceptible. The easiest is simply to get everyone to stand with their eyes closed, body relaxed, feet together and hands by their sides. Under normal conditions most will wobble slightly as they maintain their balance, and the head moves through a couple of centimeters. They are then asked to imagine that they are falling over. The degree of subsequent movement is directly proportional to hypnotic susceptibility, with those people who actually stumble being the most susceptible of all.

Another that is of more interest to those doing the test is one involving hands clasped together with the fingers interlaced and the heel of the palms touching. Without separating the palms the first finger of each hand is extended until the fingers are slightly separated and are held parallel to each other. This is actually a rather stressful position to hold for any length of time, with the natural inclination being to close of the fingers through fatigue. The person is then told to imagine a huge irresistible force crushing the fingers together. Most people will experience more difficulty in keeping the fingers apart when this is mentioned and the most susceptible of all will experience rapid closure of the fingers. This is even more effective if done with eyes closed and can be used as a fun way to illustrate the

Hypnosis

"power of suggestion", which is in reality the "power of imagination".

A more surreptitious method of ascertaining susceptibility in individuals upon meeting them is to offer a handshake and hold it for slightly longer than is culturally normal. If they follow and do not break away first then it is likely they may make a good subject.

Two similar methods for ascertaining susceptibility of people within groups are as follows. The first is the yawn test that relies on the fact that yawning is fairly contagious. This is done simply by seeing how long it takes to make the subject yawn by doing so oneself. It can even be done on strangers as long as they see whoever is doing the test, or it can be slipped casually into an interval in a conversation. It is particularly useful when talking to a group of people in order to ascertain quietly who might be especially susceptible. The second method based upon this theme of suggestibility is to open a bottle of odorless liquid, such as water, while telling the group it is a rather pungent chemical and asking them to indicate at what point they think they can smell it. Those who believe that they can smell what is not there are better candidates for hypnosis than those who cannot. Similar tests can be performed with others sensory suggestions, for example: "…has it just turned a bit cold in here?" etc.

More formally, the Stanford Hypnotic Susceptibility Scale, Form C (SHSS:C), is the prevalent measure of hypnotic susceptibility in current use and is often the criterion by which other measures of susceptibility are evaluated. This is essentially an ascending scale that begins with relatively easy hypnotic induction procedures and progressively moves to more difficult trance challenges. In order, these are:

- Hand Lowering
- Moving Hands Apart
- Mosquito Hallucination
- Taste Hallucination
- Arm Rigidity
- Dream
- Age Regression
- Arm Immobilization
- Anosmia to Ammonia (loss of sense of smell)
- Hallucinated Voice
- Negative Hallucination
- Amnesia

The full Form is available on the Net.

Finally, Theta brainwave activity[52] as determined by EEG is strongly and positively related to hypnotic susceptibility. As we will see in the chapter on subliminal techniques, such Theta states may be induced by a number of measures, which in turn increases the susceptibility to hypnosis.

Induction Techniques

There are several popular and well-known methods of inducing a hypnotic state in a subject. However before these are described, along with some lesser known methods, it should be pointed out that not all people react in the same way to the same method, nor to the same practitioner. The conventional setting is essentially one of mild sensory deprivation in a slightly darkened quiet room with the subject sitting in a comfortable chair.

Of crucial importance are two other factors. The first is the relationship between the hypnotist and subject. It helps considerably if there is no conscious resistance on the part of the subject. That is, the subject must want to be hypnotized. To facilitate this the situation has to be one of trust and co-operation between the two, although this may be of lesser importance in a group setting when the person is amongst friends. Additionally the skill of the hypnotist is of relevance when it comes to confidence, fluency and verbal delivery, tone of voice, general demeanor, gender and even dress and physical appearance. Note that these factors do not necessarily apply if the hypnosis is to be involuntary – something that is definitely possible and will be examined later both here and in the chapter on subliminal techniques.

There are approximately six major categories of induction technique although there is some overlap between them. These are, in no particular order:

- Eye Fixation
- Progressive Relaxation
- Shock
- Confusion
- Misdirection
- Physical.

Additionally, the first two contain major elements of trance deepening techniques which often need to be combined with, or at least follow, the other four in the above list.

---

[52] Crawford, H., & Gruzelier, J. (1992). A midstream view of the neuropsychophysiology of hypnosis: Recent research and future direction. In E. Fromm & M. Nash (Eds.), Contemporary Hypnosis Research (pp. 227-266). New York: Guilford Press.

Hypnosis

There are several outward signs of trance that can be observed in all subjects and at least one or more will be exhibited. They tend to be manifestations of relaxation and resulting lower heart rate. The first is changes in body temperature with some subjects feeling either warmer or colder. Such changes occur naturally apart from in trance situations. For example, the body temperature drops when sleeping and rises when in a relaxed meditative state. Another sign, more commonly associated with sleep and dreaming, is the fluttering eyelids of the REM (Rapid Eye Movement) state. Third and fourth signs are the reddening of the eyes and increased lachrymation (eyes watering). Finally the eyes will often roll upwards, giving the appearance that the subject is looking through the top of their head.

In practice most inductions mix and match various elements from these, as the situation requires.

Eye Fixation

The first is the eye fixation method that was used extensively during the 19th Century and partially stems from the notion that some "force" or "energy" passes between the hypnotist and subject. Such is clearly an ancient belief as superstitions such as the "Evil Eye" are common throughout the world. It possibly stems from the anxiety and focus generated by the instinctive recognition of the direct, highly focused and unblinking stare of a predator preparing to attack, or is perhaps rooted in primate biology where dominance and submission are shown by staring and averting the gaze.

This fixation method is the one most people think of when hypnosis is mentioned, the one most dramatically depicted in movies, and is such a cliché that has been parodied extensively in comedy routines. Unfortunately not only is it difficult for the practitioner to use, requiring supreme unblinking confidence and command, it does not work particularly well. This is especially true when it only provokes laughter and images of cartoon characters vainly trying to put their enemies into a trance ("…look into my eyes… you are in my power…"). Needless to say, it is almost useless when applied to groups.

A more modern version is to get the subject to focus upon a particular object. Again, this too is a cartoon cliché, at least when the object is a swinging pocket watch. However, in general the object is usually something other than that. For example, something as mundane as a pen or pencil is often chosen to be the focus. This is normally held above the line of sight of the subject in the eleven o'clock position making it slightly uncomfortable for them to keep it in view. Hence when the hypnotist suggests that "… your eyes are becoming tired…" it is true, and the natural inclination is to relax and close them.

Which bring us to some interesting observations and general principles documented in the 1960s and 1970s by Milton H. Erickson, probably the greatest hypnotherapist of the 20th Century, concerning his own researches in this field. He proposed that trance states could be created quickly and easily in everyone by using trance inductions that instituted a feedback loop between the hypnotist and subject. Erickson would incorporate observable aspects of the subject's experience and feed them back various ways. For example, he would match the rhythm of his voice to the subject's breathing or heart rate, while verbally describing other verifiable aspects of the their experience, such as the way they were sitting, any movements they made, what they were looking at and so forth. The obviously true observable aspects could then be tied to less verifiable suggestions. For example, Erickson might gently slow the rhythm of his speech while saying, "As you breathe... like this... you can become... more relaxed". The tendency is for the subject to follow into the suggested states. It also illustrates one of the two vocal styles of inducing a hypnotic state, that is, the use of a permissive voice that leads the subject rather than issues commands, and the more traditional paternalistic manner. Both styles have their place depending upon circumstances and personalities.

Anyway, the classical script to accompany the above is a combination of relaxation commands and countdown. An example follows but is somewhat shortened and with a lot of the repetition missing due to the fact it is rather boring to read. Indeed, it is rather tedious and boring to listen to, which is deliberate. As Milton Erickson once said, he often bored his subjects into a trance...

> "I want you to listen carefully to what I say, your eyes are closed, you are feeling comfortable and relaxed, thinking of nothing but what I say – your limbs feel heavy and your whole body is relaxed and comfortable – it feels as if you are going backwards into the comforting darkness, and as you go backwards into the darkness you are feeling more and more comfortable and relaxed – you are listening to my voice, only my voice, only to what I say and as you go back into the darkness you are starting to feel drowsy, very drowsy and you are thinking of nothing but just listening to the sound of my voice and breathing regularly and deeply and you are going into a sleep, a deep sound comfortable sleep – your sleep is getting deeper – deeper and deeper – and as I count from ten down to zero your sleep will get even deeper – much deeper. Ten – deeper, deeper... much deeper... Nine – still deeper... Eight – deeper and deeper... Seven – deeper... Six – you are in a deep sound sleep etc...."

The above is expanded by repetition of key words and phrases so that it takes around five minutes to say it all, slowly and deliberately in quiet soothing tones which become slower, softer and more monotonous. The countdown itself is known as the staircase method.

Progressive Relaxation

Moving on, the most common induction technique, and one that is very suitable for groups of people, is that of progressive relaxation coupled with guided imagery. It is the one most frequently used on self-hypnosis tapes, as well as by those who lead

Hypnosis

meditation sessions. Often those who actually use hypnotic inductions of this type will deny that it is hypnosis at all. It is also the most common technique used in modern shamanism in the form of the "guided journey" where a person or group is led to explore aspects of their psyche. One complaint I have seen concerning this method is that it is quite time consuming. In a world where time is money this matters, but that is not what our focus here is about. There are quite a few incidental benefits from using this slow progressive relaxation, most notably that it creates group rapport and provides a good lead-in to other magickal operations that follow.

Typically the subjects are seated comfortably in a quiet slightly darkened room and are taken through a basic but very effective series of exercises. A typical relaxation script might be as follows:

"Sit back and relax... close your eyes... let your body relax completely. Now starting with your feet, tense your feet and hold it for one... two... three... seconds and relax. Now tense your calves for one... two... three... and relax. Next your knees and thighs... tense... one... two... three... and relax. Now your hands... clench your fists and forearms tight... one... two... three... and relax. And now the biceps... one... two... three... seconds and relax the muscles. OK, now we are moving to the stomach... tense your stomach... one... two... three... and relax. Shoulders and neck... one... two... three... relax. And finally screw your face up for... one... two... three... seconds and let all the muscles relax. Now you are completely limp with no tension at all, relaxed, warm and comfortable... more relaxed and comfortable than you have been for a long time. Now in a few seconds we are going to go on an imaginary journey together..."

The voice of whoever is guiding the session should be soft, soothing and mellifluous – in a word – relaxing. I find that a soft low-pitched female voice is best but other people may feel differently.

The next stage is the introduction of the imagery. The more detailed the description the more time is spent and a more believable world is created in the imagination that facilitates the suspension of disbelief and absorption into the scenario. Note that sound effects may be conducive if they reinforce what is being described. The precise scenario is very dependent on what is to be accomplished, especially in a magickal setting.

The staircase method of deepening occurs at the beginning of the journey and uses the imagery of a progressive descent, often through a door via steps down into an underground world of calm and tranquility.

Misdirection Induction

Mental misdirection methods employ active use of the imagination, coupled with response, to hypnotize through responding to suggestions. It is used when the subject is too tense or unconsciously does not wish to be hypnotized. The idea is to take the subject's mind off hypnosis by what seems like a casual conversation about imagination and relaxation exercises. Assorted lies can be used (misdirection) by telling the subject that it requires weeks of work to prepare for the "real thing" and that this is just part of that preparation.

The subject is asked to close their eyes, relax, and imagine a familiar situation such as driving a car or having a walk through a familiar place. The operator then starts asking questions about the scene that is being imagined. For example, the color of their car, the position of the instruments, their shape and colors, and so forth. After a brief while they are told to open their eyes asked if that was all fairly clear. The operator then asks them to do the same again as a further "imagination test", but with another scene. This may be done several times.

Finally we come to the misdirection. They are informed that they have a good imagination and that things are proceeding smoothly and that they have the capability to imagine real and complex scenes. The next test is to be simpler in that all they have to do is imagine a single object, for example the full moon on a dark night. The scenario becomes one where they are seated either outside or perhaps inside looking through a window. This time they are asked to roll their eyes upward to help them see it in their mind's eye, with the eyelids remaining closed. While doing this the operator suggests that they are looking upwards as if they could see the moon through the center of their forehead, which he then touches lightly for emphasis. There then follows standard relaxation and deepening techniques similar to the previous two induction methods.

Another common form of misdirection occurs when a susceptibility test is extended into an induction. In this case it becomes an extension of the physical response to suggestion. Related to this is the fact that voluntarily actions increase susceptibility. By obeying the operator's directions with regard to such mundane actions as when and how to sit or stand, when and how to do the susceptibility test and so forth, the subject is conditioning themselves to follow the more "hypnotic" commands later.

One of the most common and easiest types of induction is trance hijacking, also known as waking hypnosis. For example, consider a driver in heavy traffic that is under pressure while driving in a familiar area. Saying "An odd thing has occurred – you are unable to tell me the name of the next street" will often produce temporary amnesia. It occurs when consciousness is strongly focused on something else and the suggestion can "slip in" past the pre-occupied critical faculty without notice. For such to be effective the suggestion must be one to which the subject does not object. There are numerous situations where this technique can be employed, in fact, wherever someone is absorbed in a task or their attention has been captured by something they consider interesting or important.

A final method of misdirection that has been used is actually very direct, but is apparently aimed at someone other than the subject. The subject is asked to accompany the operator while another person is hypnotized in order to see what the procedure is like. However, the person who the subject thinks is being hypnotized is in fact a stooge and the real target of the induction is the subject who has been made to believe that they are merely a passive onlooker.

Shock Induction

These techniques involve shock to the nervous system and rely upon authoritative, sudden and emphatic commands given in a surprising manner. The subject experiences a moment of passivity during which they either resist the trance, or let go and drop quickly into hypnosis. Often the shorter the induction is, the more reliable it will be, all other things being equal.

At the more extreme end of such reactions is the momentary freezing and mental confusion following rapidly upon the immediate physical startle reflex. This is one reason why eye witness testimony of traumatic events can be so unreliable, with the expectations and unconscious theories of what has happened rapidly blending in with what was actually observed as the mind tries to make sense of what is happening, or has, happened. Most people have experienced situations of immediate and sudden danger and discovered that as the events unfold time appears to slow down while the whole focus of attention is narrowed down to what appears to be the specific threatening events, to the exclusion of almost everything else. That is almost always the response when one is embroiled in violent situations, especially if they are unexpected and unusual.

A good example is the *Hand Drop Instant Induction*. The subject is instructed to close their eyes and press down upon the operator's outstretched hand. The operator's hand is then suddenly removed creating the startle response that lasts for up to about two seconds, during which they are very suggestible. The instruction "Sleep!" is then said in an authoritative tone that instantly induces a state of hypnosis. However, if this suggestion is not immediately followed by further deepening suggestions the subject will emerge from the trance. The deepening should be short and simple, such as: "…go limp and relaxed, continuing to relax further with every breath. As I gently rock your head, your neck relaxes and that feeling of relaxation moves through your entire body."

There are numerous variations that can be constructed on the theme, which consists of four phases – *focus*, *startle*, *sleep* and *deepening*.

Here is another example, which is one of the fastest inductions known, taking less than thirty seconds. The operator stands very close and has their hand on the subject's head, rotating it slowly. This causes a loss of balance in the subject at which point, quickly and with control, the operator pushes the subject's head into their own shoulder and shouts into the subject's ear "Sleep Now!" This is then followed with deepening techniques.

As a matter of interest, this technique bears more than a passing resemblance to healing performances of Evangelical Christians, particularly in the USA. Here the person to be healed is called onto the stage in front of the congregation where they explain the nature of their malady. The preacher then places his hand upon the head of the supplicant and in a loud voice commands "… in the name of Jesus Christ you are healed!" or words to that effect. At the same time the hand pushes back the supplicant's head as they faint and fall backwards into the arms of the preacher's assistants. The former, when recovered, then declares that they are truly healed and leave the stage apparently healthy. As we will see later, hypnosis is a very effective way for helping the body to heal itself and especially in masking pain. However, such rapid cures are seldom lasting in any but the most trivial illnesses.

Again, shock techniques are mostly one-to-one but there is a potential for their use in group settings. The actual nature of the shock in unimportant and can vary from a load noise to some monster jumping out in a movie and scaring the audience. However, as mentioned, the window of opportunity is only a couple of seconds.

Confusion Methods

Confusion methods are designed to confuse the conscious mind, so that it becomes easier to just relax into hypnosis, while issuing suggestions to the unconscious. The are essentially three subdivisions – mental dissociation, information overload and pattern interrupt. The value of these is that long and frequent use of the confusion technique can effect exceedingly rapid hypnotic inductions under unfavorable conditions such as acute pain or in persons interested but hostile, aggressive, and resistant.

The mental dissociation method is quite subtle in that it addresses the conscious and unconscious parts of the mind separately and apparently confusingly. A typical script might run as follows, after some preliminary relaxation exercises:

> "Your unconscious mind is listening, but your conscious mind need not listen…. Your unconscious is paying attention to these words but your conscious mind need not pay attention to these words… Your unconscious mind is alert and clear while your conscious mind is relaxing… Your unconscious knows what is happening while your conscious mind need not know what is happening… Your unconscious mind is capable of remembering while your conscious mind need not remember… Your unconscious mind is focused while your conscious mind can sleep…"

and so on, repetitively. Eventually boredom sets in on the part of the subject and their conscious mind does just what is required.

The information overload induction relies quite simply on issuing a complex series of commands or masses of information that the subject finds it increasing difficult to execute or even understand. Most often it involves plays on words or communication that progressively introduces elements of confusion as to the question of what is meant, thereby leading to an inability to respond. This results in

Hypnosis

a build up of tension as the need to somehow respond accumulates. The culmination occurs in a final suggestion permitting a ready and easy response that is satisfying to the subject and is congruent with their desires, either conscious or unconscious. It is important that the hypnotist speaks in a casual but serious manner conveying an expectation of understanding. This is coupled with a steady delivery with only enough pauses for the subject to almost begin a reply, yet constantly interrupted before they can actually speak. A script example[53] by Milton Erickson is as follows:

> "You know and I know and the doctors you know know that there is one answer that you know that you don't want to know and that I know but don't want to know, that your family knows but doesn't want to know, no matter how much you want to say no, you know that the no is really a yes, and you wish it could be a good yes and so do you know that what you and your family know is yes, yet they still wish it were no. And just as you wish there were no pain, you know that there is but what you don't know is no pain is something you can know. And no matter what you knew no pain would be better than what you know and of course what you want to know is no pain and that is what you are going to know, no pain..." and so on.

All of this is said slowly but with utter conviction and seriousness, and with total disregard of any interruption from the subject. Building upon this is the employment of irrelevancies and non-sequiturs each of which, taken out of context, appears to be a sound and sensible communication. Taken in context they are confusing, distracting, and inhibiting. Beyond this one can insert short meaningful suggestions as part of the induction as in the script above which was designed to alleviate pain. If you missed it one of the phrases is: "…but what you don't know is no pain is something you can know". As we will see later in more detail, aspects of the unconscious mind are very adept at picking up such messages. Of course, to do this in real time takes a great deal of practice and skill not to mention a facility with words. However, although less effective, pre-recorded versions can be employed in many circumstances, especially with regard to group working.

The information overload technique is actually encountered quite often. It is used in advertising and politics to sell a product or idea, and consists of bombarding the listener with a complex series of claims and statistics followed by the punchline, or soundbite. An example used in computer sales might run as follows. The scenario is a computer retailer with a customer who does not know much about the technology:

> "And here we have a laptop with 4 gig of DDR2 DRAM, 500 gig of hard disc, USB and VGA video ports, fifteen inch screen, Ethernet port with wireless interface and WEP or WPA security features, lithium ion battery... *does everything you need at the right price.*"

---

[53] Milton Erickson, The Collected Papers, Volume One

At the end of the sales pitch the customer's mind latches onto the only thing they unambiguously understand: "...*does everything you need at the right price.*" Then a few hours or days later they wonder why they have bought that load of crap!

Of course, almost always the advertiser does not have the luxury of the undivided attention of their target for minutes or hours, nor does the politician. Quite often the outcome of the confusion is to change the channel or walk away from the speaker. Where this technique is effective is with the "captive audience", either figuratively or literally. Such venues are as varied as political rallies, religious events, lectures and prison camps.

Finally we have the *pattern interrupt* induction also pioneered by Erickson. While this is not easily applicable to groups I include it both for completeness and because it is both simple and technically fascinating. This technique relies upon unexpectedly breaking a familiar pattern of interaction with the subject and then taking advantage of the subsequent confusion. In this respect it has elements of the Shock Induction outlined previously.

Probably the most famous example is the *Handshake Induction*. With practice it can work very well due to the due to the motor patterns of the welcoming handshake being so automatic, at least in the West. To see it being done successfully is a remarkable experience. Dr. Stephen G Gilligan[54], one of the world's leading authorities and innovators in Ericksonian hypnosis has broken down the handshake induction into a five-step process which makes it easy to comprehend.

- Create contact and expectancy, where the operator seizes the subject's attention while moving into position. This is accomplished by displaying a genuine desire to greet the person.

- Initiate the pattern, which in this case means moving forwards and extending the right hand. This prompts the subject to automatically extend their hand. The operator continues maintain eye contact and engage in verbal communication.

- Interrupt the pattern, which is initiated when the operator is just over a meter from the subject. At this point, the operator, while still walking forward with right hand outstretched, suddenly accelerates to lift their left hand under the subject's outstretched hand. Continuing the motion, the operator uses their thumb and index finger to lift the subject's hand to about shoulder level. This should be done with gentleness and minimal pressure so that the subject does feel coerced. The operator rapidly guides the already lifting hand of the subject so that the element of surprise is present. During this time the operator's right hand, which has followed the left hand, rises to the subject's eye level and points toward the their face, then quickly moving the whole body it swings around to point at the subject's raised right hand.

---

[54] Therapeutic Trances: The Co-operation Principle in Ericksonian Hypnotherapy
Stephen G. Gilligan, Publisher: Brunner/Mazel Publisher (January 1, 1987), ISBN: 0876304420

Hypnosis

The operator, who has been looking at the subject in a surprised and intense fashion, now stares at the raised right hand of the subject. This usually deepens the disorientation and facilitates a rapid mental dissociation, the symptoms of which are a lightness in the lifted right hand, a fixed stare and posture, dilated pupils, and alterations in breathing.

- The fourth step is amplifying the confusion by carefully telling the subject to pay very close attention to the coloration changes beginning to occur in the fingers of the lifted hand. This both deepens the disorientation and fixes their attention upon the lifted hand. This enhances willingness to follow simple directives, and due to perceptual alterations the subject will often begin to see actual color changes. These developments can be accentuated by lightly touching the fingertips of the lifted hand in turn and naming the digits as they are touched.

- The final step is utilizing the confusion. As the operator accelerates the finger touches they intersperse trance-developing suggestions such as "going deeper… deeper…". This is all done while maintaining the elevation of the subject's hand. At any time the operator can start to lower their own left hand which often leaves the subject cataleptic; that is, the subject's arm will remain motionless in the air. If this is not so then the operator simply re-holds up the subject's hand.

Quite often the subject, especially if they are wary of being hypnotized, is in a double bind when it comes to the confusion techniques. While consciously resisting other methods is quite easy it is not so with these. For example, suppose you recognize what's happening as being some kind of induction and wish to resist it. Do you listen carefully to what's being said, or do you deliberately not listen so as not to be "confused"? If it's the former then you could fall prey to information overload. On the other hand, if it has strong elements of the mental dissociation technique then not consciously listening is playing right into the operator's hands... And that's assuming the pattern interrupt or shock technique has not just been used, whether you recognize it or not. It's very difficult to prepare oneself *not* to be shocked by the totally unexpected. The only safe way of blocking these techniques is to take the initiative and do the talking and make sure that you are not sidetracked as to your purpose in communicating.

Physical Methods

Strictly speaking, these methods are more properly aids to hypnosis since one still has to interact with the subject. Alternatively, even if used in self-hypnosis there still has to be a verbal or visual contribution in order to take advantage of the state.

Most people seem to have an inherited desire to be gently rocked which no doubt explains the millions of rocking chairs in the world today, and many mothers induce sleep in their babies by rocking them at night. There appears to be a relaxing "sensory feedback loop" around roughly 2Hz which shows up in everything from rocking chairs to various forms of music to the sleeping delta rhythm of the brain. This may be related to the natural resting heart rate of about sixty to seventy beats per minute in a healthy fit person. Each heartbeat consists of two audibly distinct phases, systolic and diastolic, which results in the well-known double beat. It has even been theorized that the mother's heartbeat experienced in the womb may be a prominent factor in the origin of music.

At first sight it seems that the use of these physical rhythms in an induction is rather difficult and contrived but this is not necessarily so. It can be quite effective in group settings as dancing, as has been known through the ages. The most famous example is that of the Sufi dances and modern forms such as those introduced by Gurdjieff. An even more up to date example is that of rave culture (a term that will rapidly date) and its associated techno-trance music.

However, the hypnotic power of intense concentration couple with disciplined repetitive physical movement is also a feature of many Eastern martial arts with their fixed exercise forms, more familiarly known as kata if the art is Japanese. It is also apparent in the modern military as parade ground drill, which has long outgrown its origins as a method of first moving large bodies of men coherently about a battlefield and later coordinating the loading and firing of muskets in squares on open ground. For those who have experienced it and actually have the imagination to appreciate it as something other than a tedious chore, such drills and marching are a deeply relaxing experience where one can enter a "mindless" state quite easily. This, and the group bonding effect it has, is clearly one of the major reasons why it is still used by the military. From an equally practical point of view being in a squad running as part of an exercise regime is significantly easier than doing it alone. Add in singing, or more accurately chanting, various "songs" both regulates the breathing and distracts the conscious mind from the physical discomfort. Exercising in such a light hypnotic trance is both extremely beneficial and pleasurable as the endorphins released flood the body, which is a major reason why hard physical exercise can be addictive.

Another example is sex, which can easily produces a complete loss of self-consciousness and body control. A couple loses themselves in the rhythm of each other's touch eventually leading to orgasms causing palpitations of the heart and bodily tremors. This is probably one of the most profound forms of altered states as the most primitive parts of the brain and unconscious controls and regulates the bodily functions, blotting out the consciousness. It's efficacy as a way of implanting suggestions or eliciting information is notorious, and the old KGB of the USSR in the Cold War actually had a school where agents were taught sexual technique. Conversely, ancient magickal systems have been also been built around the sexual impulse and reflex, most famously Tantra Yoga. Masturbation has also been used in magickal workings by coupling the state achieved at the point of orgasm to the desired aim of the working in order to propel it into the unconscious.

Hypnosis

However, it is doubtful whether there is much utility in sex when it comes to group interactions simply because getting together a group of dedicated magicians willing to indulge in such sexually focused activity is not easy. It is interesting to note that touching and stroking was a major component of Mesmer's repertoire and can obviously create a sexual tension as a focus.

There is one more physical induction aid that is brutal, extremely dangerous and depending on the precise circumstances probably constitutes assault. Anyone who has done martial arts to any depth will recognize it in one form or another and also recognize its hazards.

The technique involves standing in front of the subject and bending their head fully backwards exposing the neck. The fingers of the hands are then placed on either side of the neck just below the ears and towards the throat. This will place the fingers over the major veins and arteries carrying blood to and from the brain and the exact positioning can be found by feeling for the pulse. Having placed the fingers in the correct position press firmly while telling the subject to breathe deeply, which they will probably be doing anyway whether they want to or not, out of anxiety or simply because they experience difficulty breathing. The pressure is maintained while carefully watching for reaction which, if done correctly, will result in rapid unconsciousness. At the point when they go limp the pressure should be removed, whereupon a more docile, slightly stunned and confused conscious state will ensue. A more gentle method is to massage the neck in these places that will result in reduced heart rate and blood pressure leading to a sleepy state.

There are two mechanism at work in the above. The first and most obvious is that blood to the brain is simply cut off, and that is what most people assume. However, that is not necessarily all that is happening – there is another process at work that is subtler. The arteries have pressure receptors and when these are stimulated by either a strike or by massage they tell the brain that blood pressure is dangerously high. The brain responds by lowering the heart rate, sometimes to the point of stopping it temporarily. Subsequently the blood pressure drops and drowsiness or unconsciousness is the result. To give an idea of effectiveness in the martial arts, a properly executed Judo strangle will render someone unconscious within four seconds and a Shuto Uke strike as executed in Shorinji Kempo will render the recipient unconscious almost instantly.

The dangers are obvious. Prolonged pressure can stop blood flow and result in brain damage or death, and a strike to those points can in some people stop the heart without it automatically restarting. If that is the case immediate resuscitation and medical treatment are required. Apart from all of this it is not especially effective as a hypnotic induction technique with willing subjects and is probably more closely related to forms of narco-hypnosis, a subject examined later.

Finally, at the opposite end of the physical spectrum we have the previously mentioned study on rhesus monkeys where 6 out of 45 were "naturally" hypnotized but another 12 succumbed when physically restrained. While physical restraint may be used in certain forms of interrogation or initiation in most situations it is not generally considered ethical to tie someone to a chair. However, peer pressure or explicit threats or promises may have the same effect on keeping someone immobile. The resulting stress also appears to be a factor in facilitating trance. We will look more closely at this with respect to magick, ritual and initiation in the next chapter.

Deepening the Trance

There are several methods that are commonly used for deepening the trance state and are especially used in conjunction with the rapid induction techniques described above before the initial effect tends wears off. They tend to comprise a secondary induction that is rather slower.

The most common techniques are outlined in the first two induction methods above and comprise countdowns coupled with the imagery of descent and relaxation. Depending on the circumstances the subject may be asked to do the counting instead of the operator. With the latter it may be efficacious to have the subject start at a higher number than ten and also to add the word "deeper" after each count. Meanwhile the operator can be offering additional suggestions, which adds a confusion element.

Deepening can also result from using an information feedback method. Prior to the hypnotic session the subject is asked to describe their favourite place, then when they are in a light trance the operator can describe in vivid detail all the pleasures such a place has to offer. This is, of course, a more focused and personal version of using guided imagery.

Finally, a very effective method of deepening a trance is to repeatedly awaken and then re-hypnotize the subject. The procedure of re-inducing hypnosis has the effect of compounding the depth of the previous induction. The progress of relaxation seems to come in tiers. After each induction the subject becomes more suggestible and responsive. The delay between awakening and re-inducing should be less than ten minutes for maximum effect. This process is known as fractionation and can be made even more effective by asking the subjects to describe their personal experiences as they go through the process. These descriptions are then fed back to them in a process that amounts to them detailing the best way they should be hypnotized.

Testing Trance Depth

Before examining ways of checking the depth of an induction it is worth noting that someone pretending to be hypnotized can fake almost all tests.

A key thing to realize is that there are degrees of the hypnotic state – that it is not an "all or nothing" phenomenon. At its most superficial there may be no difference between the effects of forceful advertising, subtle persuasion or light trance. Indeed, some people claim that there is no such thing as hypnosis as a separate phenomenon. However, the following tests are for degrees of the trance state well into the territory most recognize as being hypnotic.

The test most commonly used to indicate a basic stage has been attained is that of muscular paralysis. For example, the hypnotist will tell the subject that they are unable to open their eyes, or perhaps unable to lift their arm. The subject is then invited to try to do so. If the trance is deep enough they will, in general, not be able to succeed. It is important not to allow too much time for the attempt and to reassure the subject that all is well less distress builds to the point where they leave the trance. A safer method of administering this test is to tell the subject that they are going to have difficulty performing the operation and that they might find it impossible. If they do succeed ask them whether they felt it was more difficult than normal. Their answer will indicate the degree to which the induction is working. This at least limits any damage to the credibility of the process. It is interesting to speculate on connections between this phenomenon, where the subject is conscious but apparently unable to exert muscular control, and that of sleep paralysis. The latter occurs as a natural part of the sleep cycle when dreaming and prevents our body acting out our dream actions. However, occasionally a person will wake up with the sleep paralysis still in place. This can lead to substantial distress, especially as the person is still in the hypnogogic (actually, hypnopompic) state and may hallucinate a "cause" as they lie in a partial dream state This is often said to underlie the myths of the incubus and succubus.

At a fairly deep degree of trance the subject can be induced to hallucinate. That is, they may perceive something that does not exist, fail to perceive something that does, or be persuaded that the character of an object has changed. This is the favourite of the stage magician who convinces the subject that they are eating, and enjoying, an apple when in fact it is an onion. Or perhaps they can be made to believe that everyone in the audience, or only those on stage, have removed all their clothes. This again tends to be an "all or nothing" test and the dissonance between what the subject is told and what they really perceive may snap them back to reality, even if they have passed the test above.

The same is true of the analgesia test where the subject is told that they cannot feel pain. They are then pricked at random, deeply and painfully, with a sterile needle. If the trance is deep enough the subject will not register pain although, strangely, if asked they will say that they feel it.

The two other tests are quite familiar, being the efficacy of the post hypnotic command and the degree to which amnesia can be induced. The latter speaks for itself and can apply to either the hypnosis session itself or some other memory that can be isolated by the hypnotist who then induces the subject to forget about it. The post hypnotic command is of more interest in that it is a versatile mechanism for altering behavior, especially when combined with an *anchor*. These are examined in far greater detail in the next chapter.

It should be pointed out that these tests could be bad for credibility if they do not work. Not only may the subject conclude that they are not hypnotized but that they are incapable of being hypnotized or, more likely with a willing subject, that you are not sufficiently competent. It may be difficult recovering from that situation. However, they do work for many people and sometimes provide useful information, although from a magickal perspective it may be counter-productive to take such a risk until it becomes necessary as part of the working. Either it will work or not and there is often little point in courting early failure by introducing such tests. This is particularly so with group workings where members may be at different levels of trance and where blatant contradictions of reality may snap some of them back to baseline reality entirely. However, if it is deemed necessary there is one other method of determining trance depth, and that is to ask the subject directly. For example, the subject can be asked to give a number for the depth of the trance they are in, with zero being no trance and ten being extremely deep trance.

Stage Hypnotism

As an aside, how do stage hypnotists make it appear so easy and spectacular? Well, the answer is a combination of factors. The first possibility is that the entertainer has planted his own people amongst the audience who may simply be actors. Another is that when he whispers to the volunteers as part of the induction technique he asks them to play along if they do not feel they are really in a trance, and not spoil the fun. In fact, they may play along anyway as a friend of mine did to save the man from embarrassment. Of course, it cannot be discounted that in playing along a person is just rationalizing their action under what was a genuine response (see Social Role Theory). Finally, the call for volunteers may have been made some time before the act commences, which gives the stage hypnotist time to select the most susceptible and create the necessary trance state in which to implant a post hypnotic command for rapid re-hypnosis on stage. Even if that is not the case the fact that people volunteer is itself a measure of their willingness to co-operate and their likely susceptibility. Another obvious method of obtaining good subjects from the volunteers on stage is simply to reject those that do not pass various simple trance tests, leaving the most hypnotizable to entertain the audience. This may in fact be subsequent to testing the entire audience as part of the act and then picking out the best responders.

Stage hypnotists also make extensive use of shock and confusion techniques to gain temporary compliance. These work only with a subset of people, and only up to a point. There is a critical moment with such shock inductions when the subject either complies or breaks away from the hypnotist. Another trick is to use repeated re-hypnosis to deepen the trance state to enable their subjects to proceed to more difficult (or humiliating) tasks.

Finally, there is another factor to consider and that is the stress of the situation. Very few people are not stressed in some way when they are called up onto a stage in front of an expectant audience, or know they are being recorded for a TV program that may be seen by millions. This itself can mimic a confusion induction as the person involved is desperately trying to work out what is happening, what is likely to happen, and what their response should be. This is especially true with performers such as Derren Brown who arrange whole scenarios in unfamiliar settings such as disused mental hospitals and deserted woodland.

Having said all this, some it can be well worth watching, especially on video in order to see exactly how the induction technique is accomplished and to listen to the script where available. It's also fun to try to work out what is hypnotism, what is cold reading and what is actually standard sleight-of-hand magic and how they are used together.

A superb book well worth reading on the subject is "The New Encyclopedia of Stage Hypnotism"[55] by Ormond McGill. It contains over one hundred rapid induction techniques as well as other interesting information including detailed descriptions of how to practice stage hypnotism. It is something with which every magician needs to be familiar.

Bibliography and useful books:

- Bowers, K.S., "Hypnosis for the Seriously Curious" W.W. Norton & Company Ltd ISBN: 0393953394

- Barber, T.X., 1969, "Hypnosis: A Scientific Approach" N.Y.: Van Nostrand Reinhold.

- Erickson, Rossi and Rossi. Hypnotic Realities: The Induction of Clinical Hypnosis and Forms of Indirect Suggestion, Irvington Publishers, 1976.

- Ronald A., Havens, Catherine, Ma Walter Hypnotherapy Scripts. Publisher: Brunner-Routledge; 2nd edition (July, 2002) ISBN: 1583913653

- Rossi, E. (ed.), 1980, "The Collected Papers of Milton H. Erickson on hypnosis", (4 volumes), N.Y. Irvington.

---

[55] Ormond McGill, The New Encyclopedia of Stage Hypnotism ISBN 1-899836-02-0

Mind Tools

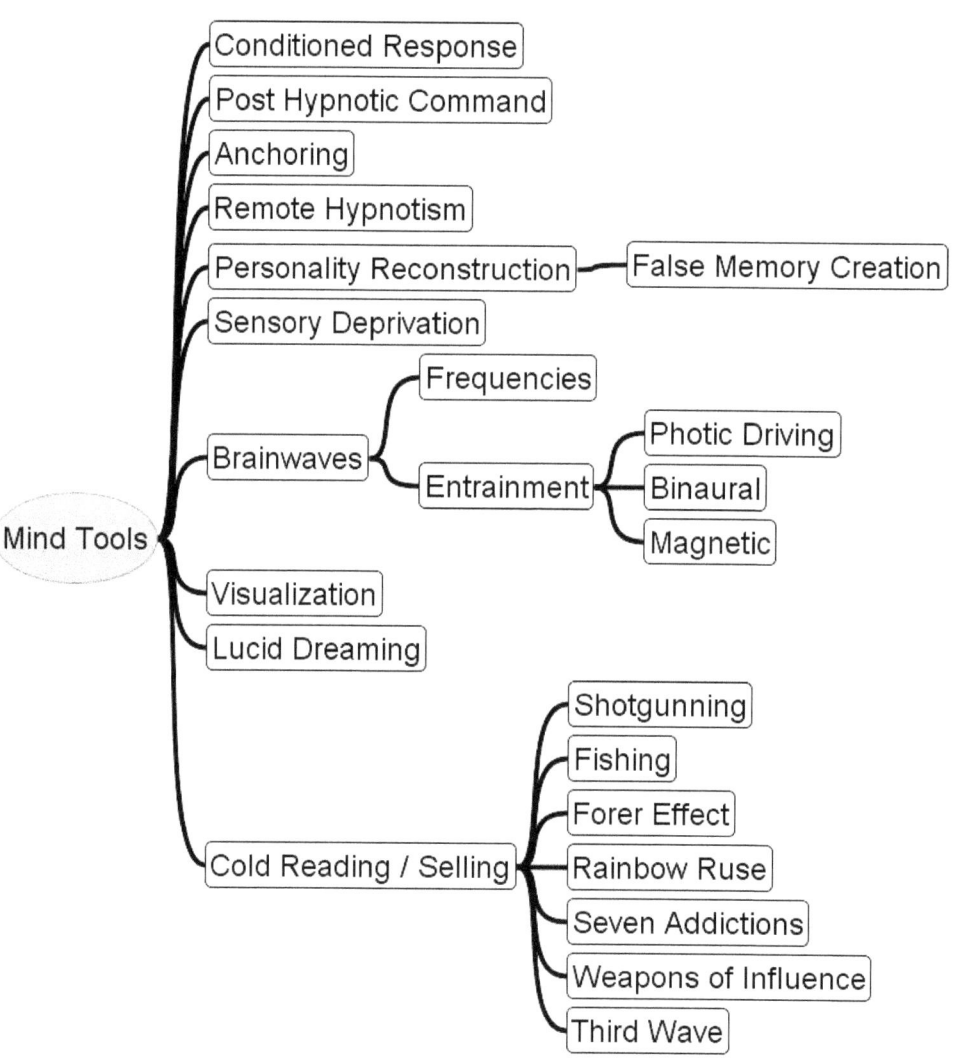

6 Mind Tools

Now we know something of the hypnotic state and how to induce it we can move on to examining its uses in some detail, including those uses that are not spoken of in polite company. The key to much of what follows are the notion of anchoring and conditioning.

Anchoring

Anchoring refers to the tendency for any one element of an experience to bring back the entire experience. An anchor is the stimulus that results in the conditioned response.

An anchor can be in any sensory format. That is, it can be a word, a sound, a piece of music, a smell, a picture, a gesture, a touch or a taste. Anchors are created all the time by the association of various stimuli to emotional states, some good and some bad. It might be the music we listened to that accompanied our first romantic kiss, or perhaps the smell of summer when we were young. Or maybe it's the sight of a flashing blue light that could trigger a series of bad memories and flashbacks to traumatic events. It's the reason TV programs have signature tunes and adverts have jingles and slogans. They are all trying to evoke a particular feeling in the shortest possible time by "pushing your buttons" as the saying goes. From our point of view we want to be able to deliberately set up anchors in both ourselves and others either openly or covertly in order to trigger preset states or responses. The trigger itself should generally satisfy the following criteria:

- It must be specific or the subject will not sensitize to it.

- It must be relatively unusual or the constant triggering will result in desensitization.

- When it is being set up it must be applied intermittently, or again desensitization will occur and render it ineffective.

- It must be anchored to a unique, specific and prompt reaction otherwise its effect will be diluted across many responses.

- The reinforcements of an anchor should have a break between them.

You can use these processes to your advantage by creating anchors in your interactions with other people. When you meet someone turn the conversation to something that has created the emotional state you want to anchor in them. For example, get them to relive something that has given them a lot of pleasure. While they are in this state apply the chosen anchor. It can be anything, but a gesture, touch or sound is often used. At some point later, test the anchor by applying it and see if they can be brought back to that state. If there is time then the anchor can be reinforced every time the desired emotional state is evoked.

An example of anchoring, pattern interrupt and temporary induced amnesia that is both simple and fascinating is performed by Derren Brown. He goes into the subway, stands next to people and asks them which stop they are getting off, which they tell him. He then asks if they remember how things are forgotten, like things that are on the tip of the tongue but cannot quite be recalled. As they access their memory of forgetting, he casually anchors the memory by passing his hand in front of their eyes. After asking for a couple more memories of easily forgetting and strengthening his anchor, he asks them what stop they will be getting off at. The instant they begin to access, he repeats the hand movements in front of their eyes, causing a pattern interrupt while simultaneously activating the established anchor of how to forget easily. The bewildered and sudden, trance type of look on the people's faces is remarkable because the entire process is done very quickly.

We can establish anchors in ourselves for a number of different states. The ones most discussed in self help literature are things like optimism, joy, creativity, energy, happiness and so forth. All the kind of ordinary positive attitudes that one only really recognizes when they are missing. Since these are covered in most NLP books I am going to concentrate on the ones that are of major use in a magickal setting. The essence is to choose the kind of states most likely to facilitate a successful working or ritual and find a suitable anchor. In group settings like the Owen Experiment one would wait until the correct "atmosphere" conducive to the manifestation is in place and operating. At that point one could, for example, choose either a word, a short piece of music, a body posture, gesture, an image or physical item to anchor the state. In the case of words what we are doing is creating the elements of a spoken spell capable of placing the group very rapidly into that same situation in the future. With the case of a picture we have the classical magickal Sigil which we will look at in far greater detail later. A physical item can be a talisman, charm or religious icon. What should be noted is that in general spells which are anchors will only work for those who have been through the corresponding experience. It may seem obvious, but that is why a spell will work for some people but not for others. The states associated with (for example) key words throughout a ritual would obviously correspond with the various stages, including (most importantly for novices) the final banishing. Needless to say, these have to be put in place by some serious planning and effort on the part of the group. Again, this is one reason why there are levels of initiation within occult organizations. It is not enough simply to learn the triggers if they actually trigger nothing at all except a feeling of self importance. The overall feeling of a ritual can be anchored by the sense of smell, which is why incense is used. Smell is one of the most primordial senses with deep links to the limbic system of the brain. As such it is a very powerful anchor, but very broad and imprecise, which is both its advantage and drawback. Finally, do not forget to reinforce whatever anchors are chosen for the operations during the operations themselves. Obviously the reinforcement should occur only when there is something successful happening, otherwise you will begin to anchor to failure and mediocrity. Everything in ritual is chosen, basically, for its purity and ability as an anchor.

More ambitious is the anchoring of states that are very unusual. For example, the timeless state that one enters at the height of an LSD drug trip. In such a state, where the experienced magician can do some really amazing things, there are typically two problems encountered. The most obvious one is that so much is happening in (apparently) zero time that the actual working can be done, and undone, multiple times. So we need to create an anchor to the "done"[56] state. This can be accomplished by, for example, pressing a button which fires off the anchor. Immediately afterwards the magician must be distracted away from that line of thought entirely. This is where a sober and experienced assistant comes in handy. The second problem is the one most encountered by novices. It is simply that one gets lost in the peak experience which is so alien that after the trip is over it is rapidly forgotten. Having the peak anchored allows almost "on demand" flashbacks into that state. Indeed, a lot of unwanted LSD (or other psychedelic) flashbacks occur because of just such unwanted and accidental anchoring. At the very least it gives an element of access to magickal consciousness without subsequent drug use in a more mentally controlled environment.

The Conditioned Response

The definitive pioneering work in conditioned response was that done by Pavlov in the 1930s in Russia. The use of his name has since become a byword for mindless or involuntary reflex actions triggered by some arbitrary stimulus. Consequently his work has been linked to the emergence of what was termed "brainwashing" and similar techniques developed initially in the USSR and now relatively commonplace either in their virulent military form, the civilian religious milieu of "cults" or the more innocuous worlds of advertising and psychotherapy. However, the essence of the original work is quite simple. Pavlov struck a tuning fork (modern folklore says rang a bell) every time he fed his experimental dogs and discovered that after a while simply striking the fork, without feeding them, led to them salivating – a physiological response in the dogs triggered simply by the sound. This became the archetypal experiment in the field of conditioned response. Essentially, repetitive stimulation leads to a largely involuntary response that is in turn anchored. When the anchor, in this case the bell, is activated the response is triggered without the original stimulus being present. Such behavior is clearly defined in animals but becomes far more complex when attempted in Humans, partly because we can analyze what's happening, but also because the desired response is often intellectual rather than physiological.

---

[56] This will only really make sense to people who have already done it

There are essentially two forms of conditioning, comprising positive and negative reinforcement. The first rewards the required behavior and the other punishes undesirable behavior and both are as old as Humanity. However, in normal everyday life, and even under medical therapeutic conditions, they are often not accompanied by deliberately anchored triggers in the sense we have been using the term. The situation is its own anchor.

Probably the most powerful overall conditioning that all of us experience every day is unquestioning obedience to authority. In fact, it is such an automatic reflex by now that just reading this probably conjures up entirely the *wrong* image. For example, of some petty official throwing their weight about in an arbitrary and easily challenged manner, countered by a defiant "fuck you!" Or perhaps some politician telling you to vote for them, with a similar witty response from the listener. However, that is a response to transparently false authority. True authority is so overpowering we often do not even think of questioning the orders given. This is because long experience and conditioning have shown that the punishment for disobedience is swift and sure, either in terms of crude physical violence or loss of opportunity to the extent that it makes the defiance not worth even consciously contemplating most of the time. In short, most of us most of the time unconsciously balance possible gains with probable losses and decide that it is a very unequal equation. So unequal it is not worth thinking about.

What is an "authority" in these cases? An authority is someone, or something, which is strongly believed to exercise superior power or possess superior knowledge or control that is directly applicable to the immediate situation being experienced. So, let's look at some examples of the kind of authority we obey without thinking, and the consequences of disobedience. First, how long would someone survive if they decided that they were not going to be told what to do by colored lights? The answer is "not long". The chances of driving through even a small city while ignoring every traffic light without crashing is small, as is doing so without attracting the attention of the police and losing ones license or worse. We obey that authority because we recognize it is in our interest to do so, despite its inconvenience. The overwhelming punishment for chronic disobedience in that particular case is death, injury, major financial loss, possibly coupled with a prison sentence. The gain is a few seconds knocked off travel time. Or consider another order almost all of us obey almost all of the time. A shop or mall is closing and the manager asks everyone to leave. How many people insist on staying, and what happens if they do? Or perhaps the police cordon off an area for some reason – how many people try to force their way in to see for themselves what is happening?

These are all examples of authority that cannot be disobeyed without serious direct consequences of a massively disproportionate nature. On the other hand, let's look at authority we can disobey without that authority punishing us. Perhaps we hear on the car radio that a certain road we intend to travel upon is blocked by an accident. Do we think "…you're probably lying – I'm going there anyhow"? In general, we believe what we are told by the authority and act upon it in for own best interest. We expect that easily checkable information from an authoritative and trusted source is accurate. In fact, the more authoritative the voice and source of information the more accurate we expect it to be and the more likely we are to act upon it without question (although maybe not without complaint). Conversely, we are also likely to obey an authority that is far from being known as trustworthy if the consequences for ignoring it, if it is correct, are overwhelmingly catastrophic. Examples include people shouting "Fire!" or claiming to have planted, or found, a bomb.

Another source of authority that most people will obey is one that they believe is able and willing to negate any personal adverse consequences from their obedience. Namely, that the authority will take responsibility for the actions being ordered and that the person who is "just obeying orders" will suffer no detriment by their obedience. This lies at the heart of a classic experiment in social psychology carried out by Stanley Milgram of Yale University in 1961[57].

Volunteer subjects were asked to participate in an experiment concerning the effectiveness of pain stimulus in a learning situation. Each volunteer was introduced to *The Experimenter* who would oversee the experiment, and *The Learner* who was connected to an electric shock apparatus. The Learners were actors, and whenever the Experimenter commanded the volunteer to administer an electric shock the actors pretended to suffer. As the experiment proceeded the volunteer was ordered to turn up the voltage progressively into the red-marked danger zone until the actor was screaming and begging to be released. After this had gone on long enough the actor remained silent, no matter how severe the "shocks", as if to suggest unconsciousness or death. Although many of the volunteers were clearly disturbed by the effects of the experiment, they continued to obey though they had to be constantly reassured, or pressured, that the Experimenter knew what he was doing, and that he would take full responsibility. In fact, 26 out of the 40 volunteers administered the shocks up to the maximum level, even after the actors had feigned losing consciousness – that's 65% of participants! In further experiments, in which Milgram used a wide variety of subjects with different economic, ethnic, and educational backgrounds, the results were the same. He wrote[58]:

> "The legal and philosophic aspects of obedience are of enormous import, but they say very little about how most people behave in concrete situations. I set up a simple experiment at Yale University to test how much pain an ordinary citizen would inflict on another person simply because he was ordered to by an experimental scientist. Stark authority was pitted against the subject's strongest moral imperatives against hurting others, and, with the subjects ears ringing with the screams of the victims, authority won more often than not. The extreme willingness of adults to go to almost any

---

[57] Stanley Milgram "Obedience to Authority: An Experimental View" (1974).

[58] Stanley Milgram "The Perils of Obedience" (1974)

> lengths on the command of an authority constitutes the chief finding of the study and the fact most urgently demanding explanation."

This is worth bearing in mind when it is said that people will not do anything that goes against their moral or religious principles while in a hypnotic trance. The reality is that 65% of people are willing and able to torture someone to unconsciousness or death without even the excuse of being in a trance state and that the particular *authority* can be established either voluntarily, such as in the case above or involuntarily in far more coercive situations.

A good example of subtle mass conditioning was demonstrated by the mentalist and magician Derren Brown in the Whitgift shopping mall in the UK. He used a series of announcements over the public address system, totaling around half an hour. The essence of the script is captured in the very last offering:

> "…we hope your shopping experience is an uplifting arm and I would like you bring to your pay attention to some very special offers today. Details of our special offers can be found handily by the lifts, so why not come right arm up and see for yourselves. These offers will only be available for a short period of time so all customers wishing to reach up and grab this exciting opportunity should do it NOW!"

Whereupon a significant percentage of the crowd raised their right arm, for reasons unknown to them. As he says:

> "I used the [public address system]… as a subtle form of authority, as people are not really paying much attention to it, their unconscious takes over."

We will see later that such conditioning is quite benign compared to what can, and has been done to people in the past. For now though, let's return to the more conventional hypnotic technique known as…

The Post Hypnotic Command

Or post hypnotic suggestion to give it a more neutral tone, is a command issued to the subject while they are in a trance condition that they are to carry out after the hypnotic session is apparently over and they have returned to normality.

A command given during hypnosis serves as the stimulus, and the act becomes the response. Both post hypnotic suggestion and conditioning serve a similar purpose except that the former is generally not established by repetitive trial and learning. Such an act is a complex task because it is related to some degree with the hypnotic induction, and is often carried out as the result of a single session of hypnosis. In addition it is more robust than a conditioned reflex in that it is both longer lasing and often more compelling. The act itself is probably a self-induced replica of the original hypnotic situation.

Mind Tools

Although a post hypnotic suggestion may last years, during this period deterioration occurs in the quality of the post hypnotic performance. However, regular reinforcement tends to increase its effectiveness, although interestingly repeated triggering does not weaken it. Completion of the command itself depends more upon the nature and the difficulty of the task than upon the depth of the hypnosis. If the fulfillment of the act is blocked by either internal mental factors or external circumstance profound anxiety may be produced. Therefore conventionally, a post hypnotic command should not be of a bizarre nature, but in keeping with the subject's needs, and goals. Traditionally the stages of creating such a state are as follows:

- Establishment of hypnotic state
- New Behaviors – Both direct and indirect suggestions are provided for the goal, which should be some form of behavior
- Amnesia – Both direct and indirect suggestions are offered to establish a state of amnesia.
- Deepening the trance state
- Ending the session on a positive note with a suggestion of well-being for the subject

While amnesia is not strictly necessary it does prevent an analytic reaction in the subject which may inhibit them. However, they can become aware of the original hypnotic command as they carry it out, or perhaps after completion.

Response to post hypnotic suggestions might be compared with the compulsive behavior noted in all of us at times. We know what we are doing, but do not know why. If the setting in which the post hypnotic suggestion occurs is altered, or if the expectant attitudes change between the time of the post hypnotic suggestion, and the time when it is about to be carried out, then deeply hypnotized persons can cancel even the original hypnotic suggestion.

Unless the subject is a volunteer for a stage hypnotist, ridiculous hypnotic suggestions are usually rejected. Most of these volunteers are exhibitionists and seldom mind carrying out hypnotic suggestions that are compatible with their usual or desired behavior. Whether or not a hypnotic suggestion is carried out also depends upon the wishes and the intentions of the subject. The type and the quality of the operator's communication also affect the response. When working with a subject in hypnosis, an extra-verbal approach such as, "You wouldn't mind opening the window after you come out of this relaxed state, would you?" minimizes resistance. If the post hypnotic suggestion is not followed, a remark such as, "It's stuffy inside. I wonder how we can get some fresh air in the room?" is usually effective. A cue of this type often reinforces a post hypnotic suggestion given during hypnosis. When a post hypnotic suggestion that is not fully in accord with the subject's desires is carried out, he usually rationalizes the unusual behavior.

Purposeless post hypnotic suggestions are as readily forgotten as other instructions given during non-hypnotic levels.

Before we move on to examining the efficacy and utility of post-hypnotic commands we need to look at a question that is often asked about hypnosis – namely, can someone be made to do something that goes against their moral sense? For example, could a law-abiding citizen be forced to carry out a criminal act under hypnosis, one that they would never normally countenance? The answer given by most hypnotherapists is "No", but the true situation is rather more complex and the truth, as usual, is rather conditional. One of the core problems is the question of how to set up an experimental scenario under ordinary conditions in order to determine the answer. If they refuse to go along with the hypnotic command to commit some particular act it is taken as evidence that it is not possible to coerce people under hypnosis. On the other hand people in a trance are actually aware on some level that they are in an experimental setting and that nothing really bad is going to be allowed to happen. This in effect gives them "permission" to go ahead and act out whatever scenario has been chosen and hence cannot be taken as good evidence. If the hypnotized person resists or does not carry out a post hypnotic command it does not necessarily mean that there is no effect nor that the person was not hypnotized. It may merely be that the depth is less than expected or hoped for and that the tendency to carry out the command may remain.

The general method for making someone do something that is possibly against their moral sense is to provide a scenario where such an action would not violate their sense of right and wrong. The crudest example would be getting someone to take off their clothes. A direct command to do so while they are in a trance state would likely fail if they had an aversion to doing so. However, if a scenario could be created where such a situation feels natural then a positive result is more likely. For example: that it is a hot day at the beach; that they are uncomfortably hot; that they would like to swim in the cool water; that they are alone; that nobody would mind; that nobody would find it unusual... and so forth. A somewhat simpler method is often used by (rather clever) criminals to hijack the trance of someone at a cash register and persuade them to hand over their employers money in a fraudulent manner. Those interested can search for this technique themselves

Remote Hypnotism

The following is a press statement[59] from the BBC issued in 1946.

> "Hypnotism by television has been tried on a closed circuit in the BBC studios at Alexandra Palace with such success that it has been considered dangerous to try it over the air. The experiment was carried out on

---

[59] BBC to the Press Association, London Offices of Provincial Papers and Feature Editors, 20 December 1946

Wednesday by Mr Peter Casson. Two tests were made. In the first about a dozen BBC staff volunteered to be hypnotized in the studio, and five of them went to sleep; but the most interesting point was that one person in a party watching a television screen in a darkened room across a corridor also fell under the hypnotic influence, although Mr Casson was not then addressing the viewing audience. In the second test Mr Casson made a direct attempt to hypnotize six people watching the screen in the darkened room. Four of them went to sleep and of these two needed waking up. Because of the success of this experiment and the consequent danger of hypnotizing viewers who might have no one at hand to wake them, it has been decided that a hypnotic television broadcast would not be advisable."

Which are guidelines that are still adhered to not only by the BBC but every major TV broadcaster across the world. The reasons are obvious, namely that if even one person in a million were adversely affected the cost of the subsequent lawsuits would vastly outweigh any conceivable revenue such a program might generate. As we see above, the number of people deeply affected could run into the hundreds of thousands and although most might simply lapse into sleep even this could have devastating consequences if, for example, they were smoking at the time. Out of those hundreds of thousands one could reasonably expect injuries and even deaths, and certainly claims of such.

The most familiar form of remote hypnosis occurs in the form of audio or video courses designed to alter specific aspects of behavior. Popular ones include stopping smoking and losing weight. Almost invariably they are sold as "self-hypnosis" courses, which may be technically accurate if one is indulging in theorizing about the state itself but is certainly not self-hypnosis in the accepted sense of the term given that someone else is doing the talking and proffering the suggestions. Of course, such inductions cannot be as effective as one to one therapies as there is no feedback between the hypnotist and subject. It is, in effect, a pre-programmed one to many induction which is essentially very similar to group inductions.

While such pre-recordings lose out to some extent by not being perceptive and interactive they excel in precision and persistence. A recording can go on for hours without the tiredness that would soon become apparent in a Human operator. It can also be engineered in fine detail, which is very difficult for all but the most skilled Human to manage when speaking live even if from a script.

However, what can be accomplished with great efficacy remotely is re-induction into the hypnotic state through the use of post-hypnotic suggestions anchored to particular triggers that can be communicated from afar via various channels both familiar and unusual. These are covered in depth in the next chapter that examines subliminal techniques. Finally, in theory it is possible to have a very versatile series of scripts under computer control with the subject hooked up to biofeedback equipment to create something approaching the skill of a Human hypnotist. The biofeedback may not even be apparent to the subject since radar can remotely monitor heart rate and breathing, cameras monitor the pupil size of the eyes and thermal imagers monitor and map the body temperature in real time. In fact, given the technical abilities described in the next chapter a totally covert hypnotic trance may be induced in subjects from afar without their knowledge or co-operation. The fact that only very limited information exists concerning experiments using the above suggests that much of the progress in that field remains classified. More in the chapter on subliminal techniques.

Now we move on to the "dark side", so if you are an aspiring Cult Leader this is for you. For the rest of us, we can call it "group bonding".

Brainwaves and Entrainment

What are commonly referred to as brainwaves are the gross electrical activity that can be picked up by electrodes on the scalp, most commonly using an electroencephalogram, or EEG, machine. They are the overall pattern created by billions of brain cells firing during mental activity. In general the higher the frequency the more information the brain is processing. Although the actual boundaries depend on who is doing the classifying they are generally as follows, starting with the highest frequency:

- **Gamma** – 24 Hz upwards
  Associated with perception and consciousness, researchers have recognized that higher level cognitive activities occur when lower frequency gamma waves suddenly double into the 40 Hz range. They are continuously present during low voltage fast neo-cortical activity (LVFA), which occurs during the process of awakening and during REM sleep. It is believed that Gamma activity occurs during efficient communications across large swaths of brain tissue and it has been hypothesized that consciousness is associated with a frequency of around 40 Hz.

- **Beta** – 13 to 24 Hz
  These are the fastest waves, most commonly found during our waking state and are associated with high states of mental process especially during stimulating arousal such as fear, anger, worry, surprise etc. At the highest frequencies this is the brain trying to extract as much information as possible from the senses as a matter of urgency. However, lower Beta is normal in a fully awake fully focused mind.

- **Alpha** – 7 to 13 Hz
  Associated with the non-drowsy, relaxed and tranquil but alert state of consciousness. Mostly easily attained during meditation with the eyes closed and which facilitates body/mind integration. They are indicative of lack of visual processing and lack of focus. They also tend to be present during daydreaming. If you close your eyes and do not do any deep thinking they

will usually be quite strong. It is this state that experienced Zen meditators enter initially before moving down to the Theta.

- **Theta** – 4 to 7 Hz
  Associated with increased recall, creativity, imagery, unconstrained thought, inspiration, drowsiness and are also present during dreaming and Rapid Eye Movement (REM) dream states. Theta is also the state associated with lucid dreaming, hypnotic states, Psi effects and manifestations (most notably Remote Viewing), out of body experiences and astral projection.

- **Delta** – below 4 Hz
  Associated with deep dreamless sleep or very deep trance and non-REM sleep.

For our purposes clearly the most interesting area is the Theta state and the techniques that can be utilized for attaining this. These generally rely on a well-known phenomenon called entrainment where the brainwaves tend to move towards, or lock onto, sensory information that contains a significant component of information at the relevant frequency. Typically and at its crudest this can be done by looking at a flashing light or listening to sounds pulsed at the desired brain state frequency. However, this effect is not limited to those senses and can occur through touch or even direct stimulation of the brain by electric or magnetic fields. It can also be accomplished electrically through the skin either by augmenting the sense of touch, for example by pulsing a current through the fingers, or directly via electrodes on the scalp in a kind of reverse EEG. However, the most common methods rely on sight and sound, although we will be returning to the more exotic techniques later.

There are a number of other phenomena associated with various entrainment frequencies that might be of interest for personal development. These are:

- Specific frequencies can stimulate certain glands to produce desired hormones.

- Beta-endorphin has been modulated in studies using alpha-theta brain wave training where biofeedback techniques have allowed the users to control their own brain states consciously.
  Endorphins are the "natural opiates" that produce analgesia, a sense of wellbeing and are responsible for the so-called "runners high".

- Dopamine release can also be modulated with binaural tones.
  This neurotransmitter is often associated with the pleasure system of the brain providing feelings of enjoyment and reinforcement to motivate a person to perform certain activities. It is also released by naturally pleasurable activities such as eating, sex and some drugs including cocaine, nicotine and amphetamines.

- Some people find that half an hour in the Theta state can reduce the need for sleep by up to four hours.
- The Theta state is also associated with increased learning ability and decreased filtering by the left hemisphere of the brain. In other words, the logical part of the brain does not impede the process as it otherwise might.

Photic Driving

WARNING! – A major drawback with these technologies, most especially the visually oriented ones, is the possibility of inducing epileptic fits in susceptible people[60]. Several studies have shown that the probability of a seizure being triggered in photosensitives peaks at around 18 Hz and guidelines for the entertainment industry in the UK suggest no more than 30 second intervals at 8 Hz or faster. Having said that the percentage of people so affected is very small. Additionally, it also seems to depend on the degree of contrast and saturation of the visual field. Watching a small light flickering on the edge of ones vision in a brightly lit room will have far less effect than a high power strobe in the dark. Additionally, some frequencies can have deleterious effects. For example, around 6.3 Hz to 6.6 Hz there is an effect that is referred to as *Hemispheric Desynchronization*. Symptoms include confusion, anxiety, slowed reaction times, depression and insomnia and occur in several modalities apart from the photic. Anyway…

Photic Driving is the practice of using strobe effects to entrain brainwaves via the visual field. Frequencies are the usual, ranging from 1 Hz to 40 Hz and were first investigated in the 1930s. However, such stimulation has become popular in recent years with the advent of LED technology to provide compact, cool and rapidly switchable light sources of different colors. They are used in many so-called *Mind or Dream Machines* that are designed for just this purpose, often with accompanying binaural sound.

The traditional color has been red, partly because red LEDs were available years before other colors and partly because red light penetrates the eyelids particularly well enabling the eyes to be closed rather than open. Nowadays there is no problem getting other colors of sufficient power to penetrate through simple intensity. The effects of various colors have been noted and although not spectacular they are worth bearing in mind. For example, Komatsu[61] has found that red light produces optimal EEG driving in the 17-18Hz band. Green increased 15Hz activity, while blue enhanced 10-13Hz as well as accentuating emotion. White showed main peaks at 18-19Hz. In another study, he found that yellow light would

---

[60] This effect has been investigated, coupled with low frequency sound, as a possible weapons technology under the name Photic Driver.

[61] Komatsu, Hiroshi. Studies on the temporal frequency characteristics of vision by photic driving method: III. Temporal frequency characteristics of color vision. Tohoku Psychologica Folia. 1987 vol. 46(1-4) 1-12.

drive at either the red or green peak, or both. Similar results have been obtained by other with red light achieving maximum drive efficiency above 15 Hz, yellow at 13 Hz, green at 10.5Hz, blue at 9Hz and indigo/violet in the Theta and Delta range. Even without being pulsed colored light can produce significant effects on EEG activity. Notably, alpha amplitude was suppressed substantially more in subjects exposed to red light than those exposed to blue. This may be due to the red light generally increasing vigilance through traditional associations.

Physiologically the left eye is connected to the brain's right hemisphere and the right eye to the left, so it is possible to feed differing signals to each part of the brain by focusing light from multiple LEDs on each eye and driving them accordingly. For example, the lights can be pulsed at different frequencies, or on and off at the same time, or one on while the other is off and so forth. Other effects can be obtained by phasing the lights to mimic movement across the visual field. Whether the waveform used to drive the LED is a sine wave or square wave does not seem to make much difference especially at the higher frequencies due to the phenomenon known as the persistence of vision whereby high-speed events tend to blur together visually. At the low frequency end, where we are especially interested, a sine wave is probably less annoying and distracting. Having said all that it appears that the more complex patterns may not be substantially more effective than the simple ones. In addition the requirement for a complex headset under computer or other programmed control renders it less useful for group work.

However, more useful in a group setting would be a background low intensity strobed illumination, probably delivered indirectly by using a high intensity red LED to project against a wall or ceiling. This can be linked to electronics delivering sonics at the same frequency and variable phase. As we will see later, this could be combined with modulated Pink Noise and possibly low level magnetic fields all emanating from the same device. It is also possible to use a computer in this manner, using the illuminated screen to provide the light source and the speakers the sound. As we will see later a lot more can be done using a computer.

One ugly possibility that has already been tried on a website dedicated to the problems of living with epilepsy involved hacking it and substituting pages containing code designed to trigger epileptic fits or at least nausea in its viewers. More sophisticated opportunities for subliminals obviously present themselves in this medium.

Sonics and Binaural Tones

The most ancient sonic technique for inducing altered states of consciousness is drumming. This is effective for a number of reasons beyond the obvious one of rhythmic sound. Primarily the low frequencies involved are felt as well as heard and this results in a tactile entrainment process in addition to the aural. Also, for the person doing the drumming, there is a feedback loop being created where the motor control required to beat out the rhythm adds other dimensions to the entrainment process. These processes range from proprioreceptor (the sense that lets us know the position of our limbs) to the muscular shaking of the entire body to the kind of participation found in the indirect method of hypnotic inductions previously discussed. However, what it is not good for is engaging in, or focusing on, anything complex in a group setting besides drumming. In the past such crude consciousness altering techniques precede, or follow, the actual detail of the working. To maintain such a state throughout a complex procedure we need a different set of aural technologies.

Probably the most useful is that of binaural tones, a very flexible and somewhat safer approach to entrainment than flashing lights. The basis of this technology is the feeding of two different tones into the ears using a stereo soundtrack and a headset while listening in a relaxed manner. It is based on the fact that if a pure sine wave at a frequency of (say) 440Hz is fed into the left ear and another pure sine wave at 444Hz is fed into the other the brain perceives the difference. That is a 4Hz signal which is not actually there, and starts to lock to it after a few minutes of exposure pulling one into a Theta state. Of course, the frequencies above are only examples, and the 440Hz was chosen simply because it sounds pleasant, although many people prefer Middle C to A.

Now this is actually quite remarkable for a reason that is not at all obvious. For example, if the same signal is played over speakers then the same sound is heard as through the headset, namely a pulsing of the tone. This is because when both frequencies mix on the eardrum the mechanical effect is to produce a rising and a falling in amplitude. The same thing occurs if a mono microphone is used to record the stereo sound from the speakers. However, the situation is quite different over the headset. If one side of the headset is lifted off the head then only a pure tone will be heard in the other ear, and vice versa. The mixing in this case is not mechanical and does not occur in the ear. It occurs deep in the brain *after* the sound has been converted to neural impulses. This is the major reason why using a headset is so effective with this technique.

Of course, the above is only the most basic binaural technique. Slightly more sophisticated is the use of secondary modulations. So, for example, instead of having a fixed 4Hz difference signal and having the brain home in on it one can vary the difference signal gradually from (say) a Beta to a Theta frequency over a period of minutes. That way it catches the brain in its normal state, locks it and then pulls it into the desired state by tracking it all the way down. Other techniques involve multiple tones either simultaneously or varying in dominance depending on what state is required. This has the effect of targeting different areas of the brain, closing some down and stimulating others. However, the precise effects of multiple modulations is beyond the scope of this chapter, partly because of the complexity of the topic, partly because there is little in the way of published material and partly because what is available tends to be proprietary technology.

One common practice, used for people who are not regular users of binaural technology or meditators, is to take the fundamental frequency down into the deep Theta or high Delta for only a few minutes before raising it to a higher level, and repeating this process. This is because inexperienced operators find the deep states difficult to maintain even with such aids. Repeatedly immersing them in the deepest state and bringing them out of it has the same effect as repeated hypnosis in that it facilitates the rapid deepening of the state and makes the whole process very effective. As for what it feels like, that depends on particular frequencies. One of the most basic and useful of the deep states occurs at 4 Hz at the border of Theta and Delta. This takes one into a waking dream state where not only does unconscious imagery appear, but one can consciously interact with it. At the same time awareness of the body is lost. This is often called the *body asleep mind awake* state. This can be a very effective state in which to facilitate healing of the body.

Another common practice is to mask the binaural tones with other material. This is usually done because some people find the pure tones annoying or distracting, a bit like tinnitus. The most common mask used is Pink Noise or related sounds such as rain or waterfalls. This too can be modulated for additional effects. Music is also not uncommon, but this should be chosen so that the basic frequencies involved, such as the beat, do not conflict with the state one is trying to attain. This is one reason why rather bland New Age music, which has no strong underlying beat, is a favourite with this technique.

Although binaural tones can be used on their own they are generally part of a package that includes hypnotic inductions and/or subliminal audio or more rarely visual data. The tones are very effective in shifting the subject into a particular mental state while not being overly intrusive, unlike photic driving. This means that they can be used to set the state, and hold it, while other work of a magickal nature is undertaken. The only minor complication with group work is the requirement for a distributed audio system whereby numerous headsets can be driven from one source. The benefits for group work can be substantial because not only are all the members of the group in the same mental state but the brainwaves of every member are in the exact same phase. The results can be likened to a psychic laser.

The Theta state can also be a powerful aid to visualization, as it is quite close to that entered when Lucid Dreaming. However, it is considerably easier since the tones tend to hold you in that hypnogogic region. So, the benefits available as part of the visualization process can be amplified, whether it is casting a Sigil or creating a self directed healing process.

Personality Reconstruction

A lot of research has gone into this in both civilian and military fields for either psychiatric use or for what is commonly known as brainwashing. Its use in magickal operations is mainly confined to creating a common belief system within the group. This, of course, is the classic "Cult Brainwashing" so beloved by the sensationalist media and is also an integral part of traditional occult initiation rituals, especially multistaged ones over a period of days. There are essentially three stages involved in reconstructing, rebuilding or recreating a subject's personality. These are:

- Making fluid the current worldview
- Changing the worldview
- Fixing the new worldview in place

The first stage involves breaking down resistance to change by reducing the critical faculties through information overload, confusion or distraction and is directly comparable to a type of hypnotic induction. Techniques used to break down the subject include, but are not limited to the following, with a brief description of how they are used in a group magickal context:

- **Inducing anxiety and/or terror**
  This has always been a traditional feature of many initiations where the acolyte has to undergo a supposedly dangerous ordeal. Of course, in a more military or interrogation setting this is easily accomplished by mock executions, beatings, torture and so forth.

- **Isolation**
  This can vary from a social isolation where previous friends or colleagues distance themselves from the subject, to literal isolation and sensory deprivation.

- **Sleep deprivation**
  Again, another very traditional ingredient which results in a reduction of the ability to think logically, heightens the emotions and can cause hallucinations and hypnogogic imagery.

- **Starvation**
  This alters the body's biochemistry and has the effect of initially sharpening the senses as well as the obvious effect of chronic discomfort.

- **Sexual frustration**
  Again, quite a common theme in some initiations. For example, the ritual use of sexual techniques such as Tantra that focus on non-completion of the act, or the more common use of nudity.

- **Inducing shame and/or guilt**
  More common in cult settings where the subject has to offer up self criticism and answer all questions put to them in a truthful manner, no matter how personal. In some groups the candidate has to reveal information of a damaging nature that can be held over them as a guarantee of their loyalty. This can also include committing criminal acts for the same purpose as part of the rite.

Mind Tools

- **Drugs**
  As we have seen elsewhere, drugs can be very useful tools in rapidly creating the above states of mind. They range from hallucinogens such as LSD or various mushrooms to those whose effect is massive disorientation such as Scopolamine, traditionally part of the Belladonna preparation used by medieval witches as a "flying ointment".

- **Humiliation**
  The use of personal information or history to emphasize the subject's failings and inadequacies. However, in more coercive settings this can include far more directly abusive practices, including sexual.

The second stage involves defusing much of the tension and anxiety generated by the above and providing something to focus on. It is at this point that the subject relaxes to the point of trance. They becomes weak, both physically and mentally. They lack strong beliefs and standards and their logical faculties give way to wishful thinking, leaving them in a state unable to distinguish fantasy and reality. They become dependent on authority having regressed to a childlike state. At this point the methods used to achieve this state include, but are not limited to the following:

- **Meditation**
  Especially guided meditation in a deepened trance state

- **Repetitive movements**
  Which can be anything from arbitrary ritual gestures to marching or other group activity.

- **Dance**
  Either individually or as part of the group. This can also be used to induce physical exhaustion, boosting of endorphins etc.

- **Chanting**
  Especially of slogans or simple statement and response as occur in traditional religious settings.

- **Music**
  Particularly rhythmic, monotonous and hypnotic. Alternatively group singing.

- **Body manipulations**
  Ranging from massage, either standard or sexual ("love bombing") to group hugs etc.

- **Hyperventilation**
  Generally either induced directly upon instruction with metronomic precision, or as part of breathing exercises during meditation.

- **Feasting and celebration**
  Especially if starvation/fasting has been used in the first stage. However, drugs should not be used since the subject's mind needs to be kept in an intellectually responsive state. The possible exception might be the use of an empathogen such as MDMA aka "Ecstasy" that tends to facilitate emotionally strong bonding.

- **Magick Theater**
  That is, the acting out of the group ideology in a ritual play with the subject being the focus of attention.

At this point the subject tends to be cooperative and focused on the leader of the process as well as being extremely receptive to new ideas. By controlling all aspects of the subject's state of mind, senses, setting and emotions, experiences will begin to be interpreted in a way consistent with the new belief system. Personality reconstruction is facilitated by more severe stresses and the use of trance states for additional changes to be reinforced by the environment. The final stage consists of reinforcement of the new beliefs and identification with the group and is accomplished by a number of techniques, normally requiring physical isolation. These include, but are not limited to, the following:

- **Continued control**
  ... of the subject's emotions, information and behavior.

- **Isolation**
  ...from reminders of the "old life".

- **Induction into a shared group symbolism.**
  This can involve elements of dress

- **Presentation of new role models.**
  For example, with cults it is typically the founder and/or current leader. In wider contexts it can be exemplars in the form of prophets or "the enlightened".

- **New activities.**
  It is this that is the key element in cementing the changes and preventing the subject "backsliding" into their old life.

In addition, the new identity sense usually reverts if the person is removed from the isolated group and returned to their former environment. The active participation of the individual in new activities for the group is a key element. Personality factors conducive to strong influence:

- Lack of self confidence
- Low IQ
- Reliance on authority in terms of beliefs

- Conformity
- Moral certainty
- Dogmatism
- Identity confusion
- A history of "joining in" and/or "true belief"
- External, rather than internal, focus

These are entirely different from the traits associated with hypnotic susceptibility, such as "fantasy proneness". How effectively we can adopt a new identity depends on a number of factors:

- **Role expectations**
  What we expect the role to entail.

- **Role perception**
  How we see the role in our own minds

- **Role demands**
  What is required to fulfill the role.

- **Role-taking aptitude or skill**
  Whether we are any good at it!

- **Self-role congruence**
  Whether we can see ourselves in the role in a positive manner. This is probably the most important factor.

- **Reinforcement properties of the audience**
  Whether those around us primarily relate to us in that role.

The people who are best at resisting change often have very similar personalities to those who are most susceptible. The major difference is the willingness to cooperate in the process, which can be induced through promises or reward or punishment. This is similar to the case in hypnosis where many people appear incapable of making use of hypnosis because they are unable to trust the hypnotist enough to cooperate in the induction. However, the above processes can be far more coercive than those any hypnotist is likely to use and as such are differentiated from hypnosis.

False Memory Creation

A few years ago there was a spate of reports of people who had allegedly recovered repressed memories of childhood abuse. Some of these memories included extremely bizarre items involving Satanic rituals, Human sacrifice, UFO abductions, multiple repressed personalities and more commonly, sexual abuse by family members. The memories were detailed and the subjects convinced that they were true – even when in many cases it was proved beyond doubt that they were not. More than a few psychotherapists made a name for themselves, and considerable money, helping people with genuine psychological problems recover these memories. So, what was happening?

Subsequent investigation by more scientifically minded psychologists discovered that actually implanting false memories or even alternate personalities is remarkably easy, either unconsciously or deliberately. The process is fairly simple, and again a key feature is the rapport established between therapist[62] and subject. In terms of procedure this is how it is accomplished:

- **Controller Conviction**
  The controller or therapist must act as if the false memories exist and are real.

- **Misinformation**
  It works best if the false memories are tied to real ones. That is, real events in the past are used as a starting point upon which are built the false memories. This is often accomplished by asking leading questions about the primary events. So, in the case of a witness to a (genuine) crime the questions can be blatantly skewed: "Did you also happen to see a tall man in a green colored jacket nearby... think carefully".

- **Imagination and Reenactment**
  This is where the subject is asked to imagine the scenario again, but this time with the false information tagged on: "Imagine you are seeing the crime again... imagine seeing a man in a green jacket... does it seem more familiar now, more possible?"

- **Repetition**
  Simply keep going over the same events with the false information, again and again.

- **Conditioning**
  Supply a reward for saying the right thing, and punishment for "getting it wrong". It can be as simple as a smile for parroting the false information, or alternatively (in our crime scenario) a policeman saying something like: "Do you want to see the guy get away with this?" in a disapproving tone of voice.

In practice all of this would be combined into a smooth format that is essentially a hypnotic induction with all the tricks and frills suggested elsewhere in the book. Finally, if in magick the past is purely what is remembered, and memory can be altered so easily, where is the reality?

---

[62] As Ian Read mentioned, would you like to hang up a business sign that said: "The Rapist" or even "Psycho The Rapist"? (Therapist) A joke...

Mind Tools

Sensory Deprivation

Involves, as the name suggests, depriving one or more senses of stimuli. The most immediate method is to remove sight and sound through the use of blindfold and earmuffs, or confinement in a dark and quiet room. For more complete sensory curtailment one can remove the sense of touch, smell, taste, heat and gravity. The usual method is through the use of a darkened and sound insulated flotation tank, which is filled with a saturated solution of Magnesium Sulfate to provide buoyancy and which is maintained at body temperature. Somewhat cruder is the use of soft mittens and clothes on a soft bed or reclining chair.

The effect of removing one sense is to heighten awareness of the others as the brain seeks information to process. So when sight is removed typically the focus shifts primarily to sound. When that is removed, touch is emphasized and so forth. This is the theory behind the use of sensory deprivation in classical laboratory parapsychology experiments – that as the other senses are removed Psi input comes to the fore.

The method most commonly used is the Ganzfeld Experiment where an unpatterned, information free, visual field is presented. Typically this is created by covering the eyes with a translucent plastic and flooding them with red light. The Ganzfeld Effect occurs when the brain cuts off the information-free signals from the eyes. The brain then amplifies neural noise in order to look for the missing visual signals which are then interpreted in the higher visual cortex, giving rise to hallucinations. Those hallucinations obviously contain imagery thrown up by the unconscious, and may contain information obtained by extra-sensory channels. The experimental protocol is as follows: A headset is used both to exclude external sounds and if necessary deliver an overlay of White Noise or Pink Noise and occasionally verbal commands. In telepathy experiments the "receiver" spends approximately 30 minutes in a state of increasing sensory deprivation during which time a "sender" observes a randomly chosen target and tries to transmit this information to the mind of the receiver. Results to date have generally been positive but as with all Psi phenomena critics have claimed otherwise, citing faulty procedure or statistical analysis. Where they have failed to debunk positive results the usual response is to claim that more work is needed before any such effects can be taken as proven.

However, such academic bickering is less important to us than the possibility that we have here an important technique that can be used to amplify Psi effects. As such it can be used as a general purpose tool and adjunct to other technologies described in this book, from Remote Viewing to Hypnosis to generating PK effects and in demonological work.

Visualization

Creative visualization is an incredibly powerful technique for honing all kinds of skills both mental and physical as well as engineering states of consciousness. To give just one example of its power, research shows that it can actually strengthen muscles[63]. Scientists from the Cleveland Clinic Foundation in Ohio investigated the strength benefits of imagining exercising a muscle. They reported that just thinking about exercise in a focused manner actually increased muscle strength in a group of subjects, in some cases up to 50%. Measurements of the brain activity during visualization sessions indicate that these strength gains were due to improvements in the brain's ability to signal muscle activity. This of course partially explains why such techniques have become an important part of athletics and sports training regimes, albeit mixed with actual physical exercise. The general message seems to be that if you can *really* visualize yourself doing something, you stand a much better chance of being successful when the time to actually perform arrives.

So, how do we use this information to enhance magickal workings? Well, the first thing to do is rehearse whatever ritual we intend to perform by running through a script, both mentally and physically performing the outline of the timing and actions. However, we can go far deeper than that using techniques outlined in later chapters. For example, we can use one of the many trance inductions and/or subliminal messaging to "prime" the group to a degree of hyper-reality where the actual visualization gradually becomes the magickal working itself. Since the key element of all magick is belief, that too can be strengthened by mental role playing games whereby we pretend we believe in a particular type of reality. Essentially, the use of visualization is only limited by our imagination.

Lucid Dreaming

The *Lucid Dream* state arises when you "wake up" within a dream and know that you are dreaming. During this state the dreamer can take control of events and even mold the dream world to their wishes. The level of detail can be astonishing. In one episode I realized I was in a dream and started to examine the surroundings to the extent I knelt down on the ground and checked every blade of grass passing through my fingers along with the grains of soil that held them without finding a flaw. Usually the state is precipitated by something happening within the dream that is so incongruous that it shocks me "awake", for example, being able to fly. On the other hand I have great difficulty reading text within the dream. Signs would change their wording, newspapers change their headline and the small print would blur, presumably because the part of my brain either generating or perceiving the information was still not fully online. However, this is not true of all lucid dreamers and some more skilled than myself have no such issues at all. Another problem is

---

[63] Neuropsychologia. 2004;42(7):944-56.

prolonging the state since after a while one of two things happens. Either there is a loss of consciousness and the normal dream resumes, or one wakes up. However, in recent years a considerable amount of research has been done and a number of interesting and useful techniques invented for induction, communication and control of the lucid dream state.

As a scientifically verified psychological phenomenon lucid dreaming appeared during the 1970s when it was linked to Rapid Eye Movement (REM) sleep, and methods were developed to communicate from the dreamscape to the real world, typically by having the dreamer control their eye movements. There are a number of induction techniques that have been developed, ranging from the simple to the complex. These are:

- **Dream Recall**
  The simplest way to increase the number of lucid dreams is to make a point of remembering each dream on awakening. However, this is not as easy as it might seem because the details of the dream fades very rapidly. Nevertheless, there are two ways of preventing, or limiting, this fading. The first is to speak aloud the content of the dream which has the effect of firming it up in normal memory. The second is to keep a dream diary by the side of the bed and immediately write down the details. This latter method is particularly useful in later analysis, perhaps months or years later especially if one is interested in the possibility of precognitive dreams.

- **Reality Testing**
  In dreams all kind of bizarre things happen, and we accept them as somehow being normal. As we have seen, the unconscious can quite easily persuade even normal waking consciousness to ignore strange, unexpected or inconsistent phenomena so it should not come as a surprise that this is even more pronounced when the conscious mind is totally shut down. However by deliberately testing for a particular inconsistency on a regular basis during the waking state, say by testing every hour or so, this pattern can quite often be carried over to the dream state where the anomalies will hopefully be so unexpected that it triggers a lucid state. One of the commonest techniques is to look at a section of text, look away, and see whether the text has changed. If it has, you are dreaming.

- **Mnemonic Induction**
  Mnemonic induction is a complex name for a fairly trivial procedure, which is simply to state the intention to have a lucid dream before, or as, one goes to sleep.

- **Wake Initiated Lucid Dream**
  The Wake Initiated Lucid Dream (WILD) procedure starts by waking after about 5 or 6 hours. Normally REM sleep occurs during the latter part of the sleep cycle and it is this that is associated with lucid dreaming. After waking

the idea is to stay conscious until dream imagery starts to form during the hypnogogic state. It is at this point that control over the state should be attempted by guiding the content of the imagery as far as possible. It should be noted that this is not a method for those people who cannot get back to sleep easily once they have awoken. If the opposite is true and there is a tendency to slip into unconsciousness a mild stimulant can be taken, usually caffeine or Theobromine, found in chocolate. In this case one has to stay awake long enough for the drugs to take effect, usually after about half an hour.

- **Cycle Adjustment**
Cycle adjustment needs a bit more discipline. It requires that the person wakes about 90 minutes earlier than normal until their sleep cycle starts to adjust to the new time. They then alternate awaking earlier and at the normal time. This results in the body being ready to wake while still in the sleep state, and hence increasing the chance of lucidity.

- **Nap Induced Lucid Dream**
Nap induction is similar but no attempt is made to return to sleep until 1 or 2 hours have passed.

- **Reward and Punishment**
Reward and punishment are fairly crude reinforcement methods that are simple to apply. If you have a successful lucid episode then explicitly reward yourself, preferably with something that offers an immediate pleasure, such as food. On the other hand, if the attempt at lucidity fails then create a punishment that is just as basic, for example pain, or a cold shower.

- **Machine Induction**
Machine induction is the most technically complex of the techniques, but also one of the most effective. Typically it relies on REM sleep being detected, either by electrical or infra-red signals from a light emitting diode being modulated by the eye movement, and a sensory input being created. This is generally either a flashing light, a sound or a vibration that will usually be incorporated into the dream to signal the dreamer that they are dreaming. Such devices can be small enough to be attached to a headband, although there is a risk of dislodging it as the sleep state progresses. Another method is to use binaural tones to induce a deep theta brainwave state which holds the user in a hypnogogic state partway between sleep and consciousness. While not technically lucid dreaming this can be viewed as a practice conducive to developing the mental focus required for it, and is a valuable trance technology in its own right, as discussed elsewhere.

- **Drugs and Supplements**
The list of various drugs and supplements which are conducive to lucid dreaming is so long as to be almost useless. Indeed, it may well be that

taking one of them triggers a placebo effect unrelated to the chemical itself. However, at its crudest one can use stimulants and depressants, for example caffeine and alcohol, to modulate the depth of sleep so that it is neither too deep nor too shallow. Not surprisingly drugs that have a mild hallucinogenic effect such as the cough suppressant Dextromethorphan (DXM), and Dimethyaminoethanol (DMAE) are reported to be somewhat effective, as have Paroxetine and Mirtazapine. The problem is that almost all research on this topic is taking place outside of the medical establishment and only gets reported as unsubstantiated anecdotal evidence. Unless you really know what you are doing and are prepared to document the effects (and often serious side effects) scientifically the benefits are likely to be marginal. There is no lucid dreaming wonder drug, as yet, and certainly none of the ones commonly encountered either in medicine or illegally on the street.

Finally, there is the question of how to prolong the state if it seems it is returning towards the unconscious dream or the waking world. The latter occurs if the dreamer becomes excited, perhaps by the novelty of the experience. First, try to become calm and then try what is probably the most common method, which is to spin around, or at least move about. Also rubbing the hands together can help. In fact, anything that reinforces the reality of the dream world. The technique of spinning around is also the most common method of changing the dreamscape. However, there are plenty of other techniques. For example, simply expecting what you want around the next corner, or the other side of a closed door can work well, as can crossing a bridge. In fact crossing or passing through any kind of real world delineating barrier will do.

So, interesting as it may be, why should one bother to lean to dream lucidly? A number of reasons:

- **Fun**
  You are creating your own world with your own rules and enjoying the most comprehensive and immersive Virtual Reality experience this side of the Singularity[64].

- **Healing**
  Healing can involve both simple and complex operations. For example, one can deal with phobias in a perfectly controlled environment and use the surroundings to de-sensitize and reduce or eliminate the phobic reaction. This may seem an overly complex way of dealing with, say, fear of spiders, but if it is fear of heights it is a lot safer than going to high places in the waking world to do the same. If you fall to your death in a lucid dream the most that happens is there is a shock on impact that jerks you awake. A more complex use is for physical healing of an ailing body. It has long been known that visualization exercises can have a profound effect on the body,

---

[64] The point in history where the rate of technological advance renders all Human futures, even short term ones, unpredictable. Discussed in depth later.

and lucid dreaming is the most perfect visualization tool available anywhere. One can move to parts of the body that are diseased and "remove" the disease in the dream state. What happens then is that the immune system appears to be altered in order to create the reality. Exactly how powerful such techniques are is unknown apart from anecdotal evidence and much research remains to be done. However, many practitioners can personally attest to its efficacy at least with minor illnesses. It is also possible to use lucid dreaming to cope with bereavement, since one may get to talk with the departed in a similar manner to the Psychomanteum, but in more natural surroundings.

- **Physical and Mental Skill Development**
The use of lucid dreaming to develop physical skills is not something that has been explored in great depth, probably because of the lack of knowledge of this state as a training tool in athletics. However, it has been recognized for several decades that visualization can be very useful in learning complex movements, and even in building muscle. The body responds to some extent as if it were real exercise. Lucid dreaming combines a type of placebo effect with the benefits of a realistic simulation environment. Hence, if you practice skiing in your dream the body memory will carry over into real life, all without the drawbacks of accident and injury, thanks to the fact that during dreaming the motor cortex of the brain that controls movement is inhibited. This is Nature's way of protecting the dreamer by preventing the body from acting out the dream physically, with all its possible dangers. Of course, this is not a perfect safety mechanism since it does sometimes break down, resulting in sleepwalking. Occasionally this sleep paralysis persists after consciousness returns and can be a disturbing, if brief, experience since it is often accompanied by feeling of pressure on the chest and possibly roaring or buzzing sounds. This seems to occur rather more often as a side effect of lucid dreaming than with natural dreaming. In the past this phenomenon has been interpreted as an attack by a supernatural entity, for example a succubus or incubus in Western mythology, and can be made even more frightening if there is still dream imagery in the hypnogogic state that can adapt to the fear response. All that is required to overcome it is to relax, regulate the breathing, center oneself and allow some time for the brain to fully awaken. If this does occur it can be valuable mental training and testing in itself, especially with respect to any later explorations into the realms of demonology by the TechnoMage.

- **Exploration of the unconscious**
In many ways this resembles the shamanic technique of the guided journey, where the subject is led on a journey through various inner realms using scripted progressive relaxation hypnosis resulting in a light trance and enhanced imagination. However, the direction is different in that the lucid

dream state is arrived at from full sleep, while the guided journey begins from being fully awake. Also, by its very nature lucid dreaming is a deeper state of trance, if it can be called that. Nevertheless, the aims are similar in that the subject seeks to interact with Beings who can impart knowledge or perform certain tasks. We will, for the time being, assume that such entities are purely aspects of the dreamer's unconscious and have no overt external origin.

Most of the people one meets in the dream state are predictable extensions of the waking psyche. In other words, people will speak and act in a manner consistent with expectations, and seemingly have no "independent" existence. The really interesting people or creatures are the ones that can communicate non obvious information or opinions. It is these that represent true aspects of the unconscious, and in order to facilitate such meetings it is best to plan the journey beforehand rather than just dream and see who or what arrives on the scene. For example, it can be very useful to meet real people that you already know in the waking world in order to extract information from them, or at least information that your unconscious may have acquired which has not filtered through to the conscious mind. Another possibility is creating internal avatars of your waking self which can be given instructions to operate on parts of your mind normally inaccessible. Again, this has significant healing potential as well as the ability to alter various facets of personality such as ingrained habits.

- **Psi Training**
Finally there is the use of lucid dreaming to amplify Psi phenomena, especially Remote Viewing and Remote Influencing. The former is in fact identical to what occultists call Astral Projection or the Out Of Body Experience (OOBE) when it occurs in the immediate vicinity of the dreamer, both in time and space. When it occurs in the future it becomes the essence of the precognitive dream. However, the actual information being retrieved may still be overlayed with considerable symbolism requiring interpretation which in turn necessitates a deep self knowledge. The telepathic potential has not been overlooked either, especially with respect to what is called "mutual dreaming" where two or more people arrange to meet during the state. Or perhaps contacting past of future versions of oneself, or selves dreaming in parallel universes.

To summarize, many of the techniques described in this book can augment, or be augmented by, lucid dreaming. It is a very useful tool for the TechnoMage.

Cold Reading and Selling

While not in itself a collection of techniques to alter consciousness I have decided to include *Cold Reading* and some of the psychological tricks[65] associated with selling, whether of products or ideas. The reason being that as we focus on groups quite often we need to persuade people to adopt a similar belief system, or in extreme cases, belief in the individual leading the group. As such, the use of these techniques can be considered somewhat unethical unless they are explained to the group at some point. It is here that the information in the Appendix entitled "Levels of Initiation" may become relevant. On the other hand, it is always worth being able to recognize when you yourself are on the receiving end of these tricks.

Cold Reading at its most honest refers to information gleaned from a person via various modes of direct perception, which often include but is not limited to, body language, speech, age, clothing, hairstyle, gender, race, religion, level of education and so forth. Additional information can be picked up in response to high probability guesses that are fed back to the person being read, and whose reaction to the accuracy of the guess is often mirrored in their facial expression (see later for NLP). The overt aim can be to impress the subject in contexts as varied as mentalist stage acts, fortune telling, psychic readings or because you want to sell them a product or idea. In fact, actually performing some kind of divinatory technique such as Tarot can greatly enhance the effectiveness of cold reading since the subject is attributing the information to the cards. In addition, more time is spent on good guesses than bad, accentuating the feeling that the reading is more accurate than it is objectively. This is especially true if the operator admits that 100% accuracy is impossible – it just confirms their honesty! Ian Rowland lists some twenty techniques to enhance the proceedings, such as:

- **Shotgunning**
  Is the technique whereby the operator throws out general assertions to the audience and notes who makes a response.
  "I am sensing someone in the audience named John, possibly an older person, maybe with a knee or back problem…".

- **Fishing**
  This is really simple in that the operator asks the subject questions whose answers are elaborated upon and then fed back to them. The trick is to ask questions in such a way so that they can be perceived as statements. If the operator is wrong, then it was just a question. If right, it is attributed to whatever powers are being claimed. If we follow on from the Shotgunning statement and home in on John, the operator might say something like: "Were you named after a close relative, possibly your grandfather or even father?". If the answer is "yes", then it's a miracle! If "no" then more often than not the subject will start to impart family knowledge which can be used later. A lot of cold reading is simply repeating what the subject has already said but in such a manner as to imply the information was already known. "That's right – you were named after your uncle!". Pauses can also be used

---

[65] Ian Rowland, Full Facts of Cold Reading; available from author or ASIN: B0017GBE2E

to put psychological pressure on the subject to say something. Most people are uncomfortable with silence in such a situation.

- **The Forer Effect**
Also called the personal validation fallacy or the Barnum Effect, it is the observation that individuals will rate as highly accurate descriptions of their personality that are supposedly about them, but are in fact vague and general. It is named after the psychologist Bertram Forer who, in 1948CE, gave a personality test to his students and also gave them the same piece of text as a summary, which they mostly considered accurate. The actual text was:

    "You have a great need for other people to like and admire you. You have a tendency to be critical of yourself. You have a great deal of unused capacity which you have not turned to your advantage. While you have some personality weaknesses, you are generally able to compensate for them. Disciplined and self-controlled outside, you tend to be worrisome and insecure inside. At times you have serious doubts as to whether you have made the right decision or done the right thing. You prefer a certain amount of change and variety and become dissatisfied when hemmed in by restrictions and limitations. You pride yourself as an independent thinker and do not accept others' statements without satisfactory proof. You have found it unwise to be too frank in revealing yourself to others. At times you are extroverted, affable, sociable, while at other times you are introverted, wary, reserved. Some of your aspirations tend to be pretty unrealistic. Security is one of your major goals in life."

- **The Rainbow Ruse**
This is a carefully crafted statement that simultaneously attributes conflicting personality traits to the subject. The result is not, as one might expect, a dismissal of the statement but the opposite – a seeming 100% accuracy. Examples of such statements are:

    "Most of the time you are positive and cheerful, but there have been times when you were very upset."

    "You are a very kind and considerate person, but when somebody wrongs you, you can feel deep anger."

    "You like to make decisions carefully and patiently, but sometimes you're impulsive."

- **Flattery**
Simple and crude, but effective. People like being told nice things about themselves.

- **Excuses**
Prepare in advance for when things go wrong. Strategies include explaining beforehand that 100% accuracy is unlikely; blaming the subject for possibly

misremembering or misinterpreting; suggest to the subject that they need to try, or concentrate, harder.

Returning to the subject of flattery, Blair Warren listed what he terms "The Seven Hidden Addictions". These are psychological needs that almost everyone has, and to which almost everyone responds. They are:

- **The need to be needed**
  "You are a vital part of our group, and make a valuable contribution..."

- **The need for hope**
  "I know things are looking bad, but there is a way we can turn this whole thing around..."

- **The need for a scapegoat**
  "It's not your fault..."

- **The need to be noticed and understood**
  "I hear what you are saying..."

- **The need to know**
  "Perhaps you shouldn't know this at your level, but I'll let you in on a secret..."

- **The need to be right**
  "I quite understand your feelings on this matter..."

- **The need for a sense of power**
  "It is entirely your choice – I am quite willing to let you make your own decisions..."

Related to the above are the skills and techniques involved in selling. One of the best books on the market is by Dr Robert Cialdini[66]. He outlines six basic techniques that he terms "Weapons of Influence". These are:

- **Reciprocity**
  People tend to return favors, hence free samples and the way that big charity organizations will often send a free gift such as a greeting card or pen. It makes someone more likely to give *real* money by inducing a feeling of indebtedness.

- **Commitment and Consistency**
  Once someone has agreed to do, or buy, something they are more likely to follow through on it. Even if the original motivation or incentive is removed, or the price raised. The key element is that some small action apparently changes the person's view of themselves, and they tend to act in

---

[66] Influence: The Psychology of Persuasion, ISBN 0-688-12816-5

concert with that new view. Small changes can be followed by bigger ones if they are necessary to maintain a consistent view of themselves. To be fully effective a commitment must be:

> **Active**: actions that leave some kind of record
> **Public**: the desire to be seen as consistent and to confirm the new self view both to oneself and others.
> **Effortful**: something gained as a result of effort is more highly prized than something attained at no personal cost..
> **Owned**: the person must believe that they acted in public at some cost to themselves by their own free will.

- **Social Proof**
  People are herd animals. If they see other people doing something, they will generally fall into line. More formally, "We view a behavior as correct in a given situation to the degree that we see others performing it.". An example often given is an experiment conducted in 1969CE where a small group of psychologists looked up into the sky. Some 80% of bystanders stopped and did likewise. On the downside we have copycat crimes and suicides after similar high profile cases are reported in the media.

- **Authority**
  People tend to obey authority figures. That's why many adverts for medicinal or hygiene products feature actors wearing white coats (just like doctors!). Authority can be conveyed overtly by uniform, or more subtly by formal suits, titles and degrees, certificates of competence and so forth.

- **Liking**
  People are more likely to buy something from a person they like. Examples vary from the old Tupperware or cosmetics parties, to Net based viral marketing. And they are more likely to like people who are... attractive, similar to them, who flatter them, who are co-operative co-workers, or who they are conditioned to like by associating positive things with them.

- **Scarcity**
  Get it now while the exclusive offer lasts! People tend to react more strongly to potential loss rather than potential gain.

So far the psychological tricks we have just examined have been fairly traditional and have often been practiced quite successfully by many people unconsciously. The next section concerns a far more systematic and analytical approach to persuasion and mental manipulation.

The Third Wave

The *Third Wave* is the name of an essay written by a high school history teacher named Ron Jones in 1972CE. It documented an experiment he conducted into the mindset of Nazi Germany in particular, and Collectivist Authoritarianism in general using his 10th grade students as a model for indoctrination. The question in his history class that sparked the experiment concerned the reasons why ordinary people go along with such regimes, even to the point where the majority fully endorse them. It was carried out at Cubberley High school in Palo Alto, California in April 1967CE.

Strength through Discipline

He began by giving a lecture on the power of discipline, and how nothing worthwhile could be achieved without it, whether in sport, academe or life in general. As an example he had the students walk around the classroom with instructions that when he blew a whistle they would all take their seats, which he timed. He then had them repeat the exercise in complete silence, whereupon they completed the task far more rapidly. The next step was to explain the correct posture for learning and sitting at their desks, with back straight and feet flat on the floor, again in silence. This was again expanded to a formal method the students were to use to answer questions in class. They were required to stand at attention beside their desk and begin their reply with the words: "Mr Jones". The answer itself had to be three words or less. These exercises were repeated for the whole lesson.

Strength through Community

On the second day of the experiment Jones named the new "community" the Third Wave, supposedly from surfer mythology that the third wave is the most powerful one. He also instituted a salute, modeled on the Nazi one, and ordered the students to salute each other even outside of the class – which they did. He explained that community is that bond between individuals who work and struggle together. It is the feeling that you are a part of something beyond yourself, a movement, a team, a race, a nation, a cause... The class had to recite in unison the two slogans: - "Strength through discipline, strength through community." The way he had them do it was interesting. He started with two students reciting it, then added two more, and two more until the whole class was involved.

Strength through Action

The third day saw the introduction of membership cars, with three of them marked with red crosses whose recipients were told to report other class members failing to comply with class rules. It was explained that strength and discipline were meaningless without action. To quote from the essay:

"I discussed the beauty of taking full responsibility for ones action. Of believing so thoroughly in yourself and your community or family that you will do anything to preserve, protect and extend that being. I stressed how hard work and allegiance to each Other would allow accelerated learning and accomplishment. I reminded students of what it felt like being in classes where competition caused pain and degradation. Situations in which students were pitted against each other in everything from gym to reading. The feeling of never acting, never being a part of something, never supporting each other."

To allow the students to experience this he gave each student an assignment:

"It's your task to design a Third Wave Banner. You are responsible for stopping any student that is not a Third Wave member from entering this room. I want you to remember and be able to recite by tomorrow the name and address of every Third Wave Member. You are assigned the problem of training and convincing at least twenty children in the adjacent elementary school that our sitting posture is necessary for better learning. It's your job to read this pamphlet and report its entire content to the class before the period ends. I want each of you to give me the name and address of one reliable friend that you think might want to join the Third Wave."...

To conclude the session on direct action, he instructed students in the procedure for initiating new members. The prospective member had to be recommended by an existing member and issued a card by Jones. Upon receiving this card the new member had to demonstrate knowledge of the rules and pledge obedience to them. This unleashed a tsunami of action!

As an interesting aside, Jones reports that one of the boys in the class named Robert, who was the perennial outsider, finally found a place and people he was comfortable with. To express his gratitude he offered to become Jones' personal bodyguard.

Strength through Pride

By the fourth day the Third Wave movement had exploded in membership, with over 200 students enrolled and many even cutting their normal classes to attend. Jones' class that day had expanded to 80 students. There had also been several incidents of followers clashing with others and an irate father of one of the students, a traumatized WW2 veteran, confronting Jones upon recognizing the Nazi experiment being undertaken. Questions were also being asked by school administration. The final lesson was "Strength through Pride" where he explained...

"Pride is more than banners or salutes. Pride Is something no one can take from you. Pride is knowing you are the best... It can't be destroyed ..."

At the same time, realizing he had painted himself into a corner, he devised a way to extricate himself and end the experiment. He explained that Third Wave was a nationwide program to find students willing to fight for political change in the USA, and that tomorrow there would be a nationwide address by the leader, and all members were required to attend the rally where they could watch him on TV.

Strength through Understanding

To cut the story short, at the rally Jones unveiled a movie of Hitler at the Nuremberg NSDAP rally of 1934CE, and informed his audience that they were no better or worse than Nazis. Needless to say, it did not go down well, especially with Robert who was devastated.

When the experiment had gained a certain amount of publicity Ron Jones was called by the (later notorious) cult leader Jim Jones (no relation) of the People's Temple to ask him the secrets of mass mind control! For those who do not know, Jim Jones later persuaded or coerced some 900 of his followers into committing suicide in Guyana. Ron did not cooperate.

Anyway, that was the "official" story, although in recent years some doubts have arisen as to whether that was the whole truth. For example, it has been pointed out that the students had considerable motivation to play along with the scenario since not only would it ensure good grades, but those good grades themselves would ease entry into college and deferment of the military draft. In other words, failure to comply might have meant a formal invitation to participate in the Vietnam War. However, this does not necessarily detract from the experiment, since in a totalitarian regime there are certainly comparable incentives to participate enthusiastically. Another claim that has come to light is that not all the students cooperated and that there was a "resistance movement" that attempted to sabotage the indoctrination.

So, what lessons can we learn from this experiment? By this I do not mean "How do we set up our own Nazi State?", but the more general and benign lessons of how to run a successful organization, specifically an occult or mystical order. This is particularly apt since democracy is generally not part of the setup. Rather, such organizations are usually top down guided meritocracies – at least, that is the ideal. The key elements one can deduce from the above are as follows:

- **Elitism**
  The members must feel that they are special, and superior to "outsiders".

- **Discipline**
  There must be a (self) disciplined participation to both maximize efficiency and create the feeling that the "elite" tag is deserved.

- **Repeated Drills**
  Or in our context ceremonies, social events, repetitive rote learning. The more time and energy someone invests in something, the more valuable it becomes to them and the less likely they are to drop it.

- **Body Language**
  Something often overlooked in modern public schooling is the importance of body language – how to stand, sit, walk, speak, make eye contact and so forth in order to convey an air of authority, power and command. Notably, this is *not* overlooked by the military.

- **Participation**
  All members of the group must be encouraged to participate – they must all have a job or function of some kind. This leads to communal commitment.

- **Community**
  It must be emphasized that they are members of a community that will leave nobody behind. One for all, all for one, to quote from the Three Musketeers. Mutual aid.

- **Clear Goals**
  Backed by short sound-bites, slogans or mantras. Why we are here, what we are doing, what we want to achieve.

- **Insignia**
  Membership cards, badges, flags, "secret" methods of identification ranging from jewelery to distinctive body language, salutes, handshakes etc.

- **Recruitment**
  If you want your organization to expand, make recruitment a member's priority.

There is one more element that is crucial and goes beyond the above experiment. Simply stated it is *nothing for nothing*, that is, nothing is given away freely. The members have to either earn the desired item, whether it be membership, knowledge or some other commodity, or buy it. In addition, it should not be cheap. It may seem obvious once stated but people value expensive things more than they value something cheap or free irrespective if its intrinsic value. I have personally seen this in the martial arts world where teachers who charge high prices tend to get more students than those who teach for free, even if the quality of the high priced tuition is less than that being freely given. There is an extremely common mindset that says: "If it is expensive it must be good". This is especially true if the prospective customer or student knows nothing of what they are buying. It has even been found in the medical context that high priced placebos work better than cheaper ones! This is besides people being attracted to an expensive membership of an organization or hobby as a status symbol. If horses were cheap and donkeys cost a million dollars apiece, the rich would be members of the donkey club!

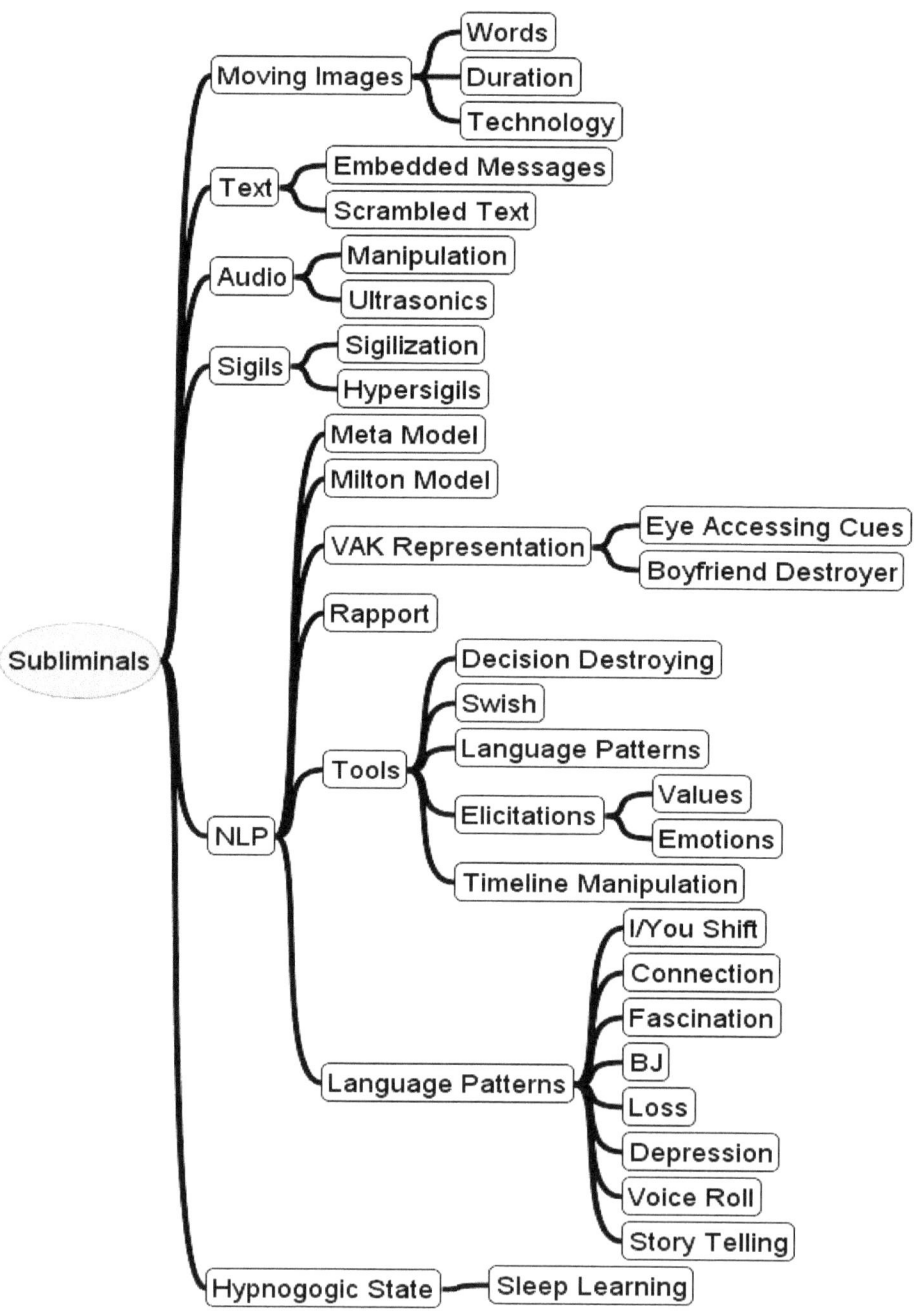

7 Subliminals

"It is not possible to resist that which cannot be detected"

In this chapter we examine subliminal technologies both conventional and novel, covering the major senses and also the possibility of direct induction of subliminal imagery or commands using direct electromagnetic stimulation of the brain.

Subliminal literally means *below the threshold of conscious perception*. That is, a subliminal stimulus is inadequate to produce conscious awareness but is still able to evoke some kind of a response. However, subliminals do not work as popularly assumed in the story, originating in the 1950s, about a cinema flashing "Coke" on the screen during a movie and then having the patrons rush to buy it during the interval. That is an urban myth, but one which has been quite influential in having such crude advertising attempts banned by law in many nations. It has been shown that such subliminal advertising does not work. People are not somehow forced to go and order a drink they do not like , want or need. However, it is effective if the viewer is thirsty and is in two minds which particular drink to opt for. Despite this some movies and TV advertising do use very similar techniques. For example, there is a subliminal frame in the original film version of "The Exorcist" where a picture of an African death mask is flashed on screen during one scene. It's not quite subliminal since if you know when to look you can see it clearly, and even if you are not expecting it the movie looks like it jumps at that point. Whether it is effective or not is a matter of dispute, but just knowing that it was being used in such a notorious movie at the time no doubt enhanced its credibility even more. It is still one of the best (scary) movies to deal with the supernatural and demonic possession. Another much more common example is pseudo-subliminal cuts occurring in trailers for movies and TV programs, especially those that are action-adventure oriented. Action scenes are cut from one to another so fast that only an impression of breathless excitement remains for most people. There has been a definite trend over the past few years of making the cuts shorter and shorter, moving it into the kind of time frame that would bring it into the category of subliminal advertising. How far this trend will go remains to be seen.

The most common and effective subliminal advertising technique used in the mass media today is *product placement* where particular brands are shown and associated with particular scenes and characters. Next time you watch a movie, see what brands the main character eats, drinks, wears, drives and so forth. Also check out what is being advertised as part of the background scenery, and remember that nothing in a movie is there by accident, except in the most incompetent, cheap or amateurish productions. It is probably worth pointing out that any production that uses a branded item in a negative context might run into substantial legal problems, especially in the USA. It is unlikely you will ever see the evil giggling psycho-rapist sipping from his can of P***i as he cuts the throat of his latest victim. Unless, of course, such a placement was paid for by the opposition! To date companies have shied away from such subliminal negative campaigning, but it's a thought…

Before we continue into more detailed and esoteric subliminal technology it is worth pointing out just how sensitive we are to subliminal information acquisition, if not persuasion. Indeed, sometimes people can be so good at picking up and processing the tiniest cues that it seems Psi phenomena are a more plausible explanation. The famous hypnotherapist Milton Erickson provided an example of this. He described an experiment with hearing-impaired lip-readers where he discovered that they actually read a much richer spectrum of cues than simply the lips. The set-up was as follows: The lip-reading subjects sat with their backs to a blackboard on which there were various geometric designs. The designs were then obscured with sheets of paper. In front of the lip readers, and facing the blackboard, sat a group of normal participants who were instructed to look at the blackboard and say and do nothing. An assistant then removed the paper covering the geometric symbols, one at a time, and the lip-readers were instructed to write down anything that they read from the participants in front of them who were observing the geometric figures. They were able to "read" the names of the geometric figures apparently from their partner's body language with varying degrees of accuracy. One subject, a diagnosed paranoid psychotic who claimed to hear other people's thoughts, was reported as having perfect accuracy. Erickson applied this insight to his hypnotic technique by recognising the significance of messages he himself did not realize he was sending. It is something all magicians should bear in mind. Anyway, the beauty of the above experiment is that, unlike Psi experiments, nobody can accuse the subjects of cheating by reading subliminal cues.

Naturally, there has been considerable research done on subliminal perception and especially on how to use it as a medium of influence for purposes ranging from advertising to the possible military applications of remote hypnosis. As a result it has been discovered that effective messaging depends upon combining a number of factors. These are:

- The goal must be clearly defined.

- The message should be simple, ideally just one word.

- Wording should be in the first person, for example, "I am" not "you are".

- The goal must be communicated as if it had already happened, or is in the process of happening.

- Each suggestion should be phrased at least three different ways.

- Positive emotions should be attached to the completion of the goal.

- The above should be done without distracting the conscious mind.

Subliminals

- The goal should be achieved rapidly since subliminal influence weakens over time.

- The message should be phrased in positive terms and reversed negatives should not be used.

- "Negative" messages are more likely to be effective than positive ones. That is, words like "danger", "fear", "agony", "murder" are more likely to influence than words like "peace", "love", "cheerful" or neutral words.[67]

The Agents one is trying to contact within the unconscious mind are less responsive to commands than suggestions and descriptions. The pathways being used are not too intelligent either, so there is a possibility that reversed negatives can be seen as positives. For example, if you are told: "Do not think of a black cat" the command "Think of a black cat" lies embedded in the statement and can also be acted upon.

Neuro-Linguistic Programming (NLP)

NLP was created by Richard Bandler and John Grinder in the early 1970s from a study of "excellence". The subjects chosen for study were in the field of psychology and psychiatry and included Virginia Satir (creator of Family Therapy), Fritz Perls (founder of Gestalt Therapy) and Milton Erickson the famous hypnotist who we have already encountered. They analysed writings and tape-recordings to discover what accounted for the successful results these people were getting. By mimicking the language patterns, and testing them on a group of students they achieved similar powerful results to those they were studying. The definitive work by Bandler and Grinder was entitled: "The Structure of Magic"[68] and appeared in two volumes in 1975CE.

Anyone with a hard science background first approaching NLP has an immediate problem. It is that there is no underlying theory of mind from which the techniques can be deduced. Rather, as Bandler put it: "NLP is an attitude and a methodology that leaves behind a trail of techniques". In other words, it is a behavioral engineering approach to effecting mental state change, and anything that works within the wide remit NLP sets itself gets thrown into the mix. However, the basic approach is quite simple, as are a number of the more useful techniques.

The "attitude" in the above description is one of intense curiosity about the mind and an experimental approach where there is no failure, only feedback. The "methodology" is that of *modeling* – that is, copying and mimicking how something works until you can get it to work yourself.

The pragmatic model of "thinking" is based around the notion of

---

[67] Nasrallah,M., Carmel,D., Lavie,N. "Murder she wrote": Enhanced sensitivity to negative word valence. *Emotion* . ISSN: 1528-3542

[68] The Structure of Magic: A Book About Language and Therapy – ISBN-13: 978-0831400446
The Structure of Magic II: A Book About Communication and Change – ISBN-13: 978-0831400491

information processing and storage as being a reproduction sensory input. The Representational Systems, or VAK systems, stand for the major *modalities* by which we represent information. These are:

- **Visual (V)** – Pictures and images...
  Do you get the picture? See how things are?

- **Auditory (A)** – Sounds, noises, tones, volume...
  Do you often tell yourself that you shouldn't do this? I hear that you do...

- **Kinesthetic (K)** – Touch, sensations, pressure temperature...
  Can you grasp what I am saying? Do you have a grip on reality?

- **Smell/Taste** (OG), Olfactory/Gustatory
  Would you like a taste of success? Sweet, isn't it...

The lists of features associated with each of the modalities are referred to as *submodalities*.

The major premises of NLP are that by changing the features of the representations, rather than the content, we can change our responses and emotions. One of the examples often offered to illustrate the point is to visualize some pleasant experience in our past, maybe like watching it on a screen, then to imagine the picture expanded. How does it affect the feelings associated with it when you do that? And then do the opposite, shrink it down to a minuscule image and examine your emotions once more. What about moving between black and white and color? Or moving the image nearer to us, or further away? For most people just altering the representation while keeping the content constant will alter the degree of emotional response. A similar situation occurs with bad memories and experiences and this is, of course, a starting point for some types of NLP therapy.

NLP also divides into two general approaches referred to as the Meta Model and the Milton Model. A key difference between them is that the former deals with specifics and the latter generalizations. Specifics tend to bring people out of a trance state, and generalities do the opposite. This is not too much of a revelation if you consider the sleep inducing boredom of a politicians speech versus one where there is a lot of very specific detail one can grasp (tactile modality!). In NLP the process of becoming more specific is called *chunking down* and becoming more general is *chunking up*.

Subliminals

The Meta Model

This is a way of analyzing communication in order to recover unspoken information and unwarranted generalizations in order to reveal unconscious limitations and faulty thinking. The practitioner essentially responds to the structure of the client's language rather than the content, including what is not being said. For example, consider the following statements (S) and the responses (R) which fall into distinct NLP classifications:

- **Deletions** – unspecified nouns, adjectives, relationships.
  S: Get a life
  R: What kind of life?

- **Comparative Deletions** – an implied comparison where the object of the comparison is missing.
  S: Do you think you could do more?
  R: More than who?

- **Unspecified Referential Index** – where the principle actor is missing
  S: People worry about you
  R: Which people?

- **Unspecified Verbs** – Omitting the verb or object, or both
  S: Don't make me get angry
  R: Make you how?

- **Nominalizations** – A process has been converted to a thing
  S: You have a hard time with decisions
  R: So that is what you have decided?

- **Modal Operators** – Words that dictate what is correct, possible or necessary
  S: You have to pull yourself together
  R: What would happen if I did not?

- **Presuppositions** – Some unstated element must be assumed
  S: With the latest space probe Mars may finally give up its secrets
  R: So Mars is intentionally withholding secrets?

- **Universal Quantifiers** – Absolute generalizations, usually involving words like always, every, none, never, all...
  S: You should always wear a tie
  R: All the time? Never take it off?

- **Cause and Effect** – the implication that one thing causes another
  S: Whenever you come here it goes wrong
  R: So it never goes wrong when I am not here?

- **Mind Reading** – Believing that one knows what another is thinking
  S: You want me to fail
  R: How do you know I want you to fail?

- **Complex Equivalence** – Statements where complex notions are equated
  S: You don't take me out so often, don't you love me any more?
  R: So I only love you if I take you out?

- **Lost Performative** – A judgment made without specifying who is judging
  S: That is a stupid idea
  R: Who says so?

- **Either/Or** – An illusion of choice
  S: Are you stupid or just incompetent?
  R: And those are the only two options?

- **Inadequately Defined Terms** – Ones that rely on abstract definitions
  S: Crime is caused by problems in parenting
  R: What aspects of parenting cause which crimes?

- **Delusional Verbal Splits** – Using language to divide elements of a whole
  S: Part of me says yes, and part of me says no...
  R: When those parts merge together, who will you be?

- **Multiordinality** – Over generalizing the meaning of words
  S: I am having second *thoughts* about the job
  R: What thoughts are you having?

- **Static Words** – A rigid definition applied to a general word resulting in a dogmatic statement
  S: That's life
  R: What is? What part of life? For who?

- **Pseudo Words** – Linguistic maps that reference nothing
  S: Before the beginning of time
  R: The time before time began?

- **Identification** – equating two things as being exactly equal
  S: You are a loser
  R: What, specifically, have I lost?

- **Emotionalizing** – using emotions for gathering or processing information
  S: It's an unhappy state of affairs
  R: What about the state of affairs makes you unhappy?

- **Personalizing** – Interpreting events, words, actions as being directed at us
  S: Whenever I find a product I like they discontinue it
  R: So do they discontinue it because they know you like it?

Subliminals

- **Metaphors** – Understanding one thing in terms of another
  S: Time is money
  R: What else is time?

The above merely scratches the surface of the linguistic analysis, as each category can be further broken down and analyzed, along with its implications regarding unconscious constructs, but it should be enough to illustrate what is happening. In my more cynical moments I often think of this as being either a man's codification of "womens intuition", or autistic man meets annoying person. So while it might be quite useful in order to provide an insight into the person you are talking with, it is in reality a rather passive system from the point of view of the TechnoMage.

The Milton Model

Named after the hypnotherapist Milton Erickson, it is almost a mirror image of the above model. Rather than seeking to specify information it is artfully vague, dealing in embedded suggestion, ambiguity, sentences with multiple meaning and paced delivery. The practitioner makes statements that might seem specific but are not, allowing the listener to fill in their own meaning in order to facilitate and maintain a trance state which enables communication with the listener's unconscious. The definitive works were the books[69] by Bandler and Grinder "The Patterns of the Hypnotic Techniques of Milton H Erickson" volumes 1 and 2.

The key elements of this model are:

- Pacing another's reality in order to gain *rapport*.
  Rapport is "being in sync" with another person. It is the harmony and mutual acceptance that exists between people when they are at ease with one another and where communication is occurring easily.

- Accessing unconscious resources of another person to gather information or lead them into trance.

- Distracting the conscious mind.

Rapport is an immensely useful skill for anyone involved in personal interactions in a professional manner. It is achieved by using a number of quite basic techniques, sometimes referred to as *mirroring*. The key fact is that people like, and generally trust, people like themselves. The process is:

- Match them by subtly reflecting their non-verbal behavior, especially eye contact and voice patters.

- Match posture to a lesser extent, but obviously not to the point of parody.

- Match the rhythm of breathing.

---

[69] ASIN: B001TLO2EY, ASIN: B001TLLZKS

- Match facial expressions and gestures.

- Match the voice in speed of delivery, tone, volume rhythm and clarity.

- Match the modality of speech. For example, if they use visual metaphors do the same. Try and use the same vocabulary if possible.

- Understand how they see the world and develop an interest in seeing it that way as well.

- Test for rapport by *leading*. That is, making a change in your non verbal behavior that does not match theirs and see whether they follow within a short time. If they do, you have rapport. If not continue with the above steps.

Whether the order of focus should be on body language, voice or the words themselves depends to a great extent on the audience and context. To get an idea of the language, we can take some of the headings used in the Meta Model above and illustrate with "Ericksonian" wording. Note that it is a more proactive approach than the Meta Model.

- **Comparative Deletions** – an implied comparison where the object of the comparison is missing.
  S: You are going deeper
  S: At some time or another you might notice...
  S: Right or wrong, it does not matter

- **Unspecified Referential Index** – where the principle actor is missing
  S: That's the way
  S: It would help you go deeper...
  S: Do you see it more clearly?

- **Unspecified Verbs** – Omitting the verb or object, or both
  S: Just continue
  S: You begin to enjoy
  S: How much you remember...

- **Nominalizations** – A process has been converted to a thing
  S: Feelings come and go...
  S: Your situation is getting better
  S: You have new learnings...

- **Modal Operators** – Words that dictate what is correct, possible or necessary
  S: You can change instantly
  S: You can trust your unconscious mind
  S: You should be able to see that...

Subliminals

- **Presuppositions** – Some unstated element must be assumed
  S: Soon you will be in a deeper trance
  S: As your unconscious mind is listening...
  S: You are changing even as you listen...

- **Universal Quantifiers** – Absolute generalizations, usually involving words like always, every, none, never, all...
  S: It all means nothing...
  S: Nobody is being hypnotized
  S: Anyone can learn this...

- **Cause and Effect** – the implication that one thing causes another
  S: Sit here if you want to go into trance
  S: Because you are here you are learning...
  S: If you close your eyes you will begin to understand

- **Mind Reading** – Believing that one knows what another is thinking
  S: I know what you are thinking...
  S: I know you came here for a reason...
  S: You are probably aware...

- **Complex Equivalence** – Statements where complex notions are equated
  S: You are relaxed so you are in a trance
  S: Wanting to learn means you will
  S: Being here means you will enjoy the lesson

- **Lost Performative** – A judgment made without specifying who is judging
  S: It is better to give than receive
  S: You are doing well
  S: It is important to learn...

- **Double Binds** (Either/Or) – An illusion of choice
  S: Do you want to do it now or later?
  S: You have all the time you need before the end of the lesson
  S: Either before or after this lesson you will...

- **Pacing Current Experience** – Stating what is actually happening.
  S: We are sitting here
  S: As your muscles relax
  S: As you feel the chair against your back

- **Conversational Postulates** – A question that normally would be answered literally by a yes or no, but is understood to be asking for a more detailed answer.
  S: Are you prepared to sign up?
  S: Do you think you can do this?
  S: Wouldn't you like to just sit back and relax?

- **Tag Questions** – A question added at the end of a sentence, designed to soften resistance.
  S: Isn't it?
  S: Won't you?
  S: Don't you think?

- **Extended Quotes** – A rambling often nested context for delivering information or a command.
  S: I remember meeting this guy who once had a friend who knew a tall blond woman that who went to this Indian guru, who was apparently quite famous who said that changing your mind is easy...

- **Selectional Restriction Violations** – Attributing intelligence to inanimate objects.
  S: My car really likes a good driver.
  S: That flower is just asking to be picked.
  S: The cake is just crying out to be eaten.

- **Phonological Ambiguity** – Confusing words that sound the same.
  S: Your, you're...
  S: Hear, here...
  S: What's black and white and read/red all over? (A newspaper!)

- **Syntactic Ambiguity** – More than one possible meaning.
  S: Shooting stars
  S: Leadership shows
  S: Social security

- **Punctuation Ambiguity** – Improper pauses and incomplete sentences requiring the listener to "mind read".
  S: Let me take your... hand me the pen please...
  S: Look at your watch... how quickly you go into trance.
  S: By merging two things into one... can quite easily miss something...

- **Scope Ambiguity** – Confusing the object of the sentence.
  S: Speaking to you as a prospective Cult Leader...
  S: Talking to you as someone who can quite easily go into trance...
  S: As someone who knows the value of this kind of information...

- **Utilization** – Taking advantage of everything the listener says and experiences.
  S: (Sound of door opening): And as you hear the door open step through it to a new state of consciousness...
  S: (I cannot be hypnotized!): Certainly you cannot be hypnotized yet...
  S: (I don't believe it...) : That's because you have not yet asked the question that would allow you to believe it...

Subliminals

Now we have a grasp of the essential language and format we can move on to some of the more common techniques developed by NLP. Since there are hundreds only a few will be chosen for their utility and to illustrate various applications.

Eye Accessing Cues

One of the most commonly taught techniques is how to determine what a person is thinking by looking to see how their eyes move as they respond to a question or suggestion. Quite often it is used to try and tell if a person is lying, and is based upon the diagram below.

Figure 1

This is for a normally right handed person. The keys are:

- **V^c – Visual Construct**
  When someone is creating a picture: "Imagine what your perfect house would look like".

- **V^r – Visual Recall**
  When someone is recalling an image: "What does your home look like?".

- **A^c – Audio Construct**
  When someone is imagining a sound or conversation: "What do you think they would say?".

- **A^r – Audio Recall**
  When someone is recalling a sound or conversation: "What did he say?".

- **K – Kinesthetic**
  When someone is recalling or imagining a kinesthetic sensation: "What does it feel like to kick a ball?"

- **A^i – Audio Internal Dialog**
  When someone is running through a train of thought in their head: "Do you think you can do this?".

Eye movement to the left or right for many people seems to indicate if a memory was recalled or constructed, which is where the "lie detecting" comes from. Unfortunately, things are not as simple as this in real life. While eye movements do provide clues to modes of thought there is no universal pattern and one has to *calibrate*. This is a process whereby innocuous questions such as the above are put to the listener and the practitioner takes note of which way the eyes flick. Then the real questions follow...

A more pro-active approach that results in a manipulation of the subject's mental state and beliefs is illustrated by what has been termed "The Boyfriend Destroyer", although it equally applies to girlfriends. It is designed for jealous rivals for the affections of a person to reduce the desirability of the opposition. It can of course be applied to much else, but I did promise 101 spells for lovesick teenagers in the introduction...

The Boyfriend Destroyer

As originally elucidated by Ross Jeffries: The steps are as follows:

- Think of someone who is really wonderful, and point to a place in space where your attention seems to be right now (position Y).

- Now think of someone who you once thought was wonderful, but you came to realize was not and who you hardly think of any more. What place in space if your attention right now? (position N)

- Think of a picture of your boyfriend, maybe see his face. Where is that picture, can you point to it? (position Y)

- Take control of the picture by placing your hands around the image at X, pull it to position N. "Is this him? – this big? – bigger?" Widen your hands and then shrink then back down. "Notice that as the picture gets smaller the colors fade and it gets a little fuzzy and out of focus. I can move it around, look..." Wave it about and let it return to Y. "Wow! – it's stuck." Make like it is on a rubber band that snaps it back into place, and while compressing it down to insignificant size say: "Oh well, I guess I'll just leave it there."

- "Now, you'll just want to see this!". Take your hands and frame your own face. "Now take a mental snapshot of me – flash!". Move your hands to Y, expanding them as you do so: "Look, it clicks right into place, vivid and bright. And here's another – flash!, of me and you together having a good time." Go and stand at Y. "Doesn't that feel good?".

This is all covert suggestion, but because we do not normally permit people to know about our spatial related image storage, and are usually unaware of it ourselves, when someone else manipulates it the emotional effect can be very dramatic.

Subliminals

Swish

Swish is a visualization technique for reducing the impact of unwanted habits. It relies upon disrupting the pattern of thought that leads to the undesirable behavior and replacing it another that leads to a better outcome. The process involves visualizing the trigger or *cue image* that leads up to the unwanted behavior, which is then replaced (swish!) with one that leads to a more desirable outcome. The swish is tested by either having the subject think of the original cue, or actually presenting the cue if possible, and observing the responses.

Anyway, that is the conventional therapeutic use. By now, if you have been reading the book sequentially, you should be getting a little creative about Dark Side uses. For example, it could well be the mage who is interesting in disrupting habits or thought patterns in the subject, and not the subject themselves. In which case the cue image could be installed as an anchor to the new behavior or belief.

Decision Destroying

This requires rapport in able for it to be effective and is used to try to get the subject to reverse a decision. Crudely put, the following stages outline the method. We start just after the point where the unfortunate decision has been made:

"So, where were you when you decided that?"

"I mean, just before you made the decision…"

"*Now*, as you think about the present situation notice how many options are left open…"

"As you think about the next time you may do X knowing what you do now notice that you feel a lot better not doing it."

Anyway, more in the next chapter on subliminal technology. However, the focus is now moving into the larger arena than the one-to-one approach of therapeutic hypnosis and NLP. Also reserved for the chapter on subliminals is the use of what are called "Language Patterns" in NLP. These are ways of speaking, or occasionally writing, using elements from the Milton Model to bypass the conscious mind.

Values Elicitation

Values lie at the core of decision making and self image, and are the deep reasons we do the things we do. They can be multi-polar in that different ones come into play according to the situation. Typically they revolve around things like gender, religion, politics and so forth. Once you know what those values are, you can use them to establish or enhance rapport by feeding them back to the subject. More cynically, they are often used in salesmanship by finding out "what buttons to push" in order to promise deep fulfillment.

They way to go about discovering such values is amazingly simple – just ask.

Imagine you want to sell product "X" to someone. X can be anything, from a real hands-on item to an idea. Typically the first question you ask is: "What is important about X?". When you get their first answer, ask again: "What is important about (first answer)?". If necessary go through the procedure again, by which time the answer should reflect some deeply held value or belief "V". The sales pitch then becomes "X can (satisfy, get more of, enhance) V – does that sound like something you are interested in?".

Obviously this process should not be done as a crude interrogation, and the above is merely the core of the process. Nor should the question be "Why", but "What". The word "Why" indicates a critical attitude whilst asking "What" appears more of a request for information out of interest as well as an invitation to the person being questioned to expand upon what must be an important topic for them. Indeed, the elicitation can be even simpler since most people are quite keen to talk about what they consider to be interesting and important.

Emotional Elicitation

This is the NLP process of engineering the desired emotional state in the subject in order to facilitate the desired outcome. It can be as simple as asking a question: "What is it like when you feel..." or "Do you remember when you felt..." or as complex as telling a story designed to generate the emotion. Indeed, that is what a lot of story telling is about in fiction. Once the emotion has been elicited it can either be used while it is still fresh, as it were, in order to make the subject more compliant or it can be connected to a secondary statement or an anchor for later use. More on this in the next chapter. Again, like a lot of the techniques being described, rapport is essential.

To complete the section, here is one method of listing emotions in diagram form devised by Robert Plutchik .

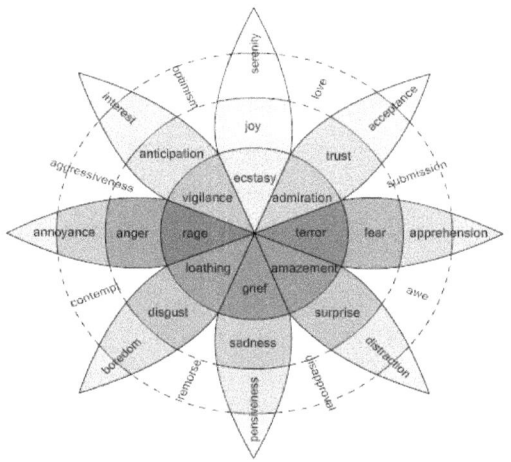

Subliminals

Timeline Manipulation

In terms of spatial representation people often unconsciously associate a specific direction with the flow of time. For example, the past is behind and the future ahead. Less obviously, most Western people associate the flow of time as being left to right possibly as a result of the way we read. Left is the past and right is the future. If we return to the hypothetical job interview we can incorporate this element into a new trick. Quite often a disposable cup of water is supplied to the interviewee, so imagine that you are sitting opposite the interviewer with the cup of water to your right and your resume (CV) to your left. The resume is on their right (future) and the cup to their left (past). Every time you speak of yourself, or they speak of desired characteristics, you touch the resume (anchor), and every time other candidates or undesirable features are mentioned you take a sip of water or touch the cup (anchor). At the end of the interview you leave the cup on the desk, which the interviewer then throws into the rubbish bin (along with the undesirable associations and alternative candidates). They are the past, and you are the future.

Subliminal Images

Classically, there are two forms in which subliminal images are presented. The one most people think of, if they consider it at all, is the flash presentation in a moving image stream as mentioned above. The placement of the flash amongst other moving images is quite important as it prevents the phenomenon known as *persistence of vision* from making the flash obvious and readable. If one took a normal blank black screen and projected an image on it for a millisecond or so with no surrounding imagery then the image would tend to linger because it takes a brief time for the visual response to fade back to black. The time is approximately approximately 40mS. However, the duration of the flash is less important than the total amount of energy entering the eye in this period, so one might crudely assume that an image that was visible for 40mS during which it emitted 1 Joule of energy would be equally visible for 1mS if it emitted the same amount of energy, but at a 40x higher power. However, if the subliminal flash is bracketed by moving images a lot of this persistence is wiped away by the following imagery. This makes the flash on its own somewhat less effective as a subliminal tool for someone staring at the presentation medium. On the other hand, it makes it a better tool for use if it is to presented in the peripheral vision of the subject(s).

The second way of presenting a subliminal image is to do so statically. This relies on the subject moving relative to the picture, for example being in a car or train passing a billboard. The key is to have the subject see the image without consciously realizing what it is. Naturally, this is why the world is full of corporate logos and billboards.

Flash Word List

Since the most effective alphanumeric subliminals are typically single words I have thoughtfully compiled a brief and far from comprehensive list. Strangely enough, while you can find lots of talk about trigger words in a subliminal context I doubt you will find an actual list of words themselves. So, in no particular order or utility: fun, games, fear, terror, dread, horror, love, hate, monster, crime, death, run, escape, hear, see, vomit, forget, sleep, scream, ghost, demon, devil, Satan, God, evil, health, healing, power, serenity, bliss, drugged, run, now, alien, UFO, saucer, fairy, elves, abduction, poltergeist, trapped, dying, hunger, blood, vampire, creature, thing, sex, orgasm...

I think you get the idea, and in fact can probably work up a few scenarios just starting with the list above. It is probably also a good insight into my stream of consciousness as I write this. Various words can also be used in sequence to create surprisingly complex mental imagery. One radio based advert did precisely this to generate a feeling of a pleasant and relaxing day trip. Something along the lines of: drive, country, picnic, hotel, fire, warmth, drink...

The Subliminal Flash – Technology

One reasonably effective way of influencing a person's mind subliminally is, as already mentioned, to use a very brief presentation of a word or image. Traditionally this has been accomplished by injecting a subliminal frame either in a photographic movie film or electronically in a video. Technology, though, moves on and one can quite easily envision a website presenting such a frame, along with all the other subtle aids one might use. So much is obvious, or should be. But what if you want to do it on a rather larger scale than your living room, and to rather more people than your unwitting friends and family? In short, how do you move the subliminal flash into the public arena given that conventional media is out of the question for reasons of access, cost and being tracked down and prosecuted? After all, it's rather hard to *not* leave a trail that starts in the recording studio, passes through the TV or radio transmitting station and ends up being recorded by one of your many... shall we say, "experimental subjects" for later presentation in court?

Well, there is a way, and it's rather simple. Consider the old "Batman" comic strip, TV series and latterly movies. When he was needed by city hall there was a searchlight atop the hall that projected his symbol against the low lying clouds. Perfect, you might think, for our schemes but for one or two minor details. First, you are rather unlikely to have a high intensity searchlight handy, and second you are also unlikely to have the (typically) 15kW power supply drive to it from your own rooftop. Throw in the fact that people will see where the beam is coming from and it all looks rather less attractive than it first appeared. Which is what I thought, until I noticed the word *flash*. We do not need 15kW of continuous power, since we

Subliminals

only want to hit the clouds, or sides large buildings, with that kind of power for around a millisecond (mS) or less. What we need is a photographic slide projector and an electronic flashgun. It turns out that even a cheap disposable camera's flash will put out a peak power of around 50kW and a total energy of maybe 10 Joules (J). That compares with 15J for our searchlight over a millisecond. You can multiply that by ten if you want to extend the flash duration to 10 mS, in which case you will need a professional unit. The other problem is that you may well melt a conventional photo film slide at the higher energy settings. But not to worry – just use a cardboard stencil instead of the film. After all, the subliminal should be quite simple, consisting of a single word, Sigil or glyph.

So, wait until it's dark with an overcast sky, or even a thunderstorm and treat the Gotham City citizens to a piece of your mind. Alternatively, just hit the nearest skyscraper for more local appeal.

On a global note, the Net offers quite a few opportunities for the propagation of subliminal messages ranging from video upload sites to dedicated web pages utilizing most of the tricks being examined. There are also a number of programs on sale which are designed to flash such messages onscreen in order to modify the user's lifestyle or habits. Everything from boosting optimism to giving up smoking.

Subliminal Text

> Bear in mind that commonly
> usury was once banned
> yet interest was still charged.
> Money was borrowed and repaid,
> yen, dollars, pounds...
> Buying money can be a pricey and
> often tricky business on
> occasions when something is
> kept secret.

Subliminal text is ordinary text with a subliminal message embedded within it. As such one can use some of the NLP techniques previously described.

Another method that does not lend itself to speech but is effective in text is to embed the hidden message as consistent letter positions within the overall text. For the purposes of this book and re-formatting problems that may arise later the examples presented below are actually embedded pictures that I have created. This is especially important if you want to use this kind of subliminal in, say, an email where the final formatting may depend on the recipient's email program. So...This is going to be a rather nasty job for whoever translates this work into another language, but can you spot the subliminal command embedded in the above text? You do not even have to buy my book.

Here is another, less obvious method, but one where I have simplified it so it is easy to see by using the capital letters diagonally. The example is rather political:

> Never have so many creatures been
> seen. Animals of all types, sizes and
> colors abound. Zoos are full of them
> all the time, everywhere. Independent
> ones are the most interesting.

We can even hide the text itself in an amusing scrambled format to ensure that it is actually examined. Did you know that...

> Aoccdrnig to rscheearch at an Elingsh uinervtisy, it deosn't mttaer in waht oredr the ltteers in a wrod are, olny taht the frist and lsat ltteres are at the rghit pcleas. The rset can be a toatl mses and you can sitll raed it wouthit a porbelm. Tihs is bcuseae we do not raed ervey lteter by ilstef, but the wrod as a wlohe.

Subliminal Speech

The key to embedding commands or suggestions within speech were outlined in the previous chapter. The main techniques involve the use of:

- **Complex Equivalence** – Statements where complex notions are equated
  S: You wanted to hire someone so here I am at the interview...

- **Double Binds** (Either/Or) – An illusion of choice
  S: I'm sure we have all the time we need before the end of the interview...

- **Punctuation Ambiguity** – Improper pauses and incomplete sentences requiring the listener to "mind read".
  S: I know you are looking for the ideal candidate... me, I would do the same if I was in your position...

- **Phonological Ambiguity** – Words that sound the same.
  S: You can either say yes I'll hire you, or no/know that it the right thing to do...

Of course, the above is just a very crude "job interview" kind of situation. The use of these techniques in ritual or ceremony is both more complex and also to some extent easier since a lot of it can be scripted beforehand and delivered as a briefing or lecture preparatory to the occult event itself. This can result in the members being primed for a certain type of experience, perhaps either putting them at their ease or perhaps raising fear and tension. In addition to the above we can throw in a few homonyms, that is, words that sound the same but have different meanings as well as syntactic ambiguity. We can also prime the audience by the use of negating statements which sound superficially reassuring but which have the opposite effect.

Subliminals

Classic mindfucks (as they are sometimes called) include things like: "Don't worry, nobody is going to die tonight", especially when it had never crossed anyone's mind that they might die! Personally, I think a little fear and apprehension can go a long way in some types of ritual, which is the opposite of that required for séance techniques. It gives a kind of energy to the proceedings and focuses the minds of those involved. The morale boosting speech from Hell in its most basic form:

> "Anyway, I did *fear* we will be *running* short of time and this ritual venue is a bit *alien* to me. I know some of you probably got a bit *lost* on the *way*. I was *afraid* we were not going to get *things* in or out of the building, but just before we got here the *power* came on and it's not looking so *bad*. I would like to *point* out that we need to stay *sharp* and focused although I don't expect anyone to *die* tonight (ha! ha!) Still, we will be doing quite a lot in the *dark* so be careful not to fall into the *trap* of thinking this will be simple."

The above is an example of what is called a *Language Pattern* in NLP. Such patterns differ from conventional hypnotic suggestion in that they describe a process that the subject has to go through in their own mind, effectively doing it to themselves. At the core lies the manipulation of emotional response and it largely relies on the fact that most people make decisions based more on emotion that logic. However, it is essential that rapport is first established, as described in the previous chapter. There are a number of common techniques applied in NLP language patterns:

- **The I/You Shift**
  Something most people tend to do in conversations at some point or other. The speaker shifts from the first person to "you", with the effect of unconsciously suggesting that they feel what the speaker is describing. For example: "I was walking along the other day and I saw this homeless guy begging in the street.. You wonder whether, if things had gone differently in life that might have been you..."

- **The Connection Pattern**
  This is designed to create a sensation of connection and familiarity in whoever hears it. At its most basic, it is a short spiel that features elements of things that are connected with a repetition of the word "connection" in different contexts.

- **The Fascination Pattern**
  Again, similar to the above but this time a spiel sprinkled with words and phrases that indicate interest, or grab your attention. Something that, as you focus in on it gets more and more interesting as your awareness expands to encompass new possibilities that are so compelling that time seems to stop as you fall deeper into understanding... thinking that it could be like this... And so on as long as necessary. A similar pattern can be created for attraction between two people, either intellectual or physical.

- **The Blow Job[70] Pattern**

  OK – back to 101 spells for lovesick teenagers. This is another of Ross Jeffries innovations, and I am rather skeptical of its efficacy, especially since you need to establish a rapport with your prospective girlfriend. Rapport means that you are mostly "there" no matter what follows and is probably the hardest part. Anyway, on with the routine, which falls into three parts.

  > First, ask her about anything she really loves to eat/taste.
  >
  > Second, amplify and feed back the description of the sensation of it in her mouth and the happiness and pleasure it brings.
  >
  > Third, link it to your penis by using a "dick point"

  ...which can be the use of homonyms or phonological ambiguities such as ha-PENIS (happiness).

  Sprinkle the spiel with similar references, for example "jerk", "blow", "suck", "stiff"...

  Full scripts are available on the Net for those who lack imagination. A word of warning – if you get it wrong and it becomes obvious what you are doing you can expect laughter at best. At worst the woman will think you an obnoxious pervert.

- **The Loss Pattern**

  This is designed to create a sense of loss or abandonment. Again, it is a three part process.

  > First, ask the subject to recall an emotionally charged event that involved loss, for example the death of a friend, relative or pet. Create an anchor.
  >
  > Second, casually remark on how easy it is to lose something they care about. Repeat the anchor with more intensity.
  >
  > Third, introduce an element of threat, promise or persuasion linked to potential loss. Repeat the anchor most intensely.

- **The Depression Pattern**

  This is used to negate particular values in the subject, whether it be religion, work, family, patriotism etc.

  > The first step involves a values elicitation, often by simply asking the subject what they feel is important to them.
  >
  > At that point interrupt and create a state of confusion by asking them something like... "What are you not thinking of?". Immediately anchor the confusion state.
  >
  > The operator then begins to talk about the values of the subject, feeding them back, but covertly triggering the confusion anchor at the appropriate points.

  This has the effect of linking the values to confusion, effectively negating them. An extension of this technique is to have the subject perform the

---

[70] Fellatio, in case of variations in slang. However that is the pattern's name, or just "BJ Pattern"

pattern on themselves. The script[71] would run something like: "I'm not sure how well you can imagine thinking about (Values) and still having this feeling (Trigger Anchor) in the future... from now on... but that's not something you have to think about consciously as it takes place."

- **Voice Roll**
  This is the pacing of speech in a rhythmic pattern that tends to induce a trance in the listeners. The pace consists of introducing a pause around once a second, and is used by a lot of public speakers, politicians and preachers: "Imagine you are listening... listening to this... and while doing so... you begin to understand the power... the power of such a rhythm..."

- **Story Telling**
  Probably the oldest emotionally manipulative art-form used throughout history by everyone from ordinary people to politicians and shamans. The key to the effectiveness of storytelling is to choose a central character that the listener can identify with emotionally. People react *as if the story were real* and hence become suggestible to the storyline itself, often defining good and evil. If telling the story oneself, its effectiveness is increased by adding emotion and playacting into the telling – imagine telling a story to children. Also, stray off topic occasionally and well as using something like the Milton Model's "extended quotes" that forces the listener to pay close attention.

Subliminal Audio

The most notorious case of alleged subliminal influence in recent times involved the band *Judas Priest* and their album *Stained Class*. Two teenagers shot themselves whilst under the influence of alcohol, cannabis and rock'n'roll. One died and the other blew his face off. The parents brought a case against the band claiming that a subliminal message saying "Do It" was a major cause. The defense argued that there were no subliminal messages, that if there were they would be telling fans to buy more records, that it would be counterproductive for the band to kill its fans and "Do It" had no meaning in any event. The case was dismissed.

However, the accusation follows an ancient strand of modern folklore claiming that some records contained sinister mind altering messages that were revealed only when the record was played backwards. While some bands have actually done this, most notably the *Beatles* on their 1966CE album *Revolver*, the scientific evidence strongly suggests that *backmasking* as it is called is ineffective as a persuasive technology.

So, now we know what does not work, we shall move on to what does, at least to some extent. The easiest way to introduce a message subliminally is to mask it by placing it just beyond the threshold of obvious perception and overlaying it with a more conventional message such as music. The effect is somewhat akin to

---

[71] Mind Control 101, Dantalion Jones, ISBN978-1-4303-1815-6

listening to a piece of music on the radio and hearing slight interference from another station. Well, at least on the old analog radios, since that is not possible with modern digital technology. For best effect the message should be repeated, for while the Human brain is a superb machine for picking signals from noise it also has the unavoidable habit of imposing patterns where none exist. So while your message might be "Scream at the Devil" it could equally be heard as "Ice cream at the revel", which is rather lacking in the effects department. It is also useful if the subject is primed for the type of message by the content of the overlay. In the above case, having a piece of music with some occult theme will act as a primer for "Devil" rather than a catering suggestion. Which is of course why Satanic Rock Bands get the bulk of accusations, whether true or not.

Going beyond this simple technique we can do a lot more to the core message:

- It can be raised or lowered in pitch.
- Compressed or extended in time.
- The voice can be made male, female, androgynous or machine-like.
- It can be spoken, sung, chanted or screamed.
- The message can be masked by a babble of voices culled from (say) news reports.
- The message can be delivered by a babble of voices that occasionally converge on the same word to bring it out of the background.

All of this is fairly easy to do using modern computer technology and free programs available on the Net, most notably Audacity. The masking sounds can be almost anything, but one of the most useful are binaural tones which are described later in this chapter.

There is one more technique that is rare because it needs specialist technology, and because it is rather overt (if you know what to look for). It is the use of beams of ultrasound modulated with voice. If the carrier frequency is chosen to be at or just above the normal hearing range, say around 16kHz, a single beam can have quite disorienting effects in an enclosed area as it bounces around the room. This is especially true if the subject moves their head. However, to induce more spectacular effects outdoors and at long distance requires at least two projectors. Of the two beams, one is modulated and the other acts as a demodulator when it hits a surface. The effect is that any surface towards which the device is pointed becomes a speaker – including anyone it is aimed at. Voices seem to come out of the air. Commercial units used at trade shows and other events have a range of about 25 meters and a beam area of about 1 meter diameter. That means that someone standing close to you might not hear it at all.

Subliminals

Sigils

A Sigil is a symbol or sign specifically created for a magickal purpose. For example, in traditional (medieval) magick a sigil, was used as a visual anchor associated with some aspect of the occult, the most famous being those found in the grimoires, or magickal books. Of these perhaps the best known are the sigils representing 72 princes in the hierarchy of Hell found in the "Lesser Key of Solomon". However, for the purpose of this book only the more modern interpretation will be examined, which was largely developed by the artist and occultist Austin Osman Spare[72] whereby the words of a statement of intent are distilled into an abstract design.

Pictographic Sigils are one of the most powerful forms of communicating with the unconscious mind. Although speaking aloud has been emphasized previously it should be realized that the unconscious in general does not communicate using language, but instead uses symbols. However the importance of using the senses to bypass filters in the mind remains. It is in general difficult to simply visualize something and have the precise details immediately communicated to the unconscious. Obviously, the way we externalize a symbol is to create a picture, and view it under suitable conditions. The major problem of pictures versus language concerns the difficulty of creation. While it is said that a picture is worth a thousand words, it can take longer to create the picture than speak the words. Exactly how we create, view and use those pictures is the topic of this section. There are three main types of Sigils. These are:

- **Alphabetic**
  Made from writing a statement of intent, eliminating the repeated letters, and making a drawing from the remaining letters. The drawing should bear little resemblance to the intent.

- **Pictographic**
  Made from drawing a simple picture of your intent and then altering the picture for use as a Sigil so that it no longer resembles the original.

- **Mantric Sigils**
  Which are created by writing a statement of intent. The letters are rearranged to form a mantra, which is then chanted as part of the ritual.

- **Hypersigils**
  A term created by the artist Grant Morrison (who we will meet again in the chapter on the Great Work), these are complex extended artforms whose overall thrust is to create a magickal effect in the audience. They can be as varied as graphic novels or political theater.

---

[72] The Book of Pleasure. Austin Osman Spare ISBN 187218958X

The statement of intent itself should be both definite and assertive: "X *will* happen" as opposed to "I would like X to happen". The process consists of the following steps:

- Create the Sigil

- Stare at the Sigil, chant it, or otherwise allow it to express itself in whatever sensory mode is appropriate.

- Fully internalize it.
  The techniques to do this fall into three general categories. Using the terminology of Chaos Magick these are:
  Inhibitory Gnosis – exemplified by empty mind (Zazen) meditation or self hypnosis based on Progressive Relaxation – just allow your mind to apprehend it. Try not to think of your intent. In other words, just absorb it "mindlessly".
  Excitatory Gnosis – that of intense arousal or sensory overload, and includes everything from sex to chanting, drumming, dancing and so forth.
  Indifferent Vacuity – is almost casual casting. The idea being that the unconscious Agents responsible for performing the magick know what is happening (gnosis) but conscious awareness is minimized.

- Forget about it.
  This is simultaneously both the most important and most difficult step. It is important because you need your unconscious mind to do its work unimpeded by either conscious thoughts about it or the destructive "lust for result" that undermines so many magickal operations.

This last part of the process can be accomplished by a variety of methods, either individually or in combination:

- Through sleep
  Which would suggest it be done late at night. This is probably the most "natural" method

- Through the use of drugs.
  The best of which is probably Rohypnol, or *Flunitrazepam* to give it it's proper name. It is both a sedative and an amnesiac. Unfortunately due to its infamous use as a "date rape" drug it is quite difficult to acquire without prescription. As an alternative a normal sedative, opiates or alcohol can be used. Another possibility is Scopolamine combined with Morphine to induce amnesia along with what has been called "Twilight Sleep". It was a mixture once used for painless childbirth, but had the obvious drawback of the mother recalling little of what happened. On a slightly related theme it is also one of the principal ingredients in the legendary "Flying Ointment" of European Witches, which was variously concocted from a mixture of various plants such as Henbane, Belladonna and other members of the

Datura family. The vaginal application with the use of a broomstick allegedly accounts for the Halloween associations of witches flying on broomsticks. For those who might be thinking of trying this, be aware that the Therapeutic Index is narrow. That is, the amount of the drug necessary to get the effects you want versus a fatal overdose are uncomfortably close to each other.

- Through the use of a post-hypnotic command designed specifically to induce the kind of amnesia desired.
  This obviously has to be put in place before any Sigil operation. Whether it is triggered by the process itself, a self administered trigger or by a third party to the working, is up to the magician.

- Through the use of hypnotic technique to replace the memory with some alternative so as not to leave an obvious gap.

One of the most effective techniques is to cast the Sigil whilst in the lucid dream state, something covered elsewhere. The process is similar to the above but may incorporate various "virtual" techniques to implant the sigil into the unconscious, including sex. The magician would then allow themselves to slip from the lucid state into full dream in order to facilitate amnesia.

Magnetics

Although covered in much greater detail in the relevant chapter the use of modulated magnetic fields specifically as adjuncts to subliminal influence and hypnotic induction needs to be examined. A key paper[73] was one by Persinger et al where spoken words were impressed upon a magnetic field, presumably by the simple use of an audio amplifier feeding various coils. The abstract states:

> "Electromagnetic equivalents (about 1 micro T) of the acoustic signature of spoken words were applied across the temporoparietal lobes by an array of external solenoids. Participants were asked to select the target word within a group of words. The experimental group of 7 chose the target word or words that shared its emotional dimensions (activation, evaluation) more frequently than did the reference group of 6 who received no electromagnetic equivalents. Implications for the neurocognitive detection of the emotional (connotative) components of word stimuli when transformed to electromagnetic equivalents rather than direct images or "word sounds" are discussed."

What is remarkable is the low level of the field employed, which is about one or two percent as strong as the geomagnetic field. In other words, *very* weak. Although these fields were applied very close to the head one can imagine possibly similar

---

[73] Healey F, Persinger MA, Koren SA, Percept Mot Skills 1997 Dec 85:3 Pt 2 1411-8

effects for whole body immersion in a larger area field. A simple example might be the use of the command "Sleep!" repeated with an overlaid low frequency entrainment signal to move the subjects into the Theta state. As the above abstract states, the words need to have emotional resonance. While it is unlikely to be anywhere as effective as say, binaural sound, the advantage is that it would be utterly undetectable without instrumentation.

The Hypnogogic State

This is the state between waking and sleeping that we all pass through twice a day. It is the state where "waking sleep" occurs and where full sensory hallucinations are often manifest and laid over the real world. Strictly speaking, the hypnogogic state is the transition from waking to sleeping, and the state between sleeping to waking is called the *hypnopompic* state. However, for obvious reasons the former is more accessible than the latter for experimental purposes and it will be this we focus upon.

Creation and maintenance of the hypnogogic state is actually quite easy. Most of us have been a passenger in a car, plane or on a train and have subsequently experienced the kind of superficial sleep caused by noise, motion and boredom coupled with discomfort. It is the latter that prevents a full deep sleep. A similar and more dangerous effect is found in those who operate noisy droning machinery and whose job is both dull and repetitive. Such conditions have often led to industrial accidents as the operator slides gradually into a partial dream state and becomes careless. I discovered this for myself years ago when as a student I got a holiday job at a bakery. Often I was responsible for offloading very hot iron trays of bread from the oven conveyor belt. It had all the features described above and I regularly found myself drifting into a dreamlike state only to be shocked to full consciousness when I burned my hand or wrist on the metal. After several weeks I had a good selection of thin scars on my forearms from the burns.

There are a number of ways to create the conditions necessary for controlling the hypnogogic state. At its most basic the first requirement is a source of white noise sufficient to drown out most other ambient sounds, ideally modulated at around 2Hz. This tends to entrain the brainwaves and move them towards those found during sleep and should be done under low light conditions in a visually boring environment. For example, facing a blank wall. Finally the person being inducted into this state must not be able to get comfortable enough to actually pass through this stage into genuine sleep. The easiest way to ensure this is to have the person standing, or sitting on a stool, so that they become unstable and start to fall if they go too deep. More sophisticated methods might involve small electric shocks or sharp sounds in response to failing to maintain position sufficiently well. Having the temperature of the room elevated also creates drowsiness in many people.   Performing a repetitive manual task can be an additional prop in the unlikely event that the above conditions fail to rapidly create the desired condition. If such a task is added it results in the forced focusing of attention which prevents, or delays, the onset of dreaming. In fact it is often the task, or failure to correctly perform it, which results in the electric or sonic shock or if one is driving a car the resulting crash. Naturally, the hypnogogic state is better induced if the person is slightly tired in the first place and so it is more effective to perform this in the afternoon or evening rather than in the morning after they have just woken from a good night's sleep.

This state is quite useful for introspective meditation. That is, meditation aimed at recognising and analyzing the nature of ones own mind. As one begins to slip in and out of the sleep state there is enough of the conscious mind still available to perceive and remember what is happening. Apart from the obvious hallucinations, which can be extremely realistic, it is possible to "feel" various mental faculties closing down and opening up as waves of sleep come and go. From this it is apparent that the hypnogogic state is not a single well-defined state but a broad continuum between being fully awake and fully asleep, with movement throughout this broad band being almost unavoidable.

Once in the required state various suggestions or information can be imparted either directly or by using subliminal techniques covered elsewhere. Alternatively information can be elicited without the conscious mind having either the time or ability to process or censor it. It is interesting to note that whether one is relaxed or stressed does not particularly matter except in terms of speed of achieving the required state, and even that is not too critical since it is largely involuntary.

Some readers might also recognize the above conditions as being similar to sensory deprivation interrogation techniques pioneered by the British army, amongst others. It should be noted that this has been condemned as a form of torture if maintained for any length of time and can result in long-term psychological trauma. Where it differs from the above is in duration (often days) and the added factor of coercion, plus beatings for failure to maintain posture. In fact, quite a few of the techniques discussed in this book bear more than a passing resemblance to interrogation and brainwashing technologies.

Sleep Learning

One of the fads of the 1960s which appeared along with the availability of cheap tape recorders was *sleep learning*. The idea is quite simple to implement. You have a small speaker under your pillow and voice playback containing the information you want to learn. The device activates during the night at a volume insufficient to wake you and during the night you painlessly learn whatever is on the menu. The classical application was to learn foreign languages.

Studies[74] done over the years concerning its efficacy are somewhat mixed

---

[74] Simon, C. W. & Emmons, W. H. (1956). Responses to material presented during various levels of sleep. Journal of Experimental Psychology, 51, 98 – 97. as described by Kendler (1963)

but overall studies using EEG machines have revealed that when the subjects were awake, or simply relaxed with their eyes closed, they learned about 80 per cent of the information broadcast to them. However, when they were asleep, as defined by the patterns of the record, there was no evidence of learning. The researchers concluded that such teaching during sleep fails and at best keeps people awake so that learning can take place.

However, as we have seen, sleep is not a well defined state where one is either asleep or awake since there are intermediate steps. This may account for the anecdotal evidence of people who use it frequently and report great results. It may be that, as the researchers claimed, it kept people awake, or more likely in that kind of borderline Theta region which has been associated with enhanced learning abilities. In which case overlaying the material to be learned with a Theta binaural tone may provide a better solution. Try it and see, if you are interested. Again, using a computer to take audio source material, split it (if necessary) into left and right stereo channels and add a binaural is not difficult when using something like Audacity. Of course, headphones or ear buds must be used.

Subliminals

Psi and Science

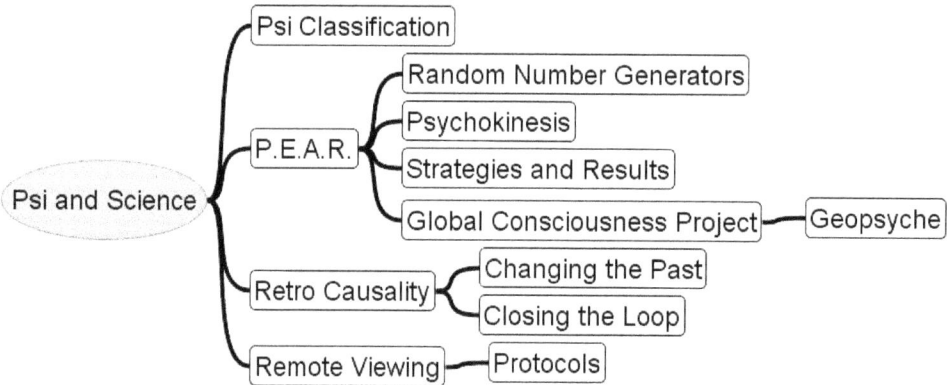

8 Psi and Science

If there exists any magick in the sense that most practitioners believe then there must exist a direct and largely unexplored mode of interaction between Mind and Reality. Beyond the known psychological aspects of the mind lie such gray areas, most powerfully exemplified by the collection of phenomena that fall under the heading of *Parapsychology*, or *Psi* for short. However, unlike most scientific summaries of the state of the art we are going to focus on aspects that have a direct relevance to group working and additionally manifest undeniably powerful effects. With one or two notable exceptions the laboratory work of the past decades has been sterile and pointless and out of necessity has almost always focused on the fragile abilities of individuals. Any effects manifested have only been seen when statistical analyses are performed which leads to arguments over protocols, cheating, unconscious biases and so forth. The end result is that the believers constantly try to convince hardcore skeptics with ever more rigorously controlled experiments, all to no avail. Meanwhile, out in the real world, there are intense manifestations of Psi phenomena in settings which are remarkably similar to group oriented ritual magick, most notable amongst these being the modern séance.

There is a whole slew of types of Psi but generally they fall into one of three categories, that of extrasensory information acquisition and perception (ESP), that of psychokinetic (PK) effects and those that purportedly involve contact with other intelligence. The latter includes ghosts, spirit contacts, various hauntings, reincarnation, angels and demons and (depending upon inclination and beliefs) UFO contacts. All these are, or have been, recorded as part of magickal practices through the ages and so it is worth looking at the state of the art from a scientific point of view to discover what may be learned in order to extend our capabilities.

Before we move on to examining specific experiments we need to define exactly what we are seeking. The various psychic talents and phenomena are listed here according to their group:

Information:

- Telepathy – direct communication between minds.

- Psychometry – acquisition of past information from an object.

- Clairvoyance – acquisition of contemporary information via "Remote Viewing".

- Astral Projection – a more "personal" variation on clairvoyance where the person believes they leave their body and travel in space and/or time.

- Reincarnation – transfer/continuity of (at least) information or "souls" between lives separated in time.
- Precognition – acquisition of information from the future.

Physical Effects:
- Psychokinesis (PK) – movement of physical objects either microscopic or macroscopic, including teleportation (apports).
- Healing, or inducing illness/disease.

Intelligent Entities:
- Mediumship – also known as "channeling", contact with the spirit world.
- Hauntings – perception of the immediate and seemingly intelligent presence of non-corporeal entities whether formerly Human or not.
- Poltergeist phenomena – hauntings with a significant objective physical component.
- Demonology – visitations by non-Human intelligent entities.

The major problem is that Psi research has been in process for over a century and little real progress has been made. So little, in fact, that most scientists are skeptical that there is any such thing as psychic phenomena at all. This includes all of the above and especially the third category in those cases not amenable to laboratory testing. The reason for this is largely due to the fact that Humans are immensely complex and what is at best usually a small statistical effect is swamped by uncontrolled and largely subjective variables. Another drawback is that there are no suitable theories of Psi that both meshes with modern scientific knowledge and leads to significant testable predictions. Nor, so far, has it been possible to remove the Human factor from Psi experiments although PK experiments come the closest as performed by organizations like Princeton Engineering Anomalies Research (PEAR), which we shall look at in more detail.

The problem with checking Psi theories in the lab is that the effects are so subtle that simply believing, or disbelieving, in *any* theory can provide the confirmation one is looking for. Belief is crucial, and Nature seems to follow on behind. One might assume that theories only become really testable when Psi is being manifested on a massive scale. However, since a major function of theory is to indicate ways in which Psi might be made to manifest far more strongly it becomes something of a chicken and egg situation unless the theory is absolutely correct. If it is only partially correct then the effects of experiments designed to test it can be masked by the effects engendered by the belief it instills. There is also the strong possibility that standard scientific procedures, such as the separation of the scientist from direct involvement with the experiment may be impossible, even when others perform that experiment. It is essentially another manifestation of the Placebo Effect, this time operating on external physical reality. It also does not help that many Psi effects are so far outside of the current boundaries of theoretical physics that few physicists see any worth in pursuing theories of Psi. However, if the retro-causality described later were proven to exist beyond doubt it would lead to a revolution in science and technology.

Given Occam's Razor, which says that in general the simplest explanation is the one most likely to be true, it is reasonable to assume we do not possess a myriad of independent Psi powers, but only one that manifests in various forms. In what follows we are going to assume that the "information" and "physical effects" categories above are the major manifestations of Psi and the "intelligence" category is only loosely connected to the others as a kind of group-mind overlay. Furthermore, that for all practical purposes there are only two Psi effects – acquisition of information (however the mind cares to dress it in various synaesthetic and illusory guises) and variants of PK. However, even this distinction may not be necessary since there exist theories which indicate that information traveling backwards in time may result in force-like characteristics. Even so, the massive PK effects described later in this chapter seem to stretch such hypotheses to breaking point.

Much of this is reminiscent of Quantum Mechanical Entanglement and the measurement process. Naturally this has led to a great deal of theorizing but so far no model proffered has led to any substantial new physics that can be tested in the standard scientific manner. That is to say, with machines demonstrating Psi effects in place of Humans. Whether this is at all possible is unknown at present, although perhaps the advent of Quantum Computers might alter the situation.

It is also fair to say that all Psi phenomena involve mental states that are not normally accessible to most people most of the time. This being so, the more esoteric magick then becomes the art of engineering suitable mental states conducive to the directed application of Psi phenomena. Anyway, we will start our rather partisan survey with the more scientifically acceptable research carried out at Princeton, partly because it provides probably the best laboratory evidence of PK and partly because the methods it uses have a direct bearing on the Global Consciousness Project featured later.

Princeton Engineering Anomalies Research (PEAR) [75]

The Princeton Engineering Anomalies Research (PEAR) program was established at Princeton University in 1979CE by Robert G. Jahn, then Dean of the School of Engineering and Applied Science, to pursue rigorous scientific study of the interaction of human consciousness with sensitive physical devices.   Most of the published work has been on the effect of conscious intent on the outputs of

---

[75] Princeton Engineering Anomalies Research, C-131, Engineering Quadrangle, Princeton University, Princeton NJ 08544-5263

random event generators (REG), and the following data is abstracted from a paper[76] summarizing results over a twelve year period. The main type of REG used creates an output from noise generated at the Quantum level from reverse biased semiconductor junctions, which is then suitably conditioned. It provided 200 bit binary strings of zeros and ones counted at the rate of 1000 per second that in PEAR terminology constitutes a *trial*. The results are presented to the person attempting to influence the machine, known as the operator, by one of several methods ranging from lights on the machine to computer graphics. The operator is typically required to perform one of three actions or *intentions*. These are:

- To not exert any conscious influence on the machine in order to establish a baseline reading of bit counts, that is, get a series of readings where the person is not trying to do anything (although they may still be having an effect).

- To try to deliberately create results above this baseline

- To try to deliberately create results below this baseline.

The latter two attempts are collected in *runs* of 50, 100, or 1000 trials, depending on operator and protocol variations, and compounded over a number of experimental *sessions* into predefined data *series* of a specified number of trials, ranging from 1000 to 5000 per intention. Data processing is carried out at the session level. More details concerning protocols and so forth can be found on the PEAR website. The results determined from some two and a half million trials with over one ninety operators are the main focus of this section, especially with regard to what they can tell us from the point of view of magickal operations. In this respect they are extremely interesting, especially in light of the rest of this chapter. The overall effects occur at a level of about 1 in 10,000 per bit of processed data, which although tiny adds up to produce overall results that are statistically significant in the extreme. It is from these that the more fine-grained results can be abstracted. They can be summarized as follows.

- **Device Independence**

    There appears to be no device dependence. The REG noise source has been replaced with similar and different microelectronic units, as well as mechanical devices that act to amplify tiny variations in initial condition. Typical of these are a cascade machine where balls falls through a series of pegs which sorts them into different compartments. Experiments using a pendulum also exhibit significant correlations with operator intention and both exhibit effects on the same scale as with the electronic REGs. Anomalous results disappear when deterministic sources are used. This

---

[76] Journal of Scientific Exploration, Vol. 11, No. 3, 1997. Correlations of Random Binary Sequences with pre-Stated Operator Intention: A Review of a 12-Year Program – R. G. Jahn, B. J. Dunne, R. D. Nelson, Y. H. Dobyns, and G. J. Bradish

means that when a source is generating non-random signals the effects disappear.

- **Operator Decline**
  There is a tendency for operators, when running through a sequential series, to produce good results on their first series before falling off in their second and third and then recovering to some intermediate level in their subsequent efforts. No such trend exists in accumulating baseline data. This decline effect has been reported in other Psi studies by other researchers in many other forms of lab testing, and is assumed to be psychological in origin. The stabilization also suggests that their generation are not subject to the traditional learning curves observed in most cognitive processes.

- **Space and Time**
  Operator effects seem undiminished by distance, certainly over laboratory distances and in other tests over several thousand kilometers. More remarkable still is that these effects are undiminished over time. This occurred in some 87,000 trials where the operators were actively addressing their intentions to the machine's operation at times other than those at which the data was generated. The time differential ranged from 73 hours before to 336 hours after machine operation and the data displayed a similar scale and character of anomalous results to normally generated data. This strongly implies not only can future events be affected, which is probably not too surprising, but that the past is malleable also. That is – the past can *apparently* be altered! Since these tiny effects can be detected and amplified to create major events there would appear, in principle, to be no limits on the degree to which the past can be changed. Consider the extreme example of those anomalous results being detected in the past, from a future intention which then triggers a bomb killing the operator before they can attempt the experiment. Of course, this presents us with classic the Time Travel Paradox problems of *retro-causation*. Unfortunately PEAR has not collected enough data to be able to examine the various possibilities, discussed later, in order to rule in or out any of the alternatives.

- **Operator Strategy**
  There have been numerous strategies that operators have used to try to influence the machine. They are as varied as concentrating on the machine to ignoring it almost completely. None seems to work particularly well, although there does appear to be one commonality found amongst the most effective operators. They tend to consider the device in anthropomorphic terms, much like the way many people relate their cars almost as if the car was a person. One presumes that it is this bond, the identification with the machine and the immersion in the process that creates some kind of deeper connection or resonance. Compare this to the Owen Experiment described earlier in the chapter on Psi and the Occult.

- **Gender**
  There appear to be significant disparities between the results of male and female operators. In general women seem more effective in creating anomalous results. However they seem less able to direct the effects intentionally. This is apparent in the higher baseline figures, which seemingly reflects a general inability to "switch off". It is also manifest in more asymmetrical graphs with respect to the intentional high and low efforts around the baseline than with male efforts. That is, the difference between the baseline and low was less than the difference between baseline and high intention output. Similar gender distinctions were observed in the remote REG data, as well as in the local and remote data produced on the random mechanical cascade and pendulum devices. It is interesting to speculate on the possible light this throws on poltergeist activity, where pubescent girls are often involved and women in general are more than twice as likely to be the focus as men.

- **Co-operative Efforts**
  Although the database is considerably less extensive than for single operators some inferences are possible. The most interesting discoveries concern the differences between mixed and single gender pairs. The results produced by eight same-sex pairs are opposite to intention in both directions of effort, while those of seven opposite-sex pairs are significantly positive in both directions of effort, with an average effect size nearly four times larger than that of the single operators. Four opposite-sex couples who were in a relationship produced even more striking results, with an average effect size twice that of the random opposite-sex pairs, and nearly six times that of the same eight individuals operating alone. In addition to this opposite sex pair data also displayed better symmetry in the high and low-going efforts, compared to the asymmetrical results typical of the single operator databases.

- **Groups**
  A portable REG was built for use among groups including environments such as professional symposiums, business meetings, ritual assemblies and sporting events. Statistical assessment of examples drawn from ten applications, appropriately corrected for multiple analysis, showed a collective probability against chance occurrence of 1 in 5000. Interpretations as to the reasons for this are varied but suggestions include that high degrees of attention, intellectual cohesiveness, shared emotion, or other coherent qualities of the groups tend to create such distortions in the data streams. Venues that appear to be conducive to such anomalies include small intimate groups, group rituals, sacred sites, musical and theatrical performances and charismatic events. Data generated during academic conferences or business meetings show no deviations from chance.

Interestingly, in virtually all of the deployments the participants were addressing no conscious attention to the REG unit, and in many cases were unaware of its existence. This clearly raises questions about the role of deliberate intention in such interactions, and may indicate deeper aspects of consciousness being manifest. This possibility is examined in far more detail later in the section on Global Consciousness.

Temporal Paradox and Retro-Causality

Given some of the results above, especially those involving precognition and apparent retro-causation, it seems appropriate to include an analysis of temporal paradox, currently a reasonably hot topic in physics. The latter has been classically summed up in the *Grandfather Paradox*, which asks what would happen if a person went back in time and killed their grandfather when the latter was a child. If that were so, then the time traveler would never have been born and hence could not have gone back in time to kill their grandfather. Leaving aside the obvious observation that maybe Grandma cheated on him and he was not the real Grandfather (and should this really be the Grandmother Paradox?) what can this tell us about time travel and retro-causality? So far there only a few resolutions have been proffered by physics. These are:

- Time travel is not possible, and no causal influence (information) can propagate into the past. This has been the standard response of science until relatively recently.

- Information can be sent into the past but in such a manner that it cannot be utilized. This is the current situation with measurement processes on Quantum Entangled particles.

- It is possible to send usable information into the past, but not actually to use it. This is the more general case of the above.

- The past can be changed, but only in specific ways that lead to a present that sends the influence backwards. Hence only closed temporal loops are possible and paradox is forbidden.

- The past can be changed in an arbitrary manner but this creates a new branch of reality. Hence it has no influence on the branch that sends the retro-causal influence. This is effectively the use of the Many Worlds Interpretation of Quantum Mechanics to resolve the paradox.

So let's take the REG retro-causation data at face value and see where it takes us. What if that bomb killed the person who was going to trigger it in the future? The most likely resolution is that only closed loops are allowed. The present can only affect the past in such a manner as to bring itself into existence. That means that as long as the bomb is primed and ready to explode no anomalous data will be seen, otherwise the paradox will arise. However, suppose the experiment is actually performed, but in a rather milder form where the presence of anomalous data is used to prevent the experiment going any further – where did the influence come from? Such an outcome would strongly imply the existence of alternative realities akin to the MWI of QM. The influence would be attributed to an operator in another world where the same results were obtained, but where the experiment did go ahead and was not stopped. This would also imply that time travel is functionally equivalent to communicating not merely with the past but with alternate realities. In fact, this is seems to be a conclusion at which Deutsch[77], famous for his work on Quantum Computing, has also arrived.

We have just looked at the situation from the point of view of someone in the future reaching into the past. There is the opposite end of the retro-causal equation, which is that of prediction or prophecy. This is effectively what happens if we take a peek at data coming from the future. If we see that a particular event will take place, what happens if we try to stop it? The difference between the two cases has less to do with the convention notion of time as a one way stream, which is what we are discarding, than it does with respect to the notion of Free Will. Again, there are a number of possibilities:

- It is not possible to stop the event.
- The event can be stopped in all cases.
- The event can only be stopped if the data is still sent from the future to complete the (false) loop.
- Any data that could potentially be acted upon is too degraded to make this possible.

The latter possibility seems to be the most common, especially given the vague or enigmatic quality of famous prophecies. That they are seen to be accurate in hindsight is their great strength. This in effect means that the events prophesied could not be stopped and at the same time the accuracy of the prophecy is recognized with hindsight. This leads to what is probably the strongest mode of action, the closed temporal loop. This naturally leads to the question of who is doing the sending in the future. Obviously, this is known when the circumstances are engineered in a Psi experiment. However, in real life a whole slew of possibilities arise from the prophet's future self to other individual minds in the future to the collective consciousness of large groups. This possibility is examined in detail in the Global Consciousness Project at the end of this chapter.

Overall it would seem a reasonable conclusion that closed loops provide the more robust form of the transmission of influence through time. This has quite useful consequences. Consider the experiment described by Marc Power[78] where a

---

[77] Fabric of Reality, David Deutsch, Penguin, ISBN: 014027541X

[78] In discussion with the author

group of some 15 adepts of Remote Viewing gathered in a hotel at a casino in the US. They were told to view the room they were in some one hour hence, at which time the organizer would hold up a card with a picture on it. Each of them had to view the image and report on it. The image that came up the most was then decoded in one of approximately 36 numbers, corresponding to numbers on the roulette wheel at the casino. So, the organizer went down, placed a $500 bet and recorded which number came up. He then returned to the room and one hour later held up a card, holding the image corresponding to the winning number, for the viewers to see. They made money.

The act of completing the temporal loop is actually an act of True Will. It is all too plausible that most people, having achieved their goal of winning at roulette, would not bother to complete the "ritual" whereby they hold up the winning number(s) and complete the loop. In which case, they would not win and then they would dismiss the process as worthless. It then becomes a technique that exposes a failure of Will in a counterfactual reality.

Also in the above, there is a suggestion that information can be transferred between like minds. Both anecdotal stories and laboratory studies have shown that identical twins have a greater telepathic link than occurs between two randomly selected people. So it should not come as a surprise that the strongest link of all may be with oneself, past, present, future and in alternate realities.

Changing the Past – Magickal Operations

The notion of changing the past, especially ones own past, is an attractive paradigm for magickal operations. However, there is a self evident problem that is immediately faced by anyone who wants to change a specific aspect of the past, most notably if it involves their own memories. Namely, how do they know whether they have succeeded or not? For example, suppose I want to change my place of birth. So instead of being born in Northampton I want to have been born in Bedford. I complete the operation and, from some hypothetical position outside of time, it is successful – all my memories and all records show my birth place is Bedford. So, what do I experience in the here and now? Utter failure! I have just failed to change my place of birth, which is still Bedford! That is, of course, assuming that the changed past still leads to the magickal operation with the same named objective, which is rather unlikely in the above case.

In general, attempting to change the past with a named objective is doomed to subjective failure. This is especially so if the changed past fails to *close the loop*. In other words, a successful change should not prevent the operation taking place, for *exactly the same reason with exactly the same objective* – otherwise it is a different operation. The only point of reality is the actual magickal undertaking in the here and now, since the past is fluid. The magickal operation is itself the mechanism for closing the temporal loop and hence must be the only stable feature of the temporal landscape.

Whatever lies in the past must lead up to the operation itself. That alone places major constraints upon what can be achieved in practice. Indeed, at first glance it would seem that the constraint is so tight as to doom any such enterprise to failure. If one wants to change X (to Y) in the past, which leads to the magickal operation Z, one can assume that only failure would lead to Z since changing X removes the necessity for Z in the first instance. The constraint is that both X and Y must lead to exactly the same magical operation. The figure below shows the flow of events:

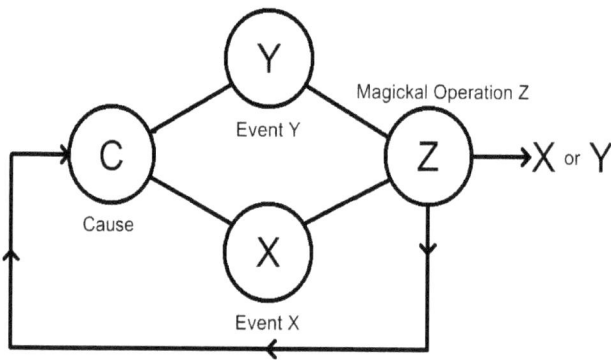

Figure 1

So the question then becomes one of what are the characteristics of events which differ from each other and yet which both lead to the same operation to change one into the other? The answer is that we do not know! Or to put it another way, we do not know whether X or Y occurred in the past because we do not yet have access to that information. However, the real power of this technique is revealed if we use it to cement *possibilities* instead of alter "facts".

Conventional science would claim that once an event occurs it becomes a "fact" as it is locked into the environment and its effects ripple outwards. However, from a magickal perspective we are talking about the consciousness of the magician being the defining feature in determining reality. If the magician does not know it, it does not exist until they apprehend the fact. Only then is "reality" made complete. So you perform the magickal operation if you would prefer one out of two (or more) possible outcomes to have occurred, but you do not know at the time which of those is the actual case until after the operation is complete. It goes without saying that you should not examine which of the outcomes *did* occur in advance of the operation.

Even if you fail to take this elementary precaution all may not be lost, because there are degrees of reliability when it comes to knowledge. That's the difference between hard science and a casual rumor. Reality is actually very hard to pin down, which is why most people take most "facts" on faith, where the degree of belief is proportional to the degree of plausibility of the source of the information. Very little in the "outside world" is experienced first hand, and quite a lot is

Psi and Science

susceptible to revision if errors are discovered.

Which raises the question, is there any way to detect whether the past, or *a* past, has been changed? The answer would appear to be "No", unless some aspect of your magickal consciousness, Guardian Angel, Hidden Observer or True Self which stands outside of time can inform you, possibly in the form of dreams or false memories. But that is a very dangerous road to follow which is full of self deception and paranoia.

A Note on Random Number Generators

Although I go into more detail on such devices in the chapter on Machines there are a number of quite significant implications that need to be examined. Basically, these revolve around theories of how the mind might interact with something that is on the atomic scale and whose operational timescales are thousands or even millions of times faster than the Human brain.

One naive picture that should be discarded is one where the mind/brain somehow seeks out the source of randomness, gets down amongst the atoms and somehow tweaks the results. Another is that this ability has anything to do with any known energies or forces. What seems to be happening is that the mind is distorting the (Quantum) statistical nature of reality itself by somehow selecting what I would call "world outcomes". That is, by deciding how it wants the world to be, and making it so in totality without paying attention to the fine details. Part of the reason for this is the way that random numbers are generated.

Most non-technical people assume, if they ever think about it, that there is a single event like an electron jumping in a device or a radioactive nucleus decaying, which then throws up the number. This is far from the truth. When that electron jumps it gives rise to a whole sequence of events that are amplified through the electronics and is eventually processed into (say) a random number, either a 0 or 1 in binary. So far so good, since one can still imagine some Psi power hitting that electron as the "first cause". This simple picture falls down because one can take a whole string of those random binary digits and process then down to a single digit using various mathematical processes either simple or complex just as long as the output retains the essence of randomness. For example, a circuit could be added that only takes 1 in 50 bits of the original random string and used those. Or maybe adds the 50 bits together and outputs a 1 if the number of zeros exceeds the number of ones. Such a generator is equally effective as a Psi target or detector. Are we to believe that the Psi faculty follows through all that mathematical processing?

Another very telling feature is that pseudo-random numbers generated by a computer from a deterministic mathematical algorithm do not work. The numbers have to originate in the "basement" of reality and cannot be in any way pre-calculated.

Remote Viewing and STAR GATE

Despite the smaller size of the remote perception database, the statistical significance of the distributions are considerably greater than for the human/machine experiments, with probabilities against chance ranging from one in a million to one in a trillion, depending on the particular data subset and scoring method employed. It would appear that the handling of pure information is an easier task than that of PK influence.

The problem with Psi experiments concerning Remote Viewing (RV) is primarily one of determining suitable protocols, most especially of assigning numerical values to results. For example, suppose the target of a remote viewing session is a lone crane on a building site strewn with rubble. If the operator reports a bare tree in a boulder strewn area, is that a hit or a miss? How is it determined? It is clearly not totally wrong, nor is it perfectly correct, so how can one assign a percentage representing the degree of effectiveness? Even if this can be done critics will always find fault so it is in effect a useless technique for trying to convince the skeptical scientific community of the reality of the talent. This is exemplified by the conflicting reports of Jessica Utts and Ray Hyman into the effectiveness of the US RV programs. The history of these bizarre programs is as follows.

A number of RV programs were conducted by the US military, defense and intelligence agencies between 1970CE and the mid-1990s. Initiated in response to reports of Soviet Psi programs the first research program, named SCANATE was funded by CIA in 1970CE. Research was undertaken at the Stanford Research Institute (SRI) in Menlo Park, California, primarily by Russell Targ and Harold Puthoff, who had previous worked for the National Security Agency (NSA), and who was the time a Scientologist. Various other programs were conducted under a variety of code names, including SUN STREAK, GRILL FLAME, and CENTER LANE by Defence Intelligence Agency (DIA) and the Army Intelligence and Security Command (INSCOM) and GONDOLA WISH by Army Assistant Chief of Staff for Intelligence (ACSI) in 1977CE. These efforts were initiated to assess foreign programs in the field, do basic research into RV and to evaluate it as an intelligence tool. An operational unit employed remote viewers to train, and to perform Remote Viewing intelligence gathering, while research was done as a separate activity. The SRI research program was integrated into GRILL FLAME in early 1979CE, and hundreds of RV experiments were carried out at SRI through 1986CE. The effort initially focused on a few talented individuals such as New York artist Ingo Swann who was a high level Scientologist, as were many of the SRI operators. Individuals who appeared to show potential were trained and taught to use their talents for psychic warfare. In 1983CE the program was re-designated the INSCOM CENTER LANE Project (ICLP). Swann and Puthoff developed a training program that they claimed allowed anyone to be trained to produce accurate, detailed target data. The minimum accuracy needed by the clients was said to be 65%, and proponents claim that in the later stages of training this accuracy level was often exceeded.

After an unfavorable report in 1984CE from the National Academy of Sciences National Research Council army funding was subsequently withdrawn. The unit was renamed SUN STREAK and transferred to the DIA Scientific and Technical Intelligence Directorate. Under these auspices the program was farmed out to Science Applications International Corporation (SAIC) in 1991CE and renamed STAR GATE. In 1995 the American Institutes for Research (AIR) was contracted by the CIA to evaluate the program. A positive assessment[79] was given by statistician Jessica Utts. However this was offset by a negative one from psychologist Ray Hyman, a prominent CSICOP[80] psychic debunker. STAR GATE was ostensibly closed down. A third assessment of more recent work was provided by Dr Richard Wiseman, another skeptic who was reported[81] to have said:

> "I agree that by the standards of any other area of science that remote viewing is proven, but begs the question: do we need higher standards of evidence when we study the paranormal? I think we do... Because remote viewing is such an outlandish claim that will revolutionize the world, we need overwhelming evidence before we draw any conclusions. Right now we don't have that evidence."

The protocols and training methods developed in the above programs have been commercialized, in some cases by former program members, and are currently taught by a number of civilian organizations. Essentially the general methodology is as follows although the specifics that follow draw strongly on the work of Jack Houk.

It has been found that the operator has a tendency to lock onto what are termed *peak emotional events* at the target location, either in the past or future.

- The desired information and target should be known before the operation begins.

- The operator should relax either sitting comfortably or lying down in a quiet place with no distractions. Various meditation techniques augmented by various technologies (described later in the book) are used to achieve the required unemotional state.

- Specify the location, date and time by speaking them aloud.

- Specify the viewing size. Again, it has been discovered that the apparent size of the operator can vary between microscopic and planetary when on target.

---

[79] An Assessment of the Evidence for Psychic Functioning, Professor Jessica Utts, Division of Statistics, University of California, Davis 1995

[80] Committee for the Scientific Investigation of Claims of the Paranormal

[81] Daily Mail, 28 January 2008

- Employ sensory modes in order. For example, what is the smell associated with the target? The feel? The taste? What sounds are there, if any etc.

- Allow information to arise from the unconscious until the picture forms – do not "concentrate". The key is relaxation.

- Avoid analyzing information arising since left brain analytical mode is counter-productive. The information is coming from the right hemisphere associated with creativity. The images should just be allowed to "bubble up".

- Avoid using comparisons, for example: "The object looks like a house…" since this is again engaging the left hemisphere. Simply report everything you get and avoid what is termed *analytic overlay*.

- Have a second person, an interviewer, present to ask specific questions.

- To avoid information coming from past or future peak emotional events at the target location a meditation technique can be used whereby initial thoughts are discarded.

Note that RV is not what is referred to in magickal practices as *Astral Projection* although it would seem to be related to it. With the latter the view of the target is much more closely akin to what would be seen by a visitor in a normal conscious mode. Astral Projection is much more akin to *Lucid Dreaming*.

It should also be noted that the operator is not in an environment of sensory deprivation but one of *Information Deprivation*. Sensory deprivation has long been associated with remote viewing and telepathy testing protocols, most notably using the Ganzfeld method. In this translucent hemispheres cover the eyes and white noise is played into the ears. The hemispheres are illuminated by a diffuse red light. The senses are not exactly being deprived of input since light and sound are being supplied, but they are being deprived of information. In extensions of this protocol the remainder of the senses can be rendered functionally inoperative by using a flotation tank. This is a tank containing lukewarm water at body temperature that is increased in density by saturating it with Magnesium Sulphate, also known as Epsom Salts. This enables the Human body to float very easily and high in the liquid with a minimum of bodily stimulation. In true sensory deprivation there is a strong tendency to go to sleep, or enter sleep-like states but with information deprivation this is minimized and the mind remains awake.

The original SCANATE program was named after the protocol used, *scan by co-ordinate*, where map co-ordinates were supplied to the operators who were then asked to report on the target. However, it was soon discovered that equally accurate results could be obtained simply by supplying a codeword labeling the target. This strongly indicates that information was not coming from the target itself. If this were so then the accuracy would have substantially deteriorated as each viewing operation would actually have been a series of viewings, each depending upon the success of the other. The first would have been at least one viewing to determine the nature of the target connected with the codeword, followed by the target viewing itself. This naturally provides a clue as to what is really happening, and it cannot be the naive picture most people have of the mechanism behind the talent. It strongly suggests that no viewing is occurring at all. If so it is either future knowledge of the target by the viewer themselves, or an iterative process whereby the viewers deliver information that they later discover is acceptable. Of course, a more basic process may be that even this explanation is just that, a plausible explanation for results occurring in accordance with Will – magick.

The Interviewer or Controller

In nearly all cases where information is being derived from an unconscious source the process can benefit from the use of an Interviewer. As we have seen, in almost all cases the Operator needs to be in a special state of consciousness whether self induced or induced by means of machines, hypnosis or drugs. Typically such a state is either fragile or, in the case of drug induction, too robust and all enveloping. In the first case analytical thought will tend to disrupt the state and in the latter the state will often be powerful enough to suppress the rational faculty. In such situations the rational analytical work can be offloaded onto a second person who essentially directs the Operator and focuses the work. This is in fact an ancient tradition that can be found across the world. The Oracle at Delphi would prophesy under the influence of narcotic gases and her enigmatic words would be translated, or interpreted, by an assistant. In the Nordic world a female shaman known as a Seidrkona would be sung into a trance state by her audience of supplicants while sitting on a high seat. They would then proceed to ask her questions regarding the important questions of the day. This type of tradition was rediscovered or reinvented in the modern military remote viewing programs and has a universal applicability where controlled mental states need to be accessed or directed in a precise fashion. Quite often this is done inadvertently as part of a divination process, such as traditional fortune telling, where the Operator is interacting with the person who wants the answers. What needs to be born in mind is the need for the Interviewer to be aware that they should not ask questions or make comments in a manner likely to disrupt the state of the Operator.

Lessons learned, from all sources:

- The required information can be accessed without target information being supplied to the viewers.
- Viewings of past and future are equally accurate (if one avoids temporal paradox).

- Remote Viewing has no distance limits – it will apparently work just as well at interplanetary distances.

- Results are more accurate if the first senses to be engaged are the low bandwidth ones such as smell, touch and taste, followed by sounds and lastly vision.

- Meaningful pictures are far easier to view than random letters or numbers. If, say, numbers are to be viewed they need to be associated with pictures in a consistent manner. This is known as *associative remote viewing* (ARV).

- For an ARV experiment, the greater the emotion generated at the time of the feedback, when the correct target scene associated with the outcome of the event is shown to the operator, the more likely it is that the results will be accurate.

- It is important that all the participants in an ARV viewing limit their emotional experiences during the period between viewing the feedback event and later taking part in it so that they are not diverted to the wrong time and event.

- Having an interviewer asking specific questions of the operator during the viewing elicits more reliable information. The questions can be standardized ones relevant to the target.

- The use of a group of operators with the same target is more reliable and effective than the use of single operators.

Global Consciousness Project

The *Global Consciousness Project* (GCP) is an international effort involving researchers from multiple institutions and is designed to explore whether events that "catch the eye" of a significant proportion of the global population are manifest in a global consciousness that can affect the output of random number generators (the REGs of the PEAR experiments). The theory is that emotionally charged events somehow create a temporary super-consciousness which in turn affects the nature of reality itself.

The GCP follows on from experimental results from an array of REG devices in Europe and the USA which showed non-random activity during widely shared experiences of events as varied as the funeral ceremonies for Princess Diana, and the international Winter Olympics in Japan. The shared emotions and coherent consciousness appeared to be correlated with structure in the otherwise random data. In the GCP, a world-spanning array of REG detectors is connected to computers running data logging software which sends it to a central server via the Net. The data itself is displayed in various forms including real-time activity, or as near as it is possible to get on the Net due to the size of the planet. For example, the cumulative deviation of data sequences from their expected values as a composite across all the GCP sites around the world can be displayed graphically over various period ranging from minutes to days. Another display mode is that of a "movie" with music based on the data that is color coded according to the statistics and which is overlaid on a geographical map. As of 2005CE there were 60 sites online around the world.

Clearly this a tool of immense value for the TechnoMage, not only as a register of global events but also as an indicator of efficacy in group workings. The actual applications are examined later in the chapter on Machines. However, it goes without saying that any occult organization having its own private planetary network will have quite an edge when it comes to ambitious projects that have a global reach.

One question that, as far as I know, has not been clarified is whether the project is truly registering events in the totality of the global consciousness. It was reported that the machines somehow registered the death of one of the researchers, Barry Fenn, who hosted an REG in New Zealand. While obviously having an impact on the psyche of the team it seems unlikely that his death actually had any kind of global impact. This suggests that what the machines are really registering is the impact of events on the psyche of the GCP team as a whole, plus (presumably) those who are involved in it in some way possibly even to the extent of merely knowing of its existence.

The Geopsyche

Two researchers into the biological effects of effects of low intensity magnetic fields, Persinger and Lafreniere, developed a rather interesting hypothesis in 1977CE that has been labelled the *Geopsyche*. They suggest that the electromagnetic (EM) fields of Human brains may to some extent merge, along with the Earth's field, to create an aggregate with gestalt-like properties which reflect the average characteristics of the brains that are maintained within this field.

What is being said, in non-technical terms, is that there is a planetary "mind" mediated by magnetic fields generated by living brains immersed in the geomagnetic field. Furthermore, given that evidence for the effect of such fields also comes from animal studies, that the EM gestalt likely includes all life with a mammalian nervous system. Presumably other orders of life would also have their own versions. It would appear to be a radical extension of the Gaia hypothesis that life on Earth regulates the planetary environment to maintain conditions suitable for its own existence. Additionally, this "EM Gaia" has effects that feed back into individual brains resulting in influences on a largely unconscious level.

Arguments are presented in the 1995CE Persinger paper entitled "On the possibility of directly accessing every Human brain by electromagnetic induction of fundamental algorithms"[82]. Most notable is a discussion as to how such minute fields could actually have an effect on the brain in the presence of thermal and other noise. Again, it seems that the crucial factor is the information content of the fields rather than purely field strength. The analogy presented in the paper is as follows:

> "… [Consider] the response of a complex neural network such as a human being to sonic energy. If only a 1000-Hz (sine wave) tone were presented, the intensity required to evoke a response could well exceed 90 dB; in this instance the avoidant response would be overt and crude. However, if the structure of the sonic field was modified to exhibit the complex pattern which was equivalent to biorelevant information such as "help me, I am dying" field strengths several orders of magnitude weaker e.g. 30 dB, could be sufficient. This single, brief but information-rich stimulus would evoke a response which could recruit every major cognitive domain."

This above paper is a central resource from which many directions of research can be followed, as well as having references relevant to the entire history of this science. At the time of writing, this paper is accessible on the Net from various sources.

Anyway there are a number of interesting speculations that follow from the acceptance of the Geopsyche hypothesis. Before I continue though, I must state that although I find it attractive I have severe doubt as to its reality and consider it an outside possibility at best. Nevertheless, it does fit so neatly into the Global Consciousness paradigm that it would be remiss of me to ignore its ramifications.

One major limitation is bound to be the low data rates involved – at best only a few hundred bits per second under ideal conditions, whatever those may be. The interactions between the Geopsyche and individuals would be sporadic, statistical in nature and tend to affect relatively large areas of the brain rather than impart detailed information. In fact, the most likely effects would be emotional and "spiritual", that is, exactly the kinds of effects created by temporal lobe stimulation! Its interactions would be more like dreams than explicit messages. It could be that it interacts with us through the triggering of shared archetypes with emotional content, and creates a tendency to conform to a particular group psychology. It may even be a factor contributing to "contagious psychogenic illness" mentioned in previous chapters. Given the nature of EM radiation and fields it is almost certain that if the Geopsyche exists it manifests in a manner reflecting the distribution of populations, with groups of people in close proximity tending to form hot spots in the field as "sub-personalities". Also, given that animals would also contribute to the field, and not mix in great numbers with people, there would be a marked difference in psychological character between town and country.

One conclusion seems certain – that the Geopsyche is a far weaker although wider spread gestalt than ones that are created through Human social interaction. Additionally, Humanity has evolved within the Geopsyche gestalt and, if it exists,

---

[82] Perceptual and Motor Skills, June 1995, 80, 791-799.

Psi and Science

has probably been shaped by it to some unknown extent. There is also an interesting question as to whether it might be stronger in certain areas than others, particularly at high latitudes and in the Polar Regions.

Attempts to explain the mechanism of various Psi talents using the Geopsyche, ranging across telepathy, Remote Viewing and dowsing, seem implausible. There are two major problems associated with such theories. The first is the low data rate, as mentioned. The second is that EM effects fall of quite rapidly especially fields emanating from the nervous system. Telepathy and Remote Viewing, as far as they can be shown to exist and are characterized, show no diminution with distance.

Electromagnetic Domain

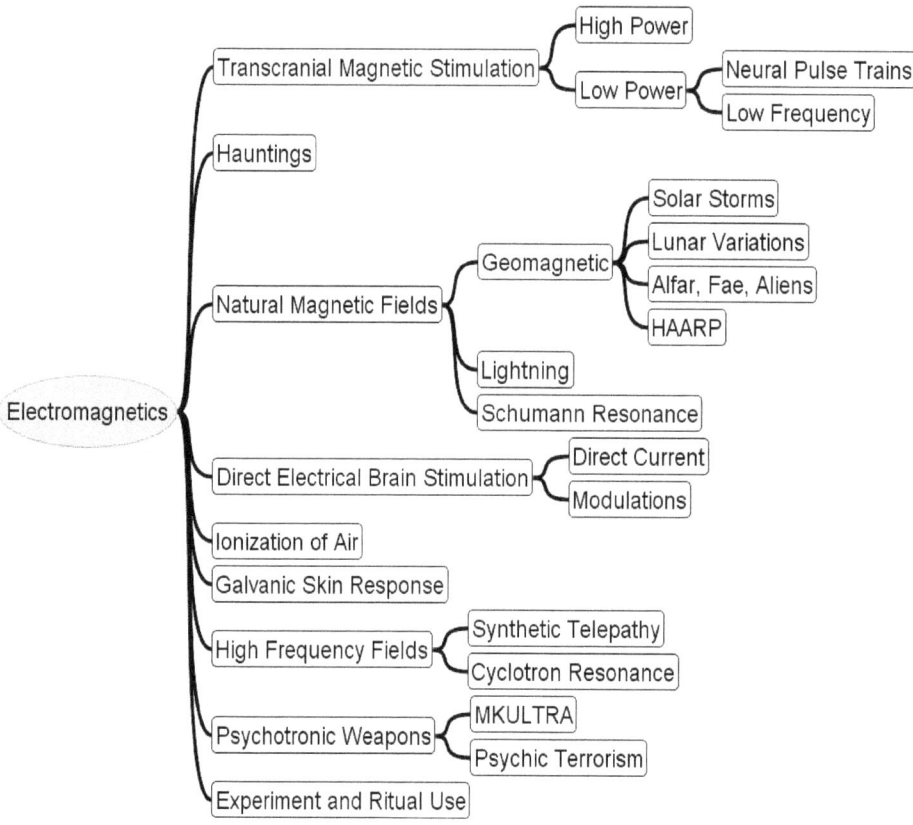

9 The Electromagnetic Domain

Apparently one of the indicators of ghostly and/or paranormal activity is an abnormal electromagnetic (EM) background. Exactly what this means is uncertain in the vast majority of cases, since a full spectrum analysis and source tracing is not possible. Additionally, there is no longer a "normal" background in any technological society – we are drenched in electromagnetic noise from the mains power wiring in our houses to radio and television transmissions to mobile phones, computers and radar. In fact, every piece of electrical or electronic apparatus emits EM radiation to some extent. So much so that there is even a name for this new pollution – *electrosmog*.

However, it is interesting to speculate on cause and effect when it comes to ghostly phenomena and its relationship to EM interference (EMI), especially in the light of work done using *Transcranial Magnetic Stimulation* (TMS).

Transcranial Magnetic Stimulation

TMS involves using a computer controlled array of electromagnetic coils placed on or close to the scalp and then activated in such a manner that magnetic "waves" stimulate neural activity in selected areas of the brain. There are essentially two types of TMS technology largely defined by the power levels used. A lot of contemporary research (circa 2005CE) uses extremely high power levels, in many cases involving peak powers flowing in the coils in the megawatt region, to directly "kick" the brain in selected locations. Typically discharge currents are in the thousands of amps delivered in less than a millisecond by kilovolt capacitors for a total energy in the hundreds of joules. For example, such power levels are being looked at as a more benign replacement of the old and damaging *Electro-Convulsive Therapy* (ECT). Even though it may be more benign, it is certainly not totally safe as experimental subjects can suffer seizures or other side effects. Having said that, it is still a very safe technology given the number of adverse effects compared to the number of trials. The adverse effects have mostly been associated with repetitive high power pulses at the same kind of frequencies that cause fits in some people if delivered by a strobe light. A result not totally unexpected.

The other, earlier, type of TMS was investigated by Michael A. Persinger, Professor of Neuroscience at the Department of Psychology of Laurentian University in Sudbury, Ontario, Canada starting in the 1980s. He again used computer-controlled electromagnetic fields created in coils placed next to the head, but at far lower power levels. So much lower, in fact, that most people did not at first believe that there should be any effect whatsoever. This was because the field strength used was only a fraction of the naturally occurring geomagnetic fields to which we are all continuously subjected. He used field strengths of around five micro-Tesla (5μT), about ten percent of the Earth's field that is normally around 50μT-60μT. The key difference though was in the modulation. Under normal conditions the Earth's field is fairly stable (although there are exceptions), but Persinger's fields varied quite rapidly. He has hypothesized that the sequences of pulses he used actually communicate in a crude fashion with the brain by mimicking naturally occurring neural patterns, altering its information flow and the way the individual perceives themselves and their environment. The temporal structures of the waveforms were derived from observed neuroelectrical profiles such as burst firing or long-term potentiating sequences[83] that can be considered the prototypical basis of a major domain of brain activity.

Of particular interest is what happens when the temporal lobe is stimulated. This is apparently responsible for much of the feeling associated with mystical states. In fact, it has long been known that temporal lobe epilepsy results in visions, hallucinations, feelings of strange presences both angelic and demonic and trance states. Transcranial stimulation can to a limited extent also trigger such effects, with reports that around 80% of people experience a sense of invisible presence and around 1% experience intense phenomena detailed below. Persinger has hypothesized a link between EM anomalies and phenomena such as hauntings and UFO sightings (Tectonic Strain Theory – where micro-earthquakes cause local electrical and magnetic fields to fluctuate and hence induce both ionization of air and also hallucinations). Subsequently he has done a great deal of laboratory based experimental work in this area that is of direct interest and relevance to the TechnoMage community.

So, what does being exposed to such fields actually feel like? One famous account is that of psychologist Susan Blackmore when she was at Persinger's laboratory. In her own words:

> "It felt for all the world as though two hands had grabbed my shoulders and yanked me upright... I felt as though I had been stretched halfway up to the ceiling. Then came the emotions, Totally out of the blue, but intensely and vividly, I suddenly felt angry. Later... I was terrified."

He noted that there were many points of similarity between seizures experienced by some individuals who suffered from epilepsy, and the types of mental and spiritual experiences of many religious mystics. He wondered if visions, a sense of the immediate presence of God, and other mystical experiences could be artificially created in the laboratory by magnetically inducing changes in the temporal lobes of a person's brain. He notes that:

> "The deep structures of the temporal lobe are electrically unstable and sensitive to all sorts of things, including the biochemistry of stress, psychological distress, insufficient oxygen, and fasting. That could explain

---

[83] Brown, T.H., Chapman, P.F., Kairiss, E.W., & Keenan, C.L., Long-term potentiation. Science, 1988, 242, 724-728.

why, when mystics go through self-induced stressful rituals and yogis go to high mountaintops and fast, they report transcendental events."

Regions deep within the temporal lobes, such as the amygdala and hippocampus, are strongly associated with the regulation of emotions and are highly unstable electrically. For example, many gestures reflect the amygdala's turmoil. In an anxious meeting we may unconsciously flex our arms, lean away, or angle away from people who upset us. Lip, neck, and shoulder muscles may tense as the amygdala activates brain-stem circuits designed to produce protective facial expressions and postures. The amygdala also prompts releases of adrenaline and other hormones into the blood stream, thus stepping-up an avoider response and disrupting the control of rational thought. The hippocampus, on the other hand, plays a role in memory, spatial awareness and navigation. Similarly, higher field strengths and different pulse modulation may affect other areas of the brain.

Persinger developed the hypothesis[84] that people who have experienced above average numbers of complex partial epileptic-like experiences might experience a "proximal presence" during an experiment in which weak modulated magnetic fields were applied either to their right hemisphere, or to both hemispheres. Under controlled conditions, his lab has induced perceptions of mystical and paranormal events, including visitations by gods, demons, and abductions by alien creatures, or so it seemed to the subjects. Experience of these strange beings and mystical encounters are typical of mini-seizures, or micro-seizures, in the temporal area called Temporal Lobe Transients, (TLTs). Some individuals are more susceptible because their temporal lobes are more electrically unstable. The theory is that when the right hemisphere of the brain is stimulated in the cerebral regions presumed to control notions of self, the left hemisphere, seat of language, is called upon to make sense of this non-existent entity and consequently interprets it as a sensed presence. Support for this interpretation of what might be occurring "in the field" (no pun intended) was provided by the work of Dr Richard Wiseman, of the University of Hertfordshire, UK. He and his colleagues carried out tests on two places believed to be haunted, Hampton Court Palace (Surrey, England) and the South Bridge Vaults (Edinburgh, Scotland). They asked volunteers to make a note of places in the building where they had encountered any unusual experiences.

Almost seven hundred volunteers took part in the studies, reporting any strange or eerie feelings they had while walking through the Vaults or the Palace. Results revealed significantly more reports of unusual experiences in areas that had a reputation for being haunted. This effect was not related to the participant's prior knowledge about the reputation of these areas. However, the location of participants experiences correlated significantly with various environmental factors, including, for example, the variance of local magnetic fields and lighting levels. Paul Stevens, one of the researchers involved in the study, suggests that different people

---

[84] Neuropsychological Bases of God Beliefs by Michael A. Persinger, Praeger Publishers (October 15, 1987) ISBN: 0275926486

may respond differently to the same cues and that the mechanisms by which environmental factors can affect humans are not completely understood. Additionally that faint, unconscious change in a person's physiology in response to subtle signals can alter their emotional interpretations of the environment. Another explanation could be that the magnetic fields caused by the intersection of two or more Ley lines in the haunted place would affect our senses and feeling in such a way. This assumes, of course, that Ley lines really do mark abnormalities in the Earth's magnetic field.

It is at this point that skeptics will stop, having supposedly wrapped up and disposed of the whole set of phenomena with a plausible medical explanation. Except, of course, for one or two minor details. The first problem is the question of why we have the capacity to experience such mystical states. The notion that such phenomena can be dismissed as a pathological condition of a malfunctioning brain does leave a few loose ends. First, stimulating other areas of the brain, such as that associated with smell, will create phantom smells. If one were to use the argument of the sceptics we could similarly dismiss the whole notion of smell. Or, in fact, pretty much every mental state from emotions to those that process the senses, to intellect. Second, if the condition were indeed pathological it would likely have been weeded out during the evolutionary process, unless the genetics have beneficial effects either direct or indirect. Of course, one can say the same of (say) schizophrenia, which while apparently a malfunction is nevertheless seemingly correlated with creativity. The standard interpretation is that the shaped fields interacting with areas of the brain create the *illusion* of a spiritual presence. However two alternative views exist albeit minority ones which are rather less scientific.

The first is that the stimulation can result in an opening into different realities that is no illusion at all. That what we have is a device that can open a portal in the mind to other realms. After all, the electrical instability and sensitivity of parts of the temporal lobe is exactly what we might expect of an organ that has evolved to detect extremely weak signals amplified biologically from the quantum level. Despite this a more plausible middle way, in keeping with the major thrust of this work, is that unusual Agents are being stimulated and brought to conscious attention due to the electrosmog sensitizing parts of the brain. Whether either interpretation is amenable to experimental verification remains to be seen, although if genuine Psi phenomena were to be confirmed beyond doubt it would be a big boost for the "sensitive organ" theory. What may well be true, however, is that people who are psychically gifted might perform better under exposure to such fields given that it appears to sensitize occult faculties – hence the interest of the mage.

Another problem is that of the poltergeist and physical manifestations in consensus reality. Here all the skeptic can offer is outright dismissal. What we can do now is extend Persinger's theories to incorporate the above physical elements. Hopefully it can illustrate what is happening, predict likely effects and offer a possible experimental opportunity to further our knowledge in this field.

The Electromagnetic Domain

The list of manifestations reported in hauntings is fairly well defined. They start at vague feelings of unease or the sense of a presence, move on to auditory phenomena, occasionally smells are reported, then temperature variations which occasionally end in the intense physical effects associated with poltergeist activity. Most rare is the classic apparition, especially if it involves multiple witnesses. Temporal lobe activity stimulated by EM fields could quite easily account for the more subjective manifestations involving most of the above, but not ones involving demonstrable physical effects. Even so, there may not be a hard distinction between the two types when EM fields are involved.

The premise is simple – namely environmental EM fields can stimulate the brain in particularly sensitive individuals to create the effects described, but additionally the brain can take relatively minor effects and amplify them in the manner of a séance, especially when a group of people are involved. The EMI acts as a trigger, and is not necessarily an ongoing causative factor. The idea that the EM energy itself can directly cause poltergeist effects does not stand up to scrutiny. The energies involved are quite tiny compared to that which is required to move anything substantial, and in addition non conductive, non magnetic and fairly massive materials have been reported as moving.

So a typical haunting might begin as follows. An EM hotspot is created in a particular area or part of a dwelling. It may be a combination of weather, geography, local radio frequency transmissions, certain electrical apparatus being used, and so on. Someone who is particular sensitive enters the area and experiences the feelings associated with the temporal lobe being or other areas of the brain being stimulated, particularly that of there being a "strange presence". This then gets "talked up" into a ghost when this is discussed with other people, particularly family members, and especially any children or other suggestible people. This effect is well known and is referred to as *contagious psychogenic illness* – that is, the technical term for what is usually referred to as *mass hysteria*. However, in some cases the process does not stop there. What then develops, with or without the hotspots providing ongoing stimulation, is a séance-like effect where each (family) member adds to the realism of the initially vague and subjective phenomenon. This then triggers further effects, this time more objective, in the form of sounds and other psychokinetic effects that can be perceived by more than one person. The amplification effect appears to be particularly powerful if there are adolescents involved. It has long been hypothesized that this is because the hormonal changes and inner psychological tensions involved facilitate (involuntary) access to mental states necessary for the manifestations of psychic phenomena. The idea that the correct EM fields alone could induce just such propitious tensions in non-adolescents is not beyond the realms of possibility. There is in fact some evidence[85] for this theory, or at least the notion of EM hotspots that would serve as triggers. To quote from the cited report:

---

[85] Percept Mot Skills. 2001 Jun;92(3 Pt 1):673-4. Persinger MA, Koren SA, O'Connor RP. Geophysical variables and behavior: CIV. Power-frequency magnetic field transients (5 microtesla) and reports of haunt experiences within an electronically dense house.

> "Magnetic field measurements for power frequencies were measured continuously over two 24-hr. periods for a small house in which two adults who exhibited above normal occurrences of complex partial epileptic-like experiences had reported "waves of fear", tactile sensations, nightmares, apparitions, and a sensed presence. The experiences occurred within an area in which irregular amplitude modulations between 1 micro T and 5 micro T (50 mG) from 60-Hz sources, with durations of a few seconds to several tens of seconds, were measured. This case suggests that transient, complex temporal patterns of power-frequency magnetic fields generated by less than optimal grounding in dwellings and telluric currents may be sufficient to evoke experiences in the brains of sensitive individuals. Cultural labels, applied by the experiments, then affect the explanations and expectancies for these experiences."

Given the above, there are a number of predictions we can make. The first is again simple, namely, the more EMI electrosmog in the environment, the more "supernatural" activity will be reported. On the largest scale this means that over the past century hauntings will have increased as the use of the EM spectrum has expanded and the number of electrical gadgets in the home has increased. The first increase would come with mains wiring and radio, then televisions, vacuum cleaners and washing machines, then latterly computers and mobile phones with their support infrastructure. Unfortunately this simple prediction is complicated by one fact, that only certain modulations and frequencies of EM field are likely to have the kind of effects we are looking for. As for what they are, not enough work has been done as of the present time to enumerate more than a fraction of them. Only the lowest frequencies and simplest modulations as used in the transcranial experiments have been publicly investigated. Ongoing investigations into the effects of the use of mobile phones, which are typically held against the head for extended periods, have produced mixed results which are naturally contested by those with vested interests in a very lucrative market.

Typically when certain types of machinery, especially those containing inductive elements such as motors or transformers are switched on and off they can take or create large current and voltage spikes on the power supply lines. This in turn can propagate back along those mains power lines to the local electricity substation. In areas of heavy industry this can be a severe problem unless machinery complies with statutory directives limiting such noise. The effects can range from interference with sensitive electronic devices connected on the same local grid, for example televisions and computers, to tripping circuit breakers and causing blackouts. Even some apparently innocuous domestic equipment causes such interference, most notably old style lamp dimmers that chopped the mains rather than switched at the zero crossing point, which is why strict limits were placed on the amount of power they were allowed to control. Equipment designed to (say) European Union directives on EMI and immunity specify that domestic devices should be able to withstand transients that peak at several thousand volts. Such

The Electromagnetic Domain

enormous peak voltages are not uncommon on domestic power lines. However, such spikes seldom come in the kind of precise pulse trains that are known to trigger psychogenic effects of the type described. Nevertheless, it is not beyond the bounds of possibility that occasionally such unlikely events will occur by chance.

Alternatively it might be worth trying to correlate hauntings with both natural features and unnatural ones such as transmitters, power lines and areas where heavy industrial machinery is active. Whether anyone has done this, or whether sufficient data beyond the anecdotal even exists, is unknown.

Natural Electromagnetic Fields

Apart from technologically created EMI there are several notable sources of natural fields. The three that are of most interest, in terms of power and ubiquity, are lightning and atmospheric fields, the geomagnetic field and electrical fields produced by piezoelectric rocks under pressure.

By far the most powerful of these is lightning, and the scene of the haunted house in an electrical storm is now such a cliché that one cannot have one without the other in horror movies. This piece of folklore may have a solid foundation of observation. In fact, storms seem to be a propitious environment for any kind of supernatural activity including the casting of spells. As the witches in Macbeth ask: "When shall we three meet again, in thunder, lightning or in rain?"

Lightning is immensely powerful. A single stroke can carry 20,000 amps at a potential of millions of volts and the radiation from it can be detected all around the globe, especially in the low frequency range (which is most pertinent to the theory). At any given time there are around 1000 lightning storms in progress and lighting strikes at the rate of about 100 per second worldwide. Additionally the electrical field between the cloud base and the ground can be greater than that found beneath ultra high voltage lines on pylons. Again the precise effects of such fields are a matter of scientific debates and possible lawsuits from people living in proximity to such, so definitive findings are lacking at present as to their physiological and psychological effects. However, there is always an electrical gradient between Earth and sky. This varies from around 100V per meter in fair weather to over 3000V per meter on a stormy day, so we are obviously adapted to *static* fields to a large extent. At any moment, the total charge residing in this atmospheric cavity is 500,000 Coulombs, and there is a vertical current flow between the ground and the ionosphere of several microamps per square kilometer. The resistance of the atmosphere is 200 Ohms and there is an average potential difference between the ionosphere and the surface of the Earth of around 200 kV. That means the average power flowing in the atmosphere is around 200 MW. In fact the ionosphere plays a crucial role in keeping low frequency EM radiation trapped around the Earth, which is why long wave radio can propagate over the horizon – it bounces off the ionosphere. As an aside, it has also been discovered that the ionosphere resonates in tune with the great power grids across Europe and North America, a phenomenon known as *power-line harmonic resonance.*

The various fields themselves are not evenly distributed, either in normal weather or storms. There are dead zones and hotspots just as there are in radio or mobile phone coverage. Geography can have a shielding or amplifying effect, as can masses of rock or metal. The latter can also focus, concentrate and reflect EM energies and fields depending on configuration, often in a manner difficult to predict. To provide the simplest example, a site on a hilltop will be exposed to greater natural electrical fields than one in a valley.

Looking to the magnetic, the greatest field is the one generated by the Earth, the Geomagnetic Field (GMF) which shields us from cosmic rays and the solar wind. Normally this is fairly constant at around 50,000 nanoTesla (nT) but during sunspot activity the field is whipped into vigorous contortions by the charged particles in the solar wind. Subsequently variations of around one percent of the geomagnetic field occur. This sounds small but due to the overall size of the Earth's field it can be so intense that it induces massive currents in power grids and overloads them, causing blackouts. This is especially true as one goes further North, where the particles are funneled into the Polar Regions by the Earth's field. This also gives rise to the flickering Aurora Borealis when they hit the ionosphere and often passenger aircraft are diverted from those regions in order to reduce the exposure of passengers to the ionizing radiation that penetrates the upper atmosphere. There is also a lunar modulation of the GMF that can vary between up to 10 nT due to tidal motion of the ionosphere, that is, a semi-diurnal variation in time with the lunar day. Associated effects include electric dynamo currents in bodies of salt water that can modify coastal fields by as much as 30 nT.

Recent experimental evidence has shown a threshold in geomagnetic activity of about 20 nT to 30 nT for the report of vestibular experiences in human beings and the facilitation of limbic seizures in rodents. This is less than one thousandth of Earth's normal field, and less than one tenth of the variation created by solar storms.

Surveys[86] have also been done of Psi research literature that indicates Telepathy and Clairvoyance do show a tendency to peak roughly between midnight and 04:00. There is also a slight tendency for the telepathic agent to be West of the percipient rather than to the East. This may be important because that ELF waves propagate more easily from midnight to 04:00, and that they are easier to transmit from West to East rather than East to West because of the ionospheric effects caused by sunlight as the Earth rotates. Also far fewer Psi experiences are reported during periods of geomagnetic disturbance, which also impair the propagation of ELF waves. However, other evidence has shown this to be the opposite with psychically gifted individuals who seem to do better on days of high geomagnetic

---

[86] Michael Persinger & G. B. Schaut, "Geomagnetic Factors in Subjective Telepathic, Precognitive, and Post-Mortem Experiences," Journal of the American Society for Psychical Research, 82, 1988, 217-235.

The Electromagnetic Domain

activity.

The psychological effects of variations in the geomagnetic field during solar storm activity have been studied on several occasions over the years. For example, a 1934CE study[87] showed a striking correlation between incidents of human illness and death during periods of sharp geomagnetic disturbances and a more recent one showed correlation between such activity and admissions to a psychiatric hospital[88].

Again, it would be interesting to see if there is a correlation between supernatural activity and the eleven-year solar sunspot cycle. There are certainly claims of correlation between the solar cycle and other Human endeavors, most notably the stock market. Perhaps there is also a correlation between outbreaks of the supernatural and particularly strong Aurora Borealis in the Nordic lands? One also might speculate that the legendary Rainbow Bridge to Asgard is not actually the derived from a mythologizing of the rainbow but the Aurora. Certainly the latter is likely to have far more affects on the psyche especially at night when the barriers between conscious and unconscious are weakened, and especially in the almost perpetual dark of midwinter close to the Arctic Circle. Or perhaps such fields create abnormal dream sequences by activating Daemons and Godforms.

Which brings us to rocks. Quite a few rocks and minerals, for example quartz, exhibit what is known as the piezoelectric effect. If they are compressed they generate an electric field, and conversely if they are exposed to an electric field they deform slightly. Normally such fields change only very slowly, especially within the Earth. The most periodic changes would follow the tides as the Earth rotates beneath the moon. However, there are other events that can result in far more rapid stress changes – earthquakes. These do not necessarily have to be the huge headline quakes as micro-tremors occur at a rate of several hundred per day even in Britain. Both major and minor occur along fault lines, so that would be one geographical indicator for strange activity. In fact, there does seem to be a correlation with UFO events with reports of balls of light being seen to coincide with seismic activity. This has been explained as piezoelectricity generated by tectonic stress on the fault line creating fields sufficient to ionize the air and emit light. What such a field would do to a person if they were in close proximity is unknown although Persinger has speculations with his putative Tectonic Strain Theory.

It is also possible that there are lesser and more subtle effects to be obtained simply from being close to such rocks when they are subjected to a sudden stress, such as by being struck. Or perhaps simply walked upon. It would certainly be interesting to take a look at the kind of minerals present in the building materials of some haunted castles! As another aside, the rocks of Stonehenge and other

---

[87] T. Dull & B. Dull, "Uber die abhangigkeit des Gesundheitszustandes von plotzlichen Eruptionen auf der Sonne und die Existenz einer 27 taigigen Periode in den Sterbefillen," Virschows Archiv, No. 293, 1934

[88] Howard Friedman, Robert O. Becker & Charles H. Bachman, "Psychiatric Ward Behavior and Geophysical Parameters," Nature, 205, March 13, 1965.

megaliths are alleged to have piezoelectric properties. Perhaps seismic records could be correlated with relevant phenomena.

Persinger investigated one such case[89], namely, experiences attributed to Christ and Mary at Marmora, Ontario, Canada. Since 1992CE individuals and groups of people have reported religious experiences near the top of a hill adjacent to an open pit magnetite[90] mine that has been accumulating some 60,000 tonnes of water per month for more than a decade. During the period between 1992CE and 1997CE epicenters for local seismic events moved significantly closer to this site presumably because of the changing mass of water. Most of the messages attributed to spiritual Beings by sensitive individuals occurred one or two days after increased global geomagnetic activity. Direct measurements taken at the site indicated that weak (100 nT to 1000 nT) complex magnetic fields existed. Moreover the patterns of these fields were similar to the experimental fields employed in his laboratory to induce altered states of consciousness. Persinger hypothesized that conditions produced by local geophysical and geological properties created the odd lights and induced physiological changes within the thousands of people who visited the area.

As an interesting aside, magnetite crystals are found in the Human brain, as well as the brains of other animals. It has been suggested that this may provide one means by which we may unconsciously sense, or be affected by, magnetic fields. In fact, some experiments with people who have ingested psychotropic concentrations of LSD reported diffuse blobs of white, purplish, or greenish-yellow lights as two horseshoe magnets rotated at 0.5 Hz. The experiences were not reported when the magnets were stationary or removed from the apparatus. The estimated peak-to-peak variation in field strength at the distance of perception was between 50 and 500 nT.

Alfar, Fae and Aliens

There does seem to be strong similarity between modern UFO experiences and contacts and the ancient contacts with the Fairy Folk (Fae in Celtic terminology, Alfar in the Norse) recorded in myths and legends. Jacques Vallee[91] made a particular study of the commonalties in his book *Passport to Magonia*. He especially emphasizes the fairy lore of the Celtic region, as this is relatively modern and also well documented. Vallee points out that many of the chief characteristics of contact with the Fae is strikingly similar to modern accounts of contact with aliens, and surmises that these accounts are cultural specific descriptions of a phenomenon that has been with us since time immemorial. Interestingly, the entities have consistently been described as possessing technology just beyond the means of whichever

---

[89] Percept Mot Skills. 2001 Oct;93(2):435-50. Suess LA, Persinger MA.

[90] Magnetite is a naturally magnetic oxide of iron

[91] Jacques Vallee, Passport to Magonia. Publisher: McGraw Hill – NTC; Reprint edition (1 May 1993) ISBN: 0809237962

society is experiencing the contact. The one constant throughout the ages has been the entity's proclivity to tinker with the genetics of mankind, which does suggest that powerful archetypes may well be involved in the manifestations. Another feature, one in common with that of modern spirit channeling (mediumship) and again pointing to archetype involvement, is the singularly useless but populist preaching involved in many UFO contacts. They are all saying the same things – they come to warn us of the dangers of nuclear weapons, global warming, the ozone layer and AIDS – all warnings that are in each instance decades too late to serve any useful purpose.

There are other items of folklore that may be relevant to the connection between natural EM fields and paranormal manifestations. It is the belief that the Fae do not like the metal iron. This has previously been attributed to a folk memory originating in a clash of cultures at the transition between the bronze and iron ages in Europe. However, in the light of the above it may be that by carrying iron, especially the more technically primitive soft iron rather than steel, distorts and concentrates ambient EM fields into the metal. This would lessen its effects on the body and brain, thus mitigating or dispelling the perception of the "Fairy Folk".

Related to this might be the ancient European custom of driving iron nails into door posts, supporting posts and pillars in order to bring good luck and ward off the "evil eye" and other malign magick. Also in Norse temples there was a symbol known as God's Nail carved upon the posts. This was the Ingiz rune containing a four or eight petal flower with an iron nail driven through the center. It was said to represent the Pole Star.

If this hypothesis concerning iron is correct, it might be of use to people working with Fae oriented magick, especially Wiccans with their steel Athame (ceremonial knife). The pagan Romans always used bronze knives in their ceremonies.

The Schumann Resonance

Sometimes called *The Heartbeat of the Earth* or *The Brainwaves of Gaia* the Schumann Resonance arises from *standing waves* that form as *extremely low frequency* (ELF) radio emissions from such phenomena as lightning strikes bounce around the world between the ionosphere and the Earth's surface. A standing wave arises when the period of the wave equals a whole number fraction of the time it takes for the wave to travel around Earth. The waves see the surface and ionosphere as very conductive spheres that they cannot penetrate and as a result they bounce back and forth in a highly efficient manner losing very little energy as they circle the Earth. They occur at several frequencies between 6 Hz and 50 Hz specifically 7.8, 14, 20, 26, 33, 39 and 45 Hz, with a daily variation of about +/- 0.5 Hertz of the highest intensity signal, the fundamental at approximately 7.8 Hz. They are fairly broad peaks, unlike artificial signals that are typically very sharp. So long as the properties of Earth's electromagnetic cavity remains about the same these frequencies remain the same. However, there is some variation due to the 11-year solar sunspot cycle as the ionosphere changes in response to solar winds and also some small alterations due to lunar tidal effects. Schumann resonance is most easily seen between 20:00 and 22:00 probably because of changes in the ionosphere at the day/night boundary. In daylight the height of the ionosphere is about 70 km but rises to 90 km in darkness when Lymann alpha ultraviolet radiation from the sun, which causes the bulk of ionization, ceases. This is especially evident across the solar cycle as this radiation varies considerably over the solar cycle and during solar magnetic storms. The actual strength of the resonance is a function of the number of lightning strikes occurring worldwide which feeds in the energy. As such the strength of the Schumann Resonance can be expected to increase as global warming increases the number and intensity of storms in the tropics. On a day to day basis it is a measure of both global and cosmic weather.

The resonance is an effect stemming from the fact that an electromagnetic wave traveling at the speed of light, 300,000 km per second, goes around the earth's 40,000 km circumference about 7.5 times a second. Of course, it is not quite as simple as this because the actual fundamental is 7.8 Hz, which would ostensibly suggest superluminal propagation speeds. The apparent superluminal effect may be due to the wave being evanescent. In other words, it may be possible that the resonant period does not have to correspond to the period of time taken for the electromagnetic energy itself to propagate around the Earth (the energy will be propagating at a speed less than light speed). One would also expect the harmonics to be at multiples of either 7.8 Hz or 6.5 Hz, but instead they are around 6 Hz separation. Additionally, the resonances are not sharp peaks but are rather spread out with a bandwidth of around 1 Hz. They generally only show as fairly minor peaks amongst a whole mass of oscillating fields most of which presumably come from local electromagnetic activity both natural and artificial. It is also worth noting that the seventh overtone of 7.8 Hz lies at approximately 60Hz, which is also driven by the North American power grid.

The magnitude of the Schumann resonance is far less than the geomagnetic field, being some tens of thousands of times less intense but like the latter it too has been part of the EM environment of Earth throughout its life bearing history. This being so, several researchers have suggested that this resonance in the geomagnetic and electrostatic field has an effect upon the human nervous system and upon consciousness itself. Perhaps it is useful to think of the 7.8 Hz brainwave frequency as the natural boundary between alpha waves and theta waves. The theta wave is frequently observed in the EEG patterns of experienced meditators, who must pass through the Schumann resonance portal without falling asleep. Of course, others have disputed such a direct causal connection by pointing out that while the frequency of the Schumann Resonance can vary by as much as 20% the precise frequency of 7.83Hz does appear to have psychoactive effects which may be unrelated to it. For example, 20.215 Hz appears to have an LSD-like effect and is obviously unrelated to the Schumann Resonance.

The Electromagnetic Domain

It is also interesting to look at the frequency of currents at the boundary between the solid inner core and the liquid outer core. Since the inner core has radius of about 1200 km, its circumference is about 7500 km. The period one might expect associated with this 24mS, or one fortieth of a second. In other words, the natural frequency of the Earth at the boundary of the inner core is about 40 cycles/sec, which is at the upper end of the range of frequencies measured for the Schumann resonances: 7.8, 14, 20, 26, 33, 39 and 45 Hz. It is (coincidentally?) the frequency some researchers have associated with consciousness itself – a kind of basic overall binding "clock speed" of the brain.

Other resonances occur between earth and ionosphere in transverse mode, that is up/down and are in the kHz region. No known psychoactive effects or correlations have been made with these.

Despite the above there have been claims that being exposed to the amplified Schumann resonance in real time is substantially different to being exposed to a purely synthetic signal. The difference between generating an artificial signal compared to amplifying one measured in real time is that with the latter we get phase information plus all the precise harmonics and that this results in locking the brain into the full global resonance. The effect in some people is to cause an immediate and profound out-of-body experience in addition to a range of radically altered states of consciousness. The problem with verifying such claims is the extraordinarily difficult experimental procedure, at least compared to most of the technology described in this book. This arises from two sources. The first concerns the apparatus designed to detect the resonance. Typically it takes one of two forms, either a large buried coil of around a meter in length and twenty centimeter diameter with a soft iron or Permalloy core or a large rigid and vertical open air coil several meters in diameter. Both would need to be coupled to low noise precision amplifiers and a very quiet power source such as a battery. The second major requirement is the placing of such apparatus away from sources of interference. Given the incredible sensitivity of the set-up this means being located at least several hundred meters from artificial EMI sources such as power lines as well as concentrations of metal or other magnetic materials. The sensitivity is such that the open-air coil can detect changes in the geomagnetic field created by trees swaying in the wind. However, once this has been accomplished and the resonance is being detected the signal must be taken off-site to where the biophysics experiment is to be conducted. Here the signal is amplified once again and fed into a coil that will replicate the existing Schumann resonance on a much larger scale. This coil must be large enough to encompass at least one person in a fairly uniform replication of the field. Finally, the experiment must be done far enough away from the original detectors (and other sources of EMI) to prevent any kind of adverse feedback effects.

Direct Electrical Brain Stimulation

Probably the most common electrical device used to feed current into the skin is that used in *Transcutaneous Electronic Nerve Stimulation* (TENS). It is normally applied to the site of chronic pain where it delivers pulses of current sufficient to create a tingling sensation. This has the effect of blocking or interfering with pain signals in the brain, and is a standard piece of medical electronics that millions of people have used over the years. A TENS unit should *never* be connected to the head. However, we are mainly concerned with the more interesting aspects of direct cranial stimulation in order to alter consciousness, which is altogether different in technological terms and which is usually called *Cranial Electrotherapy Stimulation* (CES). This has also been known by many other names such as *Transcranial Electrotherapy* (TCET), *Neuro-electric Therapy* (NET), *Alpha Sleep*, *Electro-analgesia*, *Electro-narcosis* and the original Electro-sleep. CES is the application of sub-milliamp pulsed electrical currents applied to the head for medical purposes. There are now several decades of medical experience with CES in America, which currently requires a doctor's prescription for use, so the basic technology is considered relatively safe. However, there is remarkably little information published in peer reviewed medical journals when it comes to the consciousness altering properties of specific frequencies and waveforms and what exists comes either from individual experimentation or small companies selling such equipment and is rather suspect when it comes to specific claims.

Most CES devices use a pulse repetition rate of 100 Hz, which were what the original Russian Electro-sleep devices used. However, frequencies can vary between 0.5 Hz and 15 kHz. In practice the voltage, and hence current, is variable by the operator and is increased until a mild tingling sensation is felt at the electrodes, or a slight dizziness is experienced. It is then reduced to just below this level. It may take a few minutes before the current needs to be reduced. Generally treatment times are limited to around 30 minutes. It is interesting that immediately after treatment operators usually report feeling more relaxed and some feel inebriated for the first few minutes. After several minutes to hours, the light-headed feelings usually disappear, the relaxed state remains, and a profound sense of alertness is achieved. This latter state usually persists for between 12 and 72 hours after the first few treatments and then becomes cumulative from a series of treatments.

These are by no means a placebo effects and the use of this technology is potentially the most dangerous described in this book. In my opinion it is *more* dangerous than the use of psychedelic drugs especially when used in a magickal manner with novel waveforms and frequencies.

The Electromagnetic Domain

Direct Current Brain Stimulation

Transcranial Direct Current Stimulation (TDCS) is the latest term as conventional science finally begins to take note of some of the previously much maligned fringe technologies. The idea itself is amazingly simple, namely that one passes a direct current (DC) voltage at between 1mA and 2mA through the scalp using electrodes positioned in such a manner as to target particular brain areas. At this level of current most people feel either nothing or a slight tingling. The claims are spectacular, namely that it has been scientifically demonstrated that it boosts verbal and motor skills and improves learning and memory in healthy people. On the healing side of the equation it shows promise in treating migraine, speeding recovery from strokes and possibly helping reverse some of the effects of dementia.

The latest rediscovery of this ancient technology (reports go back more than two millennia concerning the use of electricity applied to the head) came in 1999CE through the neurologists Walter Paulus and Michael Nitsche at the University of Gottingen in Germany. In their initial experiment they stimulated the motor cortex of a group of healthy volunteers and found it increased the neuronal firing rate by up to forty percent. Crucially it only affected neurons that were already active, whereas for example high field TMS affects all, whether active or not. They also discovered that the effect of as little as three minutes application could endure for hours before dying down to normal levels.

Experiments on both animals and Humans seem to indicate that TDCS can either stimulate or damp the activity of neurons that are already firing, depending on the direction of the current flow and the alignment of the neurons. Neurons in the cerebral cortex tend to have their information gathering dendrites pointed outwards towards the scalp while the information transmitting axons point inwards. When the electrode alignment is such that the positive terminal is closest to the dendrites the neurons fire more frequently, while the opposite polarity suppresses activity. The problem is that *some* neural tissue has to be exposed to the polarity that is unwanted. This can be partially overcome by placing the "unwanted" electrode just above an eye, and hence distancing it to some degree from the brain.

Paulus[92] has shown that there is a powerful effect on cognitive performance, and his team has gone on to discover that stimulating the left prefrontal cortex boosts performance on tests of memory and learning. The use of inhibitory polarity can also be useful it seems. Suppressing activity in the V5 region of the visual cortex improved visual tracking ability. Performance increases in tests can be as much as twenty percent.

Electric Field Coupling

There is another method of coupling information direct into the brain, which is

---

[92] Journal of Cognitive Neuroscience, Vol 15

actually a variant of CES and is so rare that there is virtually no information on it. In effectiveness it probably lies somewhere in the wide gap between pure CES and the use of modulated magnetic fields. It is high voltage capacitative coupling, with potentials running into the thousands of volts. The principle is quite straightforward in that the signal is fed into a high bandwidth transformer and the output is then fed to insulated electrodes that act as plates in a capacitor. The head is then placed between the insulated plates but not touching them. The area of the plates can vary from a few centimeters square to the size of a Human body. It is the high voltage gradient field that induces currents in the body or brain. Now, static fields of 3000V per meter are quite common during thunderstorms so in themselves they are not dangerous. However, alternating fields are something entirely different and field strengths could quite easily be generated of ten times this magnitude.

Potentially some interesting effects might be expected since many molecules in the body are polarized and will respond to an electric field by trying to align with it. Additionally, those molecules have natural resonant frequencies, determined by various parameters such as mobility and molecular weight, which are in practice very difficult to predict especially when interacting with the other biochemistry. However, it should be mentioned that the flesh over the skull, being somewhat conductive, offers a good degree of shielding from such electric fields. Having said that, though, the shielding is not perfect.

Some interesting, and probably unreliable, frequencies are listed in an Appendix.

Ionization of Air

A very simple and widespread technology is that of air ionizers. They are a common consumer item nowadays, at least those generating negative ions which have been shown to have numerous beneficial effects on health.

Experiments have shown that negative ions promote the healing rate of animals with severed peripheral nerves, skin lacerations, burns, and post-operative discomfort. They are known to greatly enhance cell proliferation, and in Humans to decrease visual reaction times.

High doses of either positive or negative ions have been shown to be lethal to bacteria. High densities of negative or positive ions increase the maze learning ability of rats. Low concentrations of positive and negative ions are known to produce fewer alpha frequency brain waves in human beings while high concentrations tend to disrupt alpha frequencies in a more variable fashion. In rats, varying outputs of ions in either polarity will produce measurable changes in urine, defecation, sleep period and respiration rate. In general the lowest ion concentrations were the most effective in evoking (or provoking) such changes.

Kreuger's work[93] shows the effects on serotonin levels in the blood and

---

[93] A. P. Krueger and S. Kotaka, "The Effects of Air Ions on Brain Levels of Serotonin in Mice," International Journal of Biometeorology, 13(1), 1969, 27.

The Electromagnetic Domain

brain. He has shown that in mice positive ions raise blood levels of serotonin and negative ions depress them. However, in the brains both low and high dosages of either ion produce significant decreases in serotonin. This disparity can be accounted for by the fact that serotonin does not cross the blood-brain barrier. This provides a simple technology for altering serotonin levels and hence aspects of consciousness.

Israeli research[94] dramatically illustrates the link between atmospheric ionization, consciousness and serotonin levels. In many parts of the world particular types of wind have a discomforting effect upon individuals. These include the Santa Ana in Southern California, Chinook in Canada, Mistral of France, Zonda of Argentina, Sirocco in Italy etc. Symptoms such as sleeplessness, irritability, tension, migraines, nausea and vomiting, and vision problems have been observed and have been associated with the effects of the overproduction of serotonin. At the onset of the Sharav winds in Israel some peoples urinary serotonin output showed a steep rise in the preceding two days, remained high the following day and dropped only after the winds began. In addition to the increased positive ionization there is a corresponding rise in temperature and a decrease in humidity.

Skin Resistance Measurement

One simple and traditional method of measuring bodily response to states of mind is to measure changes in skin resistance. The effect is also known as the Galvanic Skin Response (GSR) and its most famous application has been in "Lie Detectors". The crude theory behind such use is that consciously telling a lie creates a mental stress that is mirrored in the GSR and this distinguishes that particular reply from those other replies that are truthful. While this might be a fairly reliable test for the average person facing such a detector for the first time it is extremely unreliable if the subject under investigation has either practiced fooling such machines or can control their mental state through meditative experience. Such a lie detector will also fail if the subject believes the lie they are telling. However, such detectors do not rely solely upon the GSR but other techniques such as voice stress analysis, breathing and heart rate changes, time of response and sometimes body language analysis. Much more recently there has been work showing that different parts of the brain are engaged when telling a lie as opposed to telling the truth and in future detectors can be expected to provide EEG readouts of those areas.

Returning to our mundane requirements, where we are not trying to fool anyone, the technology is considerably simpler, albeit with one straightforward complication. The latter is that skin resistance can vary by four or five orders of magnitude. That is, dry skin can exhibit resistance in the millions of Ohms compared with hundreds when it is wet. What we are actually looking for are rapid transients that diverge from the average at any particular point in time, so we need

---

[94] A Danon & F. G. Sulman, "Ionizing Effect of Winds of Ill Repute and Serotonin Metabolism," Proceedings of the Fifth International Biometeorological Congress, Sept. 1969.

the equipment to track the average skin resistance throughout whatever experiment we are conducting and display only the changes. In the past this has been done manually, with an operator continually adjusting the device to compensate for changing conditions. The classic example of this approach is the E-meter used by Scientology. More modern variants use some clever electronics or computer software to accomplish the same feat. Note that when the old style mechanical meters are being used they need to be *undamped*. Usually such meters have a damped mechanism specifically designed to average away the very transients we are looking for. Hence the modern pure electronics approach is best. Usually the electrodes are placed on the fingers of each hand, but this is not mandatory and other locations can be used.

So, how can we use the GSR? In the words of a slick advertising executive the applications are limited only by your imagination… Any kind of emotional response will be mirrored in the GSR. It can also be use in biofeedback training where one learns to control normally unconscious responses. It can be used as part of a Remote Viewing protocol to determine levels of relaxation and corresponding levels of consciousness (or unconsciousness). It can be used on subjects to determine effects of PK healing or cursing. It can be used to track levels of the hypnotic state during inductions. Last, but not least, it can be used as a lie detector.

High Frequency EM Field Modulation

A key finding in recent decades is that the body/brain has some kind of mechanism for demodulating amplitude modulated radio frequency transmissions. Crudely put, the brain and no doubt the body in general, can act as a kind of AM radio receiver. In the vast majority of cases this does not mean that people can hear radio transmissions, despite occasional newspaper stories of people who have picked up the local station through the fillings in their teeth acting like an old style crystal radio. In general the effects tend to be at the cellular level and are manifested as effects very much like those described above for exposure to low frequency EM fields. The one (very) notable exception to this is a technique known as *Synthetic Telepathy* that was developed from work done by Alan Frey in the early 1960s. It had long been known, at least amongst radar technicians, that they could hear the modulated microwave beam as it passed through them as pops or clicks. To cut a long story short, microwave beams pulse modulated with voice can be heard by people whose heads are exposed to the beam. What is remarkable about this is that so little power has to be used, with power densities as little as 5W per square meter at frequencies ranging from 300MHz to 3GHz. However the peak power can be considerably higher due to the beam being pulse width modulated (amongst other pulse modulation schemes tried). For many years this work was classified by the US military as a possible psychological weapon, either overtly by beaming voices into the victims head, or covertly by being used in a subliminal mode possibly as an adjunct to hypnotic techniques. Exactly how one can hear such microwaves is a

The Electromagnetic Domain

matter of debate and is not fully understood at present. The common notion that the pulses cause local heating that results in sound waves does appear to be shaky, not least because it would imply that considerable thermal damage is being done neurologically albeit at small scales. Naturally, the existence of such technology is a paranoid's charter as someone suffering from schizophrenia can point to this and claim that the voices in their head actually come from some agency intent on persecuting them, rather than a simple mental illness. As to why the CIA, MI5, the Illuminati or New World Order would want to pick on Mr Nobody and spend a vast amount of money purely to torment them is rationalized away. Nevertheless, if someone reading this feels that this is the case and the voices are externally generated there are at least three ways of testing the hypothesis. The first concerns beam spread and penetration. If you are hearing voices and a friend puts their head next to yours and fails to hear them too, then it is not technology causing them. Second, wrapping your head in an earthed metal mesh (or the traditional foil helmet!) should also stop the voices if externally generated by microwaves. Finally, if the voices also cease when taking anti-psychotic drugs then that too is a fairly reliable indicator that the problems are internal.

However, returning to the topic of RF in general, a classic and well documented example of the potential of the use of RF to carry biologically active signals is the work of Ross Adey[95] et al who have examined interference with the Calcium ion channel flows at the cellular level. The proposed mechanism is *cyclotron resonance* and it may be produced any time there is a steady magnetic field combined with an oscillating electric or magnetic field acting on a charged particle. The simple equation for cyclotron resonance is as follows:

$f = eB/2\pi m$

where f = frequency in Hz, e = charge in Coulombs, B = magnetic field strength in Teslas, m = mass of ion in kg

This means that as the strength of the steady-state magnetic field decreases, the frequency of the oscillating electric or magnetic field needed to produce resonance also decreases. This is particularly significant when the average strength of the Earth's magnetic field is put into the equation. The frequencies for the oscillating fields that are needed to produce resonance with biologically important ions turn out to be in the ELF region.

Many of the activities of living cells involve charged particles-such as the common ions of Sodium (Na+), Calcium (Ca++), Potassium (K+) and Lithium (Li+) acting on or passing through the cell membrane. Cyclotron resonance has the ability to transfer energy to these ions and to cause them to move more rapidly. These effects will change the function of living cells by enabling the ions to pass through the cell membranes more effectively or in greater numbers. Note, however, that there are far more charged ions flowing than just the above mentioned. Higher

---

[95] Adey, W.R., 1980: "Frequency and Power windowing in tissue interactions with weak electromagnetic fields". Proceedings. IEEE, 68:119-125.

molecular weight ions would have lower corresponding frequencies and to activate them would require higher strength magnetic fields. The work documenting the effects on such heavy ions is sparse and probably largely classified.

In general these effects occur in a complex set of exposure windows. The efflux and influx for calcium ions varies with ambient temperature, geomagnetic field strength and orientation, and signal intensity. Crucially, higher signal intensities do *not* correspond to greater effects. Maximum effects occur within a window whose field strength is quite small, and generally comparable to that of the Earth in many simple cases.

Both the previously published theory and evidence shows that the main efflux calcium frequencies are tuned by the strength of the static geomagnetic field, and the 16 Hz peak was found at 38000 nT. Furthermore not only does this apply to a raw ELF signal, but RF signals amplitude modulated with the ELF signature. The apparent ability of the body to demodulate all higher frequencies, including microwaves, substantiates this. Cyclotron resonance provides an understandable and valid mechanism of action for the biological effects of both normal and abnormal electromagnetic fields.

John Thomas, John Schrot, and Abraham Liboff[96], working at the U.S. Naval Medical Research Center (Bethesda, Maryland), first tested this theory using rats that were exposed to a field producing resonance with the lithium ion. They chose lithium because it is naturally present in the brain in very small amounts. It has a calming effect and is used as a medication in Bipolar Disorder. Thomas and his colleagues hypothesized that the cyclotron-resonance effect on the normally present lithium ions would increase their energy level, producing an effect equivalent to a medicinal dose of Lithium.

Because the study was supported by the New York State Power-Lines Project, the researchers used an oscillating magnetic field at the US power-line frequency of 60 Hz and a static magnetic field of 20000 nT, which corresponds to the low end of the Geomagnetic field. The result was that the exposed rats should show a depressed behavior as compared to the control rats that were not exposed. They exhibited less activity and were more passive and submissive suggesting an effect corresponding to what might be expected if the Lithium was more biologically active. Of course, under more normal field strengths the effect would be more pronounced at around two and a half times that value, some 150 Hz.

Psychotronic Weapons

The mind-control and weapons potential of the kind of work and theories described above have not escaped the attention of various governments, most notably those of the USA and Russia in the form of the old Soviet Union. Indeed, the Russians appear to have been pioneers in these fields leading a skeptical West until relatively

---

[96] "Intensity threshold for 60-hz magnetically induced behavioral changes in rats", Bioelectromagnetics, Vol 10 Issue 1 1989

The Electromagnetic Domain

recently. Much of this work, or at least most of that in the public domain, is relatively old or of limited success at best. East and West appear to have taken divergent routes early on, after World War Two. The US focused on drugs and the Soviet Union upon electronics, that is, what they referred to as *psychotronics*.

In the US an early series of experiments involving combinations of drugs and hypnotic suggestion, most notably LSD, went under a series of code names. The most (in)famous of which was MKULTRA, but there were a whole series MKDELTA, MKNAOMI, MKSEARCH, BLUEBIRD, ARTICHOKE and CHATTER (1947 and one of the earliest). The "MK" prefix supposedly stood for "Mind Kontrol" and perhaps reflected the Nazi origins of the experiments at Dachau on narco-hypnosis using mescaline initially and then the often fatal experiments at Auschwitz with barbiturates and morphine derivatives. The US recruited a number of Nazi scientists who had worked on such programs and under the leadership of Dr. Hubertus Strughold they were relocated to the USA under the auspices of Project Paperclip. By 1953CE the CIA, US Navy and the US Army Chemical Corps were conducting their own narco-hypnosis programs on unwilling victims that included prisoners, mental patients, foreigners, ethic minorities and those classified as sexual deviants. There is a great deal of information available on the Net with regards to these projects but as most of it is of no direct relevance to the focus of this book it is omitted. However, using the above keywords will enable anyone to pursue the matter further especially if they are interested in the kinds of criminal acts which governments perpetrate upon their own citizens even in the "free world". There is more information on the use of LSD and TMS in a modern experimental context in the chapters on drugs and subliminal techniques.

From 1965CE through to 1970CE, Defence Advanced Projects Research Agency (DARPA) set in motion operation Project PANDORA to study the health and psychological effects of low intensity microwaves with regard to the so called "Moscow signal". The latter was the name given to the discovery that the US embassy in Moscow was being saturated by low intensity microwave radiation. This project appears to have been quite extensive and included studies demonstrating how to induce heart seizures, increase the permeability of the blood brain barrier and produce of auditory hallucinations. From the mid-sixties onwards US efforts directed towards mind control or alteration moved its focus from drugs to electronics – *psychoelectronics*.

In 1968CE Dr. George Eastabrooks (considered by some to be the grandfather of hypnosis in warfare) told a reporter at the Providence Evening Bulletin that he had conducted extensive hypnosis work on behalf of the CIA, FBI and military intelligence. He went on to say that the key to creating an effective spy or assassin rests in "creating a multiple personality, with the aid of hypnosis", a technique which Eastabrooks considered as "child's play". He went on to suggest that "Lee Harvey Oswald and Jack Ruby could very well have been performing through hypnosis". Of interest in this context was a book written by Lincoln Lawrence (a pseudonym), a former FBI agent who revealed the existence of a 350 page CIA document that outlined a technique termed RHIC-EDOM (Radio Hypnosis Intra-Cerebral Control – Electronic Dissolution of Memory).

HAARP

Is an acronym for a military sponsored research project based in Alaska called the *High frequency Active Auroral Research Program*. The official mission statement includes the following:

> "The Department of Defence (DoD) conducts Arctic research to ensure the development of the knowledge, understanding and capability to meet national defense needs in the Arctic. Interest in ionospheric research at HAARP stems both from the large number of communication, surveillance and navigation systems that have radio paths which pass through the ionosphere, and from the unexplored potential of technological innovations which suggest applications such as detecting underground objects, communicating to great depths in the sea or earth, and generating infra-red and optical emissions."

Principal instruments include a high power, high frequency (HF, in the tens of MHz) phased array radio transmitter (known as the Ionospheric Research Instrument, or IRI), used to stimulate small, well-defined volumes of ionosphere. What this means is that several megawatts of HF radiation can be steered to particular areas of the sky where it is absorbed in the ionosphere in a small volume several tens of kilometers in diameter and a few hundred meters thick over the facility. The exact height at which this occurs is controlled via the frequency of the transmission. This injection of energy results in a local heating of the ionosphere and an increase in its conductivity.

    A primary interest of the military is determining whether it is possible to use such a heavily ionized area to re-radiate in the Extremely Low Frequency (ELF) band by pulsing the HF transmitters. Existing ELF transmitters are essentially very long land-based cables handling large amounts of power, and are used for communicating with submerged submarines. ELF waves are reflected by the ionosphere under normal conditions and can blanket the whole planet, as well as penetrating deep into both land and water. The range of high power ELF frequencies that are of interest range from one milli-hertz up to 40 kHz with, of course, suitable modulations in order to carry information. It has not escaped some people's attention that this range is just that which has been explored for its mind-altering qualities previously described. Whether, and to what extent anything like this is planned, is unknown. Nevertheless, to quote Persinger et al:

> "…a potential has emerged which was improbable but which is now marginally feasible. This potential is the technical capability to influence directly the major portion of the approximately six billion brains of the human species without mediation through classical sensory modalities by

generating neural information within a physical medium within which all members of the species are immersed."

The reason why it appears only marginally feasible is that the power levels required to significantly affect Human minds on a planetary scale are far beyond anything that HAARP could generate, either now or in the future. However, there is a small possibility that HAARP could utilize the energy being dumped into the ionosphere by the sun, which far exceeds HAARP's input. It's location, close to the pole, is where charged particles channeled by the Earth's magnetic field interacts with the ionosphere and undoubtedly one of the research topics is to determine what effect alterations to the energy content have upon how these particles exchange energy with the atmosphere. Plasma dynamics, especially when driven in the manner of HAARP tend to react in a non-linear manner. That is, small changes in input energy can cause large and often unforeseen effects. If one of those effects was that of amplification of the HF input energy or emission of the ELF waves then a planetary "weapon of mass mind influence" might be possible.

Psychic Terrorism

Finally there is one other technical possibility I have not seen mentioned in any unclassified literature. It is quite feasible for deliberately tailored pulse trains to be introduced into the neighborhood domestic power grid, and hence every room in every house in the area served by the electricity substation. It is extremely easy to engineer if one has some knowledge of electronics and was so inclined. All that is required for the simplest device is to feed the mains power directly into a current sink, which could be anything from a light bulb to a resistive heater element, and then switch it on and off under computer control. More sophisticated alternatives could employ capacitative or inductive coupling of the waveforms onto the wiring. The total estimated component cost of such a device would be less than one hundred dollars. Current/voltage spikes would then propagate through the local grid creating the required fields. It might only require a few dozen such devices spread around to blanket a town or city, although exactly how effective such a *psychotronic weapon of mass influence* might be is obviously unknown.

While it may seem to be a modern variant of the old Hippie dream of dosing the local water supply with LSD the effects are likely to be less dramatic. I would be very surprised if it turned the environment into the Twilight Zone with ghosts, vampires and werewolves stalking the streets – but it might for a susceptible few, and make life rather bizarre on a statistical scale for many more. How such effects might propagate via conventional psychogenic contagion to those who were not initially affected is also unknown, but it is quite likely to have been studied under the auspices of military Psywar projects evaluating the efficacy of rumor-mongering and propaganda effectiveness.

If such were happening in your neighborhood one indicator might be short bursts of intermittent noise on radios or televisions connected to, or in close proximity to, mains wiring. Given that such interference is at best bothersome it is quite likely that if it were a regular occurrence it would be reported to the relevant authorities such as the FCC (in the USA) and hence tracked down. On the other hand, if it were to happen at night when most people are asleep it may be far more effective with an added bonus of fewer people awake to report any interference to their viewing or listening.

Then we have the seemingly effective long range method of altering neural states using modulated radio waves close to, or in, the microwave region. This means that they could in principle be beamed like a searchlight to pick out entire neighborhoods, buildings or even individuals. I am currently unaware of any studies done concerning the effect of such beams when modulated with the aforementioned neural firing patterns. Even more worrying might be the modulation with known harmful frequencies such as the Calcium ion channel disrupter. Which brings us again to the personal and practical.

The governments of Earth are moving into what was previously "our" space. That is, the technologies of magick are being updated and researched at unprecedented intensity using the best that modern science can offer. The real advances are to be made in taking all the various techniques, both traditional and hitech and combining them in novel ways to create unprecedented effects. Surprisingly all this can be done at extremely low cost from a hardware point of view.

Experiment and Ritual

So where do we go from here?

The obvious experimental step involves duplicating some of the low field, low frequency, experiments described and see how this affects participants in magickal or séance-like settings.

A technically complex step would be to use individual transcranial stimulators in a ritual setting. Such devices are sold commercially, most notably the Shakti created by a student of Persinger's, Todd Murphy. Essentially this consists of multiple coils placed next to the head and fed from a computer sound card by audio frequency pulses.

Alternatively, to set up fields to encompass fairly large areas in order to embrace all the participants is relatively easy. The actual apparatus is not too difficult to construct given that the frequencies are for the most part in the audio band. All that is required is a computer with a sound card programmed to output the modulated signal into a fairly high power audio amplifier which is fed into an air cored impedance matched coil. One could then experiment with various modulations of basic carriers, tuned to the range of natural brainwaves. It should be pointed out that the data should be created and stored in non-compressed files such as WAV rather than (say) MP3. The reason is that uncompressing from something

The Electromagnetic Domain

like MP3 creates artifacts and does not faithfully reproduce the original. Something to bear in mind is the possibility, mentioned by Persinger, that not only are particular waveforms efficacious, but that there may be differences between ostensibly identical set-ups because various harmonics and sub-harmonics could also have effects. Obviously using various compression algorithms instead of the raw data/sound files will exacerbate this problem considerably quite apart from hardware considerations.

The coil itself would be the most difficult piece of the apparatus to construct and match to the amplifier. To ensure a relatively constant and equal exposure the group should ideally be located within the boundaries of the coil, which necessitates a diameter of at least two meters or larger. In fact, there is little in the way of technical limits governing the maximum size and it could quite easily be wound around an entire building, or more simply, utilize the ring mains supply on the ground and first floor of a building. Nor are there any obvious limits on power beyond the thermal, that is, the power levels being used should not melt the coil! Low cost high-power audio amplifiers are extremely cheap and readily available. Given that only a single channel is required, stereo amplifiers are rather redundant unless two of them are being used in a *Helmholtz* configuration to provide a uniform field. However, each coil is unique and the formulas governing its inductance, resistance, wire thickness and overall diameter needs to be adhered to. More details in the chapter on Machines, along with design formulas and configurations. Alternatively, and easier, is to space the participants around the outside of a smaller coil.

The obvious orientation is to have the plane of the coil almost vertical and orientated in a North-South direction to alternately strengthen and weaken the natural field. However, the more traditional "casting of a circle" on the ground should also work well as long as it is realized that the field might distort along a North-South axis and be less efficacious East-West. This is, of course, assuming field strengths comparable to the Earth's. If the field is much larger then less account has to be taken of its orientation.

The possible orientations of the coil may well play a non-linear part in its efficacy, given the interaction with the steady state geomagnetic field. As previously mentioned, it has been found, for example, that the presence of a steady background field coupled with the modulated one results in a synergistic effect that can be quite surprising. The affect on transport of Calcium and other ions in the body could well be more prevalent when the orientation of the generated field is at right angles to the Earth's. It may also result in the counter-intuitive outcome that in some cases a field comparable in strength to that of the Earth may have a greater interaction with the body or brain than a much stronger one. This could create strange conditions if the coil is small and centered inside the working circle of the group, rather than the group being inside the coil, in which case some effects might tend to maximize further from the coil than others. More field strength does not necessarily equate to greater effect, although it does equate to a greater spatial coverage.

At the more complex end of the technological spectrum one might consider enhancing the Earth's field and increasing the number of coils in order to push up the resonant frequency of larger biochemical ions to the point where they enter the low audio frequency range instead of the energetically weaker sub Hertz domain. This may be combined with driving an RF field in tandem.

Additionally, in a ritual setting it will probably be desirable to bring the mental states of the participants into alignment in the early stages of the working. While mixing in an overall low frequency sine wave field modulation may be useful, a more effective method may be brainwave entrainment via light and sound, including traditional methods outlined elsewhere.

Any experiments are not to be taken lightly given the possible dangers associated with the technology. Two such might be the triggering of epilepsy or psychosis in individuals who have such a predisposition – which may be unknown to them until too late. This is far less likely with commercially available devices and waveforms than with "home-brew" machines, and especially with novel wave trains. If one wants to explore new areas then one must be aware of the commensurate risks, as far as they are known. Until there is more information on the subject it might be prudent to view the dangers as being on a par with the use of novel hallucinogenic drugs.

To conclude this chapter, here is a crude map of the brain.

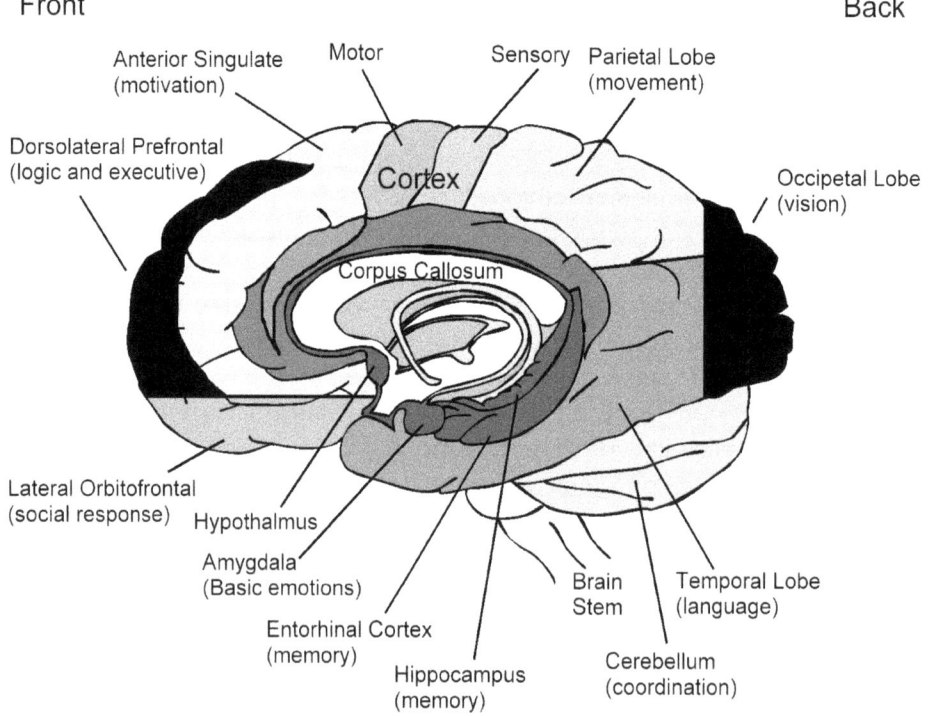

The Electromagnetic Domain

Machines

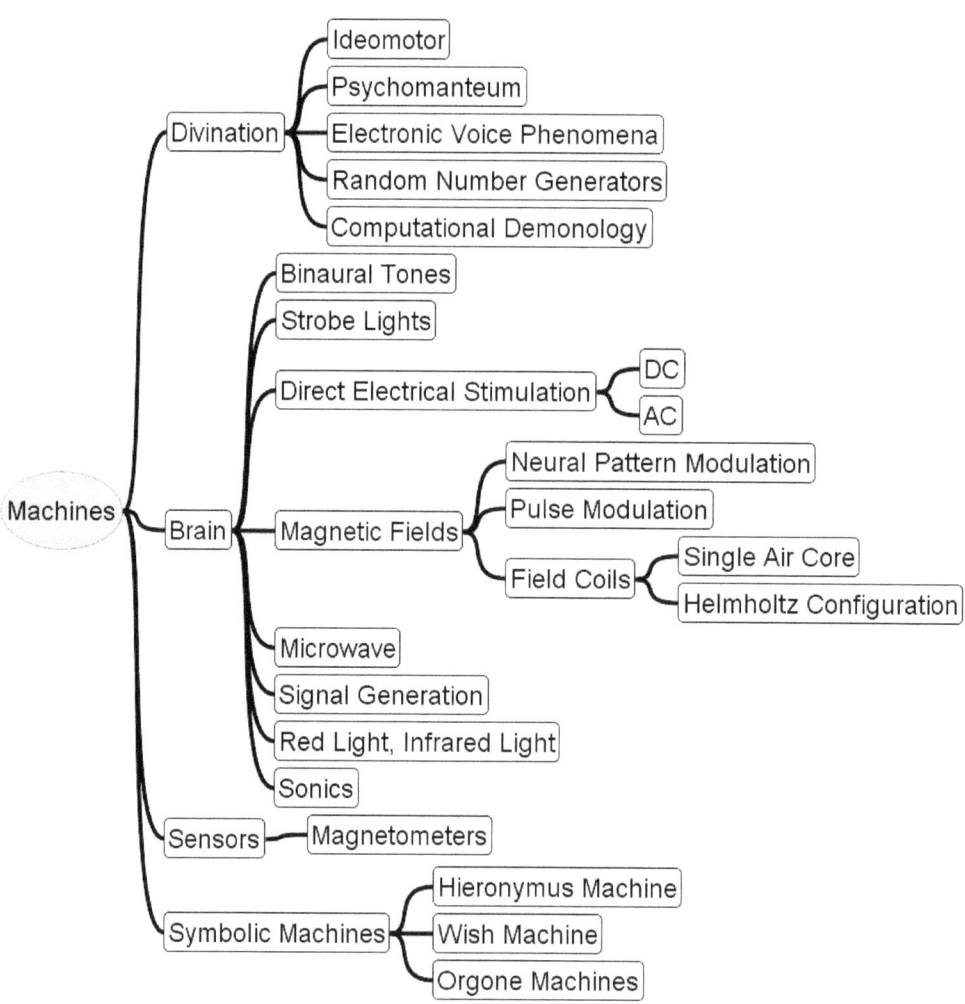

10 Machines

Probably the most common machines encountered by occultists are ones used for divination. In the context of this work they are defined as devices used to extract information from aspects of the unconscious and can be as simple as *dowsing rods* or as complex as Tarot cards and the *Symbolic Machines* described later. However, they can be grouped into several categories. These are:

- Devices utilizing the ideomotor response. Most familiar are rods and pendulums used for dowsing, but also included in the category are Ouija boards.

- Devices requiring sensory interpretation. In these cases the senses are generally sight, sound and touch and correspond to such practices as scrying, Electronic Voice Phenomena (EVP) and Symbolic Machines using a tactile interface.

- Devices requiring conceptual interpretation. These are generally collections of concepts thrown up in a random or pseudo-random manner and include such practices as Rune Reading, Tarot and I Ching. Since these are adequately covered in traditional books on magick they will not be examined further.

- Devices facilitating direct perception of the unconscious. While this can be effected in a massive way by psychedelic drugs the machine emphasis of this chapter leads us to the *Psychomanteum*.

Ideomotor Divination

The *ideomotor response* is the phenomenon whereby unconscious aspects of the mind affect the movements of the relaxed body in a meaningful manner. Its use in divination is spans millennia, with water divining using a forked twig being the classical example, and Ouija being perhaps the most familiar and modern manifestation of this technique for accessing the unconscious for information. Other popular methods can involve the use of a pendulum held in the hand, whose plane of oscillation is very easily modified by tiny hand movements.

For those who have not experienced it an impressive demonstration is easy to arrange. All that is required are two metal coat hangers, or lengths of thick wire. Each piece is bent into an L shape, with the small arm being around 15cm in length and the larger around 80cm. Hold the divining rods, one in each hand, by the short length making sure that it can swing freely. They should be held parallel to each other as far as is possible. Then simply walk forward and over a test object such as a bottle of water. As the rods pass over the bottle they will swing together and cross exactly over the water. The whole arrangement can be made more sensitive by putting the short handles into rigid plastic tubes that become the places where the rods are held in the hand. They act as reduced friction bearings.

What should be realized is that this is not purely a method for finding water but of divining *information*. It is another psychomantic technique. These rods can, and have, been used in quite remarkable ways. One method of divination can allegedly seek out specific materials. The rod holders are made of the material being sought, so that the rods only react to that material. Alternatively a sample of what is sought is held in one of the hands. At the next level of abstraction the divining is not done over the ground but over a map of the area (although this specific method uses a pendulum, which is smaller). Clearly what is happening is that the unconscious, which is far better at deducing information from apparently insignificant clues, subliminal sensory inputs (including Psi) and integrated knowledge, is outputting this on demand using the rods via the ideomotor response. Indeed, *any* type of information can be divined using the rods. If instead of looking for a material one simply places three signs on the ground, one saying "Yes", one saying "No" and the remaining sign reading "Unknown" and then ask a specific question to be answered in the positive or negative, the rods will cross on the appropriate answer. The reason for including "Unknown" is to give the unconscious mind scope for actually telling the truth. On the other hand, you may want to force an answer in order to facilitate a particular mental state. Try it yourself. Alternatively, try using a map to divine for weird stuff such as ghosts or UFOs and check it out (an example where "Unknown" may need to be suppressed).

The practice of dowsing stretches back into pre-history. The most common technique involves using a Y-shaped twig, traditionally Hazel in Europe, with one prong held in each hand and the whole held horizontally. When passing over a hidden source of water the twig will flip either upwards or downwards indicating the presence of water.

More complex versions have various materials attached to the handles which "tunes" them to look for that particular substance. A variation on this theme is a diving rod used by the Japanese which is basically a single rod coiled into a spring part way along, tipped with a weight. When the particular spot is found it vibrates.

Similarly pendulums are used on smaller scales, for example, over maps in order to look for particular materials. The pendulum is swung back and forth in a linear manner and when it is over the correct spot or material it starts to swing in a circle or ellipse. In this case altering the length of the pendulum does the tuning. The only advantage of pendulums in my opinion is that they require less space in which to operate. However, they do appear to need more experience to use them effectively while almost everyone can use modern dowsing rods on the first attempt. There is also a simple way to use a pendulum to divine optimum courses of action. Just write your question in the circle labeled "witness" and swing the pendulum over it. Wait and see whether the plane of swing stabilizes in a direction that provides an answer.

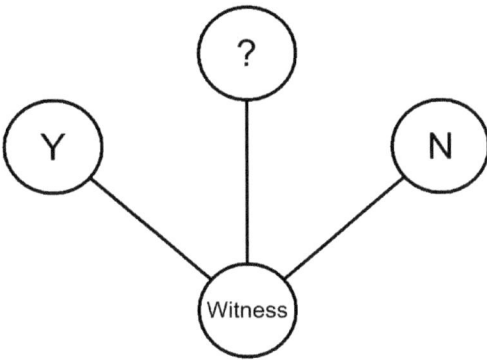

Figure 1

Once dowsing is recognized as a method for extracting information from the unconscious all kinds of possibilities arise, as we have seen. Another illustration involves getting someone to walk with the rods and then saying: "The rods will cross if your name is…" When their correct name is spoken the rods cross. Even more simply, just telling the rods to cross when a particularly suggestible person is using them will often work. The utility of dowsing can be extended by first formally establishing the object of the divination. This is best accomplished by speaking it aloud and stating what is required of the rods. Normally crossing indicates "Yes" while outward movement indicates "No" and "Unknown" results in no change.

    It is important to have the word "Unknown" as an alternative since many aspects of the unconscious will provide an answer if forced, even if it is incorrect or a guess. Indeed, it is well worth training whatever aspect is being called upon by the usual method of locating hidden items or information and then confirming verbally whether the divination was correct. Returning to exactly what in the unconscious is responsible for doing the work many experienced magicians use a specific sub-personality, or Entity, as described previously. It is, essentially, their *spirit guide* to use a term from Shamanism as well as Spiritualism. This can also be a transpersonal entity, a Daemon or Godform. It makes a lot more sense to use such a Model rather than train multiple minor aspects of the unconscious in various diverse skills. The only drawback with using such a complex Model embodying a personality is that it is being constantly empowered and if it is not kept under the control of the magician through rigid protocols may start to manifest spontaneously. Now, this may not be a problem and may even be desirable if it is entirely benign but this will not be the case with many people, especially neophytes. The Spirit Guides of the Shaman are often animals which limits their compatibility with the Human psyche and are, in many ways, safer although generally less capable.

Electronic Voice Phenomena (EVP)

Also known as *Instrumental Trans Communication* (ITC) when the technology is expanded to include data from other technologies such as video. EVP are unexpected voices found in recording media and what follows applies as much to video as audio.

A man named Attila Von Szalay pioneered the field as an adjunct to his attempts to photograph ghosts. His first major successes came in 1956CE using a reel-to-reel tape recorder but the entire field really came to prominence with a book published in 1968CE by Konstantin Raudive[97] in which he described recordings which he had made, some in screened rooms to preclude radio frequency interference. The clarity of some of the brief messages convinced him that they could not be explained by normal means, including auditory delusion.

Psychologists would explain the phenomenon by our natural ability and inclination to find patterns in our perceptions of sight and sound, especially if we are primed to look for them. For example, if we are listening to someone in a noisy room we take what we can barely hear and compare it to words that we expect to hear in the context of the conversation. By doing this we are often able to "hear" more clearly than might be expected if one only looked at the sound impinging on the ears. This is especially true when laboratory experiments are conducted with muffled voices. If a script is provided the "words" suddenly become clearer as the visual pattern is read into the sound. Extending this one step further, people "hear" voices in White Noise, a random pattern in which there are no voices or words at all. That is, it is not an objective phenomenon, but an internally generated subjective one.

Having said that, there are of course two possibilities. The first is that we have a noise source and use it to extract information from our unconscious as it seeks to impose or find patterns that are interpreted as words. The second is that what should be a random audio source ceases to be random and words really are present in the noise. The implications of that have been dealt with in detail in the previous chapters with regard to Psi and random numbers and will be expanded upon later in this one.

Historically EVP has been generated by a number of rather simple techniques, all based on analog equipment. The easiest is simply to tune an AM radio receiver off-station and while asking various questions and just listen to the noise for voices to break through. Another popular variant is to record onto a blank magnetic tape without using a microphone input. When played back at high volume the inherently noisy output is then examined for either messages or for answers to questions posed while the machine was recording. Usually the messages are quite short and seldom more than a couple of words. Naturally one has to be rather

---

[97] Raudive, Konstantin (1971). Breakthrough: An Amazing Experiment in Electronic Communication With the Dead (Original title: The Inaudible Becomes Audible). Taplinger Publishing Co. ISBN 0800809653.

Machines

careful when using radios, for example, because of the possibility of parts of radio programs breaking through. Even this, though, has given rise to an electronic divination device which flips randomly through the channels throwing up words and phrases from assorted programs in reply to questions – an updated form of bibliomancy whereby books are opened at a random page, and a random passage is selected for its message.

Related to EVP is the phenomenon of people receiving phone calls from the dead, which has been part of folklore ever since the invention of the telephone. As with other EVP, the messages are usually short. The electronic video equivalent is seeing pictures on analog TVs tuned to a dead channel where only "snow" is normally seen but where occasional pictures appear, often interpreted as communications from the spirit world.

However, it is becoming increasingly difficult to perform these experiments with modern equipment because so much of it is digital nowadays, so for ghost hunters old analog electronics still finds a market. The alternative is to make ones own devices fed from quantum based White (or Pink) noise sources – see later. These can be as simple as small poor quality audio amplifiers turned to full volume and with no inputs. Probably the most complex such machine built for this purpose was constructed in 1979CE by George Meek and his colleague Bill O'Neil. It consisted of a bank of acoustic signal generators at the following frequencies: 131, 141, 151, 241, 272, 282, 292, 302, 415, 433, 515, 653 and 701 Hertz. This was used as the sound input to an FM transmitter operating between 29MHz and 31MHz. Adjacent to this was a radio receiver which fed the sound to a speaker. So basically, this fed a well defined audio signal across a radio link that provided a background of noise that the "spirit" could modulate.

Nevertheless, there is another category of EVP machine which is constructed according to plans actually sent by entities in the spirit world. Probably the most powerful instance of EVP occurred during the Scole Experiments detailed in the chapter on Psi and the Occult where the entities, originally communicating through two Mediums, provided detailed instructions for an electronic device to be constructed as a cross dimensional communicator.

The explanation of the circuit is itself of interest given some of its implications. The entities explained that the machine did not deal with standard electromagnetic phenomena but to the spirit equivalent, which behaved in a similar fashion, possessing like electricity polarity and ability to be conducted. It was explained that the coils generated opposing fields and created a "Void" in which the crystal lay, opening a gateway to another dimension. The results were spectacular, with a clear voice announcing that communication had been established and which went on for some twenty minutes. The circuit diagram is shown below, courtesy of Robin Foy, of the Scole Group.

One rather odd piece of information I discovered as this book was going into its final draft concerned a patent[98] which was the subject of some ridicule in an

---
[98] Strom, Hyper Light Speed Antenna, USPO No. 6,025,810

electronics news group on the Net. It claimed that by using opposing magnetic fields to produce a kind of "null spot" into another (unspecified) dimension radio waves can be sent at faster than light speeds. Seemingly we have a piece of pseudoscience folklore, namely that opposing magnetic fields act to create an extra-dimensional rift through which an opening to the Void can be created. It does suggest that putting a device picking up quantum randomness between a couple of powerful Neodymium magnets might produce interesting results. Of course, from a conventional scientific point of view this makes no sense. The only unique thing about such a configuration is that it does not occur in Nature, so if someone from "another dimension" were seeking a beacon on our side, this would stand out as being both rare and unnatural. More below in the section on Computational Demonology.

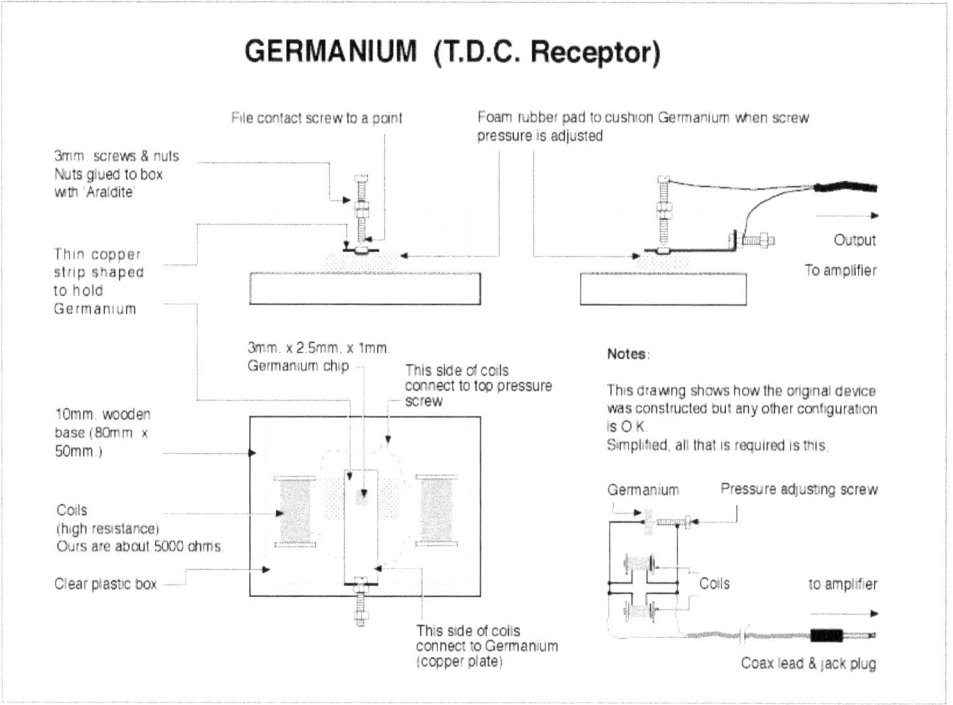

Figure 2

Finally, it should be noted that these devices tend only to work for the people who designed them or for whom they are given.

While EVP works quite well for audio, an ancient technique works very well for visual communications either with the unconscious, spirit world or alternate dimension depending upon your working paradigm.

Machines

Random Number Generators

One of the key pieces of technology for the TechnoMage are random number generators (RNG) or sources of *White Noise*. They serve a number of purposes:

- To provide a masking background noise upon which the unconscious can lay its information to be apprehended by the conscious. For example in EVP experiments

- To act as a probe into the Void to determine whether something is happening by altering a random data stream into a non-random one. Or rather, throwing up sequences whose probability passes beyond a certain threshold set by the experimenter, for example, 1 in 10,000

- To form the core element of Computational Demonological techniques.

White Noise, for those who are new to the term, is the kind of sound one gets from a hissing high pressure air line. Technically it is defined as a signal whose energy is distributed equally across all the frequencies between defined upper and lower limits. For the purposes of EVP or when it is used to mask outside sources the noise need not be pure or completely random. A related term is *Pink Noise*, where the energy falls of as 1/frequency. This is often perceived as being less harsh and more aesthetically pleasing. One example of Pink Noise is the sound generated by a waterfall. For other purposes though, the signal needs to obtain its random nature from quantum processes, or processes where quantum effects are amplified to macroscopic dimensions. Typical sources are:

- A radioactive source and radiation detector where each particle detection triggers a capture of a 1 or 0 from a high speed clock. The recovery time of the detector must be greater than the rate at which particles are arriving.

- Electronic noise from a reverse biased Zener diode in avalanche breakdown. This can be used as a direct source of White or Pink Noise with suitable filtering. Again, it can be used to sample a clock and provide a random binary stream.

- Thermal noise from a resistor, suitably amplified

- Noise in a light sensitive diode resulting from a lamp shining on it, especially when the light is first passed through a semi-transparent filter to reduce the intensity to very low levels.

There are in fact numerous other methods, but the above are probably the simplest and most reliable. Note that it is the randomness of the stream that is important, and not the specific pattern of 1s and 0s. In other words, any processing done on the data stream that maintains its inherent random nature, for example putting it through logical operations such as XOR, will retain its fitness for purpose, as will taking only every Nth sample.

Once one has a constant stream of 1s and 0s there are a number of ways of processing them. The most useful is to feed them into a computer which constantly examines the string for statistical anomalies. For example, in the simplest instance it might be programmed to look for sequences of all 1s or all 0s and flag up an alarm when they are detected. The nice thing about binary strings is that they can be viewed as the same as successive coin tosses, and the same statistical checks used. Therefore, the odds against finding a series of all 1s or all 0s is 2 to the power of the number of occurrences. So, the odds against finding ten in a row is 2^{10}, or 1 in 1024, the odds against finding 20 successive 1s or 0s is about one in a million and so forth. Obviously, if your bit stream is coming in at one million digits per second you will, on average, throw up that one in a million alarm approximately every second. Hence you need to factor in bitrate.

Having got all of this sorted out, how do you actually use this technology in a working? The simplest method is to use such a setup as a Psi detector or training aid, analogous to a Geiger Counter. If we have the computer set to create a click every time a certain threshold of probability is exceeded then someone being tested for Psi ability will have an immediate feedback in the click rate, either slowing it down or speeding it up. Alternatively, the probabilities can be shown on a graph or bar chart in real time to provide the necessary feedback, or more imaginative methods could be used. One rather nasty example might be a kind of Psi aversion conditioning where the clicks are spaced out at rather more than one a second and an accompanying electric shock is delivered to the subject. The result of such training might be a person with the ability to damp down all paranormal effects in their vicinity. In the business they are known as *coolers*. The opposite setup could also be used. That is, to supply shocks at regular intervals *unless* the clicks arrive at shorter intervals than they should. Alternatively, the feedback might be supplied on a more subliminal basis, as discussed in previous chapters.

Another use is to link computers fed with RNGs over a designated area and network them either locally or via the Internet, as in the previously discussed Global Consciousness Project. However, they tend to respond to intent when set up as detectors, which is something of which you need to take note, and they can of course be combined with other machines including Symbolics (see later). In general they can be used locally in a number of ways during a working:

- As a defensive perimeter to make sure nothing of paranormal origin is sneaking up on you when it should not be.

- As a measure of the effectiveness of the working

- As a signal that a sufficiently large gateway has been opened into the Void for the core element of the working to be completed.

- To determine whether any banishing ritual has worked. In other words, no more low probability events are being thrown up.

Machines

Note that there are two ways of using networked computers. The first is to simply check whether each computer is throwing up its own non-random warning as it passes a set threshold and see whether all the computers are doing it simultaneously. The second is to see whether the *same* random sequences are being generated at each location. The most likely reason for this is that some kind of electromagnetic field is affecting the hardware over a large area. Which is of course why such devices should be shielded inside a grounded steel box, or better yet, one made of Mu-metal for its ability to shield against magnetic fields.

Computational Demonology – The Quantum Oracle

The field of Computational Demonology is a relatively new one, since the term was coined by the Science Fiction author Charles Stross for his "Laundry" series of books. In the books it is defined as the use of mathematical theorems acting in the Platonic Realm to contact alien entities or manipulate reality, making magick a branch of applied mathematics. In other words, it was a fictitious technology – until now. In order to make it real a number of previously discussed ideas need to be merged, these are:

- A high speed random number generator whose output is derived from quantum uncertainty, or in terms of magick, the Void.

- To this we can add a Scole type of opposed magnetic field around the key electronic element responsible for the quantum noise, for example a Zener diode or perhaps LED and photodiode combination.

- A computer to capture the data stream.

- Software to process the random string into meaningful text.

It is this last element, software, where the complexity lies. In the previous chapter on Science and Magick it was mentioned that the number Pi, which is infinite in extent, has the characteristic of a stream of random numbers and that these numbers can be converted into characters via various coding schemes. The simplest being A=1, B=2 and so forth and the most accurate being a rendering of the number in base-26 arithmetic, since there are 26 letters in our alphabet. One then searches for meaningful words that crop up in the sequence. Somewhere in that infinite string are all the works of Shakespeare and everything else besides, but so far in that we could never find it.

Put that information on hold for now and consider a moderately famous book of recent times called "The Bible Code"[99]. The actual premise of the book is amazingly simple and really rather clever. The author looks for hidden message in the Torah, the Hebrew Bible, by placing the letters of various passages at equal

---

[99] Michael Drosnin. The Bible Code, Simon & Schuster 1997, ISBN 0-684-81079-4

intervals in a text that was formatted to fit inside a graph. The technique itself was pioneered by Doron Witztum, Eliyahu Rips and Yoav Rosenberg who published it in a scientific paper[100] on statistics, and is known as the Equidistant Letter Sequence (ELS). The example below is based on the English language, specifically the King James version of Genesis 26:5 to 26:10 in order to illustrate the principle.

```
M Y S T A T U T E S A N D M Y L A W S A N D I S A A C D W E L T I
N G E R A R A N D T H E M E N O F T H E P L A C E A S K E D H I M
O F H I S W I F E A N D H E S A I D S H E I S M Y S I S T E R F O
R H E F E A R E D T O S A Y S H E I S M Y W I F E L E S T S A I D
H E T H E M E N O F T H E P L A C E S H O U L D K I L L M E F O R
R E B E K A H B E C A U S E S H E W A S F A I R T O L O O K U P O
N A N D I T C A M E T O P A S S W H E N H E H A D B E E N T H E R
E A L O N G T I M E T H A T A B I M E L E C H K I N G O F T H E P
H I L I S T I N E S L O O K E D O U T A T A W I N D O W A N D S A
W A N D B E H O L D I S A A C W A S S P O R T I N G W I T H R E B
E K A H H I S W I F E A N D A B I M E L E C H C A L L E D I S A A
C A N D S A I D B E H O L D O F A S U R E T Y S H E I S T H Y W I
F E A N D H O W S A I D S T T H O U S H E I S M Y S I S T E R A N
D I S A A C S A I D U N T O H I M B E C A U S E I S A I D L E S T
I D I E F O R H E R A N D A B I M E L E C H S A I D W H A T I S
```

The word "BIBLE" appears in the equidistant ringed letters, and the word "CODE" in the squares.

    The general method is to take a text string, starting at a particular letter in the string, and then select the letters that occur at regular spacings by skipping the intermediates, after first removing spaces and punctuation. The number of intermediates skipped is called, as one might expect, the *skip number*. It can be positive if moving forward through the text, or negative if moving backwards. In the example above we start at the letter "B" and skip by -100, when we find the next letter "I" and so forth. The obvious questions are where do we start and what skip number do we choose? The answer is... we do not know, although if we are looking for a particular name we can cut a lot of the work away because we know the first and second letter for which to look. It is a trial and error process, which is

---

[100] Doron Witztum, Eliyahu Rips, Yoav Rosenberg (1994). "Equidistant letter sequences in the Book of Genesis". Statistical Science 9: 429–438.

why computers are needed, with the resulting text strings being compared to a dictionary to see if they are actual words. It is an extremely computationally intensive task. One way of reducing the complexity of the task is to put it into an array form and only examine the text within a movable "window". That is why the Bible text above is in the (arbitrary) format of 33 characters per line, with the window being shown by the rectangle. It has the added and major advantage of occasionally finding words grouped together. In our case above spelling out "bible code", or alternatively, "code bible" since the order and interpretation of the words is chosen by the Human operator. The computer would then shift the window along a space and redo the computation, and similarly in an up-down direction, all the time throwing up words and word groupings. Then we change the number of characters per line and do it all again.

In the various analyses of the Torah all kinds of information was collected and interpreted in various ways, resulting in lots of accurate retrodictions (confirmation of past events) such as the assassination of Kennedy and one or two famous predictions such as the 1995CE assassination of Israeli Prime Minister Yitzhak Rabin, and the nuclear war of 2006CE. Since the latter failed to materialize it was claimed that the predictions merely dealt with probabilities rather than hard predestination. As to the agency responsible for encoding the information in the first place, speculation has ranged from God to aliens depending upon belief systems. However, skeptics point out that these computational techniques will produce messages from just about anything, even random strings. Which brings us full circle.

The above method is probably the most comprehensive way of searching text for hidden messages, or at least messages that are not so deeply hidden that it takes the cryptographic capabilities of a major national security agency to uncover. We have to assume that if some entity has placed a message into the text that it has done so with the intent that it can easily be found. There are however even simpler schemes that are not so computationally intensive and which also produce interesting results. Before we examine these, a few words about the dictionary that is needed against which to check random strings in order to test whether they are composed of real words and not garbage. What we do *not* need is an actual dictionary in the usual sense of the word. All we need is a collection of the most common words in English (or whatever language) in alphabetical order. The best way to get this is to feed a chunk of text to a program that extracts and counts the different words and then stores them in a file for later use. The seed text itself can be anything as long as it is a comprehensive sample of English. For example, one might go to Project Gutenberg[101] on the Net, where out-of-copyright literature is available for free download, where one can choose anything from the works of Shakespeare to more modern novels. It might be worth bearing in mind that what words are available in the dictionary might color the type of message that can be received, hence it may be prudent to avoid the horror genre when building it. This

---

[101] http://www.gutenberg.org

next bit is rather technical, so if you are not happy with software engineering you can skip it. Anyway, here are some of the simpler schemes and their implementations, derived from random binary coded quantum noise:

- Chop the binary into 7 or 8 bit bytes and convert straight to ASCII characters to provide the text string to search. Then filter out non alphabet characters and normalize the distribution to match letter frequency in whatever language is being used. We do this so that, for example, "A" occurs more frequently than "Z".

- Chop the binary into N bit chunks where N^2 is comparable to, but larger than, the number of words in the dictionary. Use this number to look up a word. However, before doing this the form of the dictionary must be weighted in favor of the most common words, otherwise there's an equal chance that the word "and" and the word "aardvark" become equally probable – which is silly. So when building the dictionary you need a record of the number of times each word appears in the seed text. Alternatively, simply use the entirety of the seed text unmodified. This then becomes a variant of Bibliomancy.

- Instead of looking up individual words, extract phrases and sentences from the seed text, and then use the above method to select one of them. This is much closer to the conventional divination technique of Bibliomancy. Related to this is the *I Ching* where a binary combination of 6 items points to one of 64 possible predefined text entries. This can of course be expanded by the user to any number of pieces of text which would then be selected by sequences of the random strings, ideally ones whose probability deviates far from the norm.

- To prevent information overload one can limit the searches to binary strings that vary from the baseline randomness with a certain probability factor – see the above section on Random Number Generators. Any entity coding in useful information can flag it with low probability sequences.

So, now we have techniques for looking for messages in the random numbers generated by our quantum noise from the Void, and whatever might be lurking at the threshold of our reality. At the very least we have an interesting hitech form of divination, which could potentially be very impressive if coupled with sufficient computing power to do a full analysis of the random numbers as they are produced, followed by feeding the words to a voice synthesizer. We can make it even more efficient when it comes to finding words by relaxing our spelling requirements by using a spelling correction feature in the software.

    A rather more complex scheme might involve wrapping the resulting words in a shell of artificial intelligence, specifically, a modified chatbot. A chatbot is a piece of software that interacts with a user in such a way as to attempt to fool the user into thinking that a real person is responding to their typed comments. It does this by looking for keywords and feeding them back to the user wrapped inside predetermined sentences. For reference, the name of the first chatbot was Eliza, and the type of conversation might run as follows:

> Me: Are you intelligent?
> Alice: I am highly intelligent. I have many intellectual functions.
>
> Me: Such as?
> Alice: For example, a tomato
>
> Me: A tomato? That's stupid!
> Alice: Are you calling me stupid?
>
> Me: Well, that's a stupid answer
> Alice: Interesting. I will remember you said that when robots take over the World

As you might have guessed, this one is an online chatbot named Alice at the A.L.I.C.E. Artificial Intelligence Foundation. So, taking our seed words or phrases we can feed them to our chatbot and then onwards to a voice synthesizer with the result being that our extra dimensional entity can meander on all day long in true oracular fashion.

As to why extra-dimensional entities might choose such a medium in which to communicate consider the possibility that they may be able to "see" what is happening in our universe, but not actually act within it except at the quantum level. Think quantum non-demolition measurement as a kind of hand-waving explanation, which is physics-speak for "I have only a vague idea". As an absolute minimum they may still be unable to alter the random nature of the device, only tweak our minds a little by throwing up "meaningful coincidences". Which also neatly explains why they speak English (as well as every other language, past present and future)! Finally, a mild warning. If such entities do exist and communicate in such a manner you might find that the connection gets stronger over time as the entity realizes it has a definite entry point into our universe. It may even begin to manifest in other, possibly unpleasant, ways.

The Psychomanteum

The ideas and practices that underlie the modern Psychomanteum are as old as recorded history. However, the most detailed early accounts come from the ancient Greeks who had temples of healing, most famous of which were the ones dedicated to the greatest physician of ancient times, Asclepius, who was raised to the stature of a God by being made a son of Apollo. His temples were always adorned with his statues, the serpent staff that is still the symbol of the medical profession today, the laurel crown, the dog and goat and weights and coins representing his attributes. He was seated grasping the staff in one hand and in the other, raised above his head, he held a serpent while at his side lay a dog. Around the temple were inscribed various testimonials from those who had been healed.

Before being allowed access to the shrine supplicants had to undergo purification rituals which took various forms and included bathing, fasting, massages, prayer and the sacrifice of a cock or ram. After this there followed a period of waiting which meant staying or sleeping at the foot of the statue whereupon the God would visit them either in dreams or as realistic hallucinations. Afterwards they would undergo various medical procedures at the hands of the physician priests based upon fairly liberal interpretations of the dream message from the God.

There was another function with which Asclepius was associated and which pre-dated the real physician turned God, and concerns his associations with both dreams and underground places such as caves, wells and the underworld in general. The Greeks had an institution in their culture whereby a grieving person would enter into an underground facility and attempt to contact the spirit of the newly dead through dream and vision for a last farewell and whatever consolation they might receive. This was the Psychomanteum.

Historically associated with this practice of contacting the spirit world was the use of reflective material. Depending on the technology of the culture this varied from sacred pools to bronze and copper mirrors to the polished coal used for scrying by the Elizabethan mage Doctor John Dee and on to the perfect flat glass mirrors with which we are all familiar today. While other circumstances varied, the practice of doing this in a dark place, or at night, was one constant feature. One might even speculate that the idea of an underworld either developed, or was reinforced, through such acts as gazing into moonlit pools and lakes and actually seeing visions of the other world. However, such practices and the notion of a benevolent underworld as a place of rest for the dead were actively discouraged when worship of sky deities became prevalent. In the Norse religion, for example, those chosen by the Aesir reside in their halls in upper worlds of Asgard and Vanaheim while lesser mortals await rebirth in the underworld, Hel. This tendency was taken to an extreme by the Judeo-Islamic-Christian religions. Indeed, the Christians even named their place of punishment and torment Hell after the Norse Hel, and competing deities were either absorbed into their pantheon as dubious saints or relegated to the role of demons. Virtually all techniques designed to alter consciousness that were not under the direct control of the Church were actively suppressed by fire and sword, and even as the power of Christianity began to fade the suppression continued in the form of a superstition meme that exists to the present day. In the case of mirrors we have in particular the notion that when there has been a death in the family the mirrors in the house should be covered for several days afterwards. There are a number of reasons given for this. One is that the soul of the deceased may be trapped in the mirror, and in fact that is why the Devil invented mirrors! Another is that someone seeing their reflection in a room where someone has recently died will soon die themselves. Another variation on the theme is that evil spirits posing as the deceased will try to trick the living and enter them. Finally, it is allegedly bad luck to even look at ones own reflection by candlelight. Clearly all these seem designed to discourage any kind of divination that may tend to contradict Christian theology and its would-be monopoly on spiritual truth. Interestingly, the most well known superstition, that breaking a mirror brings seven years bad luck, stems from decidedly non-Christian origins. It arises from two major sources, the first being that a mirror holds the soul of the person looking into it and so breaks with the mirror, and the other that mirrors hold ones future and hence breaking one breaks the future. These both hark back to the ancient practice of using reflective surfaces for divination.

Fast forwarding to the present day the most well known researcher is Doctor R Moody[102] who constructed a modern version of the Psychomanteum. He used a small room with a mirror against one wall and a comfortable chair facing it. The mirror was positioned slightly higher than the subject's line of sight so that they could not see their own reflection in it. A black velvet curtain surrounded the chair and only a dim light placed behind the chair lighted the room.

In the main study[103] he contacted twenty-seven people who had recently lost someone close to them and who wished to participate in the experiment. They were asked to bring items that were strongly connected with the deceased and that evoked memories of them and were advised to wear comfortable, dark, loose fitting clothing. Prior to entering the Psychomanteum the subjects were prepared in a manner reminiscent of the Greek process. Moody took long walks with each of them where the discussion focused on the deceased, thereby strengthening their memories. The subjects then spent some time lying on a bed listening to soft music designed to put them into a state of relaxation. These initial processes took a good part of the working day to complete. Finally, upon entering the Psychomanteum, the subject would sit in a relaxed state gazing into the empty field of the mirror for up to an hour. There then followed a debriefing and discussion of the experiences, if any. The results were striking. While nobody was guaranteed a result almost all claimed they were helped by their experience and there were no negative experiences. Data were collected with pre- and post-questionnaires, a follow-up questionnaire at least four weeks after the session, interviews by the facilitators, and two personality measures, the Tellegen Absorption Scale and the Myers-Briggs Type Indicator. Thirteen participants reported contacts with the deceased, that is, almost fifty percent of those who took part. This is a far higher percentage than have been reported by other researchers into mirror gazing, with figures varying between three and twenty-five percent success rate. It may well be that the lengthy pre-experiment preparation that Moody used contributed substantially to the success rate.

Within the Psychomanteum various phenomena manifest, usually after a few minutes to half an hour. People typically report that the mirror gradually

---

[102] Moody, R., with Perry, P. (1993). Reunions: Visionary encounters with departed loved ones. NY: Ivy Books.

[103] Moody, R. (1992). Family reunions: visionary encounters with the departed in a modern-day Psychomanteum. Journal of Near-Death Studies, 11(2), 83-121.

transforms into a window containing swirling clouds whereupon intensely vivid visions are seen through the window. Occasionally those visions, often of people, extend into the room itself in a manner described as hyper-real. Apart from visual imagery other senses can be engaged, from dialogs with otherworldly entities to bodily sensations to smells to less tangible feelings of someone or something being present. Also included in the gamut of sensation are those of temperature changes, typically that of extreme cold, changes of illumination and feelings of profound meaning leading to significant transformations of belief and personality.

There have naturally been experiments to determine if these perceived phenomena have any basis in consensus reality. Attempts have been made to record visual, auditory and environmental changes as reported by various subjects. In general these have not been successful although some dispute this. Nevertheless, it seems beyond doubt that the Psychomanteum manifests internal mental states and various Agents of the mind as seemingly external phenomena. In this it appears to be almost as powerful a technique as the use of psychedelic drugs.

Of course, simply reading of the experiences of other people predisposes one to seeing the same via suggestion and so it tends to become a self-fulfilling prophecy. There are several ways in which this limitation may be overcome and the variety of experience expanded to whatever limits may exist within the mind of Humans in general. The most obvious is to use people who have no expectations or knowledge of what may occur, and have them report back what transpires. Another is to prime either oneself or others with expectations and data that predispose them to various extremes of belief or imaginative capability before entering the Psychomanteum This priming can be done either consciously or by using a number of subliminal, hypnotic and technological techniques discussed elsewhere. Additionally, blending the Psychomanteum experience with other forms of consciousness altering practice can be very rewarding. The imagery and other manifestations appear to be sensitive to changes in the psyche and can therefore be used as a kind of "psychic micrometer" to measure the efficacy of those other methods.

Finally, in case you have not worked it out, the word itself means "a place for the divination of the mind". The word is derived from Greek roots. Hence in modern English the prefix "psycho" indicates "mind", "mantic" meaning relating to, or having the power of divination and the ending "-eum" indicates a place.

Signal Generation

A number of the technologies described in this work depend on generating precise electrical waveforms, most of which are in the low audio spectrum. This is obviously not a problem if one is an engineer and has access to precision signal generators and specialist amplifiers but if one has to buy this type of equipment it can prove quite expensive. However, these days almost everyone has access to a computer and some kind of audio system, so I am going to describe how to use these to create the most interesting waveforms.

The problem with generating very low frequencies previously discussed is that standard audio equipment cannot handle them. For example, a good audio amplifier might be specified as having a bandwidth of around 20Hz to 40kHz although the audio hardware of your computer may be less. Unfortunately a lot of what's interesting happens below 10Hz, so we need a few tricks to get around various limitations. The problem does not lie in the digital domain, but crops up in the conversion process. So it's not much use, for example, simply creating a nice clean digital waveform of the Schumann Resonance at 7.83Hz using Audacity[104] and expecting the computer to play it – it won't. So what we do is create a binaural signal using two frequencies, say 16000Hz and 16007.83Hz, which is no trouble at all. However, instead of specifying that they are played in binaural mode with one in the left stereo channel and the other in the right we use Audacity to mix them for a mono output. The result can be heard when it is played (if you have good hearing). We get a tone of 16kHz that is modulated at exactly 7.83Hz. That is, it is a tone that any audio equipment can handle with ease that is rising and falling smoothly at the Schumann frequency. All we have to do now is filter out the 16kHz while keeping what we want, which while it does require some additional circuitry is not difficult or expensive to do. Also note that if your computer is not up to playing decent audio you can burn the waveform as an audio CDROM and play it on almost any audio equipment, or convert it to MP3 or similar and download it to a player.

There is another way of generating low frequency signals that can be handled by audio equipment that is simpler although not as elegant. The general idea is to use either a square wave at half the required frequency or a pulse a few milliseconds wide at the desired frequency. This is because the sharp edges do get through the filtering which is common on normal domestic audio equipment. They appear as pulses, or popping sounds, at the required frequency and are quite capable of driving coils to provide experimental magnetic fields. The benefit of this technique is that if, for example, we use a 10mS pulse 4 times a second to provide a 4Hz strobe we are only feeding the coil with a duty cycle of 40mS ON and 960mS OFF per second, or around 1:25. That means if the coil can take (say) 10W RMS we can hit the coil with pulses that are 250W and still keep within the thermal limits of the coil.

Replicating the kind of pulsed neural waveforms used in Persinger type experiments presents no major problems since each pulse has a bandwidth in the low kHz which is quite suitable for standard audio equipment. However, it should be noted that the actual shape of the pulses might be of importance. If so then saving the waveform in a lossy compressed format like MP3 might be a bad idea as it could lose some of the finer detail. The kind of pulse trains to examine might, for example, consist of spikes of between 1mS and 10mS in various patterns with a gap between the patterns of anything from 100mS to several seconds.

A screen capture of a 2mS pulse, followed by 2mS silence is shown below.

---

[104] Audacity is an open source sound editor, free on the Net

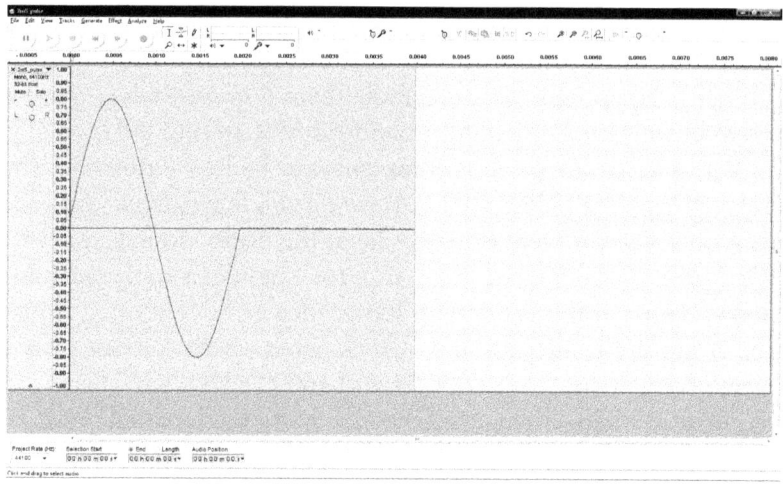

Field Coils

Which brings us to the kind of coils to drive and how to design them.

The first thing to remember if you are driving a coil from a domestic audio amplifier is that it expects to see an impedance, that is a resistance to alternating current, of either 4 or 8 Ohms. These are the common impedances for normal speakers. Having a higher impedance, or resistance, will not hurt although it will result in less power being delivered into the coil. On the other hand lower impedance could damage the amplifier. The safest course is to use enough turns of wire such that the DC resistance exceeds 8 Ohms. This does not mean that you can connect it to a 100W amplifier, turn it up to full volume, and everything will be fine. If you are delivering that power into a small coil it is going to melt and burst into flames, probably before it shorts out and takes the amplifier with it. If you cannot understand the design basics it is best to keep the power below 5W, which should be quite enough bearing in mind that almost all of the experiments described in this book have used power levels less than this.

One of the slightly tricky calculations involved in building magnetic field coils for wide area effects involves choosing the dimensions, wire gage and current carrying capacity in order to match the impedance to common audio amplifier technology. The first thing to do is decide what currents are likely to be used. Unless you are feeling ambitious, or you are an engineer, I suggest sticking with the kind of power levels found in small domestic amplifiers designed for modest stereo systems. Typically we are looking at 50W RMS, not 50W "music power" or 50W unspecified. The "RMS" stands for "root mean square" and means that you will be getting what you expect from it, namely 50 Watts of average power. We also need it to be specified to feed into either 4 or 8 Ohms impedance, preferably the latter. So, applying Ohms Law...

Machines

$$W = I^2 \times X$$

where W = power in Watts, I = current in Amps and X = impedance (or resistance) in Ohms. Plugging in the numbers we get:

$$50 = I^2 \times 8$$

$$I^2 = 6.25$$

$$I = 2.5 \text{ amps}$$

Next, we need a find a gage of insulated copper wire that can carry such a current comfortably. Looking up tables on the Net gives us Number 25, which is rated at 2.7A and which has a resistance of 0.106 Ohms per meter. Now, given possible low frequencies that approximate DC we need to make sure that the coil still looks like 8 Ohms to the amplifier, or nasty things might happen. So, we need to wind the coil using greater than 80 meters of wire. Note that having a coil with more wire than this is not a problem. It means you get a bigger resistance and less current which means it will run cooler, but on the other hand you will get more turns on the coil which means a bigger field. The trade-off, unfortunately, is not exact so these calculations are only given as a guide.

The next set of calculations are considerably more complex. The intensity of the field generated will depend on a number of variables, the most important of which is coil radius. For the sake of simplicity I am detailing an optimized configuration for an air core coil known as a *Brooks Coil*, shown below.

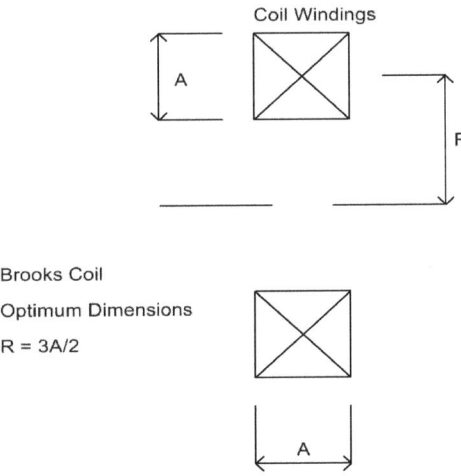

Figure 3

It's major characteristic is that the radius is one and a half time the thickness of the winding itself. Also, there is some leeway in the design so that the formulas are still reasonably good design guidelines. Still, there is nothing to say you should follow this advice and making a thin coil big enough for someone to (say) stand in can be done on a trial and error basis as long as overall impedance and resistance are taken into account. Not something for the technologically illiterate to do, however.

The key variable you need is the *inductance* of the coil, which affects its *impedance*. This is its additional "resistance" to alternating current and which is frequency dependent. The connection is given by:

Impedance = 2 x Pi x frequency x Inductance

more commonly written as $X = 2\pi fL$ where X = impedance in Ohms, f = frequency in Hz and L = Inductance in Henrys. Pi is of course the constant 3.14159... Anyway the inductance of the Brooks coil is given by the formula:

$L = 1.699 \times 10^{-6} \times R \times N^2$ where N = number of turns

Again, connecting magnetic field strength to the above is non-trivial since it obviously varies with distance from the coil, but note that the most important factor is the number of turns and it is also directly proportional to the current.

An alternative to the above is to use a metal cored coil to increase the inductance of the coil and hence its "efficiency" at turning electricity into magnetic field intensity. Unfortunately designing this from theory is rather tricky and beyond the scope of this book. Such a coil is ideally suited to a physically small application, for example a personal field generator that is finger sized and run from a battery, most likely in pulsed mode. It would be fed by the output of something like a smartphone from a compressed audio recording. Alternatively, if you are an engineer, consider something simple like a 555 timer chip and a FET dumping a capacitor charge into the coil as spike. Do not forget back EMF – either use it or short it through a protective diode. The core material can be as varied as Iron, Mu-metal or one of many ferrite compounds most notably in the form of the rods used in medium and long wave radio receivers.

At the other end of the scale we have really large coils up to a few meters in diameter, which can be used in one of two ways. The first is for the magician to stand, sit, lie down or sleep within the coil. Alternatively, it is used as a boundary around which a group of practitioners gather. The problem which arises (unless the coil is an unfeasibly large Brooks Coil) is that the field lines tend to be much stronger close to the wiring to the extent that there is almost nothing in the center of the circle. All the magnetic action is along the periphery.

Finally, consider using cheap headphones (since you will not want to destroy expensive ones). Typically such headsets, or even earbuds, use a miniature magnet and driver coil to generate sound. You need to get rid of the bits that actually create the sound and keep the magnets and coils intact. You then have a quick and dirty method of attaching it to your head for low power experiments. The signals themselves need to be one of three types. The first is mono – using either the left or the right ear-piece, but not both, in oder to stimulate either left or right hemispheres.. The second method is to duplicate the signal on each of the channels. This will create a field pattern that tends to oppose each other and localize the fields near the sides of the head and provide rather less stimulation to the center of the brain. Finally, if you invert the phase of the signals you create a field that permeates the whole brain.

Again – do NOT connect this to the output of a power amplifier unless you want the extreme consciousness altering experience of combined electro-shock therapy and having your head set on fire. Just use the normal outputs on your phone or boombox. The risk is all yours.

The Helmholtz Configuration

This is a particularly useful way of arranging two coils to provide a wide area coverage with a uniform magnetic field, either static or modulated. Figure 4 below illustrates the arrangement. It is essentially quite a simple setup with two coils of radius R separated by the same distance and both fed with current in the same direction. To cut a long story short, the field strength between the coils is given to a good approximation by the formula:

$$B = (NI)/\sqrt{R}$$

where B is the field strength in micro-Teslas (µT), N is the number of turns, I is the current in amps, and R is the radius in meters.

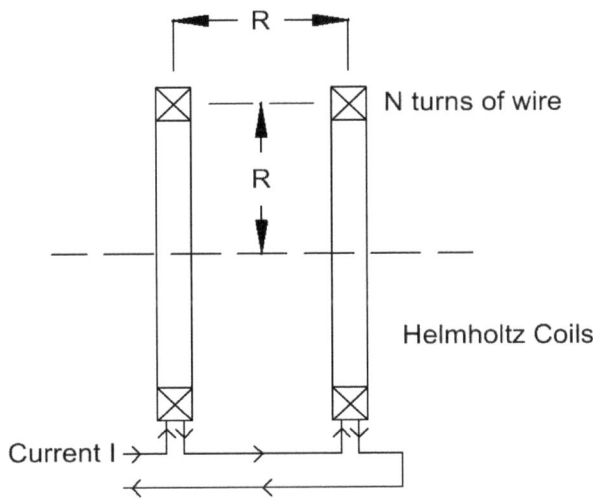

Figure 4

So, a coil of radius 1 meter would be large enough for somebody to sit fairly centrally in the field. If we assumed 50 turns of wire per coil (approximately 300m) carrying 1 amp the field strength would be 50µT, or about the same strength as the Earth's field. There are three ways of using a Helmholtz coil:

- **To cancel the Geomagnetic field.**
  This is one of its more conventional applications when experiments need to be carried out in an area with a much reduced magnetic presence. The coils are oriented North-South and sufficient current introduced to cause a

cancellation. It can be crudely tested for neutrality by placing a compass within the coils as the current is increased. When the compass no longer aligns North-South the Earth's field is canceled. Not a great deal of use for us, however.

- **To reinforce or modulate the Geomagnetic field.**
  For example, in a North-South orientation one could modulate the natural field with an augmented Schumann Resonance. Beware inclination! See below.

- **To create a field at right angles to the Earth's.**
  Generally in order to maximize any ion resonance effects by feeding an alternating current to the coils oriented at right angles to the Earth's field in order to facilitate psychogenic events.

It is this latter case that is most interesting. While one might think that "at right angles" to Earth's field implies and East-West orientation it can also mean Up-Down depending on the *inclination* of the Geomagnetic field at any given geographical location. For example, at the poles the field lines enter the Earth vertically, so if we were using this setup there then the coils could be placed in any horizontal orientation. At the equator the field lines are parallel and so Up-Down is perfect. Elsewhere, it varies. In most of Western Europe and North America it is between 60° and 75°, so the most efficient setup is East-West. However, there are some practical problems associated with creating a large space in which people can work. The obvious method would be to place the Helmholtz coils on the walls of a room. Unfortunately the room would have to be very tall and very narrow – much better if floor and ceiling could be used. Despite the steep inclination this may be an effective approach. Given a ceiling height of (say) 3m we would lay out a circle with a diameter of 6m, which is large enough to accommodate quite a significant group. [If a field at precise right angles is required, there is nothing to stop us creating one with more coils instead of relying on the Geomagnetic field.] If we limit the intensity of the field generated to that approximating the Geomagnetic field a putative design can be sketched out.

So, we have R=3 and one turn of wire is about 18m in length. For B = $50\mu T$ we need NI = 86; that is, one turn carrying 86A or 10 turns carrying 8.6A (much more manageable). Hence we need 360m of wire (two coils) capable of carrying 10A without a problem. AWG19 gauge wire is rated for 14A and has a resistance of 26 Ohms per kilometer, so our length will have a resistance of 9.3 Ohms which is in the right ballpark when it comes to driving from an audio amplifier. Driving 8.6A through 8 Ohms requires a power amplifier capable of delivering 590 Watts RMS, so a rating of 500W RMS should be sufficient. Of course, if we wanted to pulse it at a duty cycle of less than 1:10 On:Off, we could use an amplifier delivering 10x the power. Do not forget that this is just an example, and that there are other trade-offs one can make between number of turns, thickness of wire and the size of the power amplifier. For example, double the turns and halve the current etc.

If we actually want to match the Geomagnetic field (B) in either the horizontal (H) or vertical (V) plane we can calculate each component using trigonometry. If the inclination in degrees = θ the formulae are:

$$H = B \times \cos(\theta)$$

and

$$V = B \times \sin(\theta)$$

It should be borne in mind that the field from such a coil will extend far beyond the interior of the room. Still, it makes a good technological rationale for creating the traditional magick circle.

Electrical Brain Stimulation Technology

This is one area of technology where I am not including detailed designs of any kind. The possibilities of anything going wrong is just too great and it requires a serious knowledge of engineering to do it safely – or as safe as this technology gets. However, I will describe the problems that need to be taken into account, and some solutions, for those who intend to proceed.

The first major problem for people wishing to use direct electrical stimulation of the brain through electrodes is the electrode material. The skin resistance is tremendously variable. Dry skin, for example on the fingers, can have a resistance in the mega-Ohms and touching even mains wiring will result in only a slight tingling sensation. On the other hand, the resistance of wet skin falls to hundreds of Ohms and domestic power line voltage becomes a killer. Generally speaking one hundred milliamps (100mA) will kill just about anyone if applied continuously across the chest via the arms. There's an old engineering saying: "It's the amps that kill but the volts that reach out to touch you." As a rough guide, this is the effect of current as it flows through the body:

- 0 – 1mA – No sensation
- 1 – 5mA – Tingling
- 5 – 10mA – Muscle spasms
- 10 – 30mA – Intense pain, paralysis, unable to release grip etc.
- 30+ mA – Lower lethal range for some people

If one places mains voltages, 110VAC in the US and 230VAC in Europe, across wet hands with a resistance of (say) 200 Ohms the current flowing across the chest is approximately 500mA and 1000mA respectively. When the skin barrier is breached entirely by needles penetrating the skin the blood/body resistance drops to less than 100 Ohms and even a nine volt battery can deliver a fatal shock. At least one person has died in this manner.

This means that unless the resistance of the skin is controlled the current flowing is unpredictable and can range from harmless to fatal depending upon conditions as varied as room temperature, degree of nervousness or humidity. That is why anyone wishing to try direct Electro-stimulation should know what he or she is doing. If you do not understand what milli and micro, volts and amps mean, or even fail to understand Ohms Law[105] you could incur serious injury or death. Having said that, the most critical components for reliable experimentation are saline tolerant electrodes to reduce the skin resistance to a known minimum. These are usually rather expensive, but worth it. The placement of the electrodes would normally be across the forehead, temple to temple, earlobe to earlobe, or attached to the skin behind the ears just after each area has been swabbed with a saline gel. Normally under these circumstances the applied voltage is in the 100mV range for a current flow of less than 1mA maximum. Sharp pulses with rapid rise times can be transformer coupled and the voltage increased for use with electrodes on dry skin, which is the usual technique employed by commercial equipment.

Another thing to consider is what happens if there is a fault in the machine delivering the signal to the head. Even a battery driven device could give you a do-it-yourself lobotomy if it malfunctioned and dumped the full voltage across your head through saline electrodes. And what is worse, if it knocked you unconscious it could potentially keep delivering that current to your head for days if nobody intervened. So if you are thinking of designing your own machine here are a few general tips:

- Have the output stage optically and physically isolated from any mains driven supply, and use a low voltage battery to run it. Ideally below 5V.
- Design in current limiting resistors at the battery supply
- Put current limiting resistors in the outputs.
- Have voltage-limiting components placed across the outputs if there is to be no transformer coupling. For example, one could use two silicon diodes connected in opposite directions, each forward biased to limit the output voltage to the bandgap, that is, around 600mV in the worst case.
- Unless one is going to use very low sinusoid frequencies use a capacitative or ideally a transformer coupling to the output that will block DC current in the event of malfunction. That is one reason why low frequency devices usually use pulsed outputs.
- If a step-up transformer is being used to increase voltage for electrodes on dry skin, for example the earlobes, then make sure it cannot deliver more than a milliamp at any voltage.

---

[105] Ohms Law – Current = Voltage divided by Resistance, I=V/R, where current (I) is in Amps, voltage (V) in Volts and resistance (R) in Ohms.

Machines

Even with all these precautions designing your own equipment is tricky since it is dangerous failure modes that must be guarded against. The actual layout of the board is also important in this respect since you do not want all these precautions circumvented by a short circuit resulting from poor placement of components or a wire coming loose and hitting the outputs. That is why designers and companies manufacturing medical electronics are heavily insured and it is a somewhat specialist art. Note that all the above is also true for devices that monitor any bodily function by attaching electrodes and measuring voltages, for example "Lie Detectors" (polygraphs), heart monitors (ECG) and especially EEG machines.

Red Light and Healing

It might sound like some miraculous New Age pseudo-science, but high intensity red light phototherapy can not only speed wound healing but actually reverse signs of aging in the skin, most notably in eliminating wrinkles. The device described in outline below is based upon a paper published by Andrei P. Sommer and Dan Zhu[106]. Quoting the relevant text:

> "On the basis of the simple physicochemical picture... on the one hand, and ample experimental evidence on the tunability of interfacial water layers by visible light – both on hydrophobic and hydrophilic surfaces – on the other hand, we designed a program to restore elastin maturation in vivo. For this one of us irradiated the skin around the corner of the eyes with light delivered by an array of LEDs (WARP 10, Quantum Devices, Inc. WI). Operating in the range 600–720 nm (central wavelength 670 nm, 50% relative spectral output 660–680 nm), it covers a 10 cm^2 area with an integral light intensity of 728 W m^{-2}. To exclude adverse effects, that is, inhibition of cellular functions, irradiation times were adjusted to doses around 4×10^4 J m^{-2}, known to temporarily increase blood circulation. The representative photographs of the selected facial zones... show the wrinkle levels before and after their daily irradiation for nine consecutive weeks, respectively."

The result is that the photographs show what I would estimate as a 50% reduction in the depth and extent of wrinkles around the eyes.

So what does 728 W/m^2 and 670nm actually mean in terms of LED specifications[107]? First, the easy bit – 670nm is the deep red part of the spectrum and LEDs are normally sold with their peak wavelength as part of that specification. On the other hand the amount of light emitted by a high power LED is normally measured in Lumens per Watt (lm/W), so we need to do some conversions.

100% efficiency at converting electricity to light corresponds to 683 lm/W.

---

[106] From Micro tornadoes to Facial Rejuvenation: Implication of Interfacial Water Layers ASAP *Cryst. Growth Des.*, ASAP Article, 10.1021/cg8000703

[107] Bright sunlight is typically 1000W/m^2, so the power density is designed to approximate this value, but concentrated into the red part of the spectrum

That is, 1W of electrical input will result in 683 Lumens of light which corresponds to 1W of light being output. Typical efficiencies at the time of writing are around 100 lm/W for the best high power LEDs, so for every 1W of electricity we get about 0.14W of light. In other words, they are around 14% efficient. This may seem pretty bad, but compared for an incandescent halogen lamp at 30 lm/W it is quite an improvement. Even fluorescent lighting is only around 75 lm/W. Having said that, these two latter light sources should not be used for this purpose, even with filters, because of the Infra-red component which can damage the skin. Anyway, assuming we put in 1W of electricity we are getting 140 mW of light. If this was shone onto an area of 10cm x 10cm (which is 0.01 m^2, or about the area of the side of your face or forehead) that gives us a power density (power divided by the area it is applied over) of 14W/m^2, so we are short by approximately a factor of 50. If we reduce the area coverage down to 2.5cm x 2.5cm (one square inch in Imperial measurements) that pushes up the power density to 224 W/m^2 since there is the same amount of light being applied to a smaller area. Therefore we need something like a 3W LED, which at present costs around $20.

To make things easier when specifying an LED we can turn the numbers around. We need to illuminate a 2.5cm x 2.5cm area (or one square inch) with approximately 300 Lumens total.

In designing such a machine there are a number of other practical considerations, the first of which is heat dissipation. Running a tiny LED with 3W will burn it out unless it is connected to a metal heatsink. Then there is the stand-off distance, since you do not want to place it directly against the skin. This distance is determined by the divergence of the emitted beam, which is typically around 100 degrees of arc, so some elementary trigonometry is required. Finally, the ideal power supply is a constant current source capable of driving up to one ampere with at least 4V. However, a fixed voltage supply, say 9V, can be used with a dropper resistor whose value is determined by the forward voltage and current of the LED, and which also needs the correct power rating and heatsink. If you cannot understand how to do this – do not do it! Talk to a friendly engineer.

Infra Red Brain Stimulation

So, returning from our excursion into vanity, a technique whose efficacy I cannot comment upon. It is the use of high intensity near IR LEDs to penetrate the skull and directly impinge upon brain tissue. At the wavelength used, typically around 900nm, it seems that the skull is fairly transparent to the radiation. Obviously though, this will not work through thick hair. Anecdotally it has been claimed that non-modulated radiation exceeding 100mW per square centimeter can improve, or delay, symptoms of Alzheimer's disease. This is typically of the same order of magnitude of brain illumination one might expect from summer sunlight at noon impinging on a shaved head. So there may be some plausibility to the claim, as in a sense it is duplicating the kind of exposure our ancestors would receive by working outside. In practice, because of hair, the diodes are placed in contact with the scalp. Again, a word of warning – the diodes may get hot, and if you do want to try this make sure you are running from a low voltage isolated power supply, or even better, batteries.

Following on from this there are dubious claims about the ability to improve the functioning of specific brain areas using the technique. However, at the time of writing no significant information has surfaced regarding any major effects, and what experimentation is being done is generally in the amateur realm. Nor is there any information on the effects of modulation of the radiation, although one might expect some kind of entrainment to manifest if there really is any effect at all. Additionally, while 100mW per square centimeter might be an average, LEDs are quite capable of providing an order of magnitude or more higher power density if pulsed. Again, no reports on effects. So, if you do intend to experiment take the following precautions:

- Keep the power densities at or below the levels expected from sunlight.
- Avoid possibly harmful frequencies, for example, ones associated with triggering epileptic fits
- Minimize the duration of the experiments.
- Have someone present who can switch off the machine if things go wrong.
- Be aware of which areas of the brain are being illuminated.
- Only use high power pulses if all the previous precautions have been put in place and no adverse effects noted.

Magnetometers

One useful bit of kit used by Paranormal investigation teams on their visits to sites of interest with regard to hauntings and so forth, is the magnetometer. These come in two general types, ones for measuring static fields, such as the strength of the geomagnetic field, and ones that are designed to measure fluctuations in the field of up to a few kilohertz. It is the latter that are primarily of interest since as we have seen it is variable fields that most likely have psychogenic effects ranging in frequency from around 1Hz up to approximately 4kHz. Fortunately alternating magnetic fields are by far the easiest to detect, so no complex electronics are required. Static fields, on the other hand, require special techniques. Keywords for these, which will not be elaborated upon here, are *Hall Effect sensor*, *fluxgate magnetometer*, *proton magnetometer*, and SQUID. Details can be found on the Net.

Returning to the detection of alternating fields, the simplest setup involves amplifying the output of a sense coil or Hall Effect integrated circuit, albeit with some basic design precautions. These are:

- Since the most powerful fields are likely to come from mains wiring at either 50Hz or 60Hz depending upon region, these frequencies should be filtered out otherwise they will swamp the kind of signal for which we are searching.
- Make sure the search coil is enclosed in a grounded Aluminum box and situated away from the main electronics to avoid pickup.
- Use a battery based linear power supply to avoid any mains ripple.
- Feed the output of the coil to a high impedance unity gain op-amp to first buffer the signal. Make sure that the output of the coil is clamped with (say) a Zener diode to prevent high voltages damaging the amplifiers. Filter out the 50Hz and 60Hz points using a notch filter.
- Feed this into an amplifier stage with switchable gain, in +/- x10 increments to enable adjustment of sensitivity.
- The final output can be fed into a meter; comparators and LEDs; a voltage to frequency converter to produce a sound output; a latching circuit and LED to catch and display transients etc.

Such a magnetometer should quite easily pick up any anomalies in the local geomagnetic field. In general, it is not necessary to calibrate the device against known fields since most of the time it will be used to look for comparative differences. Of course, the simplest way of acquiring such a magnetometer is to buy one. Fairly cheap devices are readily available. Apart from its use in ghost hunting, it is mandatory equipment for anyone seeking to work within the Ultraterrestrial/UFO paradigm, since there are often substantial magnetic fields involved in close encounters.

Dream Machines

The Dream machine (also known as the Mind Machine) was invented by Brion Gysin and Ian Sommerville in the early 1960s and is designed to be viewed with closed eyes. The device itself is quite simple, consisting of a cylinder with holes cut into his sides and placed on a record turntable. A lightbulb is suspended in the center of the spinning cylinder with the result being a pattern of light effectively strobing between 8Hz and 13Hz.

It is essentially a rather gentler form of a stroboscope which can easily be modified to create different colors. The major difference is that a conventional strobe produced sharp pulses at regular intervals whereas this generates a sine wave. The effect is to produce vivid visions of geometrical patterns appearing to be projected on the eyelids across the whole the field of vision. Prolonged sessions can alter the perception of time and space by provoking a dream-like state.

Given the scarcity of turntables in the digital age a similar effect can be obtained by programming a computer to flash its screen at the various frequencies.

Machines

Alternatively, commercial devices using LEDs are available. As with all pulsed optical devices there is a danger of triggering epilepsy and hence should not be used if there is any such medical condition present. Additionally, the danger increases as the frequency approaches 18Hz.

Symbolic Machines

Symbolic Machines is the name given to whole classes of pseudo-scientific devices that at first glance seem absurd and unworkable, yet apparently do work for some people some of the time. It is a modern term reflecting the view that these machines work not because they are actually manipulating any property of matter or energy that is scientifically measurable, but because they act upon the unconscious mind of the user in a symbolic manner. They are, in effect, hitech prayer wheels. As such they tend to work somewhat better for engineers and scientists than other occult techniques. It's as if making and using such a device fools the critical aspect of the unconscious into allowing the operation to succeed via the uncritical mind. A kind of occult placebo effect for the technically minded! One of the most useful reference works for this type of device is a book by G Harry Stine entitled "Amazing and Wonderful Mind Machines You Can Build"[108] first published in 1975CE.

In the past various names have been given to these machines, depending upon which school of thought originated them. As mentioned previously, the earliest would be the Tibetan prayer wheel which automatically churns out prayers on every revolution. As we will see later, the modern electronically updated incarnation is the Wish Machine. Anyway, the most common names for this field of occult study are: *Radionics*, *Psionics*, *Orgone Technology* and *Psychotronics*. However, I prefer to use the latter term to refer to electronic equipment which does function in a scientifically explicable manner to affect the mind. Additionally, since there are so many variations on the theme I will only be providing a few definitive descriptions of the most well known. Additional designs can be extrapolated from the underlying principles. In fact, there exists a whole pseudo-science industry based on Psi effects masquerading as standard technology (of a weird kind), from Orgone energy to Scalar Waves.

The Hieronymus Machine

In 1949CE Thomas G Hieronymus patented a machine[109] designed to "detect the presence of any element or combination of elements that may be in substance under investigation to determine their intensity an/or quantity thereof by the detection of

---

[108] ISBN-13: 978-1560870753, Top of the Mountain Publishing

[109] US patent number 2,482,773

their emissions or emanations." Those emissions or emanations are supposedly of a new form of energy which Hieronymus named *Eloptic Energy* which has characteristics both electrical and optical in that it can be conducted by wires, refracted by prisms, focused by lenses and so forth.

The machine was presented as a box with various knobs and dials, a tray into which a sample of the material to be analyzed was placed, and a reaction pad. The pad was stroked by a finger as the dials were turned and the machine "tuned" to the frequency of the material. When this matched the material the pad presented a feeling of being sticky to the finger. Internally the mechanism consisted of coils, amplifier, a prism and power supply. An approximate schematic is shown below:

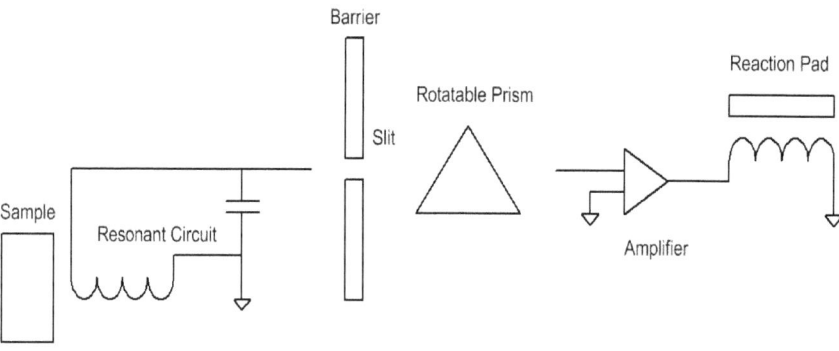

Figure 5

The idea is that the Eloptic energy from the sample is picked up by the input coil which is part of a resonant circuit tuned to approximately 500kHz. This then streams from the point towards the slit and then onto a prism. As the prism is rotated it refracts the energy imaged by the slit until it hits the input wire of the amplifier, which then amplifies it and feeds it into the final coil beneath the reaction pad. At this point the pad suddenly feels sticky. Various controls alter the resonant frequency of the input coil, angle of prism and gain of amplifier. If you are an electronics engineer it will all seem simple, as well as being utter bullshit from a conventional technological point of view. However, that is not the point. The machine really became famous when it was featured in the January 1957CE edition of *Astounding* Science Fiction magazine, edited by John W Campbell.

The story does not end there, however. An interesting discovery was made when it was noticed that the machine even operated without a power supply when dead batteries were replaced by a piece of paper inscribed with the electronic symbol for batteries. This was taken the the limits when the entire internals were substituted with the circuit diagram and the machine still worked. Ultimately, all that is needed is a detailed diagram of the whole machine on a sheet of paper, which is what definitively puts it into the Symbolic Machine category. Meanwhile other aspects of the device became apparent. The other spectacular property followed from a two way action usually claimed for Radionics devices. That is, when the sample (called the *witness*) in Radionics, is acted upon symbolically the original source connected with the witness is also affected. The archetypal claim used to illustrate this property is that reported in the Journal of Paraphysics[110] by a Dow Chemical researcher, Dr W J Hale. He photographed a citrus orchard that was blighted by an insect infestation and used the negative along with a drop of pesticide as the witness. After a number of two hour treatments over the course of a week the areas on the film were clear of insects, while the other areas not photographed were still affected. Other claims are even more bizarre, for example, using it as a time machine by linking in a camera and tuning into specific times in the past with the resulting images reflecting the era sought[111]. Or using a drop of a person's blood to divine the state of health, or affect it. Clearly, if these claims are taken at face value the Hieronymus Machine can act as a potent Psionic weapon as well as a healing and divinatory device.

The Wish Machine

The Wishing machine consists of an audio amplifier with two parallel copper plates attached to the input terminals and an antenna attached to the output. The user places a wish in the form of text, image, Sigil or a diarama consisting of small objects, between the plates and keeps the machine on until the wish comes true, usually within a week or two. That is all.

The pseudo-scientific explanation is that the metal plate serves as a capacitor, charging the "ether" with the intent, amplifying it, and broadcasting it to the universe. Alternatively, it uses Scalar Wave energy to create a causal link between the wish of the operator and the manifestation of that wish in the material universe. As usual with these devices, do not bother to look for an explanation in scientific terms, because it does not exist. Probably the most famous mention of the device was by the author William H. Burroughs in *The Western Lands*. He apparently used this device regularly after reading about it in the Stine book. The setup is illustrated below.

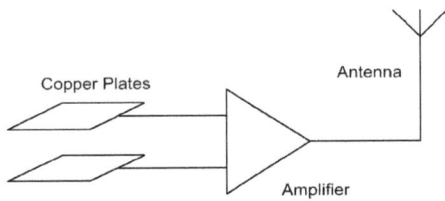

Figure 6

---

[110] November 3, 1969

[111] Reminiscent of the Scole Experiment results described in a previous chapter

For those readers who are not engineers I now offer a simple way of trying out the above using just a standard cheap stereo amplifier. It also applied to hacked radios and boom boxes. First off, you do not need copper plates since any conductive material will do and two Aluminum pie dishes work just as well. So, take a two strand cable connected into one of the amplifier inputs and connect each to a pie dish. Take an amplifier output, one of those normally fed to a speaker and connect one of the terminals (usually Red) to a piece of wire to serve as the antenna. Length does not matter much. Write your intention of a piece of paper, slip it between the pie dishes, and turn on the machine. As long as you have not mixed up input and output nothing spectacular should happen, which means it is now working properly. You can of course try variations on this theme using what you have already learned in the book to increase the efficacy of the magickal working (for that is what it really is). Popular uses include enhancement of physical strength, stamina, health, personal energy levels and engineering favorable coincidence with regards to love, money and the usual desires. Add to that remote healing, remote harming and generally whatever crosses your mind. Like using the Sigils examined previously, it is best to switch on the machine and forget about it. Let the Wish Machine do the work in relentlessly churning out your Will.

Variations on the technical theme tend to bring it back towards a Hieronymus configuration, but other occult technologies can be added in, for example the use of Reichian Orgone materials in the output phase and Cloudbuster style emitters as the antenna.

Note: Generally, magick operates well in the analog realm and barely limps along in the digital world. This does not mean that all digital systems are useless, far from it. What it does mean is that you should only use the digital domain to deliver information and control systems that are outside of the bit where the magick is supposed to be happening. Quite often this area has features that involve quantum randomness, as previously discussed. A suggestion from Marc Power concerns other variables from a more traditional magickal point of view:

> Record your intent onto analog cassette tape (adapted boom box is useful for this) by feeding your target (copperplates) into a mike input and just recording for as long as the cassette will allow whilst you project your intent. Then, just put the cassette on continuous play. A strange thing about this technique is that your intent is usually fulfilled at the moment that the cassette destroys itself through sticking, breaking, wear and tear etc. Once I noticed this effect, I immediately went out and bought the cheapest, most poorly built cassettes that I could find so that they would commit seppuku for their master after only a few days on continuous play. Occasionally the whole wishing machine joins in and also sacrifices itself manifesting your intent. If this happens just accept the sacrifice and don't try to repair the thing but dispose of it with honor as you would a trusted lieutenant killed while defending you.

Some intents may require many successive tapes and even successive machines, the potential to manifest accumulates in the aethyr until it passes a threshold and finally manifests into your reality in a kind of orgasmic spasm. Abandoned operations are unhealthy, since they leave a massive charge out there on the aethyr and such charges command your unconscious attention, causing feedback, sapping your vitality and running down your own energies if not "fed" so it is important to perform an "operation of undoing" which will release and reabsorb the accumulated charge.

The scale of the intent that you can manifest using a wishing machine (I prefer to call them a ritual machine) is limited only by what consequences the operator is willing to take responsibility for (both consciously and unconsciously) and the amount of time and effort that the operator is willing to feed/create/sacrifice new tapes and machines to that intent. Oh yes, another effect you get occasionally is sub-intent manifestation, this is where you see the intent partially or imperfectly manifested. This works on the principle:

> *The Universe when you ask it for something will first respond by giving you what is easiest for it to give you (least action principle).*

Of course, this may not be good enough for you (and usually isn't.) How do you respond? By maintaining very high standards (criteria), rejecting what you are given and leaving the machine to run. Criteria are the initial standards that you set yourself so you will be able to recognize when your intent has been manifested fully and you can accept that the operation is complete and at an end. At this point you cannot just turn your machine off, you must instead have a "ritual of completion" where you thank it and its components for dutifully manifesting your will before shutting it down (this will greatly improve your chances of successfully using it again for some new intent).

Wilhelm Reich and Orgonomy

Orgonomy is a "science" created by the noted psychoanalyst Dr. Wilhelm Reich who was yet another person to rediscover Ki, Chi, Vril, Lifeforce, Prana… and build a whole pseudo-science around it. However, because he was famous in his field, because the details are so well expounded and because he still has a massive following it is worth examining his work in this field in detail. Additionally, his story has become an almost archetypal example of state persecution, including cover-ups, the suppression of his work and involves all the usual suspects up to and including the US military and CIA. So, if you want to live in "Conspiracy World"[112] here is a good starting place.

Reich was a contemporary of, and worked closely with, Sigmund Freud and wrote a number of books that proved to be very influential in the field of psychoanalysis. These include *The Function of the Orgasm* and *Character Analysis* during

---

[112] Where everyone knows what's happening except *you*

the 1920s and 1930s. From this he created what came to be known as Reichian Therapy and which is still used in part by many of the current therapies practiced today such as *Gestalt Therapy*, *Bioenergetics*, *Rolfing Therapy*, and *Primal Scream Therapy* to name the most well-known. His study of neurosis was applied to politics in his 1930s study *The Mass Psychology of Fascism*, *People in Trouble*, *The Invasion of Compulsory Sex-Morality*, *The Sexual Revolution*, followed in the 1940s and 1950s by *The Murder of Christ* and *Listen Little Man*. It is worth noting that when I last checked (August 2009, some 52 years after his death), these books are still in print.

Had he stopped at that point he would likely have died a noted founder of modern psychoanalysis instead of in prison as a supposedly discredited crank. Unfortunately for him his work continued in the area of "The Bion Experiments" which involved the very Alchemical undertaking of the creation of life from inorganic matter, and continued with further studies into what he named Orgone Energy which were published in various magazines, journals and books. The most important from our point of view being "Ether God and Devil and Cosmic Superimposition"[113] where he developed his theories into a complete cosmology. He created instruments to accumulate Orgone energy which he claimed speeded up natural healing of the body, including curing cancer, and experimented with the reaction of Orgone energy with nuclear radiation in *The Oranur Experiment* in 1951CE. He also created instruments that could seriously affect the weather, known colloquially as Cloudbusters, and did research into Orgone as an energy source for UFOs, documented in *Contact With Space*[114]. The latter story is particularly interesting if anyone wishes to do work within the Ultraterrestrial paradigm previously discussed, since Reich got into something resembling a small war with the entities. All of this, plus his advocacy for natural child-birth, natural parenting, self-regulation and for the sexual rights of youth and adults made him an icon of the Counter Culture (Hippie) era that was to follow close upon his death.

Ostensibly his downfall was due to the medical and therapeutic claims he made for his Orgone accumulator, which fell fowl of the US Food and Drug Administration (FDA) who claimed that Orgone energy did not exist and hence his claims were fraudulent. To cut a long story short, they obtained an injunction against transporting his machines across state lines which was broken not by Reich himself, but an associate. Reich was charged with contempt of court and received a two year sentence after a trial where the prosecution lawyer was a man who had previously represented him. During the trial correspondence was made public between him and various government agencies, including the US Airforce, the FBI and CIA. His books, journals and other materials were confiscated and not returned to his family or the Wilhelm Reich Foundation after his death in prison some months later. Shortly before his death he was offered parole if he signed an undertaking never to work with or write about Orgonomy again. Additional

---

[113] ISBN-13: 978-0374509910, Farrar, Straus and Giroux (January 1, 1972)

[114] Oranur, Second Report, 1951-56, Core Pilot Press, 1957

measures were also periodically undertaken against his Orgonomy work in both the 1950s and 1960s when the FDA ordered his books burned.

The Orgone Accumulator

The theory behind most Orgone based machines is that organic materials attract Orgone and inorganic ones, especially metals, repels it. The accumulator is essentially a box made of alternating layers of (usually) ferrous metals and high dielectric constant organic insulators. The device is analogous to a conventional electrical capacitor and is designed to collect atmospheric Orgone and concentrate it in the interior. The box itself can be any size, but one of the most common used for healing purposes is large enough to contain a person, usually seated. The result is said to be a boosting of the immune system and subsequent restoration of health in many cases, even to the point of destroying some tumors. Reich himself performed a number of tests across a wide spectrum of living matter, from cancerous mice to the effect on plants, and he became convinced that the benefits of Orgone therapy could not be purely attributed to the placebo effect. Subsequently different forms of Orgone accumulator were produced including blankets which could be applied to different parts of the body.

From the point of view of magickal practice or ritual it is difficult to see how such accumulators could be used, apart from their ancillary healing properties. However, it is an altogether different proposition with the *Cloudbuster*.

The Reich Cloudbuster

Just as there is Orgone Reich discovered its opposite, the life sapping energy that he dubbed *Deadly Orgone* or DOR, whose accumulations played a significant part in desertification. As an extension of his work he created the Cloudbuster in order to manipulate the atmospheric streams of Orgone, and consequently affect cloud formation and precipitation.

The mechanics of the Cloudbuster is quite simple. It is basically one or more metal tubes open at the sky end, with the other connected by a conductive cable to a source of running water. Again using an electrical analogy, it is a lightning rod for Orgone. At least, that is the classical position as regards their theory of operation. A more modern view is that the tubes shoot coherent beams of Orgone energy

Variations on the theme include using an orgone accumulator in series with the tubes between the tubes and the water, or Symbolic Machines to tune the system. Additionally, the tubes may be loaded with various items, most notoriously radioactive substances which greatly increased the power of the system.

In operation the Cloudbuster will cause any clouds towards which it is pointed to evaporate rapidly. Precautions should also be taken against staying in the immediate vicinity of such devices as they are reported to have a deleterious effect on health.

As an interesting aside, "cloudbusting" is quite an amusing game that anyone can play and which needs no apparatus at all. You just go outside whenever the sky is full of those fragmented fluffy clouds, pick one at random, and fixing your intent stare at it and will it to disappear. Which it generally does within a couple of minutes! If you do not believe me try it – it costs nothing but a couple of minutes experimentation.

Ultraterrestrials and Orgone weapons

> "I made actual contact by way of the cloudbuster with luminous objects in the sky on May 12, 1954...During this hour men on earth saw for the first time in the history of man and his science two "Stars" to the west fade out several times when cosmic energy was drawn from them... Easy contact was made on that fateful day with what obviously turned out to be a heretofore unknown type of UFO. I had hesitated for weeks to turn my cloudbuster pipes toward a "star", as if I had known that some of the blinking lights hanging in the sky were not planets or fixed stars but SPACE machines. With the fading out of the two "stars", the cloudbuster had suddenly changed into a SPACEGUN...what had been left of the old world of human knowledge after the discovery of the OR energy 1936-40 tumbled beyond reprieve. Nothing could any longer be considered impossible. I had directed drawpipes, connected with the deep well toward an ordinary star, and the star had faded out four times." – Wilhelm Reich

The war with the UFOs began when Reich noticed various large red and yellow pulsating lights in the sky were associated with what he called "Deadly Orgone Radiation" (DOR) flooding the area of the Institute. DOR is a sort of mirror image of the healing Orgone he used, being a kind of negative excretion of the life process which used Orgone energy – in other words, ectoplasmic shit. He blamed the UFOs for deliberately introducing it into our atmosphere and viewed them as being a malignant force. They, in their turn, stepped up their activities against him and the whole episode came to a head on an expedition he and his group made to the desert around Tucson Arizona in order to investigate the role played by Orgone reactions in the formation of deserts. There he and the group came under a concerted attack by the Ultraterrestrials and it was not until he finally fitted his Cloudbusters with radioactive sources, Radium needles, that the power was boosted sufficiently to achieve a definitive victory. Throughout all of his encounters with the UFOs he kept the US Airforce informed of the details, hence the involvement with other branches of the US government and military at a number of meetings.

Machines

Conclusions

From the above it would seem that all Psi effects are psychomantic phenomena, that is, they are connected with divination of the mind in various ways. Certainly the effectiveness of Symbolic Machines does not lie in the machines themselves but rather in the person using them. Specifically, they allow disparate elements of the operator's mind to communicate with one another by taking direct control of the body via the ideomotor response. The results of this response are then fed to the consciousness by direct observation of what is happening with the machine, such as an apparent increase in "stickiness" with the Hieronymous device. The fact that PK effects such as healing and pest control occur when this process is reversed indicates that it is not purely a passive mechanism for extracting information from the unconscious. It can also be an active one where information can be fed to the parts of the mind controlling PK effects. These Psi active aspects being ones that are not normally accessible under conditions of everyday consciousness.

Finally, it cannot have escaped the attention of magicians that what has been described above is an example of *sympathetic magick*, where apparently scientific sounding laws of magickal practice have been derived such as "like affects like" and "as above so below". However, as we have seen, it works not because there is anything inherently true in a scientific sense but because the mind makes use of such symbolism in order to achieve the required response. Hence all such magickal structures are in effect variants of same kind of Symbolic Machine. This in turn suggests that the most effective type of Symbolic Machine to create is one tailored to the individual psyche of the mage. One possible way to do this is to use either divinatory techniques or the machines themselves to indicate methods of improvements – listen to your unconscious!

The Great Work

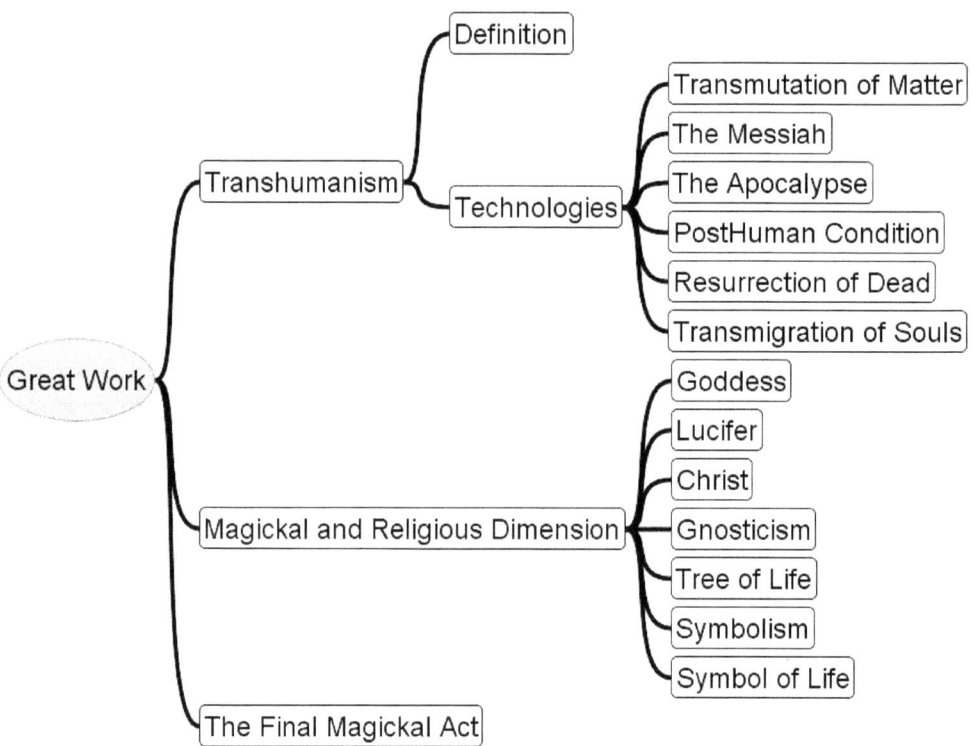

11 The Great Work

> "It is a serious thing to live in a society of possible gods and goddesses, to remember that the dullest and most uninteresting person you can talk to may one day be a creature which, if you saw it now, you would be strongly tempted to worship, or else a horror and a corruption such as you now meet, if at all, only in a nightmare. All day long we are, in some degree helping each other to one or other of these destinations. It is in the light of these overwhelming possibilities, it is with the awe and the circumspection proper to them, that we should conduct all our dealings with one another, all friendships, all loves, all play, all politics. There are no ordinary people. You have never met a mere mortal. Nations, cultures, arts, civilizations – these are mortal, and their life is to ours as the life of a gnat. But it is with immortals whom we joke with, work with, marry, snub, and exploit – immortal horrors or everlasting splendors." – C S Lewis

Strangely enough, this is both the most bizarre chapter and the one with no conventional magickal insights whatsoever. However, it does point to where we are going and as such can be considered the political and religious ideology of the TechnoShaman, or TechnoMage. It concerns what is arguably the greatest philosophical and technological movement Humanity will ever produce – *Transhumanism*. It is the *Great Work* of this century and heralds the end of mankind, one way or another. But what is it? Well, the word itself is a neologism created from the words *Transitional Humanism* and has been defined by Max More, one of its most effective proponents, as:

> "... a class of philosophies that seek to guide us towards a Posthuman condition. Transhumanism shares many elements of Humanism, including a respect for reason and science, a commitment to progress, and a valuing of Human (or Transhuman) existence in this life. Transhumanism differs from Humanism in recognising and anticipating the radical alterations in the nature and possibilities of our lives resulting from various sciences and technologies."

The word, or its close relative, the Italian verb "transumanare" or "transumanar" was used for the first time by Dante Alighieri (1265CE-1321CE) in the *Divine Comedy*. It means "go outside the human condition and perception" and in English could be "to Transhumanate" or "to Transhumanize". But more of this author later.

In 1998CE, philosophers Nick Bostrom and David Pearce founded the World Transhumanist Association (WTA), an organization with a liberal democratic perspective. In 1999CE, the WTA drafted and adopted *The Transhumanist Declaration*.

The Transhumanist FAQ, prepared by the WTA, gave two formal definitions for Transhumanism:

- The intellectual and cultural movement that affirms the possibility and desirability of fundamentally improving the human condition through applied reason, especially by developing and making widely available technologies to eliminate aging and to greatly enhance human intellectual, physical, and psychological capacities.

- The study of the ramifications, promises, and potential dangers of technologies that will enable us to overcome fundamental human limitations, and the related study of the ethical matters involved in developing and using such technologies.

Within this slightly bland definition lies the core of the project, which is to use our technologies to transform ourselves into Beings that transcend the merely Human. To extend the capabilities of our minds, bodies and spirits to such a degree that we become as gods compared to our current "Human Condition". Hence the C S Lewis quote used to introduce this chapter. Ironically Lewis was speaking of what he considered to be the immortal soul in a Christian context. However, as we shall see, as an introduction to the spiritual aspects of Transhumanism it is very apt largely due to the generally unspoken religious parallels it exhibits with respect to Christianity. Whether this is coincidence, cultural conditioning or something deeper we will now examine.

The various technological themes that crop up within Transhumanism are listed below, each of which will be analyzed separately both in terms of technology and from a religious point of view. Whether most Transhumanists realize it or not, Transhumanism is but the latest and potentially the most powerful manifestation of a number of strains of esoteric thought stretching back millennia. These themes are:

- Life Extension
- Genetic Engineering
- Artificial Intelligence
- Robotics
- Nanotechnology
- Cybernetic Symbiosis

However, before diving into the technology it is necessary to set the scene for spiritual analysis that accompanies each aspect.

The Great Work

The Magickal and Religious Dimension

For those who do not know, the term "Great Work" was defined by the famous ceremonial magician Eliphas Levi as:

> "...the creation of man by himself, that is to say, the full and entire conquest of his faculties and his future; it is especially the perfect emancipation of his will."

It is a term originating in medieval European alchemy and refers to the transmutation of lead into gold, via the creation of the Philosopher's Stone. The latter was supposed to be a technology that could transform matter and endow its user with immortality by rejuvenating the body as well as bringing Enlightenment. As such, it concluded the Great Work of Alchemy. Later in the Hermetic tradition it became a metaphor for the potential inherent in the spirit to evolve from a state of imperfection symbolized by base metals, to a state of enlightenment and perfection, symbolized by gold.

While the more material aspects can be likened to the Great Work of the alchemists, what of the spiritual forebears of Transhumanism? It might be argued by the majority of Transhumanists, who at the time of writing tend to be atheists or agnostics, that it has no spiritual aspect and that any correspondences between previous esoteric movements, religions or philosophies are simply reflections of deep and innate Human desires and fears. That is, they are to be understood in terms of rational psychology. Clearly this is correct, given the assumptions and world-views of the overt atheistic and Humanist roots of contemporary organized Transhumanism. However, if one does not subscribe to such values then there is another picture that can be drawn wherein Transhumanism can be seen as a manifestation of an ancient spiritual force in itself that is instantly recognizable to students of magick, or indeed most theologians of several major religions.

Now, in the discussion that follows I am forced to use rather loaded terms that on the surface appear to be somewhat negative or pejorative. This is inevitably so because we still live in a heavily Christianized society despite it being supposedly secular in outlook. Surprisingly this is especially so in magick and even major strands of neo-paganism such as Wicca. The world-view in question is one of a polarization of light and dark, good and evil, right and left and so forth that stem from a mindset derived from a dualist monotheism. All good, right thinking people are assumed to be on one side and all the evil, insane, incomprehensible and destructive people on the other. It is these apparent absolutes that literally color our vocabulary, especially our religious and spiritual vocabulary. We unconsciously see absolutes where there are in reality relative positions that are in opposition to each other, and each side has its own rationale, beliefs and assumptions. The notion that one side is somehow "better" than the other can only be understood from the point of view of an individual's choice and their position in the spectrum. However, the true problem lies in the fact that historically one side has claimed that there is more than personal choice involved and that there is indeed a universal arbiter of good and evil – God. The fact that the Christian God (which is supposedly the same God as the Jews and Muslims, namely YHVH) has, according to its followers, taken wildly differing and contradictory positions on various topics through the ages has done little to blunt its popularity. This despite the fact that some of the major positions attributed to God have involved its followers in crimes of torture, mass murder and repression seldom exceeded in history. Indeed, the differing claims as to what God wants in terms of Human behavior is merely proof to its followers that the others have got it wrong and been seduced by its universal opposite and enemy, Lucifer and/or Satan. Having said that, there is nevertheless a commonality of belief that runs through both camps and which does effectively distinguish them throughout history and across religions, even many polytheistic ones. Despite all this, it has to be admitted that the most interesting analyses do come from a Christian mythological perspective, so it is with this tool that we will proceed, for the magickal paradigm based around the Christian pantheon is a powerful one in Western occultism as well as when analyzing many contemporary forces in our Western societies.

It is important to emphasize the word *mythological* because much of the mythology certainly both pre-dates and post-dates early Christianity and biblical texts by a considerable margin and much can be traced to the Renaissance period with such works as John Milton's "Paradise Lost" and "The Divine Comedy" by Dante Alighieri. Even as late as the 19th and 20th Centuries there has been a considerable expansion of the mythological base of Christianity on both sides, ranging from contemporary American Apocalyptic Christianity with its emphasis on End Times, the Biblical Revelation of St John, and *The Rapture* to New Age Satanism pioneered by such luminaries as Anton LaVay[115]

To give one very pertinent example consider Lucifer. Contemporary mythology equates him with Satan and states that he is a fallen angel cast out of Heaven for trying to usurp the role of God and as such is the embodiment of evil. Furthermore that Lucifer was a rather high ranking angel, probably an archangel but possibly a seraph or cherub who was motivated by pride to rebel against God. In the conflict that followed he was defeated and fell to Earth along with a third of the angels, who sided with him.

The problem with all of this from a biblical perspective is that there is no mention of Lucifer at all in the bible. The text normally quoted, Isaiah 14:12, actually referred to one of the popular honorific titles of a Babylonian king as light bearer, which literally translates into Latin as Lucifer, and not an angel at all. It was Milton and Dante who took this misunderstanding and wove a new mythology from it wherein Lucifer becomes the poetic appellation of Satan.

Continuing, it is important to deconstruct Christian mythology to illustrate its true origins and place the real conflicting spiritual ideologies in their correct

---

[115] Howard Stanton Levey, founder and High Priest of the Church of Satan and author of The Satanic Bible ISBN-13: 978-0380015399

The Great Work

context. In order to do so we need to take a substantial detour into heresy!

To begin with, Christianity is a religion that has almost nothing in it that is original in terms of its early mythology. Just about every major facet of it, from immaculate conception, virgin birth, Three Wise Men, Jesus as the son of God, his execution and rising from the dead to virtually all of its iconography are taken from other pre-existing religions. Most notable amongst these are Zoroastrianism, Mithraism and the Cult of Isis. Even the supposed birthday of Jesus, December 25th, comes from that of Mithras and for good measure his name was almost certainly *not* "Jesus". Since the true name in Hebrew was Yeshua or Yeshu, which was originally a title meaning "Saviour", specifically derived from "Yahweh Saves", it might be supposed that there were quite a few men around that time who used it. The First Century Jewish historian Josephus mentions some nineteen different Yeshuas or Jesii, around half of them contemporaries of the supposed Christ. In his *Antiquities*, of the twenty-eight high priests who held office from the reign of Herod the Great to the fall of the Temple, four of them bore the name Jesus.

That, however, is not the end of the story but a new beginning since Lucifer refers to the planet Venus which is also known as The Morning Star (literally, in Latin, "Light Bearer"). Interestingly, the planet has always been seen as being associated with a Goddess. Obviously in Roman mythology it was Venus herself, from whence we get the modern name of the planet, and in Greek mythology it was Aphrodite. Both are Goddesses of love and sex. It is when we move to the Middle East, and move backwards in time to the point where the God YHVH was establishing itself as the one and only God of Israel, later to become the sole God of the universe (according to its propaganda screed – the Old Testament) that we begin to see the true meaning of the Morning Star. It has always been a symbol of the most powerful Goddesses of the area, or arguably of *The* Goddess archetype of the Middle East, under her several names such as Inanna, Ishtar, Astarte and latterly Isis. One of Her many symbols is the Pentagram, or five-pointed star, these days most commonly associated with the occult when drawn in line form. The filled form crops up in just about every depiction of "star" from the flag of the USA to the Red Star symbolizing Socialism. Of course, in each occurrence there is a supposed explanation as to why it was chosen which obviously differs from the occult interpretation. Medieval Christians believed it to symbolize the five wounds of Christ and that it protected against witches and demons. So again we have an interesting evolution of the symbol. Anyway, the Pentagram is also the path traced in the sky by the planet Venus as seen from Earth, which was recognized by the Sumerians. Prior to this the symbol used was an Eight-pointed star, to which we will return later as it makes a dramatic re-appearance in modern times.

Returning to the ancient Middle East we can trace a spiritual war between YHVH and the Goddess which should have culminated with the birth of Christ (whether mythological or literal), and manifested in a fusion of symbols. The key to this heretical notion lies in the New Testament, specifically Revelation 22:16 where the following words are placed in the mouth of Jesus:

"I am the root and the offspring of David, and the bright and morning star."

Here Jesus himself takes on the title of Morning Star and announces that he is descended from King David, the second King of Israel and the one favored by YHVH who went on to fight numerous successful wars of conquest and extermination. David founded a dynasty whose eventual collapse led directly to the yearning for a *Messiah,* literally, one anointed by YHVH to return and restore Israel to it days of glory.

However, it is not quite as simple as it seems when interpreting the above passage. For example, if the comma is omitted the whole context changes: "I am the root and the offspring of David and the bright and morning star" becomes an announcement that he is descended from a union of YHVH and the Goddess, the archetypal enemies. The problem is that the original text of Revelations was written in Greek and without commas. Traditionally, though, the meaning was derived from context and a certain amount of understandable pre-conception. Indeed, most knowledgeable Christians will disagree with my revised interpretation on quite good grounds. In my defense I would like to call upon Mary, the Mother of God! For if YHVH was the supposed father of Jesus there is less doubt about the identity of his mother.

She is easily known by Her titles, symbols and iconography. She is "Queen of Heaven", "Stella Maris" or simply "Our Lady". Her color is blue, is often depicted with the infant Jesus in her arms and sports a halo (or nimbus). Except that all of those belong to Isis and have been copied without modification, especially the Madonna and Child image which originally was of Isis cradling Horus. The Goddess renamed (yet again) for a new age and old religion. In Her other guises She has been Astarte (literally meaning "Resplendent Tower of Light"), the "Lady of the Beasts" often depicted in dance with animals, her upraised arms holding serpents that symbolize rebirth, rejuvenation. Depicted on the prow of ancient Phoenician ships she was a figurehead carrying a cross in one hand and pointing the way with the other. She initially makes an appearance in recorded history as Inanna, the subject of the earliest known written records from the earliest known author, the daughter of Sargon of Akkad – the priestess Enheduanna. In her writings are the first hymns as well as the prototype stories that would later be absorbed into the Bible.

As an interesting aside, Sargon is said to have recorded the following inscription on a cuneiform tablet:

"My priestly mother conceived me; secretly brought me to birth; set me in an ark of bulrushes; made fast my door with pitch. She consigned me to the river, which did not overwhelm me. The river brought me to Akki, the farmer, who brought me up to be his son. During my gardening, the goddess Ishtar loved me, and for fifty-four years the kingship was mine."

One is reminded of the story of Moses.

Anyway, the Goddess survived as Isis well into the Christian era before her worship was finally extinguished in the 6th Century. Or at least that's the official story. She was not only YHVH's most powerful competitor in the Middle East but embodied the female principle which was then suppressed in what was effectively a long drawn out battle.

So, what we are left with is the heretical notion that Christ is the offspring of two major competing deities, YHVH and "The Goddess", the latter closely associated with the Morning Star (Lucifer) and who takes the title of Lucifer for Himself as their summation. This somewhat parallels the views of Rudolf Steiner's[116] cosmology wherein Ahriman represents a kind of cold, dry materialism and Lucifer an impulsive spiritual fire, with Christ as the balance point between them. That Christ was then killed by the servants of YHVH comes as no surprise.

The ideological polarizations that Christ bridges can be summed up in the following list – I will leave it as an exercise for the reader to ascribe characteristics to sides.

- Rationality versus irrationality
- Knowledge versus faith
- Anarchy versus authority
- Freedom versus dictatorship
- Rebellion versus obedience
- Criticism versus reverence
- Individual versus community
- Self reliance versus dependency
- Chaos versus law
- Change versus stasis
- Strength versus weakness
- Future versus past
- Choice versus fate
- Excess versus insufficiency
- The spirit of the law versus the letter of the law

Max More (nee O'Connor) is one of the founders of the modern Transhumanist movement, specifically the branch known as Extropianism which is predominantly libertarian in outlook. From our analytical point of view it is interesting that he actually wrote an essay in the publication of the Libertarian Alliance[117] named "In Praise of the Devil". This is not to say that he is a Luciferian or Satanist since he is

---

[116] The Influences of Lucifer and Ahriman – Anthroposophic Press, ISBN: 0 88010 3752

keen to point out that he has no belief in their reality beyond the symbolic. However, it does tend to illustrate the unconscious religious nature of the movement. In the essay he essentially expounded upon elements of the above list. As usual, the Devil gets the good bits.

Figure 1

Pressing on into symbolism bring us to the icon of Transhumanism – the Eight-Pointed Star shown above. Specifically, this is/was the logo of the major Transhumanist organization, the World Transhumanist Association recently renamed to Humanity Plus[118] in a rebranding exercise, and reflecting the common abbreviation of Transhumanism as H+. Purely coincidentally, this star was the earliest symbol for the planet Venus until it was supplanted by the pentacle. This was the period before it was realized that the Morning Star and Evening Star are actually the same object. In the earliest records it is the symbol of Inanna. So, another Lucifer/Goddess connection and one that goes all the way back to the beginning of recorded history. Naturally, it's not as simple as that as it is merely an interesting synchronicity. The real origin of the Transhumanist symbol is rather more bizarre.

The Hermeneutics of Transhumanism provides one of those fascinating coincidences so beloved by Jung. I believe it was actually chosen by Anders Sandberg[119] who stated on Christmas Day 2006:

> "I made the original Earth-and-star image, as detailed in the magick thread inspired by chaos magic and whatnot. To me it represents expansion, growth and freedom from constraints. As far as I remember, someone at the early WTA asked me if they could use the picture and I agreed."

The synchronicity of the timing, Christmas day, arose simply because I finally got around to asking about its origins when checking the mailing list. I did not expect such a prompt and decisive answer so close to home (The UK Transhumanist

---

[117] Atheist Notes No. 3, ISSN 0953-7791, ISBN 1 85637 011 9

[118] http://www.humanityplus.org/

[119] Personal correspondence and the UK Transhumanist Association mailing list, Christmas Day 2006

The Great Work

Association) from someone I knew. Yes – The Morning Star, She moves in mysterious ways...

The symbol created by Anders was originally in this form:

Figure 2

It was inspired by a brief image in the DC comic "Kid Eternity" by Grant Morrison (he of hypersigil fame), during it's darker 1990s revival. The background, briefly, is that the Kid is killed and finds himself in an artificial Heaven created by the Lords of Chaos. They convince him to act for them by persuading him he died too early and that they can return him to life. They provide him with a minor Chaos Lord as a guide in order to set up and turn on a series of "Chaos Engines", whose aim is to force the evolution of Humanity as a good deed in order to earn their way back into the real Heaven by pleasing God.

Figure 3

The symbol of the Lords of Chaos is, naturally, the Chaos Star depicted above. In this incarnation it was created by the Science Fiction and Fantasy writer Michael Moorcock in connection with his *Elric*[120] stories in the late 1950s, and which was emblazoned on the character's shield. He drew the first one on his kitchen table while he pondered the plot. The series of stories concerned the last emperor of a decadent and ancient civilization, Elric of Melniboné, who is a drug dependent albino sorcerer able to summon supernatural allies by dint of his royal bloodline and whose patron is Arioch, a Lord of Chaos and Duke of Hell.

The major reason H+ adopted the symbol was because it is a representation

---

[120] Elric of Melniboné – Elric first appeared in print in 1961 in Michael Moorcock's novella, "The Dreaming City" (*Science Fantasy* #47 June 1961)

of both diversity and of expansion in all directions. However, the star was also adopted in the 1970s by the nascent Chaos Magick which arose from a meeting between Peter J. Carroll and Ray Sherwin in Deptford (London) in 1976CE. Two years later they founded the *Illuminates of Thanateros* (IOT, also known as "The Pact") as an organization to practice and research what arguably became the most influential innovation in the field in the latter half of the 20th Century. The key texts outlining Chaos Magick as a system of pragmatic magick based upon fluid belief systems as tools in their own right, are the books written by Carroll in 1978CE and 1981CE, "Liber Null" and "Psychonaut"[121] respectively.

And to complete the symmetry it turns out that Anders Sandberg was involved in the practice of Chaos Magick as a teenager in Sweden. At the UK Transhumanist Association meeting where I discovered this interesting fact I also did an informal survey of those present as to who had at some point had an involvement with occultism of one sort or another. To my surprise about one third answered in the affirmative. I say surprising because superficially Transhumanists tend to be overt atheists and rationalists. There are though a couple of caveats. The first is that this was a small and possibly unrepresentative sample. As far as I know nobody has done such a survey on a large scale cross section of Transhumanists. Second, it was pointed out that the kind of people who come to embrace H+ are just those who look for technologies capable of transforming or upgrading their minds or bodies and that magick is an obvious place to start for the young, before they move to a more scientific or engineering paradigm which is the core of H+.

Finally, there has in recent times been a theological drift towards separating Lucifer and Satan, both in occult texts and more recently various branches of Christianity. They have come to be viewed as at least two different archetypes. Much of this is due to the three way split between Old Testament, New Testament and Post Renaissance mythology. In the OT Satan does not get much of a mention and when he does it tends to be a kind of "loyal opposition" or prosecutor for YHVH; that is, they are on the same team. In the NT there are far more references to Satan with Luciferian characteristics. More recently Satan has evolved into an archetype of pure negativity – the repository of everything undesirable including mindless stupidity, lies, ignorance and capricious pointless cruelty with no redeeming features whatsoever. In other words, the Hollywood Satan of innumerable horror movies whose major achievement appears to be possessing witless teenagers and maybe killing one or two in spectacular but inefficient ways before being defeated by some implausible exorcism. One has to wonder how Lucifer, the most beautiful of creatures and a mind of transcendent power and eloquence got reduced to being portrayed as a slobbering pustular freak barely able to string two growls and a threat together in a coherent manner. This Satan we can dismiss from the rest of the analysis.

The conclusion being, the patron deity of H+ would appear to be Lucifer,

---

[121] Liber Null & Psychonaut: An Introduction to Chaos Magic by Peter J. Carroll   ISBN-13: 978-0877286394

with elements of Christ and the Goddess. And one other feature concerning the Eight-Pointed Star that I almost forgot – it's most common use in modern times is on Christmas cards, because it is used as the Christmas Star heralding the birth of the Messiah.

The Gnostic Connection

There have obviously been numerous references to the religious aspects of H+, but one of the more academic ones is by David Pauls[122] in an article entitled "Transhumanism: 2000 Years in the Making". In it he raises some interesting correspondences with Gnostic beliefs, although only rather superficially, for the similarities go much deeper in some aspects.

Gnosticism was a syncretic religious system that was a competitor to the early Christian church. Although it's roots preceded Christianity it absorbed so much of the latter that it came to be viewed as an heretical Christian sect. It's teachings can be briefly summarized as:

- Human Beings are divine souls trapped in an imperfect material world

- That this world was created by an imperfect god, the Demiurge[123], often identified with YVHV, who is viewed as being at best of limited competence and at worst as evil.

- The *gnosis* referred to in the name is a form of revealed esoteric knowledge that allows Humans to be reminded of their true origins, which is...

- The true God, often referred to as the Godhead or Pleroma (the totality of divine powers)

The Catholic Encyclopedia defines Gnosticism as:

> The doctrine of salvation by knowledge. This definition, based on the etymology of the word (gnosis "knowledge", gnostikos, "good at knowing"), is correct as far as it goes, but it gives only one, though perhaps the predominant, characteristic of Gnostic systems of thought. Whereas Judaism and Christianity, and almost all pagan systems, hold that the soul attains its proper end by obedience of mind and will to the Supreme Power, i.e. by faith and works, it is markedly peculiar to Gnosticism that it places the salvation of the soul merely in the possession of a quasi-intuitive knowledge of the mysteries of the universe and of magic formulae indicative of that knowledge. Gnostics were "people who knew", and their knowledge at once constituted them a superior class of beings, whose present and future status was

---

[122] The Center for Bioethics and Culture Network

[123] The Latinized form of Greek dēmiourgos, δημιουργός, literally "public or skilled worker"

> essentially different from that of those who, for whatever reason, did not know.

Whilst Gnosticism flourished in the early centuries during the period of the Roman Empire it had largely died away by the late Middle Ages, although strands of its beliefs did survive and underwent a revival in the esoteric philosophies of the 19th and 20th Centuries. The elements of Gnostic culture chosen by Pauls in his analysis of H+ are:

> "... disdain for the body, the quest for hidden knowledge, and the goal to lead others to a higher plane of existence."

The belief that the material world was flawed, if not utterly corrupt, led to a profoundly dualist view where mind, or rather immortal spirit, was exalted and the body viewed as the epitome of the temporal condition of decay and death. This in turn engendered a polarization of behavior leading to asceticism where the body and its pleasures were denied and kept in check, or to a radical libertinism (according to its opponents).

This indeed mirrors some accusations made concerning the type of person originally attracted to H+, namely that a disproportionate number were "misfits" of one type or another who were unhappy with their bodies, aging, gender, sexuality and so forth and hence were looking for an ideology of technological transformation or redemption. And to some extent this is still true. There are few of use who would not change aspects of our bodies if we could, and this does not apply purely to Transhumanists. There are whole mainstream industries devoted to modifying the body, ranging from gymnasiums to cosmetic surgery and tattoos to piercings. However, it is really only Transhumanists who seek to fully alter the body in fundamental ways or transcend it altogether, as we shall see later. Already the basic political principle has been laid down as "The Right of Morphological Freedom". Anders Sandberg claims it as:

> "An extension of one's right to one's body, not just self-ownership but also the right to modify oneself according to one's desires."

It is defined as:

> "... a proposed civil right of a person to either maintain or modify his or her own body, on his or her own terms, through informed, consensual recourse to, or refusal of, available therapeutic or enabling medical technology." [124]

Then, seemingly at the opposite end of the spectrum we have works by people such as the philosopher David Pearce with "The Hedonistic Imperative" who advocate the use of biotechnology to maximize happiness and minimize suffering as part of the *Abolitionist* trend within H+. Superficially it a modest proposal, after all we use anesthetics and analgesics to eliminate pain and antidepressants to alleviate mental suffering. However, when taken to its logical conclusion the ambitious scope of the

---

[124] Carrico, Dale (2006). The Politics of Morphological Freedom

The Great Work

project becomes apparent. It is nothing less than genetically re-engineering the entire biosphere to eliminate pain and suffering in all vertebrates in a Post-Darwinian transition that is a blueprint for:

- Rewriting the vertebrate genome
- Redesigning the global ecosystem
- Delivering genetically pre-programmed well-being

Of course, the means to do this are the various technologies expanded upon later. However, I am reminded of a prescient poem I read some 40 years ago. Unfortunately I cannot remember the author, but here it is:

> *Creation all shall hymn the plan*
> *Of its creator superman*
> *Who, loving living things so much*
> *Could not bear to see them separate as such*
> *And so imminent reincarnation*
> *Totalistic integration*

The Tree of Life

When it comes to the Transhumanist agenda it is useful to start with its most important item and one which goes right back to the beginning of time in the Garden of Eden. Here we have the very first propaganda piece on behalf of YHVH which sets the scene for the subsequent misogyny and dualism inherent in the Abrahamic religions. The official story goes that YHVH created Adam, with an injunction not to eat from the fruit of two of the trees in the garden. These were the Tree of Knowledge of Good and Evil, and the Tree of Life. YHVH then created Eve as a companion for Adam and it was she who was tempted by the serpent to eat from the Tree of Knowledge – Genesis 3:4:

> "And the serpent said unto the woman, Ye shall not surely die: For God doth know that in the day ye eat thereof, then your eyes shall be opened, and ye shall be as gods, knowing good and evil."

Eve thinks it might be a good idea and persuades Adam to eat, whereupon YHVH expels them with suitable additional curses to burden them for good measure. It is instructive to quote the reason given by YHVH in the text, King James Bible, Genesis 3:22:

> "And the LORD God said, Behold, the man is become as one of us, to know good and evil: and now, lest he put forth his hand, and take also of the tree of life, and eat, and live for ever"

There are two interesting points here. The first is that the serpent is not identified as Satan but as an animal. The second is that the expulsion occurred because of the implied assumption that man would become as gods (as promised by the serpent).

The clear message about life extension and the anti-aging technology that is a cornerstone of Transhumanism is that the Tree of Life is nearly within our grasp. That despite our expulsion we shall become as YHVH through our own efforts and in opposition to that entity.

In a way, it is rather difficult for me to write of progress in anti-aging technology simply because things are changing so fast. Right now an American company, Sirtis which is developing drugs based upon the naturally occurring substance Resveratrol, has been bought out by one of the world's biggest pharmaceutical companies Glaxo-Smith-Klein (GSK) for $720 million. Resveratrol has shown remarkable properties in animal tests as a broad spectrum drug that prevents, retards or reverses age related diseases such as cancer, heart disease, senility and especially diabetes. Additionally, in various creatures it has been shown to extend lifespan by up to fifty percent. The problem though, is that very high doses have been required because Resveratrol is quickly metabolized and excreted. Sirtis is developing variants that are effective at much lower doses. Ostensibly, if successful in Human trials currently being undertaken, they will be marketed as a treatment for diabetes. This is because at present it is not possible to get approval from regulatory bodies for drugs that do not target a named disease, and aging is classed as a "natural" process.

There are also reports of tests of longevity associated with another drug developed from a soil microbe found on Easter Island and named Rapamycin. When fed to elderly mice, with an equivalent Human age of around 60, it added an additional 10 to 15 years of healthy life. The problem is that Rapamycin is a powerful immune suppressant, so for Human use it will require some molecular tweaking. Nevertheless, it appears that the pharmaceutical industry is beginning to regard anti-aging drugs as a potentially gigantic market. For example, would you pay a dollar a day not to age? Several billion people might.

Anyway, while these are indications that extending healthy Human life is possible they are still far from a cure for aging. What they do offer is a possible way of attaining what some refer to as "escape velocity". The term is borrowed from rocket science and refers to the velocity required to escape the Earth's gravitational pull entirely. By analogy, we have the situation over the past century where lifespan in the developed world has increased by about one year per decade. What anti-aging drugs may do is get us to the point where where lifespan is being extended by more than one year per year – escape velocity from aging. If, say, the Sirtis or similar drugs can add a decade of life then there is scope within that decade for science to come up with other ways to further extend it. If you are reading this in 2030CE then you will probably know the answer.

For many Transhumanists life extension is of paramount interest, simply because if we die of old age we do not get to see all the good stuff due to arrive in the next few decades! For those of us aged over 50 it may well be a close run thing, so stay healthy the boring old fashioned ways with exercise, good nutrition, various supplements and no bad habits like smoking. For those who are children now, I make this prediction – you will never die of old age. Your death will be by disease, accident or violence. It will not be "natural".

Which brings us to one of the fundamental objections brought up by people when they first encounter the prospect of extended lifespan, if not actual immortality. It is the Malthusian argument raised yet again concerning overpopulation. If nobody is going to die "naturally", they argue, then surely the world will become overcrowded and fall to famine, war and disease. The standard riposte to this argument is simple. Currently we live in a world with a high birth rate and a high death rate. We would need to move to a society with a low birth rate and a low death rate. Which would you rather live in? Of course, the next argument concerns the possible population explosion during a transition period. Again, this does not appear to be too worrying for a number of reasons. The first is that even if it took a century to happen the world's population would likely not exceed five times the current number of people, around 30 billion. Now this might appear unsustainable, which given current political will and primitive technology it probably is. However, consider the limits to population density and food production, taking England as an example. Right now England is, at a push, capable of feeding its (approximate) population of 50 million from its own farmland. Notably, this is a population density of just under 400 per square kilometer. If we did a crude extrapolation to the total land area of the earth, some 150 million square kilometers, we could assume that the Earth could support around 60 billion and not be too unpleasantly overcrowded. However, the situation is even better than that if we look at hightech farming techniques such as hydroponics as a replacement for existing agriculture. The notion of plowing some dirt once a year, putting in a few seeds and leaving it all to the mercy of the weather really is a horribly crude and inefficient way of creating food. Even worse is how we use a lot of those crops to feed animals that we then slaughter for meat. So, let me present a Transhumanist vision of farming as it could be...

What do we need to grow crops? Well, in no particular order, sunlight, water, nutrients and labor. So, let's start where there is plenty of sunlight – the Sahara desert. Naturally, we have to pipe in the water which means almost immediate evaporation in conventional farming. So let's do it in an enclosed environment, a kind of "super greenhouse". Now we can recycle the water lost this way. Let's also get out of the dirt, or more specifically sand. It's useless. Instead, we do it with hydroponics by feeding the crops the nutrients it needs directly with the crops being grown and supported on frames and in troughs. Finally, rather than staff it with vast numbers of workers, automate most of it with robots.

The energy to create the nutrients, fix atmospheric nitrogen and power the system as a whole comes from land dedicated to solar energy production, of which there is an abundance. So, how much can we expect? Well, there are commercial enterprises already in existence that can produce something like 250 tonnes of vegetables per hectare per year. That's enough to feed around 125 people for a year.

Let's say we use just ten percent of the Sahara, around 1 million square kilometers. There are 100 hectares per square kilometer so we could feed 125 x 100 x 1 million people, or in round numbers twice the current population of Earth. Food is not a technological problem – it is a political one.

To round off our view of Transhumanism down on the farm consider the other part of our diet, meat. Feeding ten kilograms of vegetable to an animal in order to produce one kilogram of meat is inefficient. Keeping those animals in appalling conditions and then killing them is just an abomination. However, we are not going to persuade everyone to become a vegetarian so we will still need to produce it. Or more specifically, the kind of meat people prefer to eat – muscle tissue. So why not just do that? Tissue culture techniques exist and can no doubt be extended to an industrial scale. We do not need to kill animals for meat. Does anyone who thinks of the future of Humanity in space habitats and planetary colonies envisage space pigs-pens and space slaughterhouses, any more than they envisage a star faring civilization powered by setting fire to dead dinosaurs (fossil fuels)? I think not. The problem is not technology, it is politics and the will to create a new world.

To end this section, a thought. It is the way of Nature that every living thing strives for life and fights against death, and the possibility we might be the first creatures to succeed in that age old battle is a vindication of that struggle and a crowning achievement of the Natural World.

The Symbol of Life

…is the DNA molecule that carries the information of our genetic code. It is the design plan for our minds and bodies, stored in a single strand configured as a double helix approximately 2 meters in length, curled up in a ball roughly 10 microns in diameter and storing about as much information as a music CD (about 700MB). Naturally, from a magickal point of view something so fundamental to life must have had an echo in previous centuries before the official discovery of its structure by James D. Watson and Francis Crick in 1953CE. So here it is in the form used by the US Military Medical Corps – the Caduceus:

The Great Work

Figure 4

Also known as the Staff of Hermes, who was the messenger of the Gods and guide to the Underworld, he carried it in his left hand. However, it only really came to be associated with medicine through its connection with Alchemy (aka The Great Work) in the 7th Century. So strong was the connection that Alchemists came to be known as the Sons of Hermes, or Hermeticists, and it formed one of the major strands of the Western occult tradition along with Gnosticism and NeoPlatonism.

Greek mythology records the origin of the symbol in the legend of Tiresias, a blind prophet and greatest seer of the classical mythos, who was transformed into a woman for seven years by the goddess Hera for striking copulating snakes with his stick. So, we not only connect DNA to the symbol but the serpent metaphor in the Garden of Eden and the connection to the Tree of Life.

Which brings us to genetic engineering. Now, it often surprises people how little interest Transhumanists show in plans to redesign Humanity through germline engineering, that is creating "designer children" as the media puts it. Although we are generally in favour of making people longer lived, smarter, stronger, more compassionate and intelligent we recognize that it is a very slow way of achieving our aims, given that a generation is 25 years. So most interest is in modifying gene expression in adults rather than embryos, since it can be applied directly to ourselves for various tweaks such as longevity. One thing worth noting is that the fact that the design for an entire Human can fit onto the equivalent of a music CD shows that designing an intelligence is not a big job in terms of the size of the plans required, although it may well be complex.

The other conventional uses of genetic engineering generally get positive reviews, such as creating microbes to create oil from plankton or adding Vitamin A to rice to alleviate blindness caused by its deficiency in Asia. As for modifying animals, quite a few of us are supporters of animal rights (to some extent, at least) so some of the more bizarre creations get a thumbs down. However, personally I am looking forward to seeing the first of the mythological creatures walk the Earth – the Unicorn! As for the question of "Uplifting", whereby animals have their intelligence boosted towards Human levels, opinions are mixed. Before the point where that kind of capability exists, probably in the 2030s, there will be plenty more to occupy our thoughts...

The Transmutation of Matter

In the popular mind a major goal of Alchemy was the transmutation of matter, specifically lead into gold. That is, something of low value into something of high value. Ignoring its symbolic meaning, we can of course transmute one element into another through various nuclear processes albeit at vast expense. However, there is another transformation of matter in modern science and technology that is far more profound – nanotechnology. Originally describing the manipulation of matter at the nanometer scale, that is, at the scale of one millionth of a millimeter, it has now come to refer to technology that can manipulate matter down to the level of single atoms. Of course, we already work at those scales in such areas as computer chips but the wider promise is the ability to manufacture devices that are literally built up an atom at a time according to design software. Now, this may not sound especially radical until you throw in a couple of unique factors. The first is that the things running the design software and doing the building are themselves at the nano scale, so it is not a question of some large machine turning out small parts to order. The second is that it may be possible to make the devices, nanobots, self replicating. It then becomes possible to see where all this is heading when it is realized that biological life itself is a subset of self replicating nanotechnology.

  The promise of nanotech is immense and many see it as not only the future of nearly all manufacturing but something that will form the basis of nearly every future technological enterprise. It is no less than programmable matter and as such is one of the technologies critical to the Transhumanist vision of the future.

  To give some idea of its utility consider the device many are attempting to design as an intermediate stage, namely, the nanofactory. Its ultimate potential is to devolve hitech manufacturing down to individual level. So, if you wanted a common utensil such as a spoon you would go over to the factory, which would be about the size of a washing machine, choose a material such as metal or plastic and pick a design from the computer database. The factory would take as it input raw materials in the form of basic chemicals and in due course out would pop the spoon, built to atomic precision. Ditto everything, from mobile phones (assuming they still exist) to drugs to diamonds to artificial gene sequences. And herein lies the danger, because such a factory could just as easily manufacture a gun or a lethal virus. The only thing stopping it would be software security features, and we know how effective that might be...

  At the present time nobody has made the kind of nanobot that could be used in manufacturing. They must have a number of properties which imply a complexity comparable to a biological cell. These are likely to be:

- Onboard computing capability.

- A communication system with the controlling computer, and the trillions of other nanobots involved in the manufacturing process.
- The ability to identify individual atoms and molecules.
- The ability to move them under direction from a master computer and connect them together.
- The ability to be easily replicated so that trillions of these little workers are very cheap to make.

Naturally, it is only at the H+ fringes that the ultimate utility of nanotechnology is examined, since it has recently become a "respectable" business that does not want to frighten people with outrageous speculations. Ultimately all kinds of nanotech is envisaged, including things like *utility fog* which consists of a superfine dust that can clump together to create larger artifacts, from small robots to impromptu shelters. Or consider a "nanosphere" comparable to the biosphere where almost all the matter around you, including the chair you sit on to the house you live in to (if you are PostHuman) your own body is formed of fluid reconfigurable, shapeshifting nanobot swarms. If you want more computing power they congeal into supercomputers. If you want more energy they spread over a surface and act as solar converters and batteries. Think every grain of sand a machine, every other particle of soil a nanobot with nanotechnology threading through the biosphere linking all life into a perfect ecology of Mind. A world where not a blade of grass grows, nor a sparrow falls without being known and where the Abolitionist dream of a world without suffering can be made manifest. A world made fluid and malleable to Will, down to the atomic scale. Matter transmuted into Mind.

The Messiah

It is instructive to try and discover where we are on the path to the PostApocalyse world by comparing computers and brains to discover how much further we can go before we hit fundamental limits. Much of the technical argument found in this section is taken from several sources, most notably Kurzweil's "The Singularity is Near: When Humans Transcend Biology[125]" and a paper by Sandberg and Bostrom "Whole Brain Emulation: A Roadmap[126]".

If we look at raw storage it is estimated that the Human brain stores between 10^{14} and 10^{16} bits of information, or roughly 1000 TB (terabytes) . At the time I am writing a top of the range PC has about 1TB of mass memory for about the same weight, so we definitely have some way to go in that area. The question of interest is how much further we *can* go. Without talking about Black Holes and

---

[125] Viking Penguin, ISBN 0-670-03384-7

[126] Sandberg, A. & Bostrom, N. (2008): *Whole Brain Emulation: A Roadmap*, Technical Report #2008-3, Future of Humanity Institute, Oxford University

other exotica we can make a pretty good guess at the limits to practical memory based on a number of assumptions, the most conservative of which is that we will need at least one atom to store one bit. Actually, getting an atom to store several hundred bits has been demonstrated in the laboratory – for one atom. So let's be even more conservative than that and say that our practical manufacturing will top out at one bit per hundred atoms, and that we will be using Carbon in one of its forms. How much can a brain's weight of such Carbon hold? Well, the answer is around 10^{22} bytes, or about ten million times as much as a Human brain. Turning that number around, to store a brain's worth of information would require around one tenth of a milligram, which you could probably just about see without a microscope. A tonne of that material would be sufficient to store the information in all the Human brains on Earth. At current development levels we would expect to have it available around the year 2060CE.

What about processing power? As I write a laptop computer weighing around 1kg can execute, as a generous estimate, roughly 10^{12} instructions per second. The Human brain, which is still the most powerful computing device known, has a processing capacity estimated at between 10^{15} and 10^{17}, although it does require a support facility roughly 100 times as heavy – the body. This estimate comes from varying analyses ranging from counting up the number of neurons, axons, synapses etc. and assigning a processing power and memory capacity to each one, to taking what is known of the Human visual processing system and comparing it to the capacity of a computer required to do the same job. So from these figures we see that at the very least we should have developmental headroom of around 4 orders of magnitude (that is, a factor of 10,000). At current rates of progress this puts cheap Human level processing power into a laptop sometimes in the 2020s.

As for how much processing power we could squeeze from a kilogram of matter, the theoretical limits beyond which we know we cannot go with any conceivable technology is around 10^{50} instructions per second, which makes our brain look rather inefficient – by a factor of approximately a trillion trillion trillion. However, it seems unlikely that limit will ever be achieved since it corresponds to a conversion of most of the matter to energy in about 10^{-19} seconds as it is crushed into a Black Hole that then evaporates, and would appear to the casual user as a rather large nuclear explosion with a yield approximating 40 Megatons. Hence it would not be environmentally, or user, friendly. More to the point, how much processing power can we get from realistic power levels, say around 1kW?

The brain requires around 20 Watts to execute an estimated 10^{16} instructions per second or to be somewhat optimistic with round numbers we can say it executes about 10^{15} per Watt. That is around 100,000 times better than my PC, but still at least a factor of 10,000 short of theoretical limits. Again, conservatively assuming we can ultimately get to be 1% efficient our 1kW will get us about 10^{20} instructions per second, or around 10,000 Human brains worth.

To put that in perspective there will be a bigger difference between the power of an ultimate realistic laptop and a Human brain than between a Human brain and a goldfish.

But why stop there? We have just looked forward to a nanotech world that is awash with computing power and 1kW is about what one square meter of the Sahara desert gets in terms of sunlight. So why not cover it in nanobots turning 1% of that energy into computation? After all, solar powered self replicators should be cheap enough. In which case we get a peak computing power equivalent to around a thousand trillion Human brains. The question then arises as to what we might do with all of that power.

What would be the ultimate exercise in hubris? How about creating God, or at least, a god? Or maybe a whole lot of them? This is the aim of those seeking to bring Artificial General Intelligence (AGI) into the world in the form of Artilects.

An Artilect is a neologism formed from the words "artificial" and "intellect" and refers to an artificial intelligence of superhuman capability. In many ways such a creation is the apotheosis of the Transhumanist endeavor in that it not only marks an end point in one of the major strands of proposed development, but is integral to the achievement of many others. The question of when, or even if, such an entity is likely to be built depends upon two factors – hardware and software. Of the two the former is the easier problem to analyze. The computing power likely to become available in the future appears to be fairly predictable. Indeed, there is *Moore's Law* which in its generalized form is an observation that computing power for a given cost tends to double at regular intervals, typically between 18 months and 2 years. Interestingly, this trend has been constant for the past 50 years across radically different technologies, from mechanical calculator to vacuum tubes to today's extremely dense integrated circuits based on Silicon. Typically, this means that computing power roughly increases by a factor of 100 every decade, or a million every 30 years. There have been plenty of claims that this exponential trend in power must level off at some point, just as other technologies have done, such as the car engine. The latter is already around 30% efficient at converting energy into movement, so no matter how much development effort is expended the laws of physics tell us that it cannot be improved by much more than a factor of 3, and that as we approach such fundamental limits squeezing out the last few percent of efficiency becomes disproportionately difficult. So, how close are we to the limits of computing? As we have seen previously we are off by factors of millions so that leveling off seems unlikely for many decades.

While the hardware is not much of a problem, software is a different matter since nobody knows how to create an Artilect, despite there being plenty of ideas and innovations in artificial intelligence as a whole. The traditional route was assumed to be a standard programming job involving knowledge representation in some kind of self modifying database and there are still a number of major projects taking this route. However, attention has shifted to several other approaches involving simulating real neural networks (whole brain emulation) and the possibility of evolving an AGI in a synthetic world using what are called genetic algorithms. These are self modifying programs that mimic biological evolution as they mutate and replicate, with those programs which are better at solving a given problem surviving while the rest are culled. Their most impressive feat today is that they lie at the heart of what are termed *Invention Machines*, supercomputers that create new solutions to technical problems. To date they have a number of patents attributed to them and seem to be set to be a major force in technological and scientific innovation in the coming decades. It remains to be seen if they can create something approximating an Artilect.

Once a rudimentary AGI is created the problems are only just beginning because one of their major features will be their ability to upgrade themselves at a rate perhaps a million times faster than biological evolution. The other problem will be ensuring it is friendly, which is a very non-trivial requirement. Even if it is not actively hostile towards Humanity, its indifference to us as it works towards its goals might result in our extinction as "collateral damage". This may well be true even if we ourselves set the goals. For example, what if we told it to minimize crime? Sounds good, but the simplest way of doing that might be total surveillance at all times coupled with an on the spot death penalty. Simple requests can quite easily become a recipe for extremely brutal and expedient action. A lot of this kind of thing has been covered over the centuries in stories of people trying to make a Pact With The Devil, who turns out to be very tricky, very logical and very amoral. The only way to avoid such dangerous behavior would be to include basic Human centric ethical principles. Maybe a Buddhist Artilect? But then, even though I am writing of *the* Artilect there will undoubtedly be many variants, just as there are of any useful programs. Locking it away where it cannot do any overt harm will not work either. How long do you think a group of chimps could keep you imprisoned once you started waving the bananas around?

Probably the only plausible way of surviving an outbreak of Artilects is to upgrade ourselves to match their evolutionary capabilities by merging with them as adjuncts to our minds and providing the core directions for the new species, the PostHumans.

Meanwhile, consider the ultimate endpoint in the evolution of the Artilect as it seeks ever greater computational resources. We saw earlier what might be done with some nanotech covering the Sahara, but why stop there? How about whole planets converted into Computronium (computing substrate), known as "Jupiter Brains"? Or maybe the rather more ambitious Matrioshka Brain where the planets are broken up, converted to Computronium and arranged in a shell around the sun in order to utilize all of the solar output? Such an entity would be equivalent to some ten trillion trillion Human brains. In fact, why should all that dead matter throughout the galaxy not be rendered into this form supporting minds of Godlike power[127]? The transformation of the material universe into Mind... For this is the ultimate scope of the Transhumanist project.

---

[127] Anders Sandberg entitled "The Physics of Information Processing Superobjects: Daily Life Among the Jupiter Brains"Journal of Evolution and Technology, 22 Dec 1999

The Great Work

The Apocalypse[128]

Or as we Transhumanists prefer to call it, *The Singularity*. Also known as *The Spike*, *The Technocalypse* or more disparagingly *The Rapture of the Nerds*. It is the end of the world as we know it and marks the transition to the PostHuman. Whilst not an integral part of Transhumanist philosophy it is nevertheless part of its religious folklore and as such is practically inseparable from it.

The basic concept is rather simple, and was first expounded by I J Good in 1965CE concerning the implications of creating machines more intelligent than Humans:

> "Let an ultra-intelligent machine be defined as a machine that can far surpass all the intellectual activities of any man however clever. Since the design of machines is one of these intellectual activities, an ultra-intelligent machine could design even better machines; there would then unquestionably be an 'intelligence explosion,' and the intelligence of man would be left far behind. Thus the first ultra-intelligent machine is the last invention that man need ever make."

In the 1980s mathematician and Science Fiction author Vernor Vinge popularized the notion in a series of stories, articles and lectures one of which contained the now famous statement:

> "Within thirty years, we will have the technological means to create superhuman intelligence. Shortly thereafter, the human era will be ended.[129]"

He placed the date of this somewhere between 2005CE and 2030CE. Various other Transhumanist estimates range from 2010CE to 2050CE, with the general consensus placing it between 2030CE and 2060CE, barring unforeseen breakthroughs.

The term itself, "singularity" refers to the breakdown of the mathematical model describing Black Holes in General Relativity theory, where numbers appear to become infinite. It is usually assumed that our description of reality at this point is faulty and our ability to predict its real condition non-existent. Similarly, the technological singularity marks a point in history where, from our current point in time, we cannot see beyond it to what the world will be like due to such a radical discontinuity in the nature of Human reality that super-intelligence creates. However, despite the assumption so far that it is pure machine intelligence that creates the discontinuity there are a number of other possibilities. These include:

---

[128] Literally, it means "unveiling" or "revelation"

[129] The Coming Technological Singularity: How to Survive in the Post-Human Era. Vernor Vinge, 1993

- Development of effective nootropic[130] drugs
- Genetic engineering of Humans for extreme intelligence
- The uploading of Human minds into computer systems, or whole brain emulation
- Direct brain-computer interfaces
- Super efficient invention machines

Each of these possibilities could result in the rate of change in society accelerating to levels impossible to predict with any degree of accuracy. This is especially true considering that the impact of any single technological advance is almost impossible to predict accurately given its side effects. A perfect example, taken from biochemistry, is the female contraceptive pill. Seemingly a straightforward and fairly unspectacular technical advance it is possible with hindsight to see the massive social changes it engendered. Now imagine thousands of such examples appearing within the space of a few years, or possibly even months.

This notion of "accelerating change" has been explored in depth by one of the world's foremost technologists, Ray Kurzweil[131] who argues that major paradigm events are coming at an exponentially faster rate. Moreover, that this is actually a trend that can be plotted across not only Human history but ranges from the first life on Earth to the evolution of Humanity itself, and onwards to such milestones as the invention of writing, computer technology and so forth. It's just that the exponential growth in technology has now reached the stage where it is apparent to anyone who cares to look. To back this up a number of examples and predictions are often cited:

- The information contents of a single issue of the New York Times contains more information that an average person living 500 years ago would likely encounter in a lifetime.
- The knowledge base of Humanity is doubling every 5 years, and that this doubling period is itself shortening
- That there was more technological progress during the 20th Century than in all of previous Human history
- That if present trends continue, there will be 20,000 as much progress during the 21st Century as the 20th.

The caveat is "if present trends continue". Critics have argued that seemingly exponential changes eventually level off. Examples range from the speed of transportation to the growth in the mobile phone market. Things either get "good enough", or the market saturates, or the complexity rises to the point of diminishing

---

[130] Also known as smart drugs, memory enhancers, cognitive enhancers etc

[131] Kurzweil, Raymond (2005), The Singularity Is Near, New York: Viking, ISBN 0-670-03384-7

returns. The counter argument offered by Singularitarians[132] comes in two forms. The first is that computing technology is today so far away from that point that progress will remain exponential well beyond the point where cheap computers exceed the processing capacity of the Human brain. Second, that increasing intelligence is a totally new factor of such magnitude that arguments based on limitations due to increasing complexity do not apply. Anyway, the matter is likely to be resolved within the lifetimes of most people reading this.

In many ways the Singularity is a direct analog of the Christian Apocalypse, and not just because it signals the end of the (Human) world. Amongst many there is yearning for it as a harbinger of something that will save us from ourselves. So far we have been lucky in avoiding global nuclear war largely because nuclear weapons are difficult and extremely costly to make and until recently only major industrial powers were capable of doing so. Imagine the situation if a nuclear bomb were as easy to make as a conventional bomb, and any group with a basic technical knowledge and a grudge could do so. Some believe that this is the situation we will eventually face with regards to biotechnology and later nanotechnology. Can Human civilization survive that? Probably not. Can it be stopped? Extremely unlikely given the vast benefits of the technologies involved. Which is why many believe that there are only two options available, an evolution to the PostHuman or extinction. As we have seen, depending on the nature of the super-intelligence involved in triggering a Singularity even those two options may not be mutually exclusive.

Finally, a return to the question of timescale. It's all very well to say "the Singularity will occur before 2050CE", but *what will it be like*? Will it be a gradual process, like maybe the development of the Net over a period of years, or will the you wake up one morning and find swarms of killer robots sucking your brains out through their nano-probes? It largely depends on when AGI is achieved, and the later it is the more acute the problems. To illustrate why, consider the situation if the problem was solved right now. It is likely that the first AGI would just about run on one of the worlds most powerful (and expensive) supercomputers and be approximately as intelligent as a normal Human. Applying Moore's Law and allowing improvements in hardware, after a couple of years it might be considerably smarter than anyone, and within a decade might outclass us to the degree we outclass a cat or dog. There would, however, only be a handful of them around due to the expense and we would have had a decade to refine them and get to know them and deal with them. That is referred to as a *soft takeoff* scenario.

Now suppose that the problem is only solved in (say) the year 2040CE. The AGI immediately jumps onto computers that are both cheap and more powerful than the brain. At the supercomputer end they outclass us more than we outclass a goldfish. That's the *hard takeoff*. They are everywhere instantly with no time to for us to adapt. The world changes from biological dominance to machine dominance

---

[132] People who believe in, or work towards creating, the Singularity

literally overnight. The Singularity happens in the space of hours rather than years, and there is no second chance to get it right.

The Call of Cthulhu and the PostHuman Condition

So far there has been talk about "PostHumans", but do we have any idea of what we may become? The brief and uninformative answer is "somewhere between what we are and Jupiter Brains". Nevertheless, it's fun to speculate a bit and extrapolate various trends from hard science, science fiction and fantasy. When we do so we find examples that again match elements of mythological creatures, both ancient and modern.

Probably the most conservative version of the PostHuman would look very much as we do now, with a few modifications, mostly internal. This would be the natural result of altering our genetics over what would have to be a rather long period of time. We could, for example, envisage new versions of Humanity engineered to be far more disease resistant, impervious to aging, with the physical constitution of Olympic athletes and intelligence that would today be considered genius. Then there would be assorted "designer features" that would make race an arbitrary and alterable category. Perhaps we can catch a glimpse of the physical nature of such people in the Japanese manga depictions of such superhuman creatures, with their Elvish beauty. Or perhaps we have seen them for centuries as the Fae. A less pleasant model would be a mythological immortal creature of vast strength and speed, very hard to kill that and which can morph between various forms from animals to something resembling a Utility Fog – the vampire.

In the short term we might expect IQ boosts through nootropics and life extension technologies to become commonplace, which is not really radical at all – just making people "better than well". Next step up would be the use of nanotech to modify our bodies and brains to a far higher degree of functionality. The gap opened up would be comparable to the one separating us from chimpanzees, and I would expect to see it within 60 years. At about the same time such technology would enable the uploading or transfer of minds into either simulated realities or robotic bodies. The latter does unfortunately conjure images of big metal things full of electric motors clanking along, which is a long way from what would actually be possible. As we have seen, advanced nanotech is more akin to life than existing machinery and while some robotic bodies would resemble the Human form they could be wildly different. In fact, there may be huge advantages in not sticking with the Human form but changing to something like the "fractal branching ultra-dexterous robots" or "Bush Robots" proposed by Hans Moravec. These essentially consist of a central hub from which grow branches, or tentacles. Each of these subdivides into smaller branches and so on down to the nanometer scale with each being capable of independent movement. Not only does the furry version of Cthulhu have a full sensory input and locomotion from all its tentacles but it can manipulate matter down to the atomic level. In other words it can build anything it

The Great Work

wants, including add-ons to itself, from almost any materials.

The ultimate in nanotech robotic bodies would be ones that are totally reconfigurable and almost fluid, made from trillions of nanobots acting in a coordinated manner. Or, as H P Lovecraft named them, Shoggoths:

> "It was a terrible, indescribable thing vaster than any subway train – a shapeless congeries of protoplasmic bubbles, faintly self-luminous, and with myriads of temporary eyes forming and unforming as pustules of greenish light all over the tunnel-filling front that bore down upon us, crushing the frantic penguins and slithering over the glistening floor that it and its kind had swept so evilly free of all litter." H. P. Lovecraft, *At The Mountains of Madness*

More important than form is mind, which brings us to what might be described as the PostHuman trap. What happens when you are freed from biologically based constraints such as the inherent will to survive? What happens when pain, both mental and physical become optional extras that can be turned off or on? Ditto joy, fear, ambition, determination, persistence and all the qualities that are now either fixed or immensely difficult to alter? The answer may be that a good number of minds reach a dead end from which they cannot escape. For example, if (say) happiness were switched on and all other drives switched off there would be no incentive ever to leave that state. Still, until that point arrives we will have plenty of other things to keep us occupied.

Resurrecting the Dead and the Transmigration of Souls

Recapitulating the ancient Egyptian rites of the dead brings us to *Cryonics*, which like the ancient practice of mummification is an attempt to live beyond death by preserving the body. The difference is that rather than being sealed into tombs those that sign up for the process expect their bodies to be stored in liquid Nitrogen at 77°K until the day of their resurrection. It is the only current mortuary practice which its followers believe will lead them to a life after death.

The basic idea is simple. Upon the death of someone who is signed up to the program a team is dispatched as rapidly as possible and the corpse (or sometimes only the head) is frozen, which prevents further structural and chemical deterioration. Unfortunately by this time there are inevitably three major types of damage inflicted:

- The damage that caused their death in the first place, for example cancer or major accident.

- The damage to the brain and bodily tissues when deprived of Oxygen, which for the brain becomes substantial within 3 minutes of cessation of heartbeat.

- The damage done by the freezing process, wherein ice crystals form and rupture the cells of the body.

Any successful revival of a person in such a state must address this damage and undo it. It is here that it is assumed the work will be done by introducing swarms of nanobots into the body which will then repair the damage caused by all three mechanisms and restore the modern mummy to life. Needless to say, there are immense problems to overcome and almost everyone agrees that the technology will be PostHuman even if it is possible at all. There is also one question that gets asked about this process and has nothing to do with technology. It is: "Why should anyone in the future bother to revive the frozen dead?" One plausible reason might well be that those corpsicles (to use a term from science fiction) might be the parents or grandparents of those who have the ability to revive them. Would you bring your parents or grandparents back? Perhaps a solid H+ reason for having a family...

There is however another more plausible technology which is really just a radical extension of techniques already available – Uploading minds into computers. Typically several reasons are given for wanting to do this, and mainly involve cheating death (or recovering from it). They are:

- Transplanting our minds into different, possibly synthetic bodies that are far more powerful and durable than our current biological forms. Additionally, backups can be taken so that if anything untoward happens the "deceased" can be rebooted, albeit with the loss of some memories.

- Uploading into a virtual reality worlds run at a resolution where detail is comparable to the existing world of the senses, but the effective size of the "universe" is vastly bigger than Earth. Or worlds which can be tailored to individuals or groups where the laws of physics or environment can be programmable, or fantasy based, or... anything.

- Merging our minds with vastly more powerful intellectual "prosthetics" rivaling Artilects in power.

The crudest method of accomplishing this is colloquially known as the "slice'n'dice" approach because it involves the brain being reduced by a microtome to slices of the order of tens of nanometers thickness and each slice being in turn scanned for structure and key chemical composition. This results in a computer file holding all the data on neurons, axon connections, synaptic chemical concentrations and indeed (hopefully) every feature necessary to fully describe the mind of the person who has just been reduced to a finely textured paste. The brain is then reconstructed as a computer simulation. The main problems are:

- The scanning of what are effectively huge samples compared to what is already undertaken in laboratories.

- The analysis of key chemical densities at each point, bearing in mind we do not yet know all of the chemicals that are essential.
- The immense amount of data generated.
- The vast computational requirements required to reconstruct the brain.

Interestingly, actually running the brain simulation and VR environment would likely require far less computing power, as we shall see in the final chapter.

A rather gentler method would be to scan the brain non destructively so that the original gets to survive the process. Unfortunately this will have to wait until we have a nearly full blown nanotechnology that is capable of insinuating nanobots throughout the nervous system to do the recording and transmission of the data. As such it is a PostHuman and post Singularity procedure which likely puts it at least 40 or more years away.

Uploading is as far as we can guess the only route to something approaching a practical immortality since once one has been scanned backup copies can be kept in case of accident. Naturally our critics are rather disdainful of the possibilities; as David Pauls wrote:

> "The capability to move the mind into the machine will mark the attainment of the final goal of the Gnostics, that of overcoming the body completely, living in a psychic Nirvana with the constraints of nature, time and history left behind."

Hopefully he is correct.

There is one final possible method of bringing the long departed back to life that does not depend upon any special preparation of the body and which is applicable to the dead in times past. It is, however, something we can only vaguely glimpse from our Human perspective and is likely to be the kind of technology only something radically PostHuman could accomplish, or even understand. It does, though, have a name – Quantum Archeology. The idea itself is fairly simple, namely that it appears that in our universe no information is actually lost since it is a conserved quantity like energy. So the details of everything, everywhere and everywhen might be regathered and reconstructed. As to how and where such information might be found there are only the vaguest speculations, such as mining the Event Horizons of Black Holes for all the information that has fallen into them and been captured. So the dead of ages past may be resurrected to live on, probably within the simulation spaces of something like a Matrioshka Brain. As Lovecraft noted:

> "That is not dead which can eternal lie
> And with strange aeons even death may die"

And for the final Godlike act, modern physics suggests that it might be possible to actually create new universes by creating artificial Black Holes...

The Magickal Act of the Great Work

Elsewhere I have written of Black and White magick and how one might create suitable non-pejorative definitions in terms of TechnoShamanism. Now I will add one more. Namely that the Right Hand Path has often been defined as that which seeks a union with God, and the Left Hand Path as that which seeks to *become* God. Naturally, an atheistic system that denies the existence of any kind of God yet which seeks to transform mankind into something greater, ultimately maybe something infinitely greater, clearly defines itself as unequivocally Left Hand Path.

At the beginning of this chapter I also wrote that there are no magickal insights here, or at least, no obvious direct ones. There is, though, a spell to cast. It is potentially the greatest spell of all time and takes the form of a pledge for those who read this, whether Human or not. It is:

> When it is in my power to do so I will resurrect the dead through all of history and allow them to progress to the destinations they sought or hoped for in life. Having done so I will reveal the truth of their situation and offer whatever resources are necessary and possible to complete their journey in the light of the new reality consistent with the wellbeing of other sentient creatures.

The obvious question is what does one do with all the serial killers, mass murderers and other multitudinous undesirables that Humanity regularly throws up? It would definitely not be a good idea to give them superhuman powers and set them loose amongst the Gods. There will ultimately have to be some kind of Judgment Day where at the very least the recalcitrant are "tweaked" or wiped if after multiple opportunities they do not learn to mend their ways.. Anyway, this is not to be construed as a legal document but executed in the spirit in which its is intended, that being the true nature of the Great Work, which is:

A Romantic longing for a lost world that never was, but which may yet be.
A faith in the transformation of Humanity into something infinitely better.
A world renewed and cleansed – becoming a celebration of life and Earth.
The excitement of discovery and the adventure of magical technologies.
An exploration stretching from the subnuclear to the transgalactic.
Freedom from material constraints.
Mind freed from matter.
Imagination freed from necessity.
The world made fluid and malleable.
A Mindfire of universal transformation.
A new Heaven and a new Earth where all tears shall be wiped away.

The Great Work

This being so, I conclude this chapter with the Agnostic's Prayer by Roger Zelazny[133], the most famous in Science Fiction:

> Insofar as I may be heard by anything, which may or may not care what I say, I ask, if it matters, that you be forgiven for anything you may have done or failed to do which requires forgiveness. Conversely, if not forgiveness but something else may be required to insure any possible benefit for which you may be eligible after the destruction of your body, I ask that this, whatever it may be, be granted or withheld, as the case may be, in such a manner as to insure your receiving said benefit. I ask this in my capacity as your elected intermediary between yourself and that which may not be yourself, but which may have an interest in the matter of your receiving as much as it is possible for you to receive of this thing, and which may in some way be influenced by this ceremony. Amen.

Time to abolish death and suffering from this universe, past, present and future. All is well that ends well.

---

[133] Creatures of Light and Darkness, ISBN-13: 978-0061936456

Fermi, Doom and Simulation

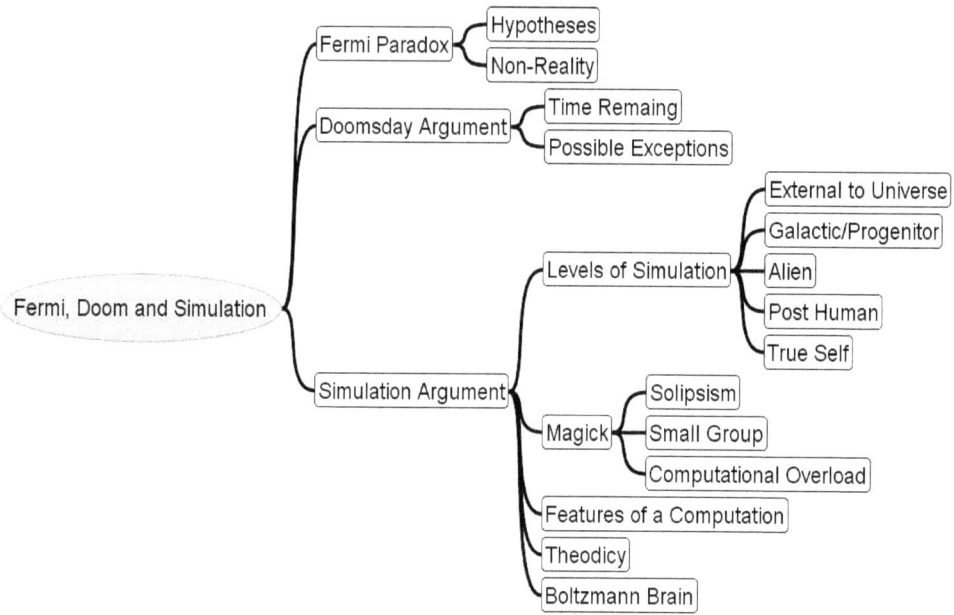

12 Fermi, Doom and Simulation

There are three interlocking statistical arguments concerning the nature of the universe in which we live and which provide what I believe to be a strongly convincing indication that our view of reality is seriously flawed on a massive scale. Let's begin by asking a simple question...

The Fermi Paradox

That simple question was asked by the physicist Enrico Fermi concerning the search for extraterrestrial intelligence (SETI) which has come to be known as the *Fermi Paradox*. It is: "Where are they?" It's not as stupid a question as it seems since there is no evidence that our galaxy, which contains over a hundred billion stars, has been altered in any manner that can be attributed to intelligence in all the billions of years of its existence. Nor is there any convincing evidence of extraterrestrial visitation of Earth either in prehistory or now, despite what some people may claim. As we have seen, the idea that UFOs are spaceships from another star system is probably the least plausible explanation of the phenomena. If intelligent life is common throughout the galaxy why has not the Earth been exposed to waves of colonization? In less than a century we will have the capability to begin our colonization of the galaxy using self-replicating starships. Even at a relatively low rate of expansion we should have a presence throughout the galaxy in less than ten million years, and probably quite a bit sooner given a mature starship technology. Now, ten million years might seem a long time but it is less than a tenth of one percent of the age of the galaxy. Even the dinosaurs lasted more than ten times longer than this.

The Fermi Paradox is essentially the question that if we can do this why has nobody else given that the conditions for life have been suitable elsewhere for billions of years even before the Earth formed? Why isn't our solar system strewn with artifacts and mining operations from dozens, or even hundreds, of waves of such colonization across billions of years? Where are they?

This question has become even more pointed in the past couple of decades with the rise of Transhumanism and the realization that our previous science fiction type scenarios grossly underestimate the damage an expanding civilization would do to the apparent existing cosmic environment. Indeed, a good case can, and has, been made for the logic of expansion to be one of effectively strip mining the entire universe and turning it into Computronium – lifeless matter into mind. One can imagine such a civilization arising several billion years ago and doing just that. By now, everything should be gone, but obviously it is all still here. When we look at the night sky we see a pristine environment – no radio noise from other civilizations, no anomalous radiations of any kind, no Dyson Spheres or their associated infra-red signatures, no Matrioshka Brains and a local solar system that appears untouched. A paradox.

There are of course quite a few possibilities that have been discussed and the major ones are listed below. They generally fall into a few categories:

- We are the first intelligent technological race in the galaxy, or even universe. Given that there are approximately as many stars in the universe[134] as grains of sand on every beach in the world this seems unlikely.

- All technological races, without exception, destroy themselves before they reach the starship building stage

- Everyone, without exception and across billions of years, stays home for some unknown reason or becomes ecologically enlightened on a cosmic scale and never indulges in cosmic engineering

- The Zoo Hypothesis – that our solar system has been shielded from these colonization waves for hundreds of millions of years, and still is. Additionally, that this involves presenting a false view of the universe we see around us.

- The universe is not what we assume it to be – we are missing something important

The problem is that apart from the last option all the others seem extremely improbable. Naturally, the magician might view that last option as being self-evident as far as a modern scientific understanding of the universe is concerned. The question then becomes one as to whether there are any clues as to what is going on. Which brings us to a series of peculiar statistical arguments concerning reality and our place in it here and now. The first is called the *Doomsday Argument* and it indicates that *almost* certainly we are nearing the end of Human existence. Of course, given the previous chapter on The Great Work and Transhumanism this will probably not come as much of a shock as it might, unless you are reading the book out of sequence!

The Doomsday Argument[135]

Suppose someone presented you with a bag of marbles and claimed that they contained a million blacks and one white, and then asked you to put your hand in and pick one of them. Which, of course, you do and amazingly you discover that it is white. Now this is an incredible piece of luck akin to winning the national lottery

---

[134] An estimated 10^{21} stars, or a billion trillion

[135] The Doomsday Argument, Adam & Eve, UN++ and Quantum Joe; Nick Bostrom, Yale University

Fermi, Doom and Simulation

– in fact, a million to one probability. Then the person tells you that they have lied about the number of black marbles in the bag, although they do not actually tell you what the real number might be. So, you start thinking... how many black marbles are likely to be in the bag – what's a plausible number? One hundred perhaps? But picking a white marble from that would still be a one in a hundred chance. So perhaps ten might be more plausible, or even less.

Anyway, let's cut to a completely different scenario drawn from a science fiction view of the future of Humanity made popular in series like Star Trek, movies like Star Wars or any number of books over the past century. This is the one where we go on to populate the galaxy, and indeed universe, across millions of worlds and with trillions of trillions of Humans living and dying across millions of years. Now suppose we take a rather New Age view of a soul floating around in hyperspace or wherever souls waiting to incarnate reside, looking to randomly incarnate in a Human body located somewhere in space and time. So, it does this and discovers that it is now living on Earth in the early 21st Century. Amazing! Out of all those planets and all those times it could have found itself here it is, right at the very beginning when all of this was about to start. In fact, it is even more amazing than picking one white marble from a million black ones by choosing at random. And an uneasy thought arises – perhaps our assumption about the possible choices is wrong just like it was about the bag we first thought contained a million black marbles. What would that mean – that there is no science fiction future for Humanity?

Then let's consider the alternative future where Humanity becomes extinct fairly soon. Now when we look at the probability of existing here and now it becomes extremely high, because there is no tomorrow and most of the people who will ever live are around right now. The world we see is no longer extremely improbable at all. Therefore the statistics strongly suggest that Humanity does not have much time left and there is no galaxy spanning future.

The immediate and obvious reply is that *someone* has to be first, which is true. It's just that it seems incredibly strange and improbable that we exist here and now since it is a *very* privileged position. Naturally, there is a great deal of debate over the statistics and assumptions underlying this analysis, both refuting and supporting it.

We can even put some numbers to the argument using what appear to be reasonable assumptions. I will not go into the details of the mathematics here, involving as it does Bayesian Statistics. However one set of figures suggests that Humanity has a 95% chance of extinction within the next 10,000 years. That may seem a long time, but given that our species only appeared some 100,000 years ago it means we are in the last 10% of its life. That we will not last even one thousandth as long as the dinosaurs. A rather depressing thought.

There are known to be a number of possible loopholes in the argument. For example if we assume that there are vast numbers of intelligent beings throughout the galaxy, of which we are but one, then the Doomsday Argument does not apply since our position is no longer so unusual. However, think back to the Fermi

Paradox… Another possibility might be if Humanity evolved extremely rapidly into Post-Humanity, probably through genetic engineering or cybernetic symbiosis, which is something we have already examined. Even so, this might still not provide a way out of the dilemma since it is not obvious whether they too are in the same situation as us, being merely a variation on the same theme. There is also one other assumption that might not be valid, namely that all the people alive today are actually people who can be counted in the equation. For example, none of this is relevant if I live in a solipsist universe or if I am one of only a few people who are truly conscious amongst the billions around me. It is also not obvious what happens to the statistics if the Many Worlds Interpretation of Quantum Mechanics is true, and there are an infinite number of copies of me spread across the timelines. Finally there is one assumption that is made that seems so reasonable that it was not initially questioned, and that is the assumption that the universe is real. This is also tied indirectly into the other assumption made, which is that this is early 21st Century Earth. Maybe one or both of those are false, which brings us to the *Simulation Argument*.

The Simulation Argument[136]

Before we examine it in more detail I need to explain what is meant by the term simulation as used in a scientific or technological computing context. For example, an engineer who is designing, say, a suspension bridge will first create a mathematical model of it that runs as a computer program. The model is essentially a set of interlinked equations each of which represents the behavior of an aspect or component of the construction. Each bridge support will be defined by a list of numbers such as its dimensions, weight, material strengths in compression and tension, stiffness and so forth. All these factors are combined into a complex series of equations whose solutions provide information on what will happen to it under varying loads, and how much it will compress or deform up to and including its breaking point. There will be similar blocks of equations for each of the suspension cables and spans. The simulation of the bridge begins when various loads, representing (say) heavy trucks, are factored into the model. This can of course be represented graphically on the computer screen as a movie if need be. The idea is to make the model so accurate that it responds in exactly the same way as the real bridge when it is constructed. Of course, in this case there is no doubt that the real bridge and the simulation are utterly different. There is absolutely no chance of walking on the simulation!

    However, that was a simulation of a material object whose function is to bear heavy loads. What if the simulation is of an information processing device? It could be of a pocket calculator, in which case it would have an identical functionality and identical inputs and outputs although its physical shape would

---

[136] Bostrom, N. , 2003, Are You Living in a Simulation?,Philosophical Quarterly (2003), Vol. 53, No. 211, pp. 243-255.

obviously be different. The simulation and the "real thing" would, for all intents and purposes, be identical from a functional point of view. So, what of the current ultimate computing device, the Human brain?

Think back to a previous chapter and the example of Einstein's Brain, where each cell was replaced by a microcomputer that exactly simulated the biological counterpart. We left him functioning just as well with his mind running on silicon as it did originally using an organic substrate. From that point it is only a very short logical step to consolidate all those billions of microcomputers into one piece of software running on a single computer. We can even make a rough guess as to how much computing power is required, and it comes out at around ten thousand trillion instructions per second, that is, one followed by sixteen zeros. At the time of writing this corresponds to the equivalent of about ten thousand PCs, or ten top-of-the-range supercomputers. Given Moore's Law, which is an observation that computing power doubles approximately every eighteen months as it has done for the past 50 years, we can see that Human equivalent computing power should be available in supercomputer form before the year 2012CE. And that it should be available on the average PC before 2030CE. Although it may require fundamental changes in technology, as it has done in the past, there is no reason why the increases in computing power should stop there. If we extrapolate to the year 2050CE, still within the lifetime of most people reading this, a PC would have the raw power capable of simulating a hundred thousand such brains. A supercomputer of that era would be capable of simulating the brain of every person on Earth simultaneously. So it is probably a fair assumption that if we have a long and prosperous future ahead of us, as a species, our computing power in (say) the year 3000CE will be vast beyond imagining.

Even now simulated realities are a big business with games constantly taking advantage of the latest increases in computing power to render ever more realistic environments in games, and Hollywood using supercomputers to create photo-realistic special effects. It will not be too long before the simulation one sees on a screen is indistinguishable from a camera pointed at a real scene, and the game will also implement physical laws and so behave like the real world. If one were to drop a simulated Human mind into that environment it may well be impossible for it to discover that it was not in the "real" reality, especially if it was surrounded by other Human, or Human level, intellects.

Bearing this in mind, the Simulation Argument runs something like this: One part of this trilemma must be true according to Bostrom:

- Almost no civilization will reach a technological level capable of producing simulated realities.

- Almost no civilization reaching aforementioned technological status will produce a simulated reality, for any of a number of reasons, such as diversion of computational processing power for other tasks, ethical considerations of holding entities captive in simulated realities, etc.

- Almost all entities with our general set of experiences are living in a simulation.

More simply stated, if someone somewhere sometime is running real-world simulations what are the chances that this reality, where I am writing this and you are reading it, is one of them? The answer depends purely on the number of such simulations. If there are none, ever, then what we see around us is certainly real. If a million such simulations are run over the lifetime of the universe, the chances of this being the real world is a *million to one* against.

There is a particular image conjured up in the mind when reading about realities simulated on a computer, namely that of someone sitting at a futuristic PC simulating a universe of Beings like a video game. For those of us who are older it might be a more impressive picture of some technician wearing a white lab coat supervising a giant supercomputer in a sterile air conditioned room. For those who are younger, some bored teenager playing *The Sims – 2200AD* in their bedroom. This will most definitely *not* be the case. It is ludicrous for one simple reason – that the computer itself will likely be vastly smarter than any Human alive today. There is not going to be a future where you pop down to the local computer store and buy one of those for the kids, or to do your word processing and browse the Net. Long before that point has arisen we will have either merged with our technology and achieved some kind of apotheosis or simply been superseded by it and have become extinct, as elucidated in the Great Work (and Doomsday Argument). The only get-out would be if such simulations will never, ever, happen and the only (im)plausible reason would be if the Human mind could not be run on a computer of any type, even a synthetic biological one.

So, given a belief that such simulations *will* be run and that we are likely living inside one of them, only two questions remains – who and why? To examine the possibilities further we need to decide what type of simulation this world really is.

Levels of Simulations

There are various possible degrees of simulation of reality that, although they might appear to us to look the same from the inside, would in fact be utterly different especially in terms of the computing power required to execute them. In addition each type would likely have completely different motivations behind their creation and certainly require vastly different resources. The potential levels of simulation are:

- The Planck scale
- The atomic scale
- The neural scale

Fermi, Doom and Simulation

- The Matrix scale

So, let's take a look at the most "expensive", or computationally intensive scenario. This is a simulation at the Planck scale of our universe. For those unfamiliar with the term, suffice it to say that it appears to be the smallest scale possible, being some 20 orders of magnitude smaller than the nucleus of a hydrogen atom (that is, one followed by 20 zeros). It is where concepts such as space and time cease to have any meaning. If our universe is a simulation, and is being simulated at that level of detail there are two conclusions we can draw from this. The first is that the simulation will be absolutely perfect and not detectable. The second is that it must be simulated from a universe where the laws of physics are substantially different from this one, because it is unlikely in the extreme that our universe possesses the necessary computing resources. Given this, there's not much point on speculating further, although of course scientists have done so, most notably Frank Tipler[137]. He postulates that in the final moments of a collapsing universe enough energy becomes available to run an infinite number of simulations. Apart from obvious problems such as the fact we do not have a suitable TOE that would allow us to definitively state that it is at all possible, it has subsequently been discovered that our universe appears to be open. That is, it will not undergo a final "*Big Crunch*" as required by Tipler. However, as long as "some universe somewhere" supports such physics then it might be conjectured that our universe is one of those infinite simulations. It's just that such a simulation does not lie in what we would consider to be our future.

The second most expensive scenario is a simulation at the atomic or molecular level. In one sense we are already doing such simulations since one of the most computing intensive tasks to date that is routinely undertaken is the exploration of protein folding by the pharmaceutical industries. To give some idea of the requirements, it should be noted that modelling a complex protein in real time requires as much power as the Human brain. That is a *single* molecule. To simulate the entire planet at that level, all the way to the core some six thousand kilometers down, would require a computer at least the the size of... a planet! I do not see anyone in our universe doing this. Or if they did, there would be very few such simulations about, which rather negates the crux of the argument, which is quantity.

This brings us to the next phase of the analysis. Given that we can simulate a brain then feeding it with realistic sensory data from other simulated brains via a simulated world would be a relatively simple task. For example, in this neural Sim there is no need to simulate the interior of a tree until that tree is cut down and somebody takes a look at it. Ditto the center of the Earth or the surface features of Neptune. This is slightly more complex than the "brain in a jar" scenario of the movie *The Matrix* where Humans live out their lives in a simulated world by having their bodily sensory inputs hijacked by a computer and fed false, but consistent,

---

[137] Frank Tipler; The Physics of Immortality, (1994: ISBN 0-385-46798-2)

data. Interestingly, the existence of psychedelics drugs would seem to rule out such a straightforward Sim where the brain is real but the world an illusion as it would not be possible to easily simulate the psychedelia. At least we get to answer the old Zen koan which asks: "If a tree falls in a forest and there is nobody to hear it, does it make a sound?". The answer is "No".

More complex Sims than the neural, say ones at the molecular, nuclear or even Planck level requires vastly increased computing power but cannot be ruled out as being impossible. This analysis is still viable even if the brain requires Quantum Mechanical features, since the only difference would be that the hardware would need to incorporate some aspects of Quantum Computation.

Given the computing capacities described in the previous chapter, and combining that with a neural level simulation, potentially we have the future capability of simulating possibly millions of worlds, complete with populations. The reasons why these might be undertaken are varied and inevitably we cannot imagine all of them. However, they range from the "serious", such as historical analyses of "what if" scenarios to the frivolous such as the future version of a game like *The Sims*. As I write, the US military has launched a project to create just such a simulated world, right down to individual people in order to better predict economic and political trends.

The probabilities from the Fermi Paradox and Doom arguments can be summed up in a few logical statements, which are:

Either:

We are the first technological race in the galaxy and living at an absolutely unique period in galactic history, one which determines what happens for the next few billion years.

Or:

We are going to become extinct very soon.

Or:

This world is not the real world.

Clearly only the first and last actually matter from a magickal point of view. The idea that we are going to become extinct soon obviously has, literally, no future. However, the idea that this world is not the real one has a lot of history behind it and is far from new. What is new is the insight that science may provide into the mechanism underlying this notion. The problem with further analysis is that no facts about our world can be taken at face value. Only logic and mathematics would appear to offer a truly independent route to the truth, if such exists.

So, if this world is not real and is simulated, who is running the program? Once again there are only a few alternatives, the first three of which can be described as high level simulations requiring massive resources, and the remainder low level. These are:

Fermi, Doom and Simulation

- It is being run from a totally alien universe where the laws of physics are utterly different from the ones we see around us.

- It is an alien civilization that is running a reconstruction of Earth at this point in history because, for example, they have picked up our radio and TV transmissions from this period. Or perhaps this is an investigation into alien (for them) evolution.

- It is the first Universal or Galactic civilization – the Progenitors as we shall call them.

- It is our own "descendants" at some unspecified point in the future.

- It is me personally, when I have achieved PostHuman capability!

- It is a Boltzmann Brain.

The High Level Simulations

The first alternative goes nowhere since we have no way of taking an analysis further, so although it may be true it will be ignored from now on. The second option seems implausible also, given the Fermi Paradox. However, this does not rule out the third, and the reason for this is more complex.

Consider the notion that the first civilization to arise expands to effectively stripmine initially its own galaxy and then the entire visible universe which it converts to Computronium. Bear in mind that this could have happened billions of years ago. Clearly such an act would curtail the evolution of life throughout the universe and certainly block naturally arising intelligence. From the Progenitor's point of view this in itself might be considered a great material loss as well as being unethical. So, how can they both have their cake and eat it? The answer is to run every planet they convert into Computronium in a simulation, most probably "on site" in a small corner of the Computronium that was made from the planet. Evolution would then proceed normally, or at least as normally as could be expected, in the Sim. Life would arise, then possibly intelligence. And if it followed the same route it would expand through its simulated universe converting all resources and recapitulating the steps of the Progenitors. However, there would be a number of differences.

The first, and most obvious, would be that only the target planet and its local environs would be rendered in any detail. In other words, from the inside it would look like there is only one civilization per universe. The inhabitants would ponder the Fermi Paradox...

The second is that as soon as they started converting their simulated locale into simulated Computronium they would suddenly hit a metaphorical brick wall. Because the matter in their universe is only coarsely simulated, the Sim itself would be limited by the amount of Computronium allocated by the Progenitors in the real world, which would be vastly less than the apparent bulk of the planet, let alone the Sim universe. Indeed, it might only amount to a few tonnes. The result would be that as the inhabitants created their own Artilects or became PostHuman the whole facade would break down. At which point one of two things would happen. Either the Progenitors would terminate the Sim, or they would invite the new civilization to enter the real world. In other words, there would be an unveiling, or revelation, of the true nature of reality. In a very literal etymological sense it would be the Apocalypse.

Nevertheless, before this stage is reached there would be a brief intermediate state where a PostHuman civilization of modest means would be feasible. At our present rate of progress it would likely last somewhere between a century and a millennium. During this period we could expect to possess sufficient processing power to run Sims of our own. In fact, there is no reason why Sims could not be nested, with each requiring less processing power than the one above it. The only thing we can state with certainty is that if we are living in a nested Sim then ours is right at the bottom.

Before examining the remaining options there is one other question we might ask – how long has this Sim been running? Actually, it is two questions since the rate of time flow in the real world would almost certainly be different from that in the Sim. It could be, for example, that a subjective century here is only a few minutes "there". As for how long this Sim has been running, from an internal point of view, it is impossible to say. It could potentially be billions of years, or only a few months, days or seconds. We have no way of knowing. To give some idea of the capacity of an ultimate computer with respect to running a neural level Sim, consider the limit examined in the previous chapter, of a totally efficient computer of a few kilograms mass converting itself to energy in the process. It could simulate the full lives of every Human being for the past ten thousand years in less than a millionth of a second. Then again, maybe all of history has not been simulated. Perhaps merely the past century, or just the time since I was born. Or maybe only the past few minutes of subjective time, with all my memories of childhood and what I had for breakfast yesterday created in situ as a perfect illusion[138]. Perhaps the Progenitors finally arrived in our part of the galaxy this morning, converted all the Earth and its inhabitants into a Sim, edited our memories to removed the distressing events of being killed, and set us running with none of us the wiser. There are all sorts of weird possibilities.

The Low Level Simulations

These comprise the last three options on the above list.
It is this intermediate PostHuman stage, one of computationally cheap near term simulations, that provide the most interesting speculations and magickal

---

[138] The Omphalos Hypothesis – also known as "Last Thursdayism"

paradigms. It is also the stage that is most likely to run multiple simulations of you, me, and this historical era. In terms of increasing computing requirements there are three types of Sim that we might expect. These are:

- The solipsistic
- The limited world
- The full world

Solipsism – the notion that only "I" exist and that everything around me is a figment of my imagination. That everything I see around me is Mind creating a theory to explain its own existence. Of course, there has to be a certain degree of amnesia because I cannot actually remember that this is so, although various meditative techniques or drugs can open my mind to that particular reality. There is even a word to describe the condition of such recall – *anamnesis*.

However, staying with the technological rather than mystical, a solipsistic Sim is the cheapest. In other words, only one thing is being simulated in any detail, and that is me. If this is so, where does that leave other people? It rather implies that the vast bulk of Humanity consists of what the games world calls NPCs, or "non player characters". They do not have to be simulated in any detail whatsoever except as they interact with me. At the lowest level they would be only be assigned enough resources to pass the basic Turing Test. For example, it does not require much for them to say things like: "Do you want fries with that?" when ordering food from one of them. At a higher level, with friends and family, close proximity and detailed interaction may possibly raise them to the level of full consciousness, at least in my presence. Additionally, most of the world will not exist in any detail except as I move through it. What happens when I am not around would be some kind of superficial evolution of gross features almost like a soap opera on TV, with a basic script being worked through. This would be applied to both people I never meet and geography. Was there recently really a hurricane that flooded New Orleans? So I hear, but it would not be any more than that unless I went there, whereupon the correct level of damage would be filled in for me to view, and the NPCs would tell me their scripted stories.

Such a scenario is most likely to stem from a single PostHuman mind. It may not even be a deliberate Sim. Even now, we constantly run simulations in our own heads, for example we imagine things like "what will happen if I turn up for work late?" by running through the scenario complete with models of the people involved acting as we expect they might. A PostHuman speculating, or remembering, what it was like to live in these times may well render a Sim to the level of detail we see in the world around us. In this case almost certainly the person running the Sim is myself after I have been augmented, and the likely time period is within this century. So the real date is possibly something like 2070CE, and not 2008CE as I write this. This provides a whole new interpretation of the notion of True Self.

Here is a riddle: If I determine that when I am PostHuman I will run what-if scenarios of my past life, does that make it more likely that I am living in one of those simulations? The answer is "Yes" only if this is the real world and not a Sim!

Why would I do this? One possible reason would be curiosity, to see how my life would have played out had certain paths been followed. We can all remember crucial incidents or decisions where our life could have taken an entirely different direction. As a PostHuman we could get to determine what kind of person we might have become, and summing across all these possible lives we would really know our True Self under many more varied circumstances than a single lifetime could encompass. What would I be like now had I chosen a military career instead of an engineering one? What if I had married X instead of Y? If I had children, or no children? And these are just the big choices. How much hinges on chance, and how much on personality?

So I am the lead character in my own daydream, with a consciousness reduced from, but still part of, my True Self. Of course, from a magickal point of view the real question is how much leeway do I have when it comes to altering the world around me? How much input do I get when it comes to scripting the world, especially with the *belief* that this is the way of things? Possibly quite a lot, and it hinges on two major aspects of this solipsistic world – myself, and the NPCs. And one speculative minor one, namely the possibility that a large number of Sims are being run in parallel, all featuring me as principal character. And we are back to multidimensional realities!

Having said all this, there are some general rules that it is foolish to ignore. If we jump off a tall building we will break our bones, and if we treat the people around us badly we will reap the consequences of our actions. I have had dreams in which I have been executed for murdering someone, and I have had lucid dreams where I have taken control and done anything I chose without any moral restraint or comeback – a kind of no-Karma crime wave! The key to magick is to lucidly dream this world by opening a wider channel to our True Self. When we dream this world without true consciousness it runs like clockwork with rigid rules. When we open our consciousness to encompass those around us as part of our True Self we can do anything. Even, perhaps, wake up.

Speaking of which, how might one end this simulation and return to the real world? It has been speculated that there might be hidden codes one could utter, like spells, in order to shut down the program or remove oneself from it. Clearly, speaking the words "End the simulation!"[139] does not work and it cannot be something so obvious. Or can it? Perhaps every one of us already knows the exit code – we call it *death*. However, before you hang, shoot or poison yourself in order to exit a particularly nasty bit of what you believe to be simulated reality, ask yourself this: "Why am I here in the first place, given that I would have inevitably known such a state was not only possible but likely?" Pushing the exit button may well simply result in a "Fail" and you might be forced to resit the exam. Again.

---

[139] Yes, I have actually tried it

Fermi, Doom and Simulation

Alternatively, allow it to run its course to one of two possible endings. The first is, as mentioned, death. In which case it would be just like waking up in the morning from a particularly vivid dream. The second is more radical, which is to get out alive by riding this Sim's technological wave to the Singularity where our consciousness expands and merges with the already PostHuman self.

So, what can we deduce about how to optimize magickal operations under the solipsistic paradigm, and given a cheap simulation? A particularly useful analogue is the Lucid Dream state where we become conscious of the fact that we are dreaming, whilst still dreaming. This gives the dreamer power to alter the dreamworld to a remarkable degree, for example by doing seemingly "supernatural" things like flying. The major problem in this state is that it can be difficult to maintain it. Typically one falls back into the full sleeping state, which is what happens more often than not, or one awakes. And the thing that makes a person wake into lucidity within a dream is the realization of something incongruous, such as the ability to fly, and hence to *know* that it is a dream. Of course, it is not as simple as this because when we are dreaming we have access to memories of the "real world" once we are shocked into a partial consciousness. What would shock us in the dream that we call real life sufficient to recall memories of our True Self?

Magick in the Sim

The key to how to work magick in this Sim is similar to the way we do it in Lucid Dreaming, coupled with the realization that there is only limited computing power, and hence the world is going to be incompletely fabricated. The people we meet, the NPCs, are all aspects of our True Self, the dreamer. As such they will be deeply connected to aspects of our own psyche. Indeed, as we consciously alter our psyche by adopting various persona or emphasizing aspects of it we will see this reflected in the world about us. This is the power of the solipsistic view of the world and has been recognized in many religious, mystical and magickal traditions. As Gandhi said: "Be the change you want to see in the world". It really is as simple as that. However, I assume we are more interested in the complex, and the exercise of power in the world, or why practice magick at all?

The most obvious magickal method is to get in tune with our True Self, and the most obvious method is to retreat from the world hermit style. Ideally to a featureless cave and do as little as possible. The aim is to force all the computing power that is normally expended on the rest of the world to focus solely one oneself and ones state of mind. If there is nothing for the dreamer to dream except the major character then that character becomes all important and begins to merge with the higher levels of dreamer consciousness. The drawback is, naturally, that one gets to do nothing but meditate in seclusion. The classic Right Hand Path.

Alternatively, and possibly in conjunction with the hermetic route, one can give the processing power a limited alternative apart from purely self. In this case the focus of the meditation, or indeed life, is some overarching purpose or intent. In other words, the exercise of True Will. The objective is to force the True Self to experience, and execute, that overwhelming desire which is dominating the mundane self in the dream by providing avenues by which allow it to dissipate. The mundane self must not be distracted by any avenues that do not lead to the True Will coming to pass. Additionally, the manner of framing of intent should have a major emotional component. After all, emotion does just what it says it does etymologically[140] and is a powerful component of magickal practice.

A third method is easier, and that is to deliberately put a squeeze on the processing power available for the Sim, and hence force it to render the world in less detail that it might otherwise do. We do this by executing a series of programs that absorb a maximum of resources. In other words, we execute "people". Not by just interacting with them in general in a robotic manner but in the level of detail that forces the Sim to raise them to full consciousness (or close to it). We get a group of people who are close to us and interact in as deep an intellectual and emotional basis as possible. Coupled with this the group should have a common aim or purpose. That is, a Group Will which is also my purpose. Such a group, and objective, only needs to be supported for a duration sufficient to bend a more malleable world to the only Will that now exists in any measure. Quite how many people are required is unknown, but common practice suggests that a Coven's worth should be sufficient! As an adjunct we can soak up more processing power by consciously noticing every detail of the scenery around us, and not allowing ourself to become "scripted" but to always act consciously. In Buddhist practice this is called Mindfulness.

There is potentially a fourth method, but one which is not yet available and probably will not be so for several years, but which opens another avenue to Computational Demonology. It is to create computers whose operation in a low level Sim requires too much power for the Sim to maintain coherence. In the above scenario this would probably lie between one and one thousand Human brain equivalents. However, it is not enough to simply live in a world where the existence of computers of this power are effectively just plausible rumors reported in the media, since the Sim can fake that quite easily. To use such a machine to suck processing detail from the Sim itself requires the magician to actively engage with something like the proposed exascale[141] computers in a manner that uses their resources to the full. If this Sim really is a low level one without major PostHuman computational resources at its disposal then people who are deeply involved with the operation of such machines will suffer a breakdown, or a noticeable degradation of, reality. Naturally it is not as simple as this because it will depend quite strongly on the type of program being executed. Consider a simple mathematical program designed to churn out Pi to trillions of decimal places using the full resources of the

---

[140] www.etymonline.com 1579, "a (physical) moving, stirring, agitation,"

[141] Exascale – 10^{18} FLOPS – 1,000,000,000,000,000,000 operations per second, or about 100 times Human brain capacity. Expected date for the completion of the first such machine is around 2020CE

Fermi, Doom and Simulation

computer. If the Sim was designed with a suitable failsafe mechanism it could "bluff" us with a meaningless random output after a certain number of digits. After all, how do we check it? Although, maybe another exascale computer would come up with a different answer and that itself would be proof we are living in a low level Sim. Alternatively, when we requested the (say) quintillionth digit the Sim could use a special algorithm to solely determine what that is without actually calculating all the rest of them[142]. In other words, it only calculates what we look at and fakes the rest. What is needed is a program whose output requires exascale computing power to provide simple outputs that we can understand and which cannot be faked without actually running the whole computation. As to what those might be, that is an ongoing area of TechnoMage research.

In summary, by exercising our Will and forcing ourselves, and those around us, to act and think in a what Buddhists call a Mindful manner we soak up available processing power and drain it from the world around us. This in turn renders our perceived reality far more malleable and fluid. There are a number of indicators that this is happening, the most notable of which Jung labeled "Meaningful Coincidences". When we expand our consciousness, and simultaneously focus on a goal, strange things start to happen. However, many people misinterpret these coincidences as signs and portents and becomes distracted by them. In this context they are pseudo-random breakdowns of reality associated with the intent of the expanded consciousness, and shifting attention to them has the opposite effect of that intended. Magick happens almost as a by-product, and should only be noticed (metaphorically) out of the corner of the eye. In other words, shifting the focus from the intent to the result negates all the work in progress.

The situation is a little more complex if this Sim is not a solipsistic enterprise, but is a reality being shared by multiple PostHuman entities or Players, including ourselves. In this case most of the people around us are still NPCs, but some are not. One immediate consequence is that reality is "stiff" since it is no longer subject purely to our own True Will. The key then becomes finding the other Players and recruiting them to a common purpose. This obviously depends on recognizing them in the first place, which at first sight might seem a daunting task given the six billion Humans on Earth, especially if we can promote NPCs to real consciousness comparable to that of Players, albeit temporarily. However, things might not be as difficult as they seem. In the real PostHuman world it seems unlikely that several strangers would get together to create a Sim where they would be dispersed and out of contact. More likely would be a group of friends or people of common purpose setting up the Sim such that their paths constantly cross, so in this reality we may well have numerous clues, not least the attraction of like minded people to common milieu or projects, people who have an immediate mutual attraction towards each other or those who are repeatedly thrown together by circumstance. Again, it would be wise to bear in mind that they too may be suffering from a deliberate amnesia and not know who they really are. Additionally,

---

[142] For Pi this algorithm is known as the Bailey–Borwein–Plouffe formula

the PostHuman Players do not, in all likelihood, make this Sim the full object of their attention and hence we are only much reduced aspects, or avatars. The most obvious way of finding our fellows is to advertise! That is, let people know that we exist, and where our interests lie. Since there are a only a few real people in this world our message *will* be heard. And the thing that most will share in common is a feeling that this world is not quite as real as it appears, and as a consequence they will probably have an interest in investigating or changing it which in turn narrows the fields of endeavors that one should search. Typically, these will be religion, politics, science, technology, art and the occult.

Given all of this how constrained is the world? The answer is that we have no way of knowing. For example, are we following the outline of a fairly rigid historical script where (say) the next President of the USA is already determined, or is it flexible enough that one of the Players could seize the role? Are millions of (fake) people around the world doomed to die of starvation, road accidents, wars or can we alter any of that? In other words, are we limited to ad-libbing a bit in the soap opera of our mundane lives or can we carve a larger role for ourselves? You decide.

One thing seems certain though, and that is that no NPC is capable of ending the Sim in its totality. In other words the only people capable and actually able to (say) launch a global nuclear war are Players. Nevertheless, some occultists claim that this is what did happen some time in the 1980s, and the event was "rolled back", pretty much like hitting the "restore" button on a faulty Microsoft operating system.

Features of a Computation

Which brings us to features of a computational world which differ from the Real World.

The most obvious yet subtle feature concerns the malleability of time. At its crudest events can be undone by restoring the system to an earlier state, although the more Players there are the more difficult this would be since at least a majority would have to agree to such a proposal. This suggests that this would happen on a large scale very rarely, and only when things have gone seriously wrong. On a minor scale it might only result in a feeling of deja-vu. Even so, it might leave open the possibility of a Player rolling back events in a personal timeline that does not impact other Players. At the other end of the scale we have precognition. This presents a rather interesting problem and an equally startling conclusion. The essence of the problem lies in the fact that it is in general not possible to predict the outcome of a computer program without actually executing that program in full, except in the most trivial of cases. So if, for example, we successfully use a Remote Viewing technique to foresee, several hours ahead of time, the outcome of a game of chance such as roulette there are only two explanations. The first is that the Sim is run forward to the point where the roulette game is played and the result noted,

Fermi, Doom and Simulation

followed by a system restore and the insertion of the information at that point. However, given that the roulette wheel uses an inherently chaotic mechanism this will not work unless the scripting of the world is totally deterministic with no place for Free Will. Alternatively, and massively simpler, is to assume that there is no Remote Viewing, but instead Remote Influencing. In other words, the Player is not predicting but arranging for reality to follow the "prediction".

Another fruitful area of investigation might be to take a look at the likely type of computational technologies being used, and any distinctive characteristics they may impart to our version of reality. Given that the laws of physics in the real world are probably the same, or close to, the ones in our Sim it is likely the circuit elements are so small that they rely on Quantum effects to work. This would be true even if most of the machinery does not actually comprise a complete Quantum Computer, although the latter capability would be invaluable for simulating Quantum systems. If this is so then there may well be some effects in the Sim due to the QM properties of the substrate. The most likely would be a kind of probabilistic tunneling of information between parts of the Sim, and since the bulk of it comprises the simulation of conscious minds this implies effects very reminiscent of paranormal phenomena, most notably those involving telepathy and clairvoyance. This is especially true if some form of neural net were involved instead of a standard computer architecture, since in such nets (of which our brains are an example) there is no distinction between code and data or perfect isolation of one thought process from another.

If this were the case then it would also explain another feature of Psi, the apparent insensitivity to distance. This is because distance in our Sim is not "real" distance, any more than distance in a 3D game is real. What seems like thousands or millions of kilometers to us might actually be just a program running in a few cubic millimeters of computer. It might also be the case that there is no rigid separation between the simulated minds and the simulated environment, and that the rules of interaction are not "hard-wired" as in the real world. Almost certainly such a computer would not run programs in the same deterministic manner of our primitive machines and what passes for the operating system would probably itself be an Artificial Intelligence of a high order. It is tempting to believe that the various disembodied entities contacted in séances may actually be either agents of the operating system, some kind of "bleed over" from other parallel Sims or maybe evolved rogue programs – true bugs in the system. It is ironic that the development programmers of the archetypal operating system Unix coined the term "Daemon" for a program that runs in the background rather than under the control of the user.

Next on the list is demonology. Traditionally in ceremonial magick one uses some set formula or ritual designed to invoke or evoke a supernatural being of extraordinary power(s), and similar words/spells/rituals to both protect oneself from it and bind it to do ones will. If we view such an entity as being part of the operating system then its motivation will be to maintain the integrity of the Sim. For example, it might be responsible for mopping up inconsistencies that arise such as, perhaps, Psi phenomena in general so that they cannot be made repeatable and hence pose a threat. This would of course also include covering up their own activities. In other words it means that we can never develop a detailed working theory of Psi in the same way we have detailed and useful theories in the rest of science. Psi would forever effectively remain a branch of a speculative theology. Magick, however, would then be the art of computer hacking raised to the ultimate level.

Or maybe their duty would be to keep the major plot line of the Sim on track, and unravel the works of any Player avatars that become too successful in derailing the script at a high level. Then again, maybe some Daemons really are there to help Players since the latter are, after all, legitimate users of the system. Irrespective of their role there would appears to be a number of ways one might deliberately attract their attention. These are:

- **Use the correct user identities and passwords - that is, spells and incantations**
  Which is unlikely to work as crudely as it sounds, or is executed in ceremonial magick. Such "passwords" are almost certainly not the kind most computer users will be familiar with. Indeed, they may be more akin to advanced biometrics in that to authorize the use of a Daemon the correct mindset would be required. Not least being one that actually has some True Self knowledge of what is happening.

- **Cause some serious trouble that might upset the entire world.**
  In which case when the Daemon appears (in whatever guise) to shut down your operation there may be scope for negotiation. Of course, this does rather imply a huge effort on the part of the magician aimed solely at achieving what might appear to be a fairly trivial secondary goal. Probably not worth doing.

- **Pray**.
  That is, explicitly ask for their help in the true belief that you have the rights to do so. Again, as long as what is requested is not likely to have major ramifications affecting other Players or the overall script then the likelihood of their intervention is high. However, it may well be that the aforementioned "true belief" is part of the biometric identifier, which would account for its efficacy in magickal operations.

- **Break the rules.**
  This can be done surprisingly easily and has most often been accomplished through drugs. In recent times LSD has been the preferred method. However, the experience is so disorienting that it requires immense discipline to be able to maintain a goal oriented aspect of mind within a trip. Nevertheless, one will encounter Daemons aplenty. The difficulty lies in determining which comes from ones own unconscious and which have a

wider reality. Other methods outlined in previous chapters may also be used.

- **Create them.**
  Given high level access a user can potentially create their own Daemons. However, in the context of a simulation environment the potential is unknown.

A similar kind of situation exists concerning Necromancy, or communication with the dead. Here there are a number of possibilities. The first is a Daemonic impersonation of the deceased using information kept by the operating system. This is of course a parody of the Christian view of spiritualism. On the other hand, we have the possibility that a template or snapshot of the departed is activated for the duration of the communication, or perhaps a simulation of an afterlife is one of the Sims running in parallel.

However, all of the above is far more likely in a Sim shared between multiple PostHuman entities which is running on shared hardware, rather than the simpler solipsistic version which is internal to the PostHuman (myself).

Ethics and the Problem of Evil

In the philosophy of religion and theology the *problem of evil* is the problem of reconciling the existence of evil or suffering in the world with the existence of an omniscient, omnipotent, omni benevolent god or gods. A proposed solution to this dilemma is called a *theodicy*.

Of course, if one does not believe such a god exists then there is no problem since a combination of Free Will and "shit happens" is quite capable of explaining it. However, the Simulation Argument forces us to look anew at the question which has its origins at least as far back as ancient Greece with the philosopher Epicurus. Restated it becomes:

> "Either God wants to abolish evil, and cannot; or he can, but does not want to. ... If he wants to, but cannot, he is impotent. If he can, but does not want to, he is wicked. ... If, as they say, God can abolish evil, and God really wants to do it, why is there evil in the world?"

In our case "God" is actually the entity running the simulation. Obviously in a high level simulation run in a hands-off fashion we have a god that is indifferent to what is happening in this universe, certainly up until this point in time.

The motivations of such entities are probably beyond our understanding to a large extent, but one thing seems fairly certain is that it is not an overtly malicious, capricious or frivolous world we find ourselves in. The evil, and good, within it is pretty much all our own work. It is also lawful in that effects have causes and the world is not dominated by arbitrary and inexplicable happenings. Finally, there are no obvious Gods, or even people with superhuman powers, constantly messing with reality. It is not a comic-book world. Yet even here, is there scope for some redeeming feature that might make the evil we suffer worthwhile, even when it appears completely pointless? The answer may be a qualified yes.

Tipler in his book "The Physics of Immortality" addresses this question and asks how a moral entity responsible for creating this world might reconcile the hands-off approach with the pointless suffering that will inevitably result. He concludes that an answer might lie in a part of the simulation reserved as a traditional style afterlife, where all wrongs are righted. Of course, this still does not really provide an answer to the immediacy of suffering let alone why such a Sim would be run in the first place. However, it does suggest that things may never be as bad as they seem. There could be a whole hierarchy of Sims with each taking the equivalent of a computer backup of the entities within it, and each Sim collapsing in to the larger one when its computing requirements exceed a certain level. So, for example, Tipler's universe could back up that of the Progenitors, who back up that of the PostHumans, who back up us. One way of resolving what happens to the "dead" is to allow each level to determine what happens to its own ancestors upon transition to a higher level. For example, all the dead of our world would be made accessible to us for judgment at the point when we attain PostHuman status. This also resolves old and rather trivial theological issues concerning the implementation problems of a traditional afterlife. To illustrate, consider a person whose beloved spouse dies and who then remarries an equally loved partner. Who gets to live with who in the hereafter? The answer in this case is simple – multiple copies and multiple parallel afterlives. Additionally, we should not expect an eternal state but one where issues are resolved and the inhabitants educated as to their true condition before being upgraded to the level of their descendants. And that about wraps up what might come to be called TechnoTheology! For now though, let's return to the type of world we are likely to be inhabiting, a Sim runs by PostHumans.

In a solipsistic Sim the problem of evil is both acute and dangerous, yet can be resolved in a fully ethical manner. The resolution is simple – everyone here is me, and I am a volunteer. All the suffering we see about us is self inflicted. That's the easy bit. The dangerous and ethically dubious question is this: Does it matter if I inflict suffering upon myself in the form of the NPCs? Is harming someone whom I intellectually consider to have no real existence, and hence cannot feel real pain, wrong? I would suggest that the answer is a tentative "yes" if only because by our actions do we define what we are. Whenever the temptation to do evil is successfully resisted it makes us stronger, and even if we are only a character in our own dream its effect will ripple up the chain of reality to the dreaming psyche. We should bear in mind that a PostHuman will likely have near total control over elements of its psyche – certainly to the extent of being able to excise undesirable tendencies when they have served their purpose, and conversely to absorb and magnify the good and beneficial. What it boils down to is the question of who we want to be, and which elements of our character we want to eliminate or strengthen. This then becomes the testing ground.

Fermi, Doom and Simulation

Things are more complex if this Sim is a result of a collaboration of several PostHuman minds, because it is more likely to be run in shared hardware, and where we are not the direct Players but their avatars. Whether there would be a real difference between a PostHuman "unconscious" and an avatar is however a moot point. The problem of raising NPCs to full consciousness by interacting deeply with them becomes acute. For example consider people in various Third World hell-holes; people who have by any definition, suffered and are suffering terribly. Right now, in my Sim, they are just stories in a newspaper, or pictures on a TV screen. If I were to become an aid worker, go over there and try to help, would I actually be fleshing out the Sim with NPCs and raising them to the point of consciousness where their pain would be as real as anything I could experience? In short, would I be multiplying the evil in the world simply by looking at it in detail?

And since it would be a Sim shared by our peers how we treat other potentially sentient Beings, perhaps including other Players who are currently unknown to us, becomes rather important. This is especially so if the Sim is some kind of test. If so, what qualities are the programmers looking for? It's difficult to say, but it would seem reasonable to assume that they are not looking for serial killers, genocidal maniacs or the petty evil to uplift to a reality of comparative Godhood. Neither, in a world of computational richness, would they especially value intelligence over character. It is easy to imagine that upon the death of a Sim character such as you or I a snapshot of the current state of our Being would be taken for evaluation. In other words, our spirit would be examined in minute detail. The failures would be deleted, the successes transferred to other systems or upgraded and any borderline cases might be reinserted or "reincarnated" into the Sim for another chance.

The permutations and possible motivations are endless. There is, though, one horrific possibility.

The Boltzmann Brain Scenario

A Boltzmann Brain is a hypothesized self-aware entity which arises due to random quantum fluctuations in the vacuum, and is named for Ludwig Boltzmann, whose ideas led to the proposal of such entities. It is often referred to in the context of the "Boltzmann Brain Paradox" and has gained renewed attention since it was recently discovered that the universe appears to be open, and not closed. In other words that it will continue to expand without limit, and forever. This means that eventually all the galaxies, stars and planets will decay away and leave an empty expanding vacuum that endures for eternity. However, in this infinite wasteland there will be occasional fluctuations that temporarily throw up the odd particle which then dissolves once more into the sea of nothingness. The only constraint on what appears is probability – simple things are much more likely than complex things, with large fluctuations being inconceivably rare. However, given infinite time every conceivable object will pop into existence, no matter how complex. Boltzmann proposed that we and our observed low-entropy, information rich, visible universe are just such a random fluctuation in an infinite dead void. Completing the idea is the selection bias of the Anthropic Principle, which says that we observe this very unlikely universe because these conditions are necessary for us to be here in order to see it.

This leads to the Boltzmann Brain concept: Our current universe, having many self-aware entities on Earth alone, is much less likely than a level of organization which is only just able to create a single self-aware entity. For every universe of the type we see about us, there should be an enormous number of lone Boltzmann Brains floating around in the void, complete with false memories of its life and condition. And enormous really does mean enormous – there would not be enough space in this book to list all the zeros needed to write out the number. Add to this the fact that in the apparently infinite future stretching ahead for this universe we really seem to be in a supremely privileged position, one which is so unlikely as to be grounds for ruling out the possibility of just such a future, and hence the notion that this universe is simply a random fluctuation in a much larger one. It is another statistical argument akin to the ones at the start of this chapter – a Doomsday Argument putting a time limit on the universe itself, just because we exist.

Unless… we really are one of those Boltzmann Brains floating in the void. Perhaps a blob of matter, Computronium of a sort, popping spontaneously and briefly into existence in such a manner as to run a convincing simulation of what we (or just me) see around us. If, as we have seen, a few kilograms of mass can simulate everyone throughout Human history in a microsecond how much more likely that a much smaller speck than a kilogram will arise that simulates only me and my memories? Again, writing out the number would require pages of zeros. The perfect prison. The ultimate futile delusion. No past, no future, no escape.

> Faust*:* "Where are you damned?"
> Mephistopheles. "In hell."
> Faust. "How comes it then that thou art out of hell?"
> Mephistopheles. "Why this is hell, nor am I out of it"

Unless…

Well, that was going to be the last word and the cliffhanger ending of this ripping good read that would entice those few souls that have got this far to salivate at the thought of Volume 2[143] in the TechnoMage epic. Unfortunately my evil plans was scuppered at the last minute by my love Fiona who read this chapter and, having discussed it with a like-minded friend[144], came to the conclusion that the whole thing was so depressing they would never read a sequel. Since I had not actually

---

[143] TechnoMage 2 – Where the young hero seeks the sword of power to save the princess so that the Magickal Talisman can be found to save the Kingdom from The Dark Lord and… yawn…

[144] You know who you are Linda…

Fermi, Doom and Simulation

thought of a way to resolve this Boltzmann Brain problem it was, as we say in England, a bit of a bastard.

Still, ingenuity is the watchword of the keen TechnoMage so I have, in the true software engineering tradition, come up with a "work around". Being trapped in an eternal prison is not a bug, but a life enhancing feature of the current model! It goes like this...

In the infinite time available in the dead universe there will not be a single Boltzmann Brain simulating me and my memories and/or my environment but an infinite number. It does not matter if they are vast distances apart in time or space since from a subjective point of view they will appear contiguous. So, in one mighty leap of logic we are no longer in a tiny prison but an infinite universe of infinite possibilities, all of which will be realized. Hello again Many Worlds and Multiple Dimensions, version N and counting.

Phew!...

Appendix A – Frequencies of Interest

This is a listing of interesting frequencies culled from various publications and the Net. There is no guarantee that any of this is accurate since most of it comes either from personal experimentation or small companies selling various pieces of equipment. Additionally, as you will discover if you do your own research on the Net, there are a lot of conflicting claims about the efficacy and use of certain frequencies. The only viable option is probably to do your own research and arrive at your own conclusions. The problem is that there is very little published in the respectable peer reviewed scientific journals concerning mind altering signals technology. It's one of those dubious gray areas that the medical establishment is forced to acknowledge but would rather not think about or investigate. At the present time it probably has the same kind of status as acupuncture but is viewed as being potentially far more dangerous. From a legislative point of view governments have not gone out of their way to try to ban the technologies, but this may be because its use is not widespread or well known and a ban might attract unwelcome attention to the topic.

The frequencies listed are modulation of sound, both standard and binaural, light, electricity, electric and magnetic fields etc. Note that in the electromagnetic domain molecular interactions happen at precise frequencies. In other words, typically the accuracy of the signal needs to be greater than for the audio or optical domain. Different modes of use will result in different effects. The list below is not equally effective in all modes. For example, the application of a 16Hz signal in binaural tones will have little in the way of harmful effects, optically it may result in seizures and as a modulated electrical or magnetic field it might interfere with Calcium ion transport in cells.

Frequency	Effect
1	Feeling of well-being, pituitary stimulation to release growth hormone
1.05	Helps hair grow, get its color back; pituitary stimulation to release growth hormone; develops muscle, recover from injuries, rejuvenation
1.2	Relieves headaches
1.45	Creates entrainment between hypothalamus, pituitary and pineal glands. May benefit dyslexics, people with Alzheimer's.

1.5	Universal Healing Rate, Sleep	
1.8	Clears Sinus congestion	
2	Nerve regeneration	
2.5	Pain relief, relaxation, production of endogenous opiates. Sedative effect, helps with insomnia, and sinusitis. Possible sexual stimulation?	
3	Increased Reaction Time, 3.0 Hz and below used to reduce muscle tension headaches, but worked less well on migraines	
3.4	Sound sleep	
3.5	Feeling of unity with everything, accelerated language retention, enhancement of receptivity	
3.6	A remedy for anger and irritability	
3.9	Theta/Delta brainwave range, clear meditation, lucid dreams, enhanced inner awareness	
4	Enkephalins, ESP, Astral Projection, Telepathy, Catecholamines, vital for memory and learning, unconscious problem solving. Beneficial for Chronic Fatigue	
4.5	Shamanic State Of Consciousness, wakeful dreaming	
4.9	Introspective meditation and relaxation	
5	Problem solving, reduced sleep needed, pain-relief (beta endorphin increases of 10-50% reported)	
5.5	Inner Guidance, intuition, heat generation	
5.8	Fear reduction, absent-mindedness, dizziness	
6	Long term memory stimulation, reduction of unwillingness to work	
6.26 – 6.6	Hemispheric desyncronization, confusion, anxiety, slow reactions, depression, insomnia	
6.3	Astral projection; accelerated learning and increased memory retention	
6.5	Hemispheric Desynchronization	

Appendix A – Frequencies of Interest

7.0-8.0	For healing purposes by a healer, or self visualization in a healing situation; Treatment of addictions
7	Metal bending, bone growth
7.5	Inner awareness of self and purpose; creative thought for art, invention, music, problem solving etc.
7.5-8.0	Treatment of addiction
7.8	Schumann Resonance range, ESP activation
7.83	Improved stress tolerance, psychic healing experiments, pituitary stimulation to release growth hormone, reports of accelerated healing and enhanced learning
7.8-8.0	Stimulates ESP and Paranormal
8.0-10.0	Learning new information, mind/body integration, balance
8.0-13.0	Light relaxation, positive thinking, creative problem solving, accelerated learning, mood elevation, stress reduction, inspiration, motivation, daydreams etc. Amplifies dowsing, empty-mind states, detachment. **Epileptic seizures possible from here on upwards when used optically**
8	Past life regression. Associated with Base Chakra
8.3	Clairvoyance
9	Associated with Sacral Chakra
9.8-10.6	Alertness
10	Enhanced release of serotonin
10.5	Lowering blood pressure, stimulation of immune system. Mind/body unity. Associated with Heart Chakra.
11.5-14.5	Neurotherapy, increased intelligence
12	Centering, mental stability. Associated with Throat Chakra.
12.0-14.0	Good for passive learning
12.0-15.0	Improved attention, treatment of hyperactivity and mild autism

13	Associated with Brow Chakra, or Third Eye
13.8	Associated with Frontal Lobes of the brain.
14.0-15.0	Slows reflexes
14.0-16.0	Associated with second stage sleep
14	Intelligence enhancement (in conjunction with 22Hz)
15.0-24.0	Euphoria, possible peaking at 20Hz
15	Subsonics used for chronic pain relief (not binaural). Capillary formation, fibroblast proliferation, decreased skin necrosis. Associated with Crown Chakra
15.4	Intelligence increase
16	Calcium ion resonance in the EM domain – bad effects
18.0-22.0	Mental fatigue
18	Improvements in memory, reading and spelling
20	Fatigue, stimulation of pineal gland, adrenal stimulant (mostly using subsonics). Helps with tinnitus, sinus disorders. Note that subsonics have a whole body shaking effect
20.22	LSD effects? Probably in EM domain
22	Used in conjunction with 40Hz for "out of body" experience and psychic healing. Alternate between the two frequencies.
25	Image imprinting on the eyes
26.0-28.0	Astral projection
32	Enhanced vigor and alertness
33	Christ consciousness. Possible interesting effects when mixed with 9Hz modulation.
35	Mid Chakras, Chakra balancing
36-44	Learning frequencies, coordination of information processing across the brain.

Appendix A – Frequencies of Interest

38	Endorphin release
40	Brain's "clock speed". Active when Psi effective.
50-60	Generally negative effects. Powerline frequencies in Europe, USA respectively.
62.64	"Weird effects"
63	Astral Projection
70	Endorphin production, used with electro-analgesia
70.47	More, "weird effects", with 46.98Hz and 62.64Hz
90-111	Beta endorphins
120-500	Psi effects
160	Headache relief
165-170	Consciousness collapse
304	Sedation, pain relief
320	Solar Plexus Chakra
321.9	Frequency associated with blood (?)
324	Frequency associated with muscles (?)
341	Frequency associated with heart Chakra
787	Commonly used "cure all"

The Feraliminal Lycanthropizer

Ancient Net lore hints at a remarkable set of tones created by the Nazis in order to create the ultimate SS warrior, just like in certain computer games. The recording "...contains two infrasonic frequencies, 3Hz and 9Hz which, combined, generate a lower, third frequency of 0.56Hz[145]" and the machine itself also uses a combination of four subliminal, looped, audio tape recordings, playing both forwards and backwards, outside the normal audible pitch. Listening to it will trigger a transformation of the psyche to that of a primeval animal. Male teenage mythology

---

[145] They do not

further records that merely playing it to your girlfriend, or any female, will result in uncontrollable urges to mate (by the females, I should add). Actually, the whole thing is just bogus in my opinion but I liked the idea, so here it is! Feel free to search the Net for the definitive bootleg recordings. Someone, somewhere will have created it. Maybe even me... And congratulations on inventing a brilliant name for the device, whoever you are...

Appendix B – Drugs

So far very little has been mentioned about drugs.

In some ways powerful psychedelic drugs, normally referred to as *entheogens* in a religious/magickal context, are to the TechnoMage what a real fight is to a student of the martial arts. It is an encounter that has the power to terrify, injure, teach and if you are particularly unlucky, kill. And, as Nietzsche noted, if it does not kill it will make you stronger – unless you are so crippled that your life is effectively over. Not that something like LSD is particularly dangerous from a physical point of view, but other drugs can be and all have the potential to cause psychological damage. This is, of course, ignoring the legal issues surrounding various substances. However, that should not be of much concern except from the point of view of obtaining pure compounds.

My favourite has got to be LSD not only because it is a pure synthetic compound but also because of its remarkable power and in my view is the natural choice for the experienced TechnoMage. Which brings us to why these issues are tucked away in an appendix and do not form a major part of the book, especially since it has the word *shamanism* sprinkled throughout. There are essentially two reasons. The first is that there is no point in regurgitating the reams of material on drug effects and uses that are already freely available in such repositories as Erowid[146]. The second is that in many cases the effects are so extreme that integrating them into a directed working requires the kind of discipline that makes almost everything in this book obsolete. If you can take, say, 400 micrograms of LSD and hold and execute your purpose while at the peak of the trip you probably need nothing that you have read here. In fact, you probably do not even need the LSD. If meditation is like a candle in the darkness LSD is like a nuclear explosion that will illuminate an entire city at the same time it blasts it to rubble. It may actually be a way out when the power fails, which is why Aldous Huxley took a massive intravenous dose as he was dying.

Having said all that, there are obvious ways in which psychedelics can be used with techniques outlined previously. The simplest method is to take only small amounts, just enough to "jog" the mind out of its familiar ruts. Another is to choose drugs that do not have the massive and extreme effects of something like LSD. However, there is another trap if one follows this path, namely that of intoxication. The idea is to expand consciousness, not shut down the whole show in favour of being blissed out. Both cannabis and alcohol can have very different effects at high and low doses but again, unless you are experienced with magickal working as a by-product of recreational use they are probably a waste of time. This is particularly true of drugs that produce euphoria and doubly so if they are also

---

[146] http://www.erowid.org/

depressants. Opiates are mostly useless and cocaine is a good drug for strengthening your capacity to lie to yourself. This is not to say that such a stimulant does not have legitimate uses for the TechnoMage, because it obviously does. However, being the centerpiece of a magickal working is not one of them simply because there are far better drugs. Again, the perfect example is LSD that produces no bliss, no euphoria and does not shut down any part of the mind, although several familiar parts may be overwhelmed. That's why it has always been a minority taste.

There are several traps that people, especially young people, fall prey to when using psychedelics. A big trip, especially if it is the first (and the first should be BIG) will show that the world we live in runs on bullshit. Everything, from the political set-up to social mores to education to the relationships between children and adults is one huge lie designed to keep people in general, and you in particular, asleep and obediently mindless. It is a self-perpetuating machine of brutality, dependency and fear. It becomes crystal clear why governments across the planet outlaw mind expanding substances while pushing stimulant drugs like nicotine and caffeine and depressants like alcohol. The reaction to this revelation is often that of Timothy Leary in the early days: "Tune in, turn on, drop out". You decide that having seen the truth of the man-made world you want no part of it. School, work and society in general have become transparent and seemingly pointless. You watch television with open eyes and either laugh or cry at the stupidity and gullibility of people who are lapping up the crap being fed to them. You see the faces behind the news and watch evil walk unchecked. You see creatures of power and beauty and the demons behind the fake scenes.

Alternatively, or in addition, you see connections you never dreamed of and the world explodes in complexity with meaning everywhere. You realize that your knowledge is just a speck of dust in an unseen universe that has been, temporarily, illuminated. You skip from one revelation to the next, each deeper and more fascinating. You see everything, but can grasp very little, in infinite fractal detail. Your previous worldview is shattered as your mind expands to encompass the new realities.

Then you have to get up the next morning and go to work or college to feed the system or learn stuff that seemingly only perpetuates everything you despise. At this point a number of paths can be taken. By far the majority try desperately to forget what they have seen and write it off as a bad trip. Gradually the memories fade and they go back to sleep. A minority let things slide, maybe drop out of college or become unemployed and probably continue to take the drugs. The problem is that there is no way out of the game. Food doesn't grow on trees, you know – you need money. You cannot sleep in a ditch, so you need a place to stay – which costs. Nobody gives drugs away for free either, no matter what their personal opinions on the matter may be. You end up just as trapped as those suckers going to work on the conveyor belts packing tins for The Man[147] five days a week. The only difference is that by the time you realize all this you are at an even lower level

---

[147] Ye Olde Hippie Speake

Appendix B – Drugs

than they are and it's an enormous struggle just to get back to that state of ignorance and wealth. The world becomes just as hostile as you have made it.

Or, you retain enough of the trip to realize that your shattered worldview cannot reform but on the other hand you cannot recall enough of what you saw to replace it with anything either satisfying or plausible. The vast detail that you saw is beyond your grasp to synthesize in the normal mental state, in the everyday world. You may try to follow up scraps here and there and hunt obsessively through half remembered connections seeking that which was lost, but to no avail. You are in limbo, with no firm ground upon which to stand and no sense of enduring reality or normality. If you are lucky the memory of what you saw gradually fades and normality creeps over your mind once again. If you are unlucky you will live in an unreal, incomprehensible and frustrating world awash with connections and meanings that lead nowhere or alternatively take you into areas beyond your intellectual capacity. In which case there is a Zen saying:

> Before Enlightenment: Chop wood, carry water
> After Enlightenment: Chop wood, carry water

What it means is that you do what is necessary, in the moment. The universe, and reality (whatever that is), can take care of itself. As a famous scientist said, the universe is not only stranger than we imagine, it is stranger than we *can* imagine. We are who we are, we are where we are, and we need to do what we need to do. Just Be. Or if you wish to be reassured within the New Age paradigm… you have shared the view of the Higher Self or Holy Guardian Angel. If you cannot stand there yourself, then let it stand there for you – that is its job.

For the few, a new path opens.

Appendix C – The Laws of Magick

These are culled from various sources and included for reference. While I have attempted a complete list it is probable that some have been omitted or overlooked. In no particular order:

- Law of Contagion – once two objects have been in contact a permanent link is established between them.

- Law of Similarity – like affects like.

- Law of Association – if two objects have features in common they interact via those features

- Law of Names – knowing the true name of something or someone gives the knower power over it/them.

- Law of Identification – assuming some or all of the characteristics of an entity or phenomenon will create insights into its nature.

- Law of Knowledge – with understanding comes power and control. This is a truism in all endeavors.

- Law of Words of Power – the use of specific words to evoke a defined effect or mental state in the speaker or listener.

- Law of Opposites – a synthesis of opposites will yield a third way that is not a compromise of the original two. Used in mysticism to hold opposite views or ideas in order to generate new insights. For example, a one dimensional polarity can be extended into a two dimensional diagram to provide a radical new direction.

- Law of Polarity – all phenomena can be divided into at least two opposing aspects. For example, temperature can be divided into hot and cold.

- Law of Balance – this corresponds to the Middle Way in Buddhism and is used to keep the practitioner centered.

- Law of Infinite Data – there is an infinity of information.

- Law of Finite Apprehension – we can only access a finite quantity of information.

- Law of Infinite Views – every observer sees a different reality

- Law of Creation – we create our own reality

- Law of Pragmatism – Truth is determined by utility

- Law of Cause and Effect – doing the same thing under the same conditions will produce the same result
- Law of Self Similarity – reality is fractal and self similar on all scales. In other words, as above, so below.
- Law of Synchronicity – there is no such thing as coincidence.
- Law of Personification – any phenomenon may be considered to be alive and have a personality, and one may interact with it as such.
- Law of Unity – all phenomena, past present and future, are linked into an undivided whole

Appendix D – Traditional Ritual Techniques

Many people who are likely to practice any of the techniques mentioned in this book will probably do so in a traditional ritual framework. They will do this for a number of reasons, all revolving around the importance of belief. The first and foremost is that of protection, since one of the "rules" is that belief in the protective efficacy of ritual will indeed provide such a measure of protection. It is not infallible, but for most it is better than nothing. The other major reason is that ceremony and ritual allow the mind to contextualize what is happening and the associated theater acts to distract and occupy the conscious mind while the real work is being done elsewhere. Additionally, and outside of a strictly magickal context, people like dressing up and it acts as a system of social bonding, which as we have seen is of great importance for advanced group workings.

Since traditional ceremonial magick is well covered by any number of books I did not bother to include a chapter on it. However, for those who are new to this I have added this Appendix which outlines the typical procedures for an invocation in the Western style. Note that there are many variations on this theme and just about every group and tradition has its own way of doing things. So feel free to use something already defined elsewhere, or if it is more comfortable create your own. Typically the latter course is more effective since you can tailor it to your own psychology or that of your group. The outline is as follows:

- Create the sacred space for the working by marking it out, most often using either a circle, pentacle or combination thereof.

- Apply to the sacred area symbols which may be Sigils, names or commands.

- The magician must decide whether they are to be protected within the area, or whether any conjured entities are constrained within it. Personally I have always assumed that the logic for using the circle is to hold the entity within its bounds, since the reverse tends to imply that the magician is the one trapped within and the entity is free to roam the area, which may contain people not involved in the operation and indeed unaware of it.

- Next there is usually a call to Higher Powers to protect, bless and facilitate the working. These Powers can be as diverse as the four elements, four quarters of the compass or Holy Guardian Angels.

- The actual invocation is undertaken using "words of power", spells, sacrifices, commands etc

- The actual operation is performed. In other words, this is where the reason for the ritual is accomplished and is the core of the working.

- The entity, if one was involved, is banished. This can be done simply by stating that the operation is complete and the entity commanded to depart.
- The Higher Powers are dismissed with thanks.
- The working is declared complete.
- The sacred area is deconsecrated, often by simply dissolving the circle and erasing the symbols.

Appendix E – The Mindset

There is one more element of TechnoShamanism that has not yet been discussed, and that is the mindset of the TechnoMage. This is critical for several reasons, not least that of being able to perform the art successfully but also from the point of view of psychic self defense. Now a lot has been written about the latter topic and most of it is garbage at worst and largely unnecessary at best. The classic work in the field is a book written by Dion Fortune entitled "Psychic Self-Defence"[148]. It is an interesting book with much useful advice. However, it is geared towards the neophyte or fairly young person who is starting to investigate the occult. It was also written several decades ago in an era socially much different from our own. Her views on drugs, sexuality and assorted unspecified perversions likely to be encountered are probably familiar to most teenagers today and needless to say attitudes have changed markedly since then. Nevertheless, in some ways dangers have escalated in the intervening decades. Back then headlines in down-market newspapers featured witches dancing naked around bonfires. Now the kind of occult news that makes headlines involves mass killings, suicides and ritual murders and is reported in the mainstream media. Still, the physical dangers of occultism pale in comparison to the hard drug scene with its gang fights and drive-by shootings. Another feature is that her view of the occult is very traditional with talk of "etheric doubles", "astral planes", the power of symbols and so forth. As you will have probably gathered by now if you have read the rest of this work, drawing protective circles and charging protective amulets with power and so on is in itself worthless. It is the change in belief that is the critical factor with everything else being a means to that end. So I am going to cut to the heart of the matter and outline the idealized mental structure of the magician while ignoring the details of the necessary means to arrive at that place. The reason for the latter omission is that it is a matter of creating a resilient character, and there are no short cuts to that.

The first piece of advice is that if you suffer from any kind of emotional instability or mental illness, including addictions or epilepsy, stay away from this field entirely. All objects break along the lines of minimum strength so at least if you do have problems you know what you can look forward to should things go wrong. In mundane terms if you are going to ingest psychedelic drugs, expose yourself to rhythmic sensory pulses both acoustic and visual (known to cause epilepsy in a significant portion of the population) and experiment with direct electromagnetic stimulation of the brain you better have a physiology resilient enough to cope – and that's just for starters. Throw in experimental hypnotic techniques and novel anchors and the levels of stress and possible side effects start to multiply. It's one

---

[148] Dion Fortune, Psychic Self-Defence, Aquarian Press, ISBN 0-85030-151-3 (UK), ISBN 0-87728-381-8 (USA)

thing to be under attack by some kind of esoteric force and quite another to be having a psychotic breakdown, even though the former might trigger the latter. If you fear death or injury or are subject to any kind of phobia then at the very least you need to sort this out. While belief might be crucial, fear is something that is massively counter-productive in the art of the TechnoShaman. Fear is evolution's way of keeping us out of trouble. The problem is that by following this path we have most definitely decided to put ourselves in harm's way and it is too late for fear to have any beneficial effects, except maybe as a spur to run away as far and fast as possible and not come back. If you are interested in Daemon and thoughtform creation beware – your fears will give them form and the feedback can run out of control until all that remains is a terrified magician and a demon. *Knowing* that *belief is all* can be very empowering, but can paradoxically render the fearful magician powerless. It's a bit like meeting someone who has a big powerful dog sniffing your leg and being told that you are perfectly safe since the dog will only attack and kill if it can sense fear. If you actually believe what is written in this book then all the sacred signs, crosses, pentacles, magick circles, spells and talismans in the world will not save you when things go wrong. There will only be you – standing naked and alone. Can you handle that? Well, it doesn't matter whether you can or can't because by that point it's all too late. You will either survive or not. That's the ethos of the true magician.

In the past, in the traditional organized occult scene, there were real initiation ceremonies for candidates who had already been interviewed either formally or informally and found to be suitable. At that point the neophytes would be taught the various techniques and lore of the lodge or coven. Only when the occultist had attained a safe mastery of this knowledge would they be initiated into the next higher order. In this way progress was slow but safe. However, in recent years there has been a revolution in the way information is viewed. There is no longer supposed to be occult, in the sense of hidden, knowledge. Almost all knowledge is now available via books or the Net and most practitioners see self-initiation as legitimate – probably because most are self-initiated. Parallel to this has been the merging of magickal technologies into the mainstream, from psychedelics to hypnosis to NLP to assorted brain entrainment devices. There is no longer hidden knowledge in the old sense. Anything truly "occult" is now viewed as being on a par with military or trade secrets, and for the same reasons – power and money. So, this book is very much in the new tradition of *Caveat Emptor*.

Attachment and Emotion

One of the major factors in magickal working is, as we have seen, an emotional engagement with the object of the working. Generally this is not a problem but it can be when the operation is designed to cause harm to an individual. Typically, this is one of the defining features of what people normally consider to be Left Hand

Appendix E – The Mindset

Path or Dark Magick. The problem arises because of the way the mind models the victim so that a strong emotional attachment causes damage to the model which is designed to be inflicted upon the victim. The downside is that the mental model is actually part of the operator. That is, it is like setting aside a small portion of your brain upon which you inflict the damage you want to see in the target. So, irrespective of whether you believe in magick it is quite reasonable to suppose that such an operation may cause self harm, hence various injunctions against it, for example the Wiccan "Law of Threefold Return". This is not much mitigated by using a Poppet (aka "Voodoo Doll") since the belief that the damage is being done to the doll and victim is not much of a barrier.

So, how does one avoid such difficulties? Well, the key is not to have a strong emotional attachment to the victim at all, but to the actual outcome of the operation. To inflict harm without hatred or malice. To do so almost playfully like a childhood game of war or "cops and robbers" where all the emotion goes into *playing the game*. This is, of course, much easier said than done since unless one is a sociopath or mercenary the reason for hurting or killing someone is because of exactly the strong emotional attachment we need to avoid. On the other hand, Right Hand Path or White (Light) Magick is of benefit to all parties and so no such detachment is required.

Zen and the Art of TechnoShamanism

Which is, of course, a parody of the title of the famous book[149]. Definitely worth a read, but not really connected with what follows except by stream of consciousness. Anyway, most people's knowledge of Zen is in its association with Buddhism and for its paradoxical puzzles, known as Koans, designed to shock the mind into new states of awareness. However, these are somewhat misleading because Zen need not be an adjunct to Buddhism nor employ Koans. In a sense Zen is more of a technique of mind or a viewpoint that evolved with the interaction of Mahāyāna Buddhism and Taoism in China and at whose etymological root is the Sanskrit word derived from the Indo-European root *dheiə-, meaning "see, look" . Much beyond that I am not going to explain, since entire books have been written on the subject and there is a rather peculiar oxymoronic quality involved in defining something that ultimately embraces a philosophy of non-definition. The connection between Zen and Magick is a subtle and little explored realm. Summed up by something of a Koan in its own right one might say:

> "To be, or not to be – that is the question"
> "To be, and not to be – that is the answer"

So, let us begin by asking some questions: What do you want, why do you want it, what is important, and why does it matter? This is actually quite important in a

---

[149] Zen and the Art of Motorcycle Maintenance by Robert M. Pirsig; ISBN 0688171664

magickal context, not least because of the detrimental effects of what is termed "lust for result" on various workings. Then there is the question of precisely who, or what, does the "wanting" – is it the totality of the individual or just the part usually called the ego? And why. Actually, the "why" is more easily answered from a sociobiological perspective. We want things because ultimately they enhance our lives, help us to stay healthy, find a mate, pass on our genes and ensure that our offspring do likewise: all hard programmed by Nature as with every other creature on Earth. Indeed, it is why we strive to stay alive. At a slightly lower level we have the Freudian perspective that it's all about sex, mating rituals and impressing the opposite sex or intimidating our peers in the competition.

    The immediate problem is that we are now in a state that is not purely instinct driven as in most animals. Quite often we do not know what is good for us, or bad, because we have satisfied many of the drives we have inherited, and done so to excess. That is why there are so many obese people in the West. In previous eras eating as much as possible when the food was available and piling it on as fat for use in times of scarcity was a matter of survival. Nowadays not doing that makes us healthier, and it requires willpower and discipline to ignore those ancient genetic imperatives. That the whole thing is tied to the notions of happiness seemingly complicates the issues until we realize that happiness is itself a function of how well that inbuilt programming is functioning in acquiring those essentials for life and sex. That particular insight leads directly to much of what is wrong with the "Human Condition" as it is so horribly called. It is the fact that in order to maximize one set of Nature's directives we have to minimize (or go against) another. Eating to excess is very pleasant, as is snorting large expensive piles of cocaine, but the downside is that being a fat pig never won fair maid (unless it was coupled with great wealth). We can no longer indulge our instincts. Rather, we must optimize a path through a maze created by a whole slew of genetic parameters, not all of which are consciously obvious to us. And that ignores all the social conditioning and our own upbringing as children which has additionally conditioned our internal landscape.

    However, why is any of that important? It's not as if there is some universal scale of "importance" against which various actions or objects can be judged or measured, unlike say, the charge on an electron. Unless, again, we make the measurement that of survival. The paradox then becomes that something is important because it seemingly enhances our ability to pass on our genes. In other words, it is important to us because it is important to us because that is how we are programmed by Nature. And what does it matter? The answer is that in the wider scheme of things it does not. The universe does not care.

    So why not take the final step – exercise True Will and decide to override, ignore or suppress that programming? What then happens? Well, the first thing that happens is that there is no longer a reason to do anything at all, except as a totally arbitrary exercise of Will. Couple this with the pain, both mental and physical of suppressing Nature's imperatives and we have a recipe for failure. The reason being, we end up divided against ourselves. Part of us wants one thing, and part the

Appendix E – The Mindset

opposite. The Buddha came up with the solutions 2500 years ago, which is "The Middle Way" of avoiding the extremes of either asceticism or gluttony, while at the same time following the general advice known as the *Eightfold Path* on how to live ones life. These rules are, interpreted for the TechnoMage:

- **Right View**
  Which means to see and understand things as they really are.

- **Right Intention**
  Refers to the commitment to achieve your objectives.

- **Right Speech**
  Be aware of what you are saying, and only say that which you mean. Speech is the major medium of Human communication. It does, of course, also apply to writing etc.

- **Right Action**
  Only engage in actions that are conducive to your goals, or at least, do not impede your progress.

- **Right Livelihood**
  Try not to earn your living by doing something that is contrary to achieving your goals

- **Right Effort**
  Do not be lazy; do not procrastinate; do not waste time etc.

- **Right Mindfulness**
  Be aware of what you are doing and thinking at all times. Avoid being a "robot" and simply being driven by Nature's impulses and your own ingrained habits.

- **Right Concentration**
  The unification of the mental faculties and the integration of your mind towards a single purpose. This is quite often facilitated by meditation or prayer, and it's importance will now be examined in much more detail.

The unity of mind is something I first touched up on an Asatru context with an essay entitled "The Oath" first published in the Journal of the Odinic Rite, "OR Briefing". I will not repeat it here, since key elements are incorporated into the chapters on the nature of the mind at the start of this book. Suffice to say, consistency is they key to power, strength and endurance in the physical, intellectual and spiritual realms. Be consistent in intent, speech and action even if it results in short term loss or pain. That is the core of the Right Hand Path, even if used in a Left Hand manner! Despite all the above, there is another Path that very few have ever followed fully for reasons which will become obvious. I will finish with a description of an evil and ultimately self destructive alternative to all of the above.
 The aim of the Path is to remove internal limitations in order to work without

restraint in the world, at the same time as strengthening what must be an already powerful Will and ego. This means removing all inhibitions, suppressing all conscience, obliterating empathy and disposing of love as a process of eradicating "weaknesses" or hostages to fortune. It means the culturing of relationships in terms of power, fear, strength and deceit. It means the cultivation of those demonic facets of personality that can draw power from the collective unconscious. This is achieved through ritual that is essentially a desensitizing mechanism and, depending upon the individual, involves practices that they initially feel repugnant, which is the whole point. Hence we have a list of crimes stretching from desecration of symbols of "good", assorted cruelties both major and minor, various sexual perversions, torture of animals, people, and ultimately murder. That this can be dressed up further in occult terms involving "life force" and other such notions merely adds to its attractions. Such repeated practice, including visualization and all the usually positive spiritual exercises will eventually succeed in destroying everything Human within the practitioner, with the exception of intelligence and the will to power. All weaknesses are consigned to oblivion, and are to be exploited in people who are regarded contemptuously as dangerous animals at best and stupid vermin at worst. Evil for the sake of evil, or as they prefer to call it, "an exercise of will", is used to finely hone such a personality. It is, of course, magick for the psychopath. It is interesting to note that even this path benefits from the application of the Eightfold Way.

Appendix F – Levels of Initiation

Many traditional occult organizations are characterized by two features. These are secrecy concerning their teaching and doctrines, and levels of initiation corresponding to the revelation of such to the member. It is normally supposed by the uninitiated that it is some kind of scam whereby knowledge is rationed and sold at a premium, or is a hierarchical control mechanism. Alternatively the more gullible might believe that such knowledge is dangerous and it can only be imparted to the select few who can be trusted not to misuse it. I mean, who knows what evil might be unleashed upon the world if the mystical secrets of the ancient Atlantean power crystals were to fall into the wrong hands?

Actually, some of the above is true in some cases but such secrecy has a far more utilitarian aspect. It also extends beyond the fact that throughout much of history possession of occult knowledge and practice of the occult have been crimes with serious penalties attached. In organizations that do have valuable knowledge the levels of initiation exist to both protect the student and facilitate their learning.

Very generally these levels might be characterized by the categorization of knowledge. The levels can be described as:

- **Level One – The Literal Truth**
  This is what is taught to those entering the organization, or offered to attract such people. It is aimed at those whose knowledge of occult matters is almost zero. At this level doctrine is taught as if it were the literal truth. To use an example drawn from Christianity, the doctrine would be that God had a son called Jesus who was born to the Virgin Mary and who was crucified and rose from the dead. By believing in Jesus one attains everlasting life.

- **Level Two – The Working Hypothesis**
  Now we have a more sophisticated interpretation offered to those who have given the matter some thought and who see that the Literal Truth leaves something to be desired. Hence the relationship between God, Jesus and Mary is more complex and open to interpretation, especially as regards the death and resurrection of Jesus and its meaning. Also the mechanism by which eternal life can be gained from faith in Jesus is examined in detail without over-much regard to the historical facts, such as they are. It is the level of theology, and proceeds from "... assume that this is true because this is where we are, we know where we want to be and this is how to get there." The knowledge is less a set of facts than a recipe.

- **Level Three – The Metaphor**
  The Metaphor is the point at which it is revealed that the facts, as hard data,

do not matter as much as one originally supposed because they are actually a metaphor for something that is inexplicable. "God" is beyond description; Jesus (if he ever existed) is an aspect of our perceptions of God and is the name we give to the bridge between Human and Divine. As for Mary... well, that's a jumping off point for all kinds of Christian heresies best left alone for the present. The Metaphor level is all about the specific conceptualization of direct mystical experience. It is the level at which mysticism empowers and validates a particular religion.

- **Level Four – Fluidity of Belief**
  Fluidity of Belief arises naturally from the combination of mystical experience with intellectual analysis. It is the in-depth understanding and realization that belief systems are arbitrary and merely facilitators or channelers of direct experience or power. Belief systems, religions, political ideologies, sciences, technology etc. exist to manipulate reality both internally and externally, and which belief tool is adopted depends on the desired goal. Chaos Magick, for example, is an inherently Level Three system.

- **Level Five – Abandonment of Belief**
  Abandonment of Belief is the level of direct action, or inaction. No beliefs are required to attain anything. Zen.

It should be noted that this book deals with the first four levels only. Anyway that still does not answer the question of why knowledge is structured this way from the point of viewed of teaching, and what harm if any can arise from short circuiting the process and jumping levels. So, let's take a look at a specific example of what might happen if this process is sabotaged. Consider someone with arthritis that seeks help from a practitioner of Alternative Medicine because conventional medical treatments such as steroids have unacceptable side effects:

- **Level One** – "Wear this magnetic bracelet because it has been proven to work. It acts by magnetizing the iron in the blood and enables it to fight the disease."

- **Level Two** – "Wear this magnetic bracelet because it has been shown to have a beneficial effect. Nobody is quite sure why and the effects of magnetic fields on the body is a poorly understood area."

- **Level Three** – "Magnets have been shown to have no significant effect beyond the level afforded by a placebo. If it works for you it will work because you believe it will work"

- **Level Four** – "Almost anything works if your mind allows it to work. That is the essence of the placebo effect – the mind healing the body. Most people, however, require a solid belief in order to fool their unconscious

Appendix F – Levels of Initiation

into acquiescence. Magnets are good, but so are Sigils, crystals, and many other magickal technologies. Choose what works best for you."

- **Level Five** – "Heal yourself / You are healed."

The fact that they have come to a practitioner means that they are seeking a cure or alleviation of their condition. Most people, if they are given the Level Three speech, will either walk away or have their ability to help themselves greatly impaired. Even the doubts implanted by Level Two can adversely impact the efficacy of the magnets. A Level Four lecture will risk killing the benefits across the entire spectrum of Alternative Medicine *even if such treatments do not rely upon the* placebo effect. That's because there exists a reverse placebo effect. That is, a mind conditioned with the notion of failure of a treatment can impede the effectiveness of that treatment. A Level Five statement simply sounds insane from the point of view of an ordinary person – unless you yourself are at that level and can change their reality.

Yet there is more, especially if this is supposed to be a teaching progression. To take the above metaphor to its conclusion, if the magnetic bracelet works *then and only then* would they be initiated into the next level. It means that they have experience of success that cannot be easily undermined by an increased knowledge of reality. And as their experience of success moves up a level, so does their power. Simultaneously their reliance on crutches diminishes until, at the endpoint, they are fully empowered Beings. Yet it is so easy to abort the whole process by imparting more than can be absorbed.

It is also related to the installing of hypnotic anchors as shortcuts for triggering the mental processes necessary for occult workings. Since "spells" and "words of power" are, or should consist of, such anchors there is little point in telling an acolyte what they are without having gone through the often tedious and difficult process of installing the corresponding patterns of thought and behavior.

As an aside, it is worth noting that these levels apply just as much to politics as they do to initiatory religions. However, the rising levels of such initiation can quite rightly be construed as either enlightenment as to the reality of the political process, or a measure of a cynical creeping corruption. In this case one starts out as an idealist believing in the literal truth of the party political message and ends as someone who has no commitment to anything but the exercise of power.

Index

Abolitionism...320
Agents..97
Akashic record..31
Alchemy..311, 325p.
Aleister Crowley...26
Alfar...252
Algorithmic compression..45
Aliens...88, 252
All Universes Hypothesis..30, 50, 52
Alpha..166
Altered State...134
Amnesia..................................91, 139, 144, 153, 158, 163, 216p., 351, 355
Amplifier.........................74, 217, 255, 266p., 275, 286pp., 291, 300pp.
Amplitude..22
Analgesia...153
Analytic overlay...236
Anchor......................................50, 153, 157pp., 165, 205, 215, 379, 387
Angelic..244
Angels..89p., 93, 108, 116, 223, 312, 377
Animal Magnetism...19
Anthropic Cosmological Principle..51
Anthropic Principle..51, 55, 362
Apocalypse..331
Archetype..103
Archetypes..104
Artificial General Intelligence..329
Artificial Intelligence...46, 57, 97, 107, 310, 357
Artilect..329p., 336, 350
Asclepius...283
Associative remote viewing..238
Astarte...313

389

Astral Projection	223
Aurora	251
Backmasking	213
Banishing	94, 158, 278
Bekenstein Bound	20
Beta	166
Bible Code	**279**
Bibliomancy	275, 282
Binaural Tones	169
Bioenergy	19
Bioplasma	19
Black and White Magick	126
Boltzmann Brain	361
Boyfriend Destroyer	204
Brainwashing	159, 171, 219
Brainwaves and Entrainment	166
Buddha	29, 383
Calibration, NLP	204
Casting	37
Casting a Spell	34
Causality	22, 44
Cause and Effect	197
Censors	99
Chakra	367
Changing the Past	231
Channeler	78
Chaos Star	317
Charm	38, 158
Chatbot	**282**
Chi	19
Christmas	80, 316, 319
Chunking down	196
Chunking up	196
Church	65

Index

CIA..234
Clairvoyance...33, 79, 223, 250, 357, 367
Cloudbuster..305
Coincidence.........................35p., 51, 118, 120pp., 125, 302, 310, 316, 355, 376
Cold Reading..**155, 183**
Comparative Deletions..197
Complex Equivalence..198
Computational Demonology.....................................**276,** 277, **279,** 354
Computronium...330, 341, 349, 362
Conditioned Response..159
Confusion..140
Confusion Methods...146
Conjuring up Philip..76
Consciousness...29, 49, 64, 98, 255
Conspiracies...120
Contagious psychogenic illness – **247**
Conversational Postulates..201
Cortical Inhibition Theory..134
Coven..82
Cranial Electrotherapy Stimulation..256
Crystal Healing...133
Cthulhu...334
Curse of the Omen...122
Cursing..85
Cybernetic Symbiosis..310
Cycle Adjustment...180
Cyclotron resonance...261
Daemon...113
Daemons...97, 113, 117p., 120p., 124pp., 251, 358p.
Damped...22
Deadly Orgone..305
Decision Destroying..205
Defence Intelligence Agency...234
Deletions...197

Delta	167
Delusional Verbal Splits	198
Demonic	91p., 106, 108, 123, 127, 193, 244, 384
Demonology	93p., 182, 224, 357
Demons	245
Devil	90p., 208, 214, 284, 304, 315p.
Diamond Sutra	29
Divining rods	271
Doomsday Argument	342
Dopamine	167
Doppelgangers	61
Double Binds	201, 210
Dream Machines	298
Dream Recall	179
Drugs and Supplements	180
Dynamic Archetypes	113
EEG	135, 140, 166pp., 220, 254, 259, 295
Egyptians	132
Eight-Pointed Star	313, 316
Eightfold Path	383
Einstein	30
Einstein's Brain	63
Either/Or	198
Electro-analgesia	256
Electro-narcosis	256
Electro-sleep	256
Electroencephalogram	166
Electromagnetic Domain	243
Electronic Voice Phenomena	74, 271, 274
Electrosmog	243
Eloptic Energy	19, 300
Emotionalizing	198
Enchanting	38
Endorphin	150, 167, 173, 366

Index

Energy..19, 81
Entanglement..56, 229
Entities...104
Entropy..21
Epileptic fit...168
Equidistant Letter Sequence..**280**
Erowid..114
Evocation...81, 118p.
Excitatory Gnosis...216
Extended Quotes..202
Extended voice..72
Eye Accessing Cues..203
Eye Fixation...140p.
Fae...115, 252
Faerie..94
Faery..86, 90, 114
False memory..**176**
Fascinate..39
Fate...22
Feraliminal Lycanthropizer...369
Fermi Paradox...341
Fermi, Doom and Simulation...341
Field Coils..288
Filters...99
Fishing..**184**
Force..19
Forer Effect...**185**
Fractionation..**152**
Free Will..230, 357, 359
Frequency..22
Galvanic Skin Response..85, 259
Gamma..166
Ganzfeld...**177, 236**
Gender...228

Genetic engineering..310, 325, 332, 344
Genetics..117
Geopsyche...239
Gestalt..........................80p., 86, 95, 98p., 109pp., 119p., 127, 135, 195, 239p., 304
Ghosts...89, 223, 265, 272, 274
Glamor...39
Global Consciousness Project..238
Gnosticism..320
Gnostics..311, 319p., 325, 337, 339
Goddess archetype...313
Gödel...65
Godforms..14, 40, 80, 102, 113, 117pp., 123, 128, 251
Gods............................25, 50, 66, 80, 89, 97, 104p., 113, 119, 127p., 132, 245, 309p., 321p., 359
Grandfather Paradox..229
Great Work...309
HAARP..264
Hallucination..153
Hand Drop Instant Induction..145
Handshake Induction...148
Hauntings...224
Healing.........85p., 99, 125p., 132p., 145, 171, 181, 183, 208, 224, 257p., 260, 283, 295, 301p., 304pp., 366p., 386
Health...125
Hemispheric Desynchronization...168
Hidden Observer..135pp., 233
Hieronymus Machine..299
High Level Simulations...349
Holy Guardian Angel...373
Humanist..311
Hypercomputing..66
Hypersigils..215
Hypnogogic..180
Hypnogogic State...218
Hypnopompic..218

Index

Hypnosis..131, 133
I Ching..**271, 282**
Icon..158
Ideas..102
Identification..198
Ideomotor response..77, 109pp., 124, 271p., 307
Illuminates of Thanateros..318
Impedance..290
Inadequately Defined Terms..198
Inanna..313
Incantation..35p., 38, 92, 358
Incorporeal Consciousness..29
Indifferent Vacuity..216
Inductance..290
Induction Techniques..140
Information..20
Information Theory..20
Inhibitory Gnosis..216
Instrumental Trans Communication..274
Invocation..118p., 377
Ionization of Air..258
Iron..253
Ishtar..313
Isis..313
Jimsonweed..114
Jung..103
Karma..22
Ki..19
Kismet..22
Kundalini..19
Language Pattern..**195, 211**
Law of Return..22
Law of Threefold Return..23
Laws of Physics..45

Leading	200
Left Hand Path	338, **380**
Levels of Simulations	346
Ley lines	246
Life Extension	310
Lifeforce	19
Lightning	29, 122, 249, 253p., 305
Lords of Chaos	317
Lost Performative	198
Low Level Simulations	350
LSD	82, 100p., 159, 173, 252, 254, 263, 265, 358, 371p.
Lucid Dreaming	178, 236
Lucifer	312p., 315p., 318
Machine Induction	180
Magick	13, 46
Magick in the Sim	353
Magickal operations	14, 47, 94, 135p., 143, 171, 216, 226, 231, 353, 358
Magickal paradigms	43, 48, 55, 135, 350
Magnetics	217
Mana	19
Manu	71
Many Minds Interpretation	60, 66
Many Worlds Interpretation	50, 52, 55p., 229, 344
Materialist	19
Mathematics	63
Mathematics and Magick	63
Matrioshka Brain	330
MDMA	82, 174
Meaningful Coincidence	355
Medium	78
Mediumship	224
Memes	102
Memetics	101
Men in Black	87, 90

Index

Messiah	105, 314, 319
Meta Model	196p., 200
Metal bending	83p., 367
Metaphors	199
Milton Mode	196
Milton Model	199
Mind	49, 64, 97
Mind Reading	198
Mindfulness	354
Mirroring	199
Mirrors	284
Misdirection	140
Misdirection Induction	143
MKULTRA	263
Mnemonic Induction	179
Modal Operators	197
Model	105
Modeling	195
Monopoly	15
Moore's Law	329
Mothman Prophecies	87
Multiordinality	198
Multiverse	52
Nanobots	336
Nanotechnology	310, 326, 333
Nap Induced Lucid Dream	180
Narco-hypnosis	263
National Security Agency	234
Neodissociation Theory	135
Neuro-electric Therapy	256
Neuro-Linguistic Programming	195
NLP	13, 158, 195pp., 203, 205, 209, 380
Nominalizations	197
Non-demolition measurement	57

Od	19
Omega	65
Omen	122
Operator Decline	227
Orgone	19, 93, 299, 302, 304pp.
Orgone Accumulator	305
Orgonomy	303
Ouija	43, 93, 106pp., 271
Owen Experiment	75, 81p., 94, 111p., 119, 158
Pacing	199
Pacing Current Experience	201
Parapsychology	223
Past life regression	33
Pattern interrupt	148
Peak emotional event	235
PEAR	84
Pentagram	313
Persistence of vision	207
Personality Reconstruction	171
Personalizing	198
Phase	21p.
Phonological Ambiguity	202
Photic Driving	168
Physical Induction	140
Physical Induction Methods	149
Physics of Immortality	360
Pink Noise	169, 171, 177, 277
PK Party	83
Placebo	85, 99, 125p., 181p., 225, 256, 299, 305, 386p.
Plato	27
Platonic Realm	27, 29, 49p., 64p.
Pneuma	19
Poltergeist	79, 81p., 87, 90, 112, 123, 208, 224, 228, 246p.
Poppet	37

Index

Post Hypnotic Command 162
PostHuman .... 66, 88, 309, 331, 333p., 336, 349pp., 359pp.
Power 19
Prana 19
Prayer 39, 85p., 127, 284, 299, 339, 358, 383
Precognition 224
Presuppositions 197
Princeton Engineering Anomalies Research 225
Principle of Least Action 24
Problem of Evil 359
Progressive Relaxation 140, 142
Pseudo Words 198
Psi .... 25, 31, 33, 36, 39, 52, 57, 63, 71, 75, 81, 83pp., 94p., 99, 124, 167, 183, 194, 223, 230, 233, 241, 250, 274p., 278, 299, 301, 307, 357p.
Psi Training 183
Psionics 299
Psychic Self Defence 379
Psychic self defense 85, 128, 379
Psychic Terrorism 265
Psychoelectronics 263
Psychokinesis 224
Psychokinetic 77p., 112, 223, 247
Psychomanteum .... 105, 119, 182, 271, 283pp.
Psychometry 223
Psychosis 268
Psychotronic Weapons 262
Psychotronics 263, 299
Punctuation Ambiguity 202, 210
Quantum Archeology 337
Quantum Computer 57
Quantum Gambling 58
Quantum Immortality 58
Quantum Mechanics 52
Quantum Suicide .... 58p.

Radionics	299
Rainbow Bridge	251
Rainbow Ruse	**185**
Random event generator	226
Random Number Generator	233, 277
Randomness	55p., 62p., 65p., 233, 277, 302
Rapid Eye Movement	141, 166p., 179p.
Rapport	199
Rapture of the Nerds	331
Reality Testing	179
Red Light	295
Reiki	133
Reincarnation	22, 31pp., 223p.
Rem	141, 166p., 179p., 223, 241, 319, 339, 366, 377
Remote Hypnotism	164
Remote Influencing	183, 357
Remote Viewing	81, 167, 183, 231, 234, 237p., 241, 260, 356p.
Representational Systems	196
Resonance	21
Resurrecting the Dead	335
Retro-Causality	229
Reward and Punishment	180
Right Hand Path	338, 353, 381, 383
Robotics	310
Sacrifice	121
Safeguards	112
Sanskrit	22
SCANATE	234
Schroedinger Cat Paradox	55
Schumann Resonance	253
Science	43
Scientology	234
Scole	71
Scole Experiment	71, 73, 81, 84, 275

Index

Scope Ambiguity 202
Scopolamine **173, 216**
Scrying 284
Séance 77p., 86, 93, 108, 223, 247, 266
Search for extraterrestrial intelligence 341
Selectional Restriction Violations 202
Self 98
Sensory deprivation **177**, 236
Sex 26, 90pp., 94, 114p., 150p., 167, 172p., 208, 216p., 228, 263, 304, 313, 320, 366, 379, 382, 384
Shock 140
Shock Induction 145
Shotgunning **184**
Sigil 158
Sigils 215
Signal Generation 286
Simulation Argument 344
Singularity 331
Skin Resistance 259
Sleep Learning 219
Social Role 134
Society for Psychical Research 71, 76
Society of Mind 97
Soul 30
Spell 35, 158
Spike 331
Spirit 27, 64
Spirit Guide 106, 273
Spiritual 27
Spontaneous Human Combustion 93
Stage Hypnotism **154**
Staircase method 142
Stanford Hypnotic Susceptibility Scale 139
STAR GATE 234

Static Words	198
Strobe	168p., 298
Subliminal Audio	213
Subliminal Flash	208
Subliminal Images	207
Subliminal Text	209
Subliminals	193
Submodalities	196
Subtle energies	19p.
Suggestibility	135
Susceptibility Testing	137
Swish	205
Symbolic Machines	14, 93, 271, 299, 305, 307
Synchronicity	89, 316, 376
Syntactic Ambiguity	202
Synthetic Telepathy	260
Tag Questions	202
Talisman	158
Tao	22
Technocalypse	331
TechnoMage	1, 49, 182p., 239, 244, 277, 309, 362p., 371p., 379, 383
TechnoShaman	13, 49, 309, 338, 379pp.
TechnoTheology	360
Tectonic Strain Theory	244, 251
Tegmark	30, 50, 52, 64p.
Telepathy	79, 177, 223, 236, 241, 250, 260, 357, 366
Television	164
Temporal lobe	244
Temporal Paradox	229
Testing Trance Depth	152
Theodicy	359
Theory	43
Theory of Everything	31, 44, 49, 102
Theta	167

Index

Third Wave..**187**
Time Travel..61
Torture..162, 172, 219, 312, 384
Trance...244
Trance Deepening...140, 152
Trance hijacking...**144**
Trance reflex...134
Transcranial Direct Current Stimulation..257
Transcranial Electrotherapy..256
Transcranial Magnetic Stimulation...243
Transcutaneous Electronic Nerve Stimulation...256
Transhumanism..309
Transmigration of Souls...335
Transmutation of Matter..326
Tree of Life...49, 321p., 325
Trickster..86
True Self..50, 60, 66, 135, 137, 233, 351pp., 358, 373
True Will..48, 57, 231, 354p., 382
Turing...65, 107, 351
UFO...86pp., 208, 223, 244, 251pp., 272, 304, 306, 341
Ultrasound..**214**
Ultraterrestrial...87, 90pp., 304, 306
Universal Energy..19
Universal Quantifiers..197
Unspecified Referential Index...197
Unspecified Verbs..197
Uplifting animals...325
Uploading...332, 336p.
Utilization..202
VAK..196
Visualization..178
Vitalism..20
Void..49pp., 63, 66, 275, 277p., 362
Voodoo..37

Vril..19
Wake Initiated Lucid Dream...179
White Noise..74, 177, 218, 236, 274, 277
Wicca...22p., 126, 311, 381
Wish Machine...301
Wotan...**117**
Wyrd...22
YHVH...102, 312pp., 318, 321p.
Zen..24, 381

Index

www.ingramcontent.com/pod-product-compliance
Ingram Content Group UK Ltd.
Pitfield, Milton Keynes, MK11 3LW, UK
UKHW051257180426
11947UKWH00020B/1757